The publisher and the University of California Press Foundation gratefully acknowledge the generous support of the Sue Tsao Endowment Fund in Chinese Studies.

Empire's Tracks

AMERICAN CROSSROADS

Edited by Earl Lewis, George Lipsitz, George Sánchez, Dana Takagi, Laura Briggs, and Nikhil Pal Singh

Empire's Tracks

INDIGENOUS NATIONS, CHINESE WORKERS,
AND THE TRANSCONTINENTAL RAILROAD

Manu Karuka

UNIVERSITY OF CALIFORNIA PRESS

University of California Press, one of the most distinguished university presses in the United States, enriches lives around the world by advancing scholarship in the humanities, social sciences, and natural sciences. Its activities are supported by the UC Press Foundation and by philanthropic contributions from individuals and institutions. For more information, visit www.ucpress.edu.

University of California Press
Oakland, California

Chapter 1 was previously published in Alyosha Goldstein, ed., *Formations of United States Colonialism* (Durham, NC: Duke University Press, 2014), and is republished by permission of the copyright holder, Duke University Press.

Library of Congress Cataloging-in-Publication Data

Names: Karuka, Manu, 1977- author.
Title: Empire's tracks: indigenous nations, Chinese workers, and
   the transcontinental railroad / Manu Karuka.
Description: Oakland, California : University of California Press, [2019] |
   Includes bibliographical references and index. |
Identifiers: LCCN 2018038417 (print) | LCCN 2018040802 (ebook) |
   ISBN 9780520969056 (Epub) | ISBN 9780520296626 (cloth : alk. paper) |
   ISBN 9780520296640 (pbk. : alk. paper)
Subjects: LCSH: Railroads—United States—History. | Capitalism—United
   States—19th century. | Chinese—United States—Economic conditions—
   19th century. | Indians of North America—United States—Economic
   conditions—19th century.
Classification: LCC HE2751 (ebook) | LCC HE2751 .K37 2019 (print) |
   DDC 385.0978/09034—dc23
LC record available at https://lccn.loc.gov/2018038417

28 27 26 25 24 23 22 21 20 19
10 9 8 7 6 5 4 3 2 1

The engines of this valley have a whistle, the echoes of which sound like iterated gasps and sobs.

JEAN TOOMER, Cane

This is The Beast, the snake, the machine, the monster. These trains are full of legends and their history is soaked with blood. Some of the more superstitious migrants say that The Beast is the devil's invention. Others say that the train's squeaks and creaks are the cries of those who lost their life under its wheels. Steel against steel.

ÓSCAR MARTÍNEZ, The Beast

Indigo took her seat in the dark parlor car and watched the stars; no matter how fast the train moved and the earth moved, the stars remained unhurried on their slow journey.

LESLIE MARMON SILKO,
Gardens in the Dunes

CONTENTS

ILLUSTRATIONS

PREFACE

In 1871, Stone Calf, a Cheyenne man, told an audience at New York's Cooper Union, "Before they ever ploughed or planted an acre of corn for us they commenced to build railroads through our country. What use have we for railroads in our country? What have we to transport to other nations? Nothing. We are living wild, really living on the prairies as we have in former times."[1] In his statement, Stone Calf highlighted a persistent gulf between industrial development, in the vehicle of railroads, and his nation's political economy. He invoked histories of independent trade, defying U.S. arrogations to sovereign control over Cheyenne lands, defying also the colonialist alibi of "improvement." Prior to any attempt to impose ranching or agriculture on an industrial scale, he pointed out, the United States built railroads. Amidst these transformations, a distinctly Cheyenne way of life persisted.

Three years earlier, Americans had assembled at a place they recently christened "Promontory Point," in a territory they claimed to control under the name of Utah, on a May afternoon. Political and business leaders, and journalists, had all traveled by rail, from the east and from the west, to arrive in time for the ceremony. A cohort of working men, carrying in their bones the accumulated dirt, wood, and steel that led them here, watched from a distance, some of them perhaps feeling a sense of envy, dreaming of their own possible futures, or perhaps sharing a sense of contempt at the uncalloused hands of power, detecting a certain nervousness among these barons of capital standing before the interrelated weight and gravity of sledge and stake. Two men, moving officiously, clothed in a desperate pompousness, anxiously projecting expectations of deference, stood at the center of the assembly. After a pause for photographs, as the gathered crowd watched, one of the men lifted a silver-tipped maul. Perhaps you could hear the breeze in the anticipatory hush, as he arced the hammer down toward a golden spike. He missed the spike altogether. The word "Done" was immediately telegraphed across the continent.[2]

Leland Stanford's failure at the climax of the golden spike ceremony to symbolically finish the first transcontinental railroad in North America was an act of truth.[3] Against this failure, Stone Calf spoke to a collective lie, a mythology of the United States as a nation and not an empire. This book follows in the trajectory of Stone Calf's rebuttal. The domestication of this continent under a national political economy is no more "done" than was the domestication of Cheyenne collective life three years after the railroad. In this place called North America (among other names), we live and think in an ongoing situation of colonial occupation.

Three major themes undergird the arguments of this book. First: *continental imperialism.* To conceive of the United States in national terms is to naturalize colonialism. There is no "national" territory of the United States. There are only colonized territories. There is no "national" U.S. political economy, only an imperial one, which continues to be maintained, not through the rule of law, contract, or competition, but through the renewal of colonial occupation. In the U.S. framework, there is no "national" law that can be distinguished from conquest. The United States claims and maintains control over its "domestic" territories at the nexus of war and finance.[4]

Second: *countersovereignty,* a position of reaction to distinct Indigenous protocols governing life in the spaces the United States claims as its national interior. Recognition of prior and ongoing Indigenous collective life provides a substructure to stabilize U.S. property claims. The United States declares its existence in reaction to complex networks of relationship between humans, nonhuman life forms, and inanimate processes that together constitute a distinct place in the world.[5] Countersovereignty, as a mode of political authority, is closely linked to counterintelligence, counterinsurgency, and counterrevolution, all modes of reactive anxiety, fragile modes of power that can take overwhelmingly violent form.[6] These are core modes of U.S. authority.

Third: *modes of relationship.* The history of capitalism is multiple and multifaceted. To invoke a phrase from Marx's *Grundrisse,* the struggle to comprehend actually existing capitalism, whether historically or in the present, is a struggle to comprehend a differentiated unity.[7] Capitalism bears distinct colonial and racial histories. Against a vision of a unitary capitalism subsuming noncapitalist modes of relation under its logic, *Empire's Tracks* examines how capitalism proceeds in reaction to prior and ongoing modes of relationship. This book theorizes capitalism itself as a mode of relationship, involved in the production of relationships, relationships that are situated in and with specific places.

A surfeit of representations of the transcontinental railroad occupies university library shelves, popular media, and gaseous political oratory. Beginning with the telegraph, "Done," a reader notices the repetition of particular anecdotes, citations of a shared group of documents, and perhaps, a more generalized narrative form. I call this the "Race to Promontory Point": two interwoven narratives careening back and forth from chapter to chapter, describing two railroad corporations racing to cover as much ground as possible before meeting each other, culminating at Promontory Point, Utah, where the Union Pacific and Central Pacific railroads joined tracks. Even works that depart from this narrative form are often constrained by the linearity of its trajectory, considering capitalism as a coherent and discrete system that emerged elsewhere and expanded onto Indigenous lives and territories, presuming the U.S. nation and its economic infrastructure as the culmination of the story, so that the U.S. nation-state, and U.S. capitalism, incorrectly appear as fixed end-points whose preeminence is both obvious and permanent. Indigenous nations and Chinese workers appear, if at all, as contextual backdrop, colorful diversions from the main story. *Empire's Tracks* steps outside of these confines to construct another narrative form, one more attentive to the reactive nature of imperialism.

Empire's Tracks is driven by a historical materialism that considers analysis of gender, race, and colonialism as starting points for a history of capitalism, examining the interrelationship of imperialist expansion with the structural legacies of slavery in the wake of emancipation. The following chapters locate gendered relations of race and colonialism in the production of capital, not only in the management of labor and differential pay rates, but also in production schedules, investments in machinery and physical plant, and even in mechanisms of credit and finance. The emergence of capitalism as a world system, or the reproduction of capital on an expanding scale, was and remains dependent on and reactive to the socially lived space and time of racialized and colonized people. *Empire's Tracks* charts the co-constitutions of the racial/colonial state and the modern corporation, analyzing attempts to control where and how bodies move, tracing out disruptions of that control through the renewal of relationships against the enforced isolation and partitions of imperialism, relationships that are foundations for possible futures which persist, albeit in transformed manner, in the present moment.

The golden spike did not suture the Union after the Civil War; it symbolically finalized the industrial infrastructure of a continental empire where none had existed before. An anticolonial internationalist perspective enables consideration of the emergence of industrial and financial institutions in relation to the emergence of the modern imperial state. I call this railroad colonialism: territorial expansion through financial logics and corporate organization, using unfree imported laborers, blending the economic and military functions of the state, materializing in construction projects across the colonized world. Railroad colonialism was central to the co-constitutions of the modern imperial state and finance capitalism, in the latter half of the nineteenth century.[8]

Before proceeding, let me pause to briefly describe the organization and aims of this book. This is not a work of historical recovery, nor does it focus on "encounters" between Chinese migrants and Indigenous peoples. Instead, *Empire's Tracks* offers structural analyses of capital and imperialism from distinct colonial standpoints, crossing the borders of discrete subfields of Indigenous and ethnic studies in its citational practice and in its theoretical and methodological approaches. The arguments in this book move between the abstract and the concrete, between theory and history, in order to flesh out the differentiated unity of imperialism, or actually existing capitalism.[9]

The first two chapters of the book introduce two of the book's core arguments. The first chapter examines how countersovereignty has shaped the archive of U.S. colonialism in North America, so that the historiography of U.S. nationalism naturalizes colonialism. The second chapter argues that Ella Deloria, Sarah Winnemucca, and Winona LaDuke have theorized modes of relationship, providing us with crucial tools for the critique of political economy. These are followed by five historical chapters. The book's third chapter, on railroad colonialism, charts the history of railroads across Africa, Asia, Australia, Latin America, and North America. The following chapters suggest particular universalities from below: system-wide perspectives of historical change through Lakota, Chinese, Pawnee, and Cheyenne histories. My focus in these chapters is not on recovering the phenomenological richness of precolonial or colonized alterity. Rather, my focus is on historicizing and theorizing core concepts from the critique of political economy—namely, expanding reproduction, the labor theory of value, the origins of private property, and the declining rate of profit—through these particular histories. Reading these chapters together, the railroad functions as a phantom subject and capitalism appears as multiply refracted. This refraction is, itself, a historical outcome of capitalism.[10] These historical chapters are followed, in turn, by two theoretical chapters. The book's eighth chapter theorizes "shareholder whiteness," a structural transformation in whiteness following emancipation that aligns with the development of the modern corporation and finance capitalism. This is followed by a chapter that reads Du Bois, Lenin, and Turner to provide a conceptual apparatus for understanding continental imperialism, the means by which the United States asserts control over its "homeland." The book concludes with an analysis of imperialism in the current conjuncture, drawing from the core arguments—continental imperialism, countersovereignty, and modes of relationship—to argue that decolonizing North America is a significant anti-imperialist imperative.

There is a way in which the terms of value for academic work, so far as they are couched in expectations of novelty and uniqueness, actually proceed from and renew the logic and relations of the Doctrine of Discovery. The seeming novelty of scholarship produced on these lines of value often reaffirms questions that have already been asked. Hortense Spillers wrote, "For all that the pre-Columbian 'explorers' knew about the sciences of navigation and geography, we are surprised that more parties of them did not end up 'discovering' Europe. Perhaps, from a certain angle, that is precisely all that they found— an alternative reading of ego."[11] Against the impulse of discovery, the desire for novelty, my method here is more closely akin to meditation, which I understand as a practice of liberation: effort to realize questions and capacities that have been here all along.[12]

ONE

The Prose of Countersovereignty

IN AUGUST OF 1877, AS Central Pacific Railroad construction moved into Paiute territory a month after Chinese workers went on strike, Central Pacific employment of Chinese labor dropped precipitously, never to reach the same giddy heights as those required during the slog through the Sierra Nevada summit wall. According to Charles Crocker, director of construction for the Central Pacific, Chinese workers heeded fantastical stories spread by Paiutes. He wrote to his associate:

> The most tremendous yarns have been circulated among them and we have lost about 1000 through fear of moving out on the desert. They have been told there are Snakes fifty feet long that swallow Chinamen whole and Indians 25 feet high that eat men and women and five of them will eat a Chinaman for breakfast and hundreds of other equally as ridiculous stories.[1]

It was their irrational fear, stoked by the stories told by Native people, Crocker suggested, that limited the employment of Chinese workers for the railroad. The ultimate controlling factor for employment rates was, in his telling, neither the needs of capital nor the demands of labor, but rather the imperial interaction: the encounter of Paiutes with the agents of colonialism in the form of railroad workers and managers. To explain the unfolding of negotiations over production between Central Pacific directors and Chinese workers, Crocker resorted to a third party, the people whose territory the railroad was built over and through. There is an anxiety that shows its face here, about the ongoing, unfinished nature of a colonial process that must confront the simple fact of Paiute survival and continuity, and about the incomplete sanctity and integrity of the capital that emerges from continental imperialism, which grounds its claim in an assertion of countersovereignty.

My invocation of "countersovereignty" proceeds, first, from a sense that settler invocations of sovereignty require recognition of Indigenous modes of relationship, however muted or displaced, in order to maintain any semblance of stability or coherence. This can be seen in the land grants that fueled Central Pacific Railroad production. Underlying any stability and coherence of Central Pacific claims of exclusive land ownership was recognition of the prior Paiute, and other Indigenous, claims on that same land. Barring any such recognition, however displaced or muted, Central Pacific claims to land would themselves be vulnerable to the same relations of conquest, whether through market terms or through force, that established and sustained a colonial order over Paiute territory. Countersovereignty, as visible in Central Pacific land grants and elsewhere, was a project of balancing the chaos and violence of colonialism on one side of the ledger—that of the (implicitly recognized) Indigenous sovereign—in order to establish political and economic space for the settler sovereign.

Colonial sovereignty is always necessarily a reactive claim: it is accurately considered a claim of countersovereignty. Recognition of Indigenous sovereignty takes form through fact and empiricism, capital and value. While prior sovereignties of Paiutes haunted Central Pacific colonialism, the railroad also relied on an imported labor force managed under conditions of racial violence. Chinese workers were integral to the Central Pacific's construction process, and decidedly not as enfranchised members of Nevada settler society. The possibility of Chinese claims to full participation in countersovereignty threatened the colonial economy. Chinese labor (disciplined by Chinese merchant capital) sustained and expanded the production of capital in the colonial political economy, and by doing so, sustained and expanded colonialism over Paiute lives and territory. The possibility of Chinese workers engaging of their own accord with Paiutes threatened the political economy of countersovereignty. Claiming a status of fact for that countersovereignty, such possibilities of alien and Native interactions were cast as rumors. Was Central Pacific Railroad capital, which derived from federal land grants and the surplus produced by railroad laborers, vulnerable to being slowed by a rumor? The location of Crocker's story was, itself, set in place at a crossroads of federal Indian and railroad policy. The secretaries of the interior and treasury communicated over the path of the railroad, and of land grants, "fixing a point at the Western base of the Sierra Nevada Mountains, through which the main line of the Pacific Rail Road shall pass."[2]

For a historian working in the Central Pacific Railroad archives, Crocker's story raises questions rather than answering them, and begins a line of inquiry rather than providing an exotic sidebar. This, after all, may be the only mention of Chinese and Paiute interactions in the archive of Central Pacific Railroad production. To find more, we must turn elsewhere. Lalla Scott, for example, recorded a story of a Chinese railroad work gang who shared food with a group of Paiutes living near their work camps during one segment of railroad construction near Humboldt Lake, in Nevada Territory.[3] Interactions between Chinese and Paiutes are recorded as rumors in the archives of Nevada settlement and colonization. These interactions open possibilities of a history in which colonial claims to legitimacy and authority are seen as properly peripheral, coercive, and reliant, ultimately, on violence.

Following the strategies of railroad capitalists, attempts to write a history of Chinese and Paiute interactions in the nineteenth century rely on speculation as a method. While capitalists speculate on ways to maximize future profits, historical speculation looks to the past to mine objects, rumors, and tangles of contracts in order to map a field of possible interactions between Chinese migrants and Paiutes. Casting shadows back onto the behemoth of expanding capital, these histories underscore the speculative enterprise of a history of U.S. expansion under the banner of abstract universal Capital, moving from a Newtonian universe of colonial justification to a quantum field of historical and political probability. The history of countersovereignty is part of the rumor community of continental imperialism, constantly repeated in the present, a testament of faith in colonialism.[4] Speculation, grounded only in the power to end the prospect of life and its reproduction—this is the limit of history.

Historians often seek access to the voice of the colonized, the voice of the people, through rumors. Dim echoes sounding through the caverns of colonial archives, these rumors appear at a remove from their community of meaning and interpretation. This remove, a gulf between a living, supple rumor and its cold reduction into fact, is one of those chasms productively shaping the historiography of colonialism, reaching across the social and subjective constraints of the colonial historian's institutional location.[5] To dismiss rumors as problematic sources misses the point that rumors indelibly shape the historiography of colonialism.

In the analysis of rumors, questions of their origins and causes are often irrelevant. Rumors veer away from the metaphysics of colonial knowledge and justification, which carry neatly ordered sequences that flatter colonizers' or elites' pretensions to power. Instead they focus historians' attention on the social reproduction of meaning, the repetition and transformation of "local knowledge," and on the social effects of those processes.[6] The community of a living rumor—its authors and audience—outlines its boundaries as it echoes through times. To speak, hear, and repeat such messages is to participate in a rumor's community: the rumor of the colonized is an inclusive, democratic form of communication.

A rumor does more, though, than create a community of shared knowledge. It also breathes life into a community of interpretation, a particular vantage point on a colonial situation.[7] Implicit within rumor is a distrust of colonizers and local elites. Instead, the community of interpretation called into motion by rumor grounds itself within shared experiences, interpreted through a common repertoire, maintained and nurtured as a basis for navigating the collisions, collusions, and traumas of colonialism. In this way, rumors can provide historians access to an anticolonial politics, whose organizational forms emerge from the daily life of colonized people.[8]

Rumors as they appear in colonial archives often share more than a critique of colonial power; they also outline a field of possible responses. Here, again, the boundaries of a rumor's community become significant.[9] Shared knowledge and planned response must be guarded and policed, lest they fall into the hands of those who collude with the agents of colonial coercion. Hence, the repeated appearances of rumors in the archives of colonialism, in which colonial bureaucrats and corporate and military authorities see their work as rooting out rumors and preempting assaults on their power and reason. Rumors appear in the colonial archive laden with fear and anxiety, with the awareness that the antiseptic face of colonial authority is only maintained through a constant escalation of violence, an overtly aggressive and nervous stance.[10]

Rumors in settler colonial situations are distinct from the sweeping outline rendered above. Rumor is usually taken to provide access to the voices of the colonized, the people, or the masses; in settler colonial situations, rumors may have played an important function in delineating and substantiating the claims and contours of a colonialist identity, speaking to the historian of settler nationalism with a sort of ancestral voice.[11] In nineteenth-century Nevada Territory, rumors played just such a role. These were communities that took their founding impulse in rumors of precious metals, information shared through informal networks alongside government reports and mass media. Until the development and expansion of a continental telegraph network, information about Indians, in particular, passed through newspaper exchanges that reprinted information without attribution, often contradictory, and couched in speculation and rumor.[12] Terry Knopf described functional interpretations of rumors: "Rumors . . . explain what is not clear, provide details, answer questions, aid in decision-making and, above all, relieve collective tension."[13] These rumors were, at the same time, important circuits for the reproduction of paranoid fantasies of racial supplantation, whether by Indigenous nations, racial aliens, or others.[14] Rumor was the flame that heated the melting pot.[15]

To claim membership in the nascent community of late nineteenth-century Nevada was to claim participation as audience and co-author of the constitutive rumors of the community. Across language, cultures, and histories of migration and settlement, rumors forged a community of interpretation among those who came to call themselves "Nevadans" and "Americans." The rumors that spread within this community, preserved in its archives, record the perspectives shared in the community, and its interpretation of a common situation. We might follow Tamotsu Shibutani's analysis of rumor as a collective transaction, one involving a division of labor that works to settle on a shared interpretation of events, "a collective formation that arises in the collaboration of many."[16] This community of interpretation has an afterlife in the historiography of continental imperialism that covers rumor's ideological birthmarks in the costume of dispassionate fact.[17] Gary Fine and Patricia Turner remind us: "What people believe is true reflects how they perceive themselves, their associates, and the conditions under which they live."[18] With no particular point of origin, spreading through official and informal means, elaborated upon and improvised through repetition and reinterpretation, the rumors that grounded Nevadan settlers in place lent themselves to a sort of democratic possibility, a shared claim to ownership that could simultaneously allow for and preserve hierarchy and social difference within the community, while delineating boundaries and borders for who was included. Ralph Rosnow and Gary Fine argued that rumors are most often fueled by "a desire for meaning, a quest for clarification and closure."[19]

To participate in the political trappings of Nevadan society—to vote, to claim rights in property or in court—is, then, to participate in the rumor of countersovereignty, the absurd claim that has to be continually repeated in order to enfold itself in a shroud of legitimacy, beyond the threat of violence which lingers in the silence following its utterance. Rumor manifests here as a form of collective problem-solving, the problems being: the prior occupancy and ongoing existence of Indigenous communities, and the social reproduction of imported labor.[20] In Paiute histories, this threat was often realized in cata-strophic violence inflicted by whites upon Paiute communities, and settlers' rumors of countersovereignty played a part in this.[21] This repetition, moreover, is about much more than an interpretation or a story. It is the foundation of a set of policies, of a way of acting, couched in invasion and occupation.[22] Rumor thrives in situations of war and politics, those constitutive elements of counter-sovereignty.[23] What Knopf described, of rumor's function in another context, is applicable here: "rumors are not only a refinement and crystallization of hostile beliefs, but a realization of them as well—a confirmation by 'reality'— reality as perceived by the group of people involved."[24]

A critical historiography of continental imperialism would necessarily participate in rumor control rather than rumor interpretation—rumor con-trol that is grounded in the authority, not of the empirical fact of the colonial expert, but of Indigenous nations. This critical historiography would refuse its function as part of the communication channels and institutional chan-nels of the rumor community.[25] It would turn away from the standards of evidence that shape the rumor community.[26]

An anticolonial approach to U.S. history calls for rumor control as one of its contributions. Rumors of countersovereignty, themselves, emerge at the very intersection of colonialism and historiography.[27] Like all rumors, they are couched in nonnormative evidence. Claims of countersovereignty made through the repetition and dispersion of rumors, masquerading as empirical fact, deviate from the experiential memories of Paiutes who controlled their territory.[28] Rumors raise questions of the competence and trustworthiness of sources, questions central to empiricist approaches to telling history, which often mask the violence patchily recorded and enacted in archives of coun-tersovereignty.[29] Hence, in the folklore of the settler community, we see moments of origin in contact, fantasies of Indigenous disappearance, and paranoia about invasion and displacement from the South or the West, from those who cannot share entirely in the authorship or reception of the rumor of countersovereignty.

Rumor takes its place, in the Nevada / U.S. colonial order, as part of a speculative counterpoint, trumpeting its melody amidst the euphonic pap of colonial society. This was a community, after all, founded in speculation, in the feverish futurity of gold rush. Colonists arrived in the region and scanned riverbeds and ledges, imagining likely sites to tap a vein, strike a lode. Theirs was an extractive social order. The landscape, and the people on it, were insig-nificant or irrelevant to their dreams and plans. Stories circulated about what kind of place was more likely to produce gold or silver, or about poor miners who struck it rich, fueling a shared community, directing and shaping desires, cohering into collective speculations on the possibilities contained in the land. In the speculative milieu of Nevada mining society, rumors were an example of talk that had actual value.[30]

Speculation also arose through relations and management of risk among the colonists' community, and the Paiutes it sought to displace. In the months following the discovery of the Comstock Lode in 1859, the white population in the vicinity swelled from 200 to 6,000.[31] Because of the nature of the gold and silver deposits in the region, mining relied on mechanization, which lent itself to concentration of production in mining corporations, and reliance on financial investments from San Francisco and New York.[32] The risks that the colonists faced were spread unevenly across their community, and these risks were often displaced onto Paiutes and other Native communities in the area, where they took material form as impoverishment, hunger, and violence.

Paying so little heed to Paiutes' productive work that created and nurtured the necessities for life, the colonialist community of rumor turned ravenously on the landscape, pulling out stands of trees, diverting streams, hunting and fishing the waters and land clean of fish and game animals.[33] The community of rumor radically reshaped the landscape of Paiute life. Those trees were vital sources of piñons, those streams and hills sources of meat and fish.[34] Risks arising from industrial development were socialized outward, displaced onto Indigenous nations, and settler survival was ensured by the increasing precariousness of Paiute individual and collective life.

Indian Bureau census records of Paiutes themselves read as speculative estimates of population by gender, age group, and willingness to work for wages, alongside estimates of commodities, which list items by kind, dimensions, and number. Although colonizers obsessed over census-making in order to collect, organize, and deploy "facts" toward extending and maintaining colonial rule, these records are based less on empirical fact than on conjecture. The availability of commodities at certain prices, at specific times, mirrors conjectures about the size and makeup of Paiute communities, fixing them in time and place, and recording their receptiveness to capital. Interest in wage labor and "industriousness" were key forms of information recorded on these census forms.[35] The political economy of colonialist rumor in Nevada has shaped the historiography of the region, producing empiricist history grounded in rumors masquerading as facts. This is especially the case when it comes to seeming knowledge and expertise about Native peoples.

Recapitulating rumors as facts, historians and their audiences assume membership in the rumor community, breathing new life into the rumor of countersovereignty with each variation, with each retelling. What historical actors saw clearly as nakedly political claims, as stories of justification after the fact, subsequent readers take for facts, for the whole story. It is in this small way that rumors of Chinese and Paiute interactions recorded in the archives of nineteenth-century Nevada might take on a broader significance. These particular rumors expose the broader workings of the colonial archive, of the political claim trumpeted by the faceless reporters, territorial legislators, journalists, and corporate leaders who compiled these records in the heat of the moment, or with the ruminative remove of some months or years. This is the claim of countersovereignty. In these rumored interactions between Paiutes and Chinese people, the function of the colonial archive, and the historiography that proceeds from it, is the prose of countersovereignty.

In its form of address, its mode of authorship and transmission, and its content, the prose of countersovereignty orients itself toward delegitimizing Indigenous modes of relationship and solidifying a colonial sovereignty unmoored from them. Its genres are well known: Indigenous disappearance, social evolution, and the inevitability of the bourgeois political economic order. It works seductively, enticing listeners to participate in its founding fictions, to seek redress in the rights and recognition which it delegates, rights and recognition that, as they are based on a foundation of rumor, can be swiftly and capriciously revoked or amended once they are granted.

It is this prose of countersovereignty that is visible in the archival appearances of interactions between Paiutes and Chinese people in nineteenth-century Nevada Territory. It is the record of these groups embalmed in the pages of history, named as disappearing natives on the one hand, and threatening aliens on the other, that delineates the space in between: the rumor community of countersovereignty, the colonialists who naturalize their history and presence on the land. In the rumors that record interactions across these communities, this legitimacy, this presence that refuses to provide an explanation for itself, that scoffs at any request for an explanation, frays and unravels, underscoring the institutions and ideas of Nevada and the United States as not native, but alien; not natural, but reproduced through colonialism.

The rumor that began this essay—Charles Crocker reporting that Paiute stories dissuaded Chinese desires to work on the Central Pacific Railroad in Paiute territory—appears at a junction in the tracks of corporate and immigration policy, in questions of access to and control over racially marked land and labor. The Central Pacific Railroad embodied the large-scale processes that brought Paiutes and Chinese workers into contact with each other. Responsible for the western leg of the transcontinental railroad, the Central Pacific held a charter from the state of California, and was fueled by Congressional land grants and railroad rights-of-way. Passing through the southern edge of the Pyramid Lake Reservation, for example, the Central Pacific augured a controversy over reservation boundaries that remained unresolved for over a decade.[36] Central Pacific directors struck an agreement (they referred to it as a "treaty") with Paiutes that allowed them to ride atop trains and flatbed railcars, free of charge.[37] Paiutes adapted railroad mobility to meet their own needs, riding trains to places important to them, to seek wage labor, and to meet in social gatherings.[38] Significantly, this travel appears in Indian Bureau archives, in instances where agents attempted to control the movements of starving Paiutes and Shoshones seeking food in towns along the railroad line, or preventing the movement of people from the Walker River Reservation after a smallpox outbreak, in order to prevent the spread of the disease to nearby towns.[39]

As the Central Pacific moved incrementally through the Sierra Nevada, Chinese workers composed the majority of its workforce. The use of Chinese labor was integral to the business plans of the Central Pacific directors. This is consistently clear in the speculative plans that the directors laid for railroad production, in their ongoing efforts to recruit Chinese workers in California and in southern China, and especially in their responses to the Chinese workers' strike of July 1867. For their part, railroad labor brought Chinese workers far from the established centers of the California Chinese community in San Francisco, Stockton, and Marysville. Chinese merchants followed workers, selling provisions, contracting, and managing work gangs.[40]

What to make of Crocker's story? The story shifts attention from the abuses of the Central Pacific Railroad, which led the workers to strike. Moreover, it provides a convenient shift of attention away, a clearing of the conscience, from the brutal means of breaking the strike, when the Central Pacific managers colluded with Chinese merchants who supplied food to the work camps, to prevent food from going to the camps until the workers could be starved into submission. The Central Pacific would likely have been reluctant to hire Chinese workers in the same numbers after they struck once, and especially after the most grueling part of construction, the summit tunnel, was completed. Crocker provided this improbable explanation less than a year after he and his managers broke the strike. Did he invoke this story rather than explain the construction managers' distaste for Chinese labor, now a liability after the most difficult terrain was traversed, after the cost of their labor increased? The bilious irony is that construction proceeded much more quickly and easily, with less loss of life and exposure to harsh winter conditions, once the summit tunnel was complete. Knowledge of these rumors drew its community into relations of insiderdom and control, carefully managed and concentrated, of the railroad production process.

Paiutes may have had their own reasons for circulating these stories among Chinese workers, as a calculated attempt to delay railroad construction through their territory, or perhaps in an attempt to open space for their own employment. They were, by this time, involved in the mining economy of the region as wage laborers. If this was the case, they may have improvised stories to the moment. Perhaps Paiutes fed these stories to Chinese workers in an effort to derail the smooth progress of railroad construction through their land. It is interesting to note that after the Donner Party passed through their land, Paiutes associated whites with cannibalism.[41]

The Chinese workers may have had their own reasons for telling such stories. Why fear giant cannibals elsewhere, when Chinese workers were already caught in the ravenous maws of the Central Pacific Railroad Company? Perhaps they concocted this story in order to leave difficult work conditions by subterfuge, after direct confrontation failed to succeed.[42] Facing the devastation of a broken strike, they may simply not have had the collective morale to continue working under such abusive and risky conditions. A reluctance to move further away from the Pacific Coast and its community institutions, further away from more direct connections to their home communities in Guangdong, might have provided another motive. Significantly, one of their strike demands was the right to leave work when they wished, and telling these stories, explaining or feigning the depth of their fears, might have been a way to wrest this right from their bosses, even after their strike was broken.

Ultimately, an empirical, settled explanation of this story is impossible for the historian. Working with these stories, the historian is drawn into the rumor community, which naturalizes exploitation of Chinese labor and expropriation of Paiute modes of relationship. As such, this record operates as the prose of countersovereignty. For an anticolonial historiography, this rumor is significant, not for revealing limits to the power of railroad capitalists, or those capitalists' ability to shift the blame for firing Chinese workers. Rather, this rumor underscores the ongoing process of displacing anxieties about the unfinished and incomplete colonial project that underlays capitalism in North America. Crocker invoked a rumor that Paiutes may have passed through Chinese work camps near the Sierra Nevada summit tunnel in the spring and summer of 1867, and the two groups of people communicated with each other in language and idioms they both understood, to answer questions about railroad production and railroad profits.

In a second case, archaeologists have excavated what they identify as Chinese medicinal vials from a historic late nineteenth-century Paiute campsite in the Mono Basin.[43] This particular finding, so material and concrete in itself, raises questions about the objects, their use and meaning, and their distribution. Holding such a tangible object in hand, the scholar can only ask intelligent questions, and answer them with intangible, speculative answers. The historiography of continental imperialism follows the methodological boundary lines of archaeology in this instance.[44] These questions and answers, the meanings we ascribe to these objects, are the prose of countersovereignty.

This prose works by presenting presumptions as certainties, arriving at plausible stories that exclude other perspectives, other possible trajectories of power and authority, and flatter the coherence of a trajectory of countersovereignty. If the Mono Basin was not terra nullius, then it was perhaps a place without history. The spatial bias of archaeologists resonates in sympathy with the temporal bias of national (colonial) historians, scribes of countersovereignty who situate objects within cause-and-effect chains foreordained to end in the plenary power doctrine.[45] It is a short step from here to what Ranajit Guha has exposed as "geography by history."[46]

Instead of telling a story, these vials raise a host of questions that cannot be answered. These unanswered questions animate the prose of countersovereignty. Paiutes interacted with Chinese workers whose work camps passed through their lands, and with Chinese workers and merchants in the towns and cities that were built through their lands. Some Paiutes, for example, bought opium from Chinese merchants to seek some relief from hard labor.[47] Glass collectors and archaeologists have narrowed down the particular qualities and identifying characteristics of the glass bottles typically used to store Chinese medicines, as a way to access the history of Chinese people in Virginia City.[48] However, we have no certainty that Paiutes received these bottles directly from Chinese people, nor about what was stored inside the bottles and what those materials were used for.[49]

What does this hint of interaction between these two communities—one bearing the full brunt of a virulent, violent process of colonization, the other existing at the edge of labor importation, racist violence, and surveillance—tell us about the prose of countersovereignty, about the invention and justification of countersovereignty from the echoing fragments of a shabby melody? Can these objects help us understand the maintenance of that fiction standing as prose through the consolidation of colonial control in the region, from the late nineteenth century to the present?

These are unanswered questions, and the answers proffered draw their speakers and audience into the rumor community of countersovereignty. The unanswerability of these questions is itself a product of colonialism, and of the evasions that colonized and racialized communities necessarily made in order to sustain themselves. Indian Bureau authorities took a particularly strong stand against Paiute medical practices and practitioners, and attempted to supplant them with white nurses and doctors, a policy that only intensified in the early twentieth century.[50] Paiutes, themselves, turned to their own medicinal knowledge to treat smallpox, and other new diseases introduced by colonists.[51] Where the settler ear turns toward the objects and boundary lines that justify its claims to control, these medicinal vials are objects that speak other languages, intone other histories. The rumor community of countersovereignty is unable to hear these histories clearly. The colored glass of the vials refracts and distorts a history that looks clear at first glance.

Pointing neither to a pristine prehistory before the arrival of whites on Paiute land, nor to an unvarnished modernity organized under the gears of State and Market, these medicinal vials instead point to other possibilities, of material and cultural exchange that emerged out of histories of colonialism and capitalism, but that developed independently of it. Can colonizers acknowledge themselves as peripheral in their own stories, in their own rumors?

Another rumor of Paiute interactions with Chinese people on their lands finds its general location in cemeteries. These stories circulated, most often, through that exemplary genre of the rumor community, the settler memoir. It is striking that in these memoirs, Paiutes and Chinese are held aside from other social groups and social markings, organized under their own chapter headings, ethnographic asides from the telos of the main story. The two groups converge, most often in these memoirs, in cemetery scenes, which might constitute a stock pattern in the rumor of countersovereignty, so concerned with establishing its preeminence over what is has displaced, so anxious about what might displace it. In these cemeteries, spirits of the past and portents of the future haunt the prose of countersovereignty.

These stories are most often set in Chinese cemeteries. They begin with a break from the general narrative, often a coming-of-age story, or a narrative of migration and settlement, to provide some ethnographic details on Chinese burial practices and customs, which also provide details on Chinese communities in the area. These are some of the only places in these memoirs where Chinese people appear independent of their connections to whites.

It is when the portrayals turn to food, in conjunction with burials, that Paiutes enter the narrative, tricking superstitious Chinese mourners by feasting on the food left at graves.[52] The white narrator, and implicitly, the white audience, is here privy to the entire exchange from a position of amused detachment.[53] Insulated from the ravages of hunger caused by their colonial presence, on solid ground in their ability to command a hegemony of burial practices, of ways of relating to the dead, the rumor community establishes itself, in part, by looking at other people's dead, at other people's activities at cemeteries.[54] Portraying these interactions between Chinese mourners and Paiutes through comic vignettes, the rumor community also displaces other possibilities that could arise, of the recovery or production of a common sense of humanity through funerary ceremonies, of the sort that Vincent Brown described among Black mourners in Jamaican slave society.[55] Northern Paiute histories cut against these comic stories, with memories of white people robbing Paiute graves.[56] Chinese people are playing dead here, continuing to be foreign even after their death. The rice left on their graves, which Paiutes spit away in disgust, exemplifies their alienness to the landscape. Paiutes, on the other hand, figuratively eat the dead. Holdovers, relics from a time that pre-dates the rumor community, theirs is a prehistory that continues only at the margins of life and death.

At the same time, both Paiutes and Chinese people exemplify anxieties of the replacers being themselves replaced in the rumor community in these anecdotes. Chinese people, buried in the ground and building their own cemeteries, might supersede here the claims of whites, who populated the hills and valleys with their own dead as part of their process of staking a claim of control and ownership. In this way, the Chinese dead haunt white racial control of colonial space, for example, in regulations that restricted Chinese miners to specific places.[57] The structure of the rumor—its nervous repetition, its focus on comic details and displacement, its suggestion of the dispassionate observer—itself records an anxiety about the sanctity of the colonial order.

Kalpana Sheshadri has written that "all comic stories about natives carry within them the anxious joke of Whiteness." In her argument, comedy functions in colonial contexts to veil anxieties and ambivalences of colonial whiteness.[58] This is apparent with the focus on Chinese spirits, whose graves are stark reminders of nightmare future possibilities of racial invasion and supplantation. Moreover, Paiute people continued to survive and maintain their collective lives against the violence of colonization. Unassimilated into the ceremonial mores of Christianity or the prerogatives of bourgeois rationality, they refused to be controlled by others. As Paiutes survived the advent of colonialism, they laid claim to the dead who were buried in their land. There is an anxiety about the coherence of the prose of countersovereignty in the face of these basic realities.

One more instance of Paiute and Chinese interactions recorded in the archive of continental imperialism outlines the possibility of a political encounter, the participation of Paiute men and women in anti-Chinese rallies in Nevada Territory during the 1870s and 1880s. Paiute and Chinese conflicts over the bottom rungs of the racial division of labor spilled into fuller archival view, providing some context to the larger political economy of Nevada society during this period, and the positions of Paiutes and Chinese people within it. Paiutes who marched in these rallies carried placards and signs that repeated the demands and slogans of anti-Chinese whites in the area. Namely, that Chinese workers drove down the wages of working men, and degraded the status and position of (working) women. Paiutes took up the slogans of white nativist politics. They decried Chinese workers for driving down wages and siphoning money to China. They participated in white protests that culminated in physical violence and threats of massacre.[59] Despite the appearance of repetition and engagement, these charges and accusations, as uttered by Paiutes, carried somewhat different meanings than those uttered by white townspeople and city dwellers.

Most of the Paiute conflicts with Chinese men were over access to resources and to waged labor. For example, a group of former Chinese railroad workers was allowed to live in the vicinity of Winnemucca Lake, sustaining themselves by fishing, until they started selling the fish to local whites, thereby undercutting the Paiute fish trade.[60] Paiute men competed with Chinese men during this period of Nevada history in two primary forms of waged work. The first was teamstering. Men from both communities competed to transport goods via wagon and mules. For Paiute men, this often involved working for the Indian Office.[61] The second was competition over lumber; specifically, the stumps of trees that had been felled by earlier rounds of settlement, which had been used up for construction material and heating fuel. After this round of development, the hills had been largely stripped clean of trees.[62] Indian agents saw lumber as a key commodity, not only as a possible source of wage labor for Paiute men, but also as a necessary resource in building the physical plant of Paiute reservations: agency buildings and homes for reservation residents. This dovetailed neatly with the interests of Nevada settlers in economic development, using federal appropriations to Paiutes as a subsidy for colonial development. In 1863, James Nye, governor and superintendent of Indian affairs in Nevada, wrote to the secretary of the interior reporting on plans to use annuities to establish a sawmill and begin lumber production on the Truckee River Reserve, which would be available for settlers to use.[63]

As one of the largest corporations in the area, the Central Pacific Railroad attempted to claim control of vital timber resources on Paiute land. The Central Pacific subcontracted with local concerns to provide wood for the railroad. For example, the company contracted with J. B. Chinn, a Nevada settler, for 150 cords of pinewood bolts in 1869.[64] It is unclear who cut and processed the wood, but this was the kind of wage labor—short-term piecework contracts for unskilled, strenuous labor—that Paiute men turned to for survival during these years. Once the railroad was built, groups of Paiutes built encampments near the tracks, and significant numbers of Paiute men found employment with the railroad company.[65]

Claims on Paiute lumber were important to Central Pacific Railroad Company business strategies. According to the surveyed line of the track, the Central Pacific would pass through the southern part of the reservation, which held most of the valuable timber and agricultural land within its boundaries. Railroad claims to Paiute timber were also part of Indian policy. As T. T. Dwight, superintendent of Indian affairs, explained to the commissioner of Indian affairs, "The rapid construction of the Pacific Railroad running as it will directly through these reservations, will necessarily consume the greater portion of the timber as well as scatter the Indians from their present locations."[66] In 1868, the commissioner of Indian affairs notified the secretary of the interior of his support in opening the timber reserve on the Truckee River to Central Pacific grants.[67]

The railroad company and the Pyramid Lake Paiutes entered into a longstanding dispute on whose claim took legal precedence. The Central Pacific claimed lands on the Truckee River Reservation that gave access to the productive fisheries there, fisheries that were lucrative in the 1870s.[68] Land claims seamlessly blended with control over Chinese labor in the Central Pacific's business plan. E. H. Derby, a booster for the Central Pacific, wrote in 1869,

"As respects ties, the line has great resources in the lumber of the Sierra Nevada. It can command Chinese labor and resort to the rolling mills of San Francisco, for the renewal of its rails."[69] In this description, Chinese labor joined Paiute land as basic prerequisites for railroad construction. Paiutes, themselves, vanished from the company register and the historical record, buried in subcontracting schemes, or simply pushed aside in the seemingly bloodless conquest of private property.

Later railroad companies attempted to make their own claims on Paiute lands. Writing in support of the Virginia and Truckee Railroad Company's application for a right-of-way through the Walker River Reservation in 1880, John Kincaid, then governor of Nevada, wrote:

> The company desires the right of way through that reservation. I favor it for reasons above set forth and for the further reason that in my judgment, the Walker Lake reservation is productive of no especial benefit to the Indians.
>
> You are aware that in our State the proportion of agricultural land is very limited. The Walker and Pyramid Lake reservations cover a very considerable portion of our available land in that direction. The close proximity of railroads make their reservations simply loafing places for the Indians. They go there when annuities are paid only, the balance of their time is spent in living upon the whites along the lines of railway, of course there are exceptions, a good many of the Piutes prefer to live as the whites do by farming, notably at Big Meadows, Humboldt Co, the proportion of this class to the whole tribe is small ... I believe the entire system of Indian matters in this state should undergo a very thorough reformation ...
>
> The extension of the V. and T.R.R. south will certainly open up a very important mining region, besides bringing into market the product of Mason and other agricultural valleys contiguous to, and adjoining the Walker Lake Reservation, and I consider that any judicious aid rendered by the Government of our state will be wise policy.[70]

The railroad, according to the governor's argument, enabled the modernization and tilling of Nevada soil for the fertile fruits of capital. Paiute sovereignty, as recognized by the federal government, stood as an impediment to this process, an impediment, in his logic, for both colonists and Paiutes alike. A few months later, James Spencer, the agent at Pyramid Lake, wrote to the commissioner of Indian affairs on behalf of Walker River Paiutes, inquiring after $750 pledged by the railroad company in a contract made with the community. According to Spencer, "They distinctly understand that they are to have free rides for themselves, their fish, game, &c., and though it is not stated in the contract, being as I understand an after-thought, it was also verbally agreed that all government supplies for the Indians should be trans-ported free over that road."[71] He wrote this during a period of rank destitu-tion and struggle for food and shelter. Spencer had reported, just two months before, "There is now a great scarcity of food among these Indians and a greater scarcity yet to come."[72]

For adult Paiutes, wage labor was an important means of ensuring the survival and maintenance of their communities. For Paiute men, digging up the roots of the old, massive trees, and cutting and stacking them into bun-dles of firewood, was an important source of income, especially because it was grueling, backbreaking work that few others were willing to do, except, that is, for Chinese men.[73] For Paiutes, this was partly a question of control over resources, with Chinese workers turning the refuse of colonization, such as the roots of piñons, which had provided a basic food source for Paiutes before colonists tore the trees down in their search for heating fuel, into commodi-ties of some meager value. The conflict did not preclude other kinds of exchange, with Chinese merchants selling alcohol and opium to Paiutes, in an uncanny aftershock of the British opium trade.[74] The exchange drew the attention of local authorities, who attempted to manage and police both communities. In April of 1866, H. G. Parker, superintendent of Indian affairs in Nevada, wrote to the commissioner of Indian affairs about a growing trade in gunpowder between Chinese merchants near Nevada towns and Paiutes who sought to head off colonists' violence toward them. This was, again, based in rumor, as was Parker's response. As he reported,

> I could not prove the charge against any one or more of them in particular, because they all look so much alike it is almost impossible to tell one from another. I think however, I have succeeded in stopping this trade in future, though I have secured the assistance of detectives in order to apprehend them, and shall punish them severely if possible, in case I find they continue the practice.[75]

Many Paiute women, for their part, sought employment in the forms of domestic work and laundry work, which again was work that few whites in the area were willing to do.[76] This was feminized work, and white women in these jobs could garner comparatively higher wages than in other places. Paiute women gained reputations for themselves among employers as good workers, appropriate to their employers' own needs and desires of station and status.[77] Chinese men, as a group, were the only group of men to cross gender lines and compete for this work.[78] They were employed as domestic workers, as well as cooks in restaurants.[79] Their washhouses were centralized sites for washing, especially for poorer settlers.[80] Conflicts between male Chinese workers and Paiute men and women over wage labor were profitable, driving down wages and pushing the limits of wage labor subsistence for both groups.

Paiute men and women marching in anti-Chinese parades were participating in the settler order, but they were not assimilating into whiteness as the fantasies of Indian policymakers of the era would have it. Their actions were born out of commitments to the continuity of their communities and desires to stay on their lands, and they worked out strategies that would allow them to do so. Paiute critiques of the role of Chinese workers in making the conditions of life more difficult for them, then, bore a double-edge in the context of the white nativist movement. For here, "native" whites' anxieties about the possibility of invasion and supplantation by Chinese people was exposed as an anxiety about the function of whiteness itself, in relationship to Paiute and other Native people in the area. White nativism was exposed as a claim of colonial control. In Virginia City, for example, Mary McNair Mathews listed the local secret societies: the Knights of Pythias, the Order of the Red Men, and Anti-Chinamen.[81] As John Higham argued about racial nativism, "The concept that the United States belongs in some special sense to the Anglo-Saxon 'race' offered an interpretation of the source of national greatness."[82] Paiutes' presence in nativist marches belied this interpretation. If Paiutes carried posters charging that "The Chinese Must Go!" then what of the whites they marched with?

In capital, the figures of Native and Alien were enfolded into a process that enabled the maintenance of communities and cultures through invasion, occupation, and importation, underscoring unresolved tensions of conquest and slavery that fueled the expansion of industrial capitalism in the nineteenth-century United States. This is apparent in the directors of the Central Pacific Railroad: proud abolitionists, who decried violence against Indigenous people in Nevada and California, whose own business plans rested on the racial exploitation of Chinese labor and on corporate inroads on Paiute sovereignty.[83]

In this process, interactions between Chinese and Paiutes were reduced to rumors. Instead of the triumphal procession of capital, pushing back the frontier to strike a path toward the riches of China, here was the labor of China moving eastward, engaging Indigenous people whose autonomy survived the enclosure of their land and lives. This rumor is a nightmare for U.S. continental imperialism. It cannot be resolved into fact, leaving loose threads in any attempt to relegate the history of conquest safely to the past.

The prose of countersovereignty, which is the history of the United States as a nation, remains, essentially, an unanswered question. Rumors constantly repeat with subtle variations, only to be answered in increasingly frustrated terms. The historian crafting narrative through the prose of countersovereignty will remain on frustrated terrain. For no matter how polished the horn, the tune remains defiantly forlorn. It can find no proper resolution, only endless deferrals. Emil Billeb, for example, relayed a visit to his San Francisco office by Sam Leon, a Chinese migrant, his unnamed Paiute wife, and their children.[84] This kernel only raises more questions. What brought them together? What were their names? How did they experience the city? Where did they go next?

How to control and contain the prose of countersovereignty, with its countless tongues and countless mouths, its voice of iron? We are on grounds here that Sharon Holland previously traversed: "Memory must be animated so that it can subvert the effects of its manipulation by the nation."[85] Moving from a common frame of history, with its fossilized pretensions to truth grounded in colonial authority, we might imagine histories that are transient, always at play in a field of changing politics, shifting emphasis from evidence to interpretation, from the historian who intones, to an audience that calls up and invokes histories in order to more fully critique their present, and imagine their future.

TWO

Modes of Relationship

IN THIS CHAPTER, I ARGUE that Ella Deloria, Sarah Winnemucca, and Winona LaDuke theorize modes of relationship. My reading of their work shifts emphasis of a critique of political economy from the production and reproduction of capital to the production and reproduction of relationships. This shift of emphasis can sustain a focus on capital, as a process and a relationship, not a thing in itself; an insight, Marx argued, which is particularly clear in colonies.[1]

Marx moved from "theoretical expressions" of economic categories to the social relations of production, produced by people "closely bound up with productive forces." The emphasis, for Marx, is on change. Changes in productive forces lead to changes in modes of production, which ultimately change "all their social relations." The emphasis, for Marx, is on social relations. Focusing on modes of relationship can help us to understand that collective Indigenous relationships in and with place are concrete, not mystical. Focusing on modes of relationship emphasizes that consciousness does not determine existence. Social existence determines consciousness. The emphasis is on relationships, and it is on change. Marx wrote, "All that exists, all that lives on land and under water, exists and lives only by some kind of movement." The movement of wind and water, of grass species, of massive buffalo herds, and of groups of people who follow them, are dynamic and interrelated. Modes of relationship theorize dialectics in place. Marx argued that the existence of capital is predicated on the interrelationship of wage labor with "monopolized earth."[2] The central question is the relationship between the expropriation of Indigenous relations in and with land, and the exploitation of Indigenous and nonindigenous labor, the historical and structural basis of imperialism.

In *Waterlily,* Ella Deloria presented a way of thinking about consciousness in relationship to place. After giving birth alone, while her community is on the move, Blue Bird, in a moment of deep awareness and presence, observes herself, surrounded by beautiful flowers in full bloom, which seem to draw out an even deeper awareness. In this sustained awareness, her attention blurring between the flowers and her newborn, Blue Bird takes notice of her child, beginning to name their relationship. Intersubjectivity, in this passage, cannot be separated from an awareness of presence in place, but place is not an inert, lifeless mass. Intersubjective relations in and with place are the foundation for materialist critique. Blue Bird recalls a moment from her childhood, when her brother gathered earth beans from a mouse's nest, and she scolded him for taking their food without leaving something for them to eat. After her grandmother, in turn, scolded her for her tone, they decided to leave some dried corn for the mice. Deloria theorized Dakota practices of property and distribution, in relationships between humans and other species, recirculating food to enhance well-being. Property renews relationships across gender, generation, and species.[3]

This insight is repeated, on a larger scale, in a story told by the storyteller Woyaka to the children, about a time when their ancestors were unable to find food, and were guided by a holy man to hunt a herd of buffalo who freely offered themselves. He spoke of the relationship between Dakota people and the buffalo. Killing with reverence, renewing relations with the buffalo, is a precondition for enjoyment of the buffalo's gift of food. There is, however, a line distinguishing humans from other animals in the text. In the aftermath of a smallpox epidemic, Waterlily finds herself in a tipi with eight relatives, the sick and the healthy living side by side. Quarantine, the narrator states, would have been shocking and unthinkable to all members of the family. It would have been "a gross repudiation of fellow human beings." To be in relationship with fellow humans is to share distinct kinds of vulnerability.[4]

At the novel's outset Blue Bird seeks solitude as she goes into labor, in order to lessen the vulnerability of her community while they are on the move. Her brow dampening with sweat, Blue Bird draws on her memories to orient herself, struggling to maintain a coherent line of thought, trying to remember something she once overheard her grandmother tell someone about the best position for a quick birth, or for an easy birth. It flashes to mind. Blue Bird's awesome power to create life is compounded by awesome discipline: silence that would not draw attention to herself, or her people, in a moment of utter vulnerability.[5]

Blue Bird and her grandmother are the sole survivors of an attack on their family, and she carries the memory of loss as a definitive aspect of her identity. Her grief does not isolate her from her adopted community. Instead, it provides an occasion for support and sympathy. Alone in their new home, Blue Bird and her grandmother are finally able to express their grief, joined by their women neighbors. Shared grief, shared vulnerability, is a precondition for forging and renewing collective relationships. Elsewhere, in the story "A Woman Captive and Her Baby," Deloria described a Dakota woman, taken captive to the west, who resolves to escape. After careful planning, she flees with her infant son, following the sunrise. Realizing that she is wandering in circles and running out of food, she comes upon a group of men, contentedly feasting on a buffalo. In this moment, her infant cries out in hunger, causing the six men to immediately vanish. As they flee, she overhears the men speaking Lakota. The men had left her food, as well as tracks that she follows home to the Black Hills. Deloria related a particularly gendered vulnerability, the recipient of collective care, even when unintended. I read this story as a rigorously materialist account of a specifically Dakota mode of relationship.[6]

Deloria presented the tiospaye, "a larger family, constituted of related households," as a core unit of community life among Dakotas. Cooperative living in a tiospaye entails a collective mode of relationship, so that, for example, "all adults were responsible for the safety and happiness of their collective children." The narrator discusses children's feelings of "security and self-assurance." "Almost from the beginning everyone could declare, 'I am not afraid; I have relatives.'" Deloria theorized community as providing personal security through collective relationships, individuality arising through interdependence. Later in the novel, Waterlily, now a young woman seeking advice from her mother as she considers a marriage proposal, comes to understand her decision in the context of collective relationships and interdependence. While she is hesitant to accept the stranger's proposal, the horses he offered as gifts would allow her uncle, who had helped raise her, to honor his mother-in-law, her grandmother. Blue Bird reminds her daughter that relationships cohere through personal generosity, before leaving Waterlily to make her own decision. In a moment of elation, struck by the dense and interwoven web of loving care involved, Waterlily decides to accept the proposal. Her individual choice can only be understood in the context of her relationships.[7]

At the very beginning of the novel, Blue Bird, after giving birth, rejoins the line of relatives who are moving their village. As she looks for her family, a young woman, a social cousin, has her sit on a travois, to be carried along the way. An act of recognition and care, a rejuvenation of chosen bonds of relationship, marks one of Waterlily's first interactions with her community. Deloria described a mode of relationship exceeding the biological, appearing through particularly significant moments of care and accountability. This is social kinship. Kinship provides support, but it also carries obligations. Waterlily later experiences this while developing new relationships with her new husband's relatives. Through careful observation, she slowly begins to "integrate herself" into the tiospaye in which her husband lives. The observation and fulfillment of relationships, the result of lifelong experience, cohere a distinctly Dakota way of living in collective relationship to the places that Dakota people claim as their home.[8]

Late in the novel, the narrator describes a community in crisis after a murder. An elder exhorts the shocked and grief-stricken community to adopt the murderer in precisely the relationship they held with his victim, by giving him their most valuable possession. Here is a theory and practice of property that revolves around forging and renewing relationships of care and mutual obligation. Deloria outlined a critique of political economy. The community decides to counter the destruction of life by fostering new relationships in order to restore peace. The elder remarks, "Now two lives have been destroyed, the one for the other. Let us forget the nasty business and try again. It ought never to happen among men of the universal kinship of humans. Let us have peace once more." The universal kinship of humans he intones is an articulation of the principle of internationalism. Internationalism can be understood through distinct Indigenous modes of relationship.[9]

A Dakota mode of relationship, as Deloria presented it, is oriented around the creation of life, the expansion of kinship relations, and the establishment and maintenance of peace. It is, in other words, the social reproduction of peaceful interdependence. The emphasis is on social forms of relationship. Deloria described motherhood, for example, as a social, and not a biological, relationship. Gender is itself a social relationship, with a boy who is allowed to follow girls' pursuits "liable to come under a spell that would make him behave in a feminine manner all his life." Masculinity is denaturalized, a site of training. What is at play is not an aversion to the feminine, but instead the cultivation of a masculinity that is interdependent and intertwined with the feminine. Deloria staged one scene of this interdependence in a Sun Dance where a youthful Lowanla has made an "extravagant pledge" in order to mourn his father's death. After his ordeal begins, his uncle steps in to bear some of the burden, until his aunts rush in to shoulder the rest. Far from devaluing Lowanla's sacrifice, the people hail this as an unforgettable act, as "'the loftiest expression of kinship affection.'"[10]

Waterlily repeatedly returns to a focus on "kinship training." The core of this process is relationships between grandmothers and grandchildren. Rather than chiding young Waterlily for making too much noise when the older children are amusing her, her grandmother gently addresses all of the children, and when this is not enough, she speaks directly to Waterlily's older brother. Her grandmother's method of instruction helps Waterlily realize her individuality through interdependence. Her relatives begin to hold her more accountable as she begins to draw on memories of past experiences to guide her actions. Individual and collective memory is central to this mode of relationship. "'Do not forget, grandchild. Keep remembering, or you will die.' Remembering means being conscious."[11]

Remembering means being conscious, a predicate for fulfilling relationships. Property, on the other hand, "comes and goes and comes again." Property, Deloria suggested, is not something to be accounted in itself, something to be remembered when gone, but for forging and renewing relationships. "The idea behind it was this: if everyone gives, then everyone gets; it is inevitable." Giving enables the creation of more life, and the establishment and maintenance of peaceful relationships. Following a successful hunt, Black Eagle's relatives, feeling compelled to share the abundance, flag down people passing by, even sending out young people on horses to invite strangers to join the feast. Abundance is not for hoarding. Hoarding would be antithetical to the true purpose of property: to foster relationships. Deloria theorized property: not for the realization of the self-interested individual, but instead, for enabling collective life.[12]

Waterlily ends with a scene of women and children harvesting berries in a river bottom, at once a "communal enterprise" and a "sociable excursion." After spreading out blankets and shade, arranging for babies and small children to be supervised, the women disperse "in all directions among the countless bushes dotting the valley on both sides of the river as far as one could see." In a scene of pleasure and delight, Waterlily experiences "the dear sounds rising from the women below: unrestrained feminine laughter and good-natured banter, occasional mock scolding or lusty joking by those with an earthy and robust bent, sudden cries of happy surprise upon the finding of another bush even more lavishly laden or with still bigger and sweeter berries, shouted warnings to mobile children forever gravitating toward danger or mischief the instant backs were turned." Labor is the basis of intergenerational, gendered, collective relationships, the basis of pleasure, and of sustenance, drawing upon and enacting "The cumulative wisdom of Dakota women, gained through experience from way back." Labor, as Deloria theorized it, is a basis for individuality through interdependence.[13]

Deloria provided windows to analyze colonialism. At its core, colonialism involves repetitive failures of relationship. Blue Bird and some visitors discuss observations of life at a U.S. military stockade, sharing incredulity at the violent way the whites slap, spank, and otherwise profoundly disrespect their children's individuality. It is difficult to explain, and difficult to understand. Fear seems to be the operating principle. Individuation, for the colonizers, is predicated on relations of fear, not interdependence. Blue Bird, sympathizing with the whites' children, concludes that the children must become so frightened that they lose the ability to think. A colonial mode of relationship blocks consciousness, interrupting the process of thought. Failure to fulfill relationships is a defining feature of colonialism. Later in the novel, Red Leaf's father defends his friend, insisting that there are some good white men. His wife wryly responds, "'I suppose you would die to save him—would he die to save you?'" Against the universal brotherhood of humans, colonizers can be expected to refuse solidarity in the precise moment when solidarity is most necessary.[14]

Colonialism transforms abundance into scarcity, interdependence into isolation. Deloria presented colonialism as a profound failure at being human. Waterlily, staying in the village of Good Hunter, her husband's father, witnesses worry and anxiety about white people's effect on the village's food supply. "They wantonly kill off our friends (the buffalo) and leave them spoiling on the plains. What manner of men are they, to be so wasteful? Are they children? Do they not yet have their senses? If this keeps on, we shall all starve!" Such profligate, unthinking killing and waste, failing to respect the interrelations of collective life across species, is incomprehensible. The whites must have never matured beyond their childhood, to be so insensible. To be so insensible, they are unaccountable. They are profoundly dangerous to life.[15]

I turn now to Sarah Winnemucca's theorization of a colonial mode of relationship. Winnemucca helps us understand the accumulation of capital on Paiute lands as predicated on active relations of war and occupation. She described a moment when a "whole band of white people perished in the mountains, for it was too late to cross them." The whites, lacking relationship with the place or its people, unknowingly put themselves at death's door. "We could have saved them," Winnemucca wrote, "only my people were afraid of them. We never knew who they were, or where they came from."[16]

What was the reason for their fear, which prevented them from assisting these errant strangers? News had already spread to Paiutes from neighboring communities that whites "were killing everybody that came in their way." People were fleeing into the mountains for refuge. Winnemucca's own family joined this exodus, where mothers warned "that the whites were killing everybody and eating them." The children, filled with fear, imagined monstrous cannibals arriving every time the wind kicked up dust in the valleys below. Such fears were rooted in empirical observation. Winnemucca recorded a conversation between older women: "Surely they don't eat people?" "Yes, they do eat people, because they ate each other up in the mountains last winter." These observations are keys to Winnemucca's theorization of a colonial political economy, which is to say, a colonial mode of relationship.[17]

Winnemucca theorized colonialism as a relationship of war, manifesting in sexual violence. A group of white men regularly came into her village at night, demanding sexual access to her sister. Later, her mother launched a lacerating critique. "They are not people; they have no thought, no mind, no love. They are beasts." Winnemucca's mother took the prevalence of rape as evidence of white men's failed humanity. Winnemucca provided another window into the colonial refusal of relationship, when a group of settlers found and burned her village's winter supplies. Colonialism transforms abundance into scarcity, security into vulnerability. Along with sexual violence, Winnemucca observed, the destruction of food is a key method of colonial warfare. The occupiers refuse to abide by professions of brotherhood, refusing, even, to treat Paiutes as fellow humans.[18]

For Ella Deloria, theorizing a Dakota mode of relationship, collective and individual relationships with place are the basis for consciousness. For

Winnemucca, theorizing colonial warfare, lack of relationship is a basis for the violence of invasion and occupation, through a refusal or incapacity for consciousness. This includes ecological destruction. Moving up the Carson River, Winnemucca and her family met a relative who shared the devastating news that scores of their relatives had died after drinking water from the Humboldt River, which settlers had poisoned. Violence against Paiute lands and waters is an attack on Paiute collective life.[19]

Colonial warfare entails conscription to colonial violence. Winnemucca's grandfather regaled others of fighting alongside whites against Mexicans, but his participation made him newly vulnerable, forcing him to hide from those he had fought against. What ends does colonial warfare serve? Can the ravenous appetites of the occupiers possibly be sated? Winnemucca theorized a relationship between cannibalism and capitalism among the whites. They will stop eating each other by consuming the foundations of Paiute collective life instead. The accumulation of capital on Paiute lands cannot be disentangled from colonialist war. Colonial property claims justified barbaric violence against Paiute communities. A company of soldiers passed through a Paiute village in 1865, accusing them of stealing some cattle from settlers. The next day, after traveling sixty miles, the soldiers came upon a Paiute camp and massacred almost everyone there, mostly older people, younger women, and children. The sadistic brutality was predicated on, and justified by, colonial property claims.[20]

Winnemucca demonstrated an inverted truth concealed beneath accusations of thievery: colonialists accuse Paiutes of stealing what they, themselves, have stolen from Paiutes. There is a double-edge of colonial theft, providing the origins of colonial property relations, while providing an alibi to renew the violence on which those property relations are predicated. Winnemucca recalled a conversation with an Indian agent at the Malheur Agency, who told the assembled Paiutes, "Nothing here is yours. It is all the government's." A man named Egan stood, asking her to translate:

> Did the government tell you to come here and drive us off this reservation? Did the Big Father say go and kill us all off, so you can have our land? Did they tell you to pull our children's ears off, and put handcuffs on them, and carry a pistol to shoot us with? We want to know how the government came by this land . . . Do you see that high mountain away off there? There is nothing but rocks there. Is that where the Big Father wants me to go? If you scattered your seed and it should fall there, it will not grow, for it is all rocks there. Oh, what am I saying? I know you will come and say: Here, Indians, go away; I want these rocks to make me a beautiful home with!

Egan articulated a brilliant critique of a colonial mode of relationship. The U.S. government violently drives Paiutes off their lands in order to claim possession, on quasi-theological grounds of civilizational progress and uplift. The role for Paiutes, in this colonialist mode of relationship, is not to disappear. It is to inoculate the occupiers against the colonial violence that forms their relationships with each other, and with the land they have stolen. A recognition of Paiute presence, and Paiute claims on land that seems to be barren and useless now, is productive for colonial futures, providing new spaces for accumulation, especially in moments of crisis. This is a core dimension of what I call "countersovereignty."[21]

Colonialism, as Winnemucca presented it, entails a transformation from abundance to scarcity. Describing a visit by three relatives who had crossed deep snow in the mountains, she remarked, "Bread and meat tasted very good indeed. It put one in mind of old times when meat and bread were plenty." Later, during her work as an interpreter, she noted that agency officials withheld seventeen wagons full of supplies. Hunger and impoverishment are compounded by stark isolation. After colonial occupation, "We shall no longer be a happy people, as we now are; we shall no longer go here and there as of old; we shall no longer build our big fires as a signal to our friends, for we shall always be afraid of being seen by those bad people." Colonialism produces profound loneliness. Capital accumulation on Paiute lands is predicated on the rupture of relationships.[22]

Winnemucca described how her family was forced to leave their homelands for California, leaving her "poor papa" behind. What was the effect of scarcity and isolation among Paiute survivors of colonialism? "My people have been so unhappy for a long time they wish now to *disincrease,* instead of multiply. The mothers are afraid to have more children, for fear they shall have daughters, who are not safe even in their mother's presence." Colonialism provides an organizing structure for capital accumulation, by decreasing Paiute life. The accumulation of capital on Paiute lands takes place through the expropriation of Paiute women's intergenerational relationships. The Central Pacific Railroad was part of this infrastructure of gendered expropriation. Prior to the railroad, Paiutes had dug a mile-long ditch for the construction of grain and timber mills. While the United States had appropriated $25,000 for the mills, they were never built. The Central Pacific Railroad took Paiute timberland, and settlers later used the ditch to irrigate their fields. The infrastructure of colonialism on

Paiute land revolves around the expropriation of land *and* the exploitation of labor.[23]

After moving to Stockton, California, her brother informed the family that their white host asked them to stay, for the women and girls to work in the kitchen, and the boys to work as ranch hands. A gendered division of labor within Winnemucca's family appeared to provide the domestic and pastoral basis of colonial life, behind which lurked sexual violence and colonial war. After recording her grandfather's exhortation to work, and the beneficence of the wage, Winnemucca noted, "All that time, neither my uncles nor my mother had told what the white men did while we were all left alone." Wage labor, and its accompanying vulnerability to sexual violence, are elements of colonial warfare. Colonialism transforms the fruits of Indigenous labor into the pangs of starvation. Winnemucca described how, after Paiutes carefully and methodically taught themselves to grow wheat, enjoying a successful harvest, a local missionary took their fine wheat and gave them poor quality flour in return, "ground just as you would grind it for hogs," leading to illness and deaths. "At first," Winnemucca recalled, "Father Wilbur and his Christian Indians told us we could bury our dead in their graveyard; but they soon got tired of us, and said we could not bury them there any more." Colonialism leaves no room for Paiutes, even after death.[24]

Paiute labor constitutes a source for colonial revenue. Without providing any seed, or any instruction in wheat cultivation, the Indian agent demanded taxes in hay and wheat, threatening to take wagons and to banish people from the reservation on nonpayment. Instead of distributing beef among Paiutes, to fulfill treaty obligations, "those that have money can come up and buy. Those that have none stand back and cry, often with hunger." Indian agents turned the administration of the colonial state toward personal enrichment, enforced by another kind of Paiute labor. The agent appointed a police force of Paiutes, "a useless office, for Indians could not arrest either an Indian or a white man. They really were nothing but private servants to the agent."[25]

Winnemucca argued that decolonization entails the restoration of Indigenous modes of relationship. At its core, as Winnemucca presented it, this is about relationships between Paiute women. Early in the text, she described a frightening morning, when news that "some white people were coming" sent everyone running. Her mother fled with little Sarah and her baby sister, but Sarah was paralyzed with terror, unable to move her feet. Winnemucca's aunt caught up with them, and the mothers buried the girls, shading their faces with sage, warning them not to make any noise, "for if we did they would surely kill us and eat us." Winnemucca demanded that her readers imagine what it felt like to be buried alive, "thinking every minute that I was to be unburied and eaten up." I take this as a searing demand to consider the lived experience of colonialism. To be buried alive in one's own homeland, every moment at risk of being violated and cannibalized by the occupiers. Heart throbbing, Sarah stilled her breath throughout the day and into the night, despairing that she and her sister had been forgotten. She heard whispering and footsteps approaching, steeling herself for the end, and then heard her mother's voice. From being buried alive, to being found, disinterred, taken back to the others, brought back into the circle of care. We can read this as a programmatic description of decolonization.[26]

KILLING WITHOUT REVERENCE

For Winona LaDuke, Indigenous relations with nonhuman animals, plants, rocks, and waters, "our older relatives—the ones who came before and taught us how to live," form the foundations for Indigenous collective life. The ongoing violence of colonialism centers on the mass destruction of older relatives. On the North American Plains, for example, prairie ecosystems, buffalo, and Indigenous nations have co-evolved for thousands of years. Colonialism seeks to rapidly block that process of co-evolution, to eradicate the accumulated knowledge of that process, and to impose an altogether alien conception of life and value that takes flight from an ornately parochial theology. At the core, LaDuke argued, Indigenous modes of relationship are about bolstering the capacities to support more life in a place.[27]

Relations of interdependence provide the context for individuality. LaDuke interviewed Fred Dubray, president of the Inter-Tribal Bison Cooperative, who told her that domesticating buffalo, such as by removing their horns to make them easier for humans to manage, changes the way that buffalo relate to the land, which changes the land itself. His insight involves relating to the herd overall, rather than to individual buffalo, and for Dubray, this reflects core lessons on Lakota struggle as collective struggle. LaDuke theorizes an Indigenous mode of relationship which is collective, which spans myriad species, and which fosters more life in a place. Colonialism, on the other hand, seeks to annihilate the collective, destroying and homogenizing life and consciousness in place. Where Indigenous modes of relationship work through interdependence, colonialism works through dependency. Where Indigenous modes of relationship provide a context for individual voices to differentiate themselves, colonialism homogenizes. LaDuke wrote, "To kill incorrectly, many would say, affects and disrupts all life." We might sharpen our understanding of imperialism as killing incorrectly: killing without reverence, killing without awareness, killing without a sense of relationship, killing solely with an eye to eating.[28]

Renewed state-sanctioned slaughter, domestication, and management of buffalo is a renewal of colonial violence. Colonialism produces a desolate and lonely wasteland, through mass destruction of life, and mass destruction of the consciousness of life. With their vaunted scientific method and rule of law, colonialists seem to remain blithely unaware of the horrific and barbaric toll of their mode of relationship. Colonialism is predicated on mass extinction and genocide. LaDuke drew a direct link between the cultural and political destruction of Indigenous life, and the loss of biodiversity. Mass destruction of life has a specific geography, which in North America is concentrated in many of the ongoing centers of Indigenous life on the continent. Colonialism destroys the ways that a place can sustain life. The prairie, "the single largest ecosystem in North America," was cultivated by massive, roaming buffalo herds. A century and a half after the initial colonization of the region, the ecosystem has been remade to support the cattle industry, "from feed crop monoculture to feedlots, from underpriced public permits (a holdover from old reservation leases) to drawdown of the aquifers, agricultural runoff, and soil erosion," destroying the biodiversity, and much of the life, in the largest community of plants and animals on the continent.[29]

Imperialism excels at proliferating capital into progressively fewer hands, and it does so by wrecking the ecological and social basis of life, through the interrelationship of state and corporation. The Plains was first colonized through the coordination of railroad corporations and the U.S. Army. The ongoing occupation of the region is maintained through federal subsidies to agribusiness and energy corporations, in coordination with police, National Guard, vigilantes, and mercenaries. By the end of the twentieth century, more than 270 million acres of land under federal control were being leased to cattle interests, generally at subsidized rates. Turning the land over to the industrial cultivation of domestic livestock constrains the ecosystem's ability to support wild species. After a century and a half of aggressive industrial colonization, few Indigenous species remain on the Great Plains. LaDuke cited a 1990 study that found only 20 percent of the region remains capable of supporting natural plant communities. Continental imperialism has murdered the older relatives. This is one way to tally the balance sheet of imperialism, and the task ahead for decolonization.[30]

LaDuke gives us a central anti-imperialist question: "Who has the right to make the earth anew, and how is it made so?" Imperialism works through territorialization, circumscribing places with territorial lines, within which imperial states enact monopolies on violence. Territorialization proceeds through terror, inscribing a certain space as a space of violence. Scholars of territory have drawn an etymology for the term not to terra, meaning land or terrain, but to terrēre, to frighten, so that territory and terrorism are profoundly linked in conceptions of imperial sovereignty. The historiography of the settler "nation" has a territorializing function. Territorialization also occurs through military occupation and infrastructure development. Territorialization spans species, involving a direct assault on Indigenous modes of relationship. During the exceptionally cold winter of 1996–97, for example, the buffalo herd from Yellowstone National Park moved to lower elevations in search of food, crossing a border between the park and the state of Montana, where they were captured and sold for meat, or shot on public and private lands. Representatives of the colonial state killed 1,100 buffalo that winter, drawing down the total herd from 3,446 to just 1,700 by the end of the season.[31]

Territorialization proceeds through infrastructure development. Infrastructures are central to the reproduction of distinct modes of relationship, lines of interconnection, shaping distinct terms of relation, and shaping the terms of relation across distinct social spaces. Treaties, for example, are infrastructures, alongside railroads, reservations, and borders. Focusing on infrastructures can help clarify how prior modes of relationship can persist alongside novel infrastructures of colonial domination. Infrastructures are often layered, superimposed over previous networks, producing possibilities for the irruption of supposedly vanished or dormant terms of relationship within and against colonial policies. Within infrastructures we can feel both the imperative and the imminent possibility of decolonization. For imperial states, infrastructures are sites of vulnerability, sites to assemble and deploy technical and political knowledge in order to preempt the break-down of imperial authority. Infrastructures of colonialism are infrastructures of policing and military occupation, and have been central to the experimental statecraft and social engineering of colonial power. Railroad colonialism entailed not just the production of imperial infrastructure, but just as important, the development of the modern imperial state form. To understand the transcontinental railroad in terms of continental imperialism is to understand the development of the United States of America as an imperial state.[32]

The infrastructure of continental imperialism in North America centers on building capacities to make war, and to extract energy from the soil and water. Countersovereignty, as a mode of reaction, projects itself into the future, through what LaDuke described as "advanced exploration infrastructure." Imperialism captures (LaDuke's word is "pillage") and exports resources to sell them elsewhere. Indigenous nations are left bereft of the ability to maintain their own modes of relationship, and even from the ability to benefit from the destruction as consumers.[33]

The ever-increasing energy consumption habits of the United States present a threat to the planet's ability to sustain collective human life, and are located in infrastructures of expropriation and encroachment on Indigenous lands in North America and beyond. These infrastructures are the concrete basis for continental imperialism, for the mythical projection of a "domestic" space of the "nation's interior." Open pit and strip mining of high-quality coal in and adjacent to tribal landholdings in Wyoming and Montana provide electricity to Los Angeles and Seattle. LaDuke listed owners of the Colstrip 1–4 mines, first established by the Northern Pacific Railway, which abut the Crow and Northern Cheyenne reservations: Montana Power Company, Pacific Corporation, Puget Sound Power and Light, Pacific Gas and Electric, Western Washington Power, and the Los Angeles Department of Water and Power. Industrial hydropower, coal, and oil involve destructive relationships with Indigenous places and with Indigenous nations. The nuclear industry throughout the world locates itself in or near Indigenous lands and waters. Two-thirds of uranium, one-third of low-sulfur coal, as well as major hydroelectric, oil, and natural gas reserves, are located in Indigenous communities. Egan's critique of a ravenous colonial political economy holds true, a century and more after it was spoken.[34]

Continental imperialism has proceeded with a destructive approach to energy production. It has also proceeded through controlling water. LaDuke wrote, "The Bureau of Reclamation has irrigated 9.1 million acres and constructed 322 reservoirs, 345 diversion dams, 14,490 miles of canals, 34,990 miles of laterals, 930 miles of pipelines, 218 miles of tunnels, 15,530 miles of drains, 174 pumping plants, and 49 power plants in the United States, much of it in the arid West." The drawdown of the Ogallala Aquifer from the Northern to the Southern Plains, over decades, has enabled the further concentration of monopoly agriculture and ranching. Thirsty corporations have depleted the aquifer. The related erosion of a third of the region's topsoil through the overcultivation of land, overgrazing of livestock, deforestation, and improper irrigation techniques has resulted in desertification. Early travelers from the United States described the Plains (presumptuously) as a "great American desert." A desert is what the United States has actually produced.[35]

Imperialism, as a mode of relationship, is historical and ongoing in North America. The invasion of Indigenous lands and waters has not lessened in intensity in the present day. It is usually sanitized, if acknowledged at all, through the colonialist mythology of settler "nations." The ecological devastation of the Great Plains, and the resultant massive loss of life and biodiversity, has its origins in the initial colonization of the Plains, including 90 million acres of land grants to railroad companies. The mass slaughter of the Plains buffalo herd proceeded in waves, corresponding with the construction of railroads, "the vehicle for an astonishing slaughter." In North America, the accumulation of capital is predicated on relations of theft and mass slaughter, resulting in social and ecological catastrophe.[36]

In this book, I argue that continental imperialism proceeds through the interrelationship of state and corporation, and more specifically, through the war-finance nexus. A central anti-imperialist task is to break these interrelated modes of domination, as historical processes that constrict the present and foreclose futures. LaDuke quotes Loretta Pascal, a Lil'wat grandmother, who gives us what I take as core anti-imperialist questions in North America: "Where did you get your right to destroy these forests? How does your right supersede my rights?" Working out answers to Pascal's questions, we might collectively renew a practice of anticolonial internationalism on these lands. To begin working out an answer to Loretta Pascal's questions, it may be helpful to think about the relationship between settler state formations and real estate. Claims to land as private property are enforced by the military and police, and mercenaries operating with state sanction. This includes the declaration of "public lands" by state authorities. Winnemucca focused on mechanisms of taxation to steal wheat from Paiutes. At White Earth, taxation was used to steal land, with the state of Minnesota grabbing a quarter of a million acres as tax payments.[37]

The history of capitalism in North America is not a history of a free market, governed by the principles of competition between self-interested individuals. It is, in large part, a history of the administration of colonial control over Indigenous communities through the accumulation and valorization of corporate capital. This is what Winnemucca analyzed with the capitalization of "beef contracts" to administer Paiute reservation life. On the Plains, LaDuke noted, "Feeding those whom the government had deprived of food and sustenance became a major business and a new commercial opportunity for the fledgling western cattle industries." U. S. agriculture subsidies, which severely depress the livelihoods of farmers in the global South, have origins in Indian Office purchases of beef from western cattle industries. Up to 50 million pounds of beef are purchased by federal agencies for distribution to reservation communities. Many of the meat commodities that the United States distributes to Indigenous households originate in livestock grown in industrial conditions on captured Indigenous lands. LaDuke described this as an "intergenerational distortion of subsistence," which might be another way to define a colonial mode of relationship.[38]

Many of the world's most powerful multinational energy and agriculture corporations had their spawning grounds in the administration of continental imperialism, in the occupation of Indigenous lands and water, which continue to be places of renewal for corporate profits. The capitalization of Indigenous lands, waters, and resources have provided value, at no cost or risk, to some of the largest corporations in the world. Over two centuries, U. S. courts have prioritized the ongoing accumulation of corporate capital as a central function of the racial / colonial state, granting powers to corporations, and treating them as persons before the law. In the end, the fruits of continental imperialism redound to corporate shareholders.[39]

Continental imperialism, the co-constitution of settler states and corporations, leads to war at ever increasing scales of destruction. Colonialism, Winona LaDuke suggests, captures Indigenous peoples in a "time warp" of permanent war. Colonial occupation renders Indigenous nations as trespassers on their ancestral lands. Indigenous homelands in North America have become central sites for war preparations, testing new weapons, and training in new techniques, on the colonialist alibi that these are "empty" lands, devoid of human habitation. Who is the enemy? In the mid-1980s, six NATO allies—Belgium, Great Britain, West Germany, Netherlands, the United States, and Canada—joined in low-level flight training in Nitassinan, touted by the Canadian government as "wilderness interior free of human habitation," after increasing European resistance to low-level flight training over densely populated areas. Low-level flights produce shockwaves that are excruciating to human ears and bodies, and cause temporary insanity in birds and animals in their path. The Indigenous Innu, LaDuke wrote, asked, "Who is the enemy in the forest?" Imperialism proceeds through war, its primary mode of relationship.[40]

Against the renewal of relations of war, LaDuke argues that "America and industrial society must move from a society based on conquest to one steeped in the practice of survival." Shifting from conquest to survival, and a corresponding delinking from growth, are core anti-imperialist challenges today. Indigenous modes of relationship, in other words, are at the heart of anticolonial internationalism, to enhance, rather than destroy, the qualities of life on this planet. Ella Deloria wrote about the "universal kinship of humans," which I read as an invocation of internationalism. In the twentieth century, the great breakthroughs in the struggle against imperialism were achieved through alliances between the urban proletariat and the peasantry in the peripheries of capitalism. In the early twenty-first century, our urgent task is to develop and proliferate a new synthesis in the relationships between the urban poor, the peasantry, and Indigenous nations. LaDuke suggests, "It is quite the time to reconcile the hunter and the peasant." Once we accurately see North America as a space of hundreds of colonized Indigenous nations, we can begin to understand that imperialism, in North America, is a chain that is built out of weak links.[41]

Decolonization, as Mohawk activist Katsi Cook frames it, is a feminist question. "How are we going to recreate a society where the women are going to be healthy?" I take this as a core challenge for anti-imperialist thought and practice. The establishment of locally controlled renewable energy infrastructures fulfills a decades-long call for the development of liberation technologies across Indigenous North America. The long-standing underdevelopment of tribal communities, LaDuke suggests, now provides an opportunity, because "Native peoples are less addicted to fossil fuels than the rest of the country." The reestablishment of traditional agriculture materially renews relationships with the land. Indigenous planning for a buffalo commons renews the relations between Indigenous nations and the buffalo, and renews the Plains as a site of international coordination between Indigenous nations.

Infrastructures of decolonization renew Indigenous modes of relationship, and they do so by undoing the logic and relationships of the war-finance nexus. These are examples of actually existing decolonization, and they should be supported, and proliferated, as significant anti-imperialist modes of relationship.[42]

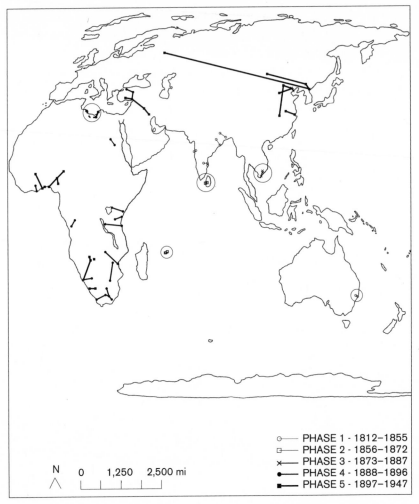

PHASE 1 · 1812–1855
PHASE 2 · 1856–1872
PHASE 3 · 1873–1887
PHASE 4 · 1888–1896
PHASE 5 · 1897–1947

N   0   1,250   2,500 mi

MAPS 1 AND 2: Railroad Colonialism. Cartography by Elsa Matossian Hoover.

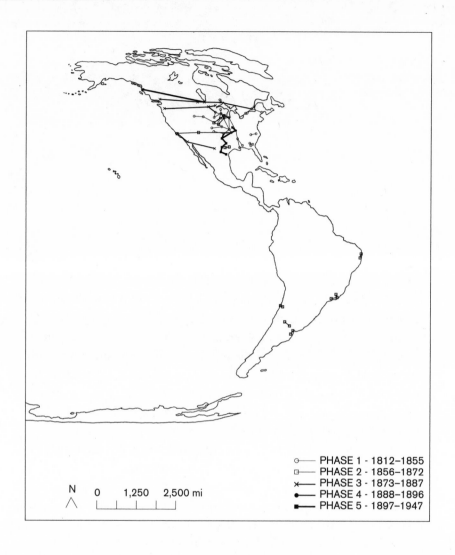

N   0   1,250   2,500 mi

○——— PHASE 1 - 1812–1855
□——— PHASE 2 - 1856–1872
✕——— PHASE 3 - 1873–1887
●——— PHASE 4 - 1888–1896
■——— PHASE 5 - 1897–1947

THREE

_____

Railroad Colonialism

THE UNITED STATES OF AMERICA is profoundly unexceptional. The Central Pacific and Union Pacific railroads are manifestations of a broad historical process that I call railroad colonialism. North American railroads linked with railroads elsewhere in the colonized world. Imperialists across the Americas, Africa, Asia, and Australia built railroads as infrastructures of reaction, as attempts to control the future. Infrastructure, in other words, played a police function, materializing not through liberal universalism, but proliferating distinctions and comparison along the lines of community, nation, race, gender, caste, and respectability. Railways enabled the circulation of colonial commodities throughout the imperial core, and even more importantly, they made the large-scale export of financial and industrial capital to the colonies a central feature of global capitalism.[1]

In Britain's Asian and African colonies, direct state management, arising from administrative and military concerns, would contradict the free market alibi of British imperialism. The Missouri-Kansas-Texas Railroad crossed Indian Territory in the United States, connecting key U.S. military posts deep in Indian country, "strung together by the iron rail, like barbed wire on fence posts." Across the colonized world, railroads carried the devastation of industrial warfare. Even relatively short rail lines transformed possibilities for capital accumulation and imperial jurisdiction. The internationalization of the cotton industry drove railroad construction in North America and South Asia in the years before the U.S. Civil War and in British East Africa in the early twentieth century. In addition to cotton, railroad colonialism facilitated the development of South African gold, Malayan tin, Central African copper, and Indian iron and steel, each organized under imperial control. In North and South America, railroad colonialism transformed bountiful prairie lands into massive monocrop areas for beef, pork, and grain production. In the last quarter of the nineteenth century, railroad colonialism turned decisively away from any entrepreneurial pretense and toward active colonial state planning, heightening inter-imperial competition and destabilizing British domination of the world economy.[2]

Colonial monopolies materialized through control over the physical characteristics of rail networks. In North America, corporations built railroads along the U.S.-Canada border, and U.S. corporate control over railways in Mexico resulted in a continental railway network largely conforming to U.S. infrastructure standards. Imperial powers built rail networks over neighboring territories in idiosyncratic gauges, the distance between the rails. At the junctions of tracks built at different gauges, goods and passengers had to transfer from one train to another. Imperial railroads often constricted people and goods within a specific imperial network, producing economies of isolation. At the end of the twentieth century, it was still cheaper to ship goods from Europe or North America to Brazil than to ship regionally within Latin America.[3]

Railroad colonialism was produced through great suffering. By the early twentieth century, infrastructure development in African colonies involved the impressment of "political labor" to build rail lines in Nigeria and Kenya, two months of forced labor authorized in Uganda to build rails, and compulsory labor on public works in Kenya and Nyasaland. British and French imperialists employed horrific work conditions and a wanton carelessness with worker's lives, categorized as "public works," to build railroads for the profits of engineering, construction, and steel corporations, and for the reorganization of African societies around cash crop exports. Catastrophic death rates littered railroads across the colonized world. In some places, each mile of railroad cost upward of a thousand human lives.[4]

Colonial railroads sometimes reintroduced large-scale unfree labor, such as in Mauritius at the turn of the century, where French colonial administrators turned to compulsory Native labor after finding it unsatisfactory to contract Italian, Indian, Chinese, and Malaysian workers. Railroad construction often attempted to remake Indigenous labor markets in order to capture and control existing Indigenous infrastructures. In eastern Africa, for instance, railroads superseded a long-standing porter-based transportation network, which settler farmers viewed as a drain on their supply of agricultural workers. In Tanzania, German railway development destroyed an ecologically efficient long-distance porter-based trade network, resulting in the emergence of a nascent working class oriented toward coastal plantations.

Railway building, in many parts of the colonized world, augured the introduction of new, hierarchical systems of management tying wages and skills to racial distinctions. The racial organization and management of railroad labor saw some of the earliest and most significant forms of struggles over wages, technology, and the working day. Workers' struggles developed alongside armed insurgencies and campaigns of industrial sabotage, sometimes blending into struggles for self-determination and freedom.[5]

Investors on colonial railroads invested in more than the futures of railroad corporations. They invested in the futures of colonialism. Railroads reordered modes of relationship across the colonized world, seeking to confine myriad possible futures into the death threat of imperialism: there is no alternative.[6]

FEEDER LINES

The first phase of railroad colonialism began in 1812, lasting until 1855, primarily in North America and South Asia. The United States granted its first railroad charter, for a line linking the Delaware and Raritan Rivers, less than a month after the Battle of New Orleans. Over the years of railroad expansion, the United States would organize twenty-four states, half before the Civil War, the other half, prior to large-scale settlement, after the war. The vast bulk of the space claimed as domestic territory by the continental United States was incorporated during the era of railroad building.[7]

The earliest technical labor for U.S. railroads originated in the U.S. Army. Amid a shortage in engineers, U.S. railroad companies turned to engineers from West Point, who surveyed more than twenty railroads between 1827 and 1838. Many of these engineers would leave the army to work directly for railroad companies, some of them moving on to supervise railroad construction in other empires. The U.S. Army is one place to look for the rise of management bureaucracies and administrative hierarchies, both understood as hallmarks of the industrial corporation. The history of the corporation cannot be separated from the history of colonial warfare. By the early 1840s, amidst debates about the support of frontier garrisons, railway promoters in the United States began sketching out railway networks for the occupation of Indigenous lands, blending military and real estate logics. Railroad promoters anticipated the exchange value of Indigenous lands, even before the onset of colonial jurisdiction.[8]

The late 1840s saw the beginnings of railroad colonialism in India, where, between 1845 and 1875, taxes levied on Indians guaranteed 5 percent returns on British investments of about £95 million in Indian railroads. "Public debts," Hobson noted, "ripened in the colonies." During these years, the East India Company inoculated its shareholders from risk through land grants and supplies of cheap labor alongside guarantees on investments, while claiming powers to supervise and control the railways. Railroads transformed India into a captive market for British capital. British manufacturers lobbied for state support of Indian railroads, to enable the shipping of mass-produced British textiles into the interior, pushing for cotton cultivation in western India in order to drive down U.S. cotton prices. After the end of the U.S. Civil War, British cotton manufacturers switched back from Indian short staple cotton to the long staple cotton of Alabama and Louisiana, prompting financial collapses in Bombay. Through 1924, colonial railroad policy in India stipulated the purchase of rails, locomotives, and nonspecialized track fittings from British manufacturers, providing a sphere for the circulation of idle British capital. Railway debts alone made up over half of Indian debt. While railways in India played a major role in the destruction of artisanal industries, especially in textiles, the colonial monopoly also arrested the emergence of machine and heavy industries in India.[9]

In the United States, claims of possession over Indigenous lands acted as a "proprietary anchor" for railroad investments. In 1850, the United States made its first railroad land grant, to the Illinois Central Railroad, granting lands in Mississippi and Alabama, which the Illinois Central immediately began selling, bringing hundreds of settlers to the southern states only two decades after removal. By the middle of the decade, U.S. rail mileage nearly equaled the total rail mileage in the rest of the world, and by the end of the decade, total mileage and total investments in the U.S. rail network had more than tripled. U.S. railroad land grants often included provisions requiring troop transport at reduced rates, or for no charge, provisions first invoked on October 15, 1855, when the Illinois Central Railroad transported members of the Tenth Infantry Regiment from Pennsylvania to Fort Armstrong in Illinois and Fort Snelling in Dakota homelands. To the north, the Grand Trunk Railway in Canada, built in the 1850s, was the longest international railway of its time, reflecting both the prerogatives of imperialist expansion and settler interests. In Australia, railway construction began in New South Wales in 1850, at a time when the settler population was probably equal to the Indigenous population. In their successful bid for state funding, leaders of the Sydney Railway Company argued that economic development in the wake of railroad construction would stall the emigration of settlers to California gold fields. The Sydney Railroad was infrastructure to produce white territoriality. By 1859, railway construction began in New South Wales, importing equipment, materials, and labor from overseas. British construction firms organized the migration of tens of thousands of British railway workers, including paid travel advances for their families.[10]

In the United States, core institutional forms of plantation, corporation, and frontier post often blended in the same entity. The construction of a rail network in the southern United States relied on enslaved Black women, children, and men. The Virginia and Tennessee Railroad, in 1856, would have ranked the sixth largest plantation in Virginia, and the Southwestern Railroad in 1850 would have been the third largest plantation in Georgia. The enslaved, for their part, responded to the situation with the full ensemble of actions in plantation settings, including running away. In addition to cotton, trains shipped captives for the internal slave trade. Train depots across the Upper South were places of terror, violation, and grief for Black people being wrenched southward. Jacob Stroyer remembered a train arriving at a depot, "when the noise of the cars had died away, we heard wailing and shrieks from those in the cars." On the train itself, enslaved people were often forced to ride in the dangerous, hot, noisy car behind the engine. Brazilian rail projects relied on slave labor through the 1860s, and British-controlled railway companies continued to purchase slaves decades after the British abolition of the slave trade.[11]

Railroads became instruments of warfare in 1855, with the construction of the Balaklava Railway by a British company as part of the Crimean War, two years after the firm had contracted to build the Grand Trunk Railway. Following the 1857 rebellion in India, colonial policy supported rapid railroad construction, not only to move troops and military supplies, but also to enforce a new strategy of imperial rule through social difference. In 1860, Indian railways introduced a "coolie class," built on the model of cattle wagons, in which doors were locked, and opened only at select stations. Passengers squatted on the floor. Amendments to the Indian Railway Act in 1871 and 1890 would give British railway employees powers of jurisdiction, rendering passengers liable to arrest for not paying excess fare, intoxication, or public nuisance. Indian railroads segregated women on the lines of caste, class, and religion. In North America and South Asia, imperial and racial governance were enacted, in part, by where a person could ride a train.[12]

From the late 1850s through the early 1870s, corporate management began to cohere from military origins, to oversee the movement and containment of people in colonized space. Railroad building in North America and South Asia occurred through the war-finance nexus, breathing life into imperialism. War over slavery's futures took place on railroads. The U.S. Civil War primed the pump for railroad expansion in North America, both in financial and spatial terms, with the U.S. rail network expanding by almost 35,000 miles by the end of the war. Northern railroads posted regular and secure profits over the course of the war. This was the first war to regularly employ railroads for massive and rapid troop movements, using rails to supply troops deep in enemy territory. By the end of the war, rail sabotage by retreating soldiers, haphazard repairs, and occupying forces left the southern rail network in massive disrepair. Rebuilding this infrastructure would be a key task of reconstruction, an arena of struggle over the meaning of emancipation.[13]

The development of a managerial class and the expansion of a bureaucratic and professionally administered state, in the years afterwards, reflected lessons of using railroads for war. The war facilitated the rise of a generation of military leaders, such as Grenville Dodge and William Sherman, who would deploy railroads for the invasion and occupation of Indigenous lands in the coming decades. While military officials looked to railroads for control over territory, U.S. railroad corporations drew upon military resources in the pursuit of financial profit. U.S. officials were keenly aware of how railroads remade Indigenous ecologies. Interior Secretary Jacob Cox remarked in 1870 that "the building of the Union Pacific Railroad has driven the buffalo from their former hunting grounds." Significant post–Civil War railroad construction in the United States can be organized into two groups: five transcontinental lines that capitalized vast territories functionally under Indigenous control, and four "Granger" lines that transformed the Plains into a global supply center of pork, beef, and grain. Post–Civil War railroads extended U.S. jurisdiction on a continental scale through military occupation, remaking Indigenous prairie lands through an economy revolving around meat and grain exports, providing the caloric basis for imperialism.[14]

The 1870s saw a transformation in the global movement of people and resources. A combination of rails, canals, and ports effectively decreased the distance between Western Europe and the rest of the world. Dutch investment in North American railroads during these years, particularly in Minnesota, a few years after the Dakota uprising, and Red River lands, just after the Red River uprising, as well as New Mexico lands under the Maxwell Land Grant, accompanied the promotion of Dutch emigration to these lands. After 1870, military strategy became a primary rationale for railroad building in India, inspired by the use of railways in the U. S. Civil War, to enable rapid troop movements and ease perceived climate stress on English troops, a kind of industrial inoculation against malaria and sunshine. Over time, the military rationale for Indian railroads would shift from counterinsurgency to imperial competition, to counter Russian expansion in Central Asia and French expansion in Southeast Asia.[15]

Jardine, Matheson & Company, one of the principal firms that had spurred the first Opium War, built the first railroad in China, between Shanghai and Woosung. Local people promptly dismantled it. Meanwhile, in Peru, beginning in 1871, an immigrant from the United States began contracting more than five thousand Chinese workers to build railroads. Amidst a growing anti-Chinese popular movement in California, Peruvian officials began recruiting Chinese labor in California, as well as thousands of workers from Chile and Bolivia. Construction managers found that Indigenous Andeans could work harder at high altitudes than imported workers. Iron, coal, even food supplies, came almost entirely from outside of Peru. In the United States railroads superseded canals as the primary form of infrastructure development, and the railroad system east of the Alleghenies was largely completed by 1870. From 1867 to 1873, railroad mileage almost doubled, mostly in the Upper Mississippi Valley. Foreign capital, almost entirely British, financed this rail expansion. Most foreign investment from Britain in the last third of the nineteenth century went to Britain's settler colonies, to Argentina and Uruguay, and to the United States, primarily in the form of secure loans to railways and public utilities, rather than high-yield forms of investment. In 1871, the United States made its last significant railroad land grant, to the Texas and Pacific Railway Company. By this time, the United States had granted more than 170,000,000 acres of land, much of it not in its functional control, to about 80 different railroads. By 1943, railroad companies would claim title to 131,350,534 acres, about 90 percent of it located west of the Mississippi River. Land grants to railroad corporations, key instruments of the war-finance nexus, facilitated the growth of finance capital.[16]

From 1873 to the late 1880s, an international financial crisis led to the direct management of railroads by imperial states. Bookended by insurgency on the North American Plains and in Sudan, it was a period of territorialization through military administration, in which railroad labor around the colonized world was organized in work gangs, using rudimentary tools. The onset of the Panic of 1873, triggering a five-year, systemic economic crisis, coincided with the collapse of the Northern Pacific Railroad, which had been sold to investors for its military utility, the railroad's charter baldly contradicting the 1868 Fort Laramie Treaty. Lakota military resistance to the illegal occupation of their lands triggered the collapse of the Northern Pacific Railroad. The resolution of the ensuing global financial crisis would lie in railroad construction in African colonies, followed by China. In 1871, the rival Southern Pacific Railroad had announced that it would employ Chinese laborers, spiking Southern Pacific bond sales, and the Crédit Mobilier scandal broke in 1872, exposing the capture of U. S. federal debt for Union Pacific Railroad construction by private interests. These investments remade the continent, isolating and transforming Indigenous places into productive spaces for capital accumulation. After the 1873 crash, Freedmen's savings banks and cotton prices followed the tightening credit, hastening the concretization of debt peonage across slavery's heartland.[17]

The year 1873 also marked a transition point in Brazilian railroad policy. After two decades of railroad building by British companies, the Brazilian state became directly involved in railroad operations. Following the financial crisis, Argentinian railroads underwent a wave of consolidation, channeling exports to Britain on rail networks funded through British investments. In the midst of the global financial crisis, Indian railroads began to miss their guarantees to investors, and the colonial government switched to direct funding. With the charade of free trade becoming increasingly brittle, British imperialists searched for other alibis. As financial crises triggered a series of famines in India, colonial authorities discussed moving food and relief supplies on railroads, and with the 1878 Afghan campaign, Indian railways received an additional, fresh military impetus. Devastating waves of famine would reoccur in 1896–97 and again in 1899–1900, amid colonial expenditures on railroads and war, to the detriment of irrigation and education. Railways were one of the first major industries to employ large numbers of

Indians, hired by contractors and agents, paying along caste and religious lines. Railroad construction in India was labor intensive, drawing whole families from villages near the tracks, with women making up about 40 percent of the workforce. For tasks like plate-laying, the strongest workers were organized into small gangs of 12–13, under the charge of a headman, closely supervised by British inspectors. Tunnel construction in India relied on the most rudimentary materials: pick, hammer, basket, kerosene lamps and mirrors, and muscle power.[18]

As the financial crisis resolved into a renewed social crisis by the end of the 1870s, European powers competed to control and capture resources and territory through the state-managed development of railroads. French railways in West Africa, and British railways in West and East Africa, were all being built under state supervision. In 1879, British and French merchants submitted proposals for railroads in the Gold Coast, to link interior palm oil, cotton, and rubber producing districts with the coast, proposing a railroad to gold mines in the western province, newly occupied after the Ashanti War of 1873–74. The 1881 completion of a seven-mile railway line from Tangshan to Xugezhuang set in place the spine of a main trunk line connecting northern China with Manchuria. Competition over access to southwestern China spurred French colonization of northern Vietnam. The French built the area's first railroad for counterinsurgency, failing to quell Vietnamese anticolonial guerillas. Within a few years, the French had built railways through isolated areas of Vietnam, neglecting more heavily populated areas. Tens of thousands of migrant Chinese workers died while building these railroads. The loss of a tributary relationship with Annam spurred renewed debates in China over the strategic use of railways for defending territorial integrity.[19]

In 1877, workers in North American cities rose up in mass protest against railroad labor conditions, tipping from labor agitation into political demands. Amidst the financial crisis, completion of the Southern Pacific Railroad through Arizona, and into New Mexico, cemented the occupation of Mexican territory. The large-scale usurpation of Indigenous lands, spurred by the construction of railroads, became a regular part of state policy, auguring Yaqui and Maya uprisings in Sonora and Yucatán. Railroad construction tied the Mexican economy to a relationship dependent upon U.S. economic interests, and the usurpation of Indigenous landholdings enabled the expansion of the Porfirian regulatory state. In Sudan, British railroad construction on the Wadi Halfa–Abu Hamad line facilitated counterinsurgency operations against the Madhi's followers. Beginning in 1884, and initially planned to extend into Darfur, it was finished in August 1897. It was a military railroad, administered by British military officers until 1925, built by Egyptian Sa'idis (working in gangs, supervised by a headman), Mahdist prisoners, and former slaves. In 1885, Métis people rose up for the second time against Canadian power along the Red River, only two years after the Canadian Pacific Railway was completed through their country. Their rebellion was precipitated by railroad land grants, and the routing of the railroad away from Saskatchewan, which deepened an economic depression. Back in 1869, Canada had to wait until spring to dispatch troops to suppress the earlier uprising, but now the Canadian government rushed troops by rail to Saskatchewan to violently suppress the resistance.[20]

DIPLOMACY, OR REAL ESTATE

From 1888 through the turn of the century, railroad colonialism centered on inter-imperial competition over the African continent, before taking off in China, and to a lesser degree, in the Ottoman Empire. In Africa, imperial competition for resource monopolies proceeded through preemption and humanitarian alibis, relying on both labor importation and militarized labor management, opening moments of conflict between settlers and empires. In China and the Ottoman Empire, railroad colonialism proceeded through concessions to European empires and corporations.

In 1888, Lobengula, the Ndebele king, signed a treaty, the so-called Rudd Concession, ceding gold rights north of the Limpopo River, with an agent of Cecil Rhodes, but within months he renounced the treaty, arguing that the written text did not correspond with the actual agreement. Meanwhile, Rhodes had incorporated the British South Africa Company to realize his vision of British continental imperialism, inspired partly by the transcontinental railroad in North America. The British government upheld the BSAC territorial claim, and a crisis of political authority and economic stability pushed the collapse of the Ndebele state by 1893, the searing flame of anti-settler insurgency flaring almost immediately. Following railway development to Lobengula's capital, the bulk of Ndebele land and cattle passed directly into the hands of settlers. After cracking down on a first wave of Shona and Ndebele uprisings in 1896, the BSAC instituted a series of taxes, attempting to induce Africans to work for railroads and mines. Within a few years, railway workers in Southern Rhodesia were being housed across ethnicity, unlike the strict ethnic separation in the Transvaal mines, lending to the development of new solidarities among African workers.[21]

A year after the Rudd Concession, representatives of the major imperial powers convened at the Brussels Anti-Slavery Conference, to launch an imperialist antislavery campaign, advocating "the construction of roads, and in particular of railways." Humanitarian agreements aside, the imperialists competed to capture African resources through railroad construction. The race to build railroads into the West African interior was a race between corporations, but it was also a race between imperial states. An economic boom in southern Africa, spurred by the 1898 discovery of gold, had been enhanced by railway construction linking the Transvaal with Lourenço Marques, the key port in Portuguese Mozambique. Boer leaders actively sought German and Dutch investment for railroad construction, including the promotion of Dutch emigration to southern Africa, attempting to increase settler independence from the British empire. The BSAC built a northern rail link, successfully capturing the African copper belt for British imperialism. BSAC railroad work relied heavily on the manual labor of unpaid Ngwato warriors working under forced conditions and disciplined with violence. BSAC managers adjusted construction calendars to the cycles of Shona and Ndebele agriculture, building extensively during slack seasons. In German East Africa, a retreat of high finance and industry from the colonies resulted in a vacuum filled by settlers who enforced a brutal regime of industrial labor.[22]

The 1895 Treaty of Shimonoseki, ending war between Japan and China, spurred inter-imperial competition between Japan and Russia over Manchuria, leading Chinese officials to develop a system of concessions for railway construction. Within three years, Chinese officials invited Americans to become involved, vainly attempting to offset the more powerful financial and military cartels. Railroad concessions resulted in the construction of over 6,500 miles of track, and the Europeans began to directly negotiate with each other over their interests in China. Railroad concessions granted rights to employ labor, invest capital, manage railways, enforce security, issue currencies, and exploit natural resources, hollowing out the Chinese state's administrative control over territory. A corresponding decline in the Chinese waterborne commercial system, alongside the growth of treaty ports, further increased Chinese dependency on foreign powers. The Chinese population responded to such encroachments with almost immediate local campaigns of sabotage. Ottoman officials also tried to grant railroad concessions strategically, at the end of 1899, granting a preliminary concession for a railway from Konya to Baghdad and Basra, to the Anatolian Railway Company, headed by Deutsche Bank. By 1906, as construction made its way through Turkish territory, activists floated plans for German colonies along the rail line.[23]

By the close of the century, railroad colonialism continued to rely on labor importation. In 1896, in the midst of a famine, four hundred Punjabis enlisted to support construction of the Uganda Railway, which was built through what is now Kenya. An 1892 report on the Mombasa railway, presented to the British Parliament, had anticipated importing labor from India, budgeting for a certain number of deaths, planning to recruit south Indians to work coastal areas, and north Indians for work at higher altitudes. A plague outbreak in April 1897 halted the shipment of workers, in turn halting railroad construction until October, when migrants quarantined in camps under medical supervision were sent by rail to Karachi, to depart for British East Africa. In German East Africa, a force of two thousand African workers built the Tanga line under the management of small contractors. The Germans also recruited Indian laborers and masons who had deserted from British East African colonies. German officials initially planned for a Chinese workforce to construct the Central Line, but instead drew upon Nyamwezi porters of the long-standing caravan trade. In Congo, imperial infrastructure initially revolved around steamships moving rubber along the river. Before railroads, porters carried disassembled steamers inland from the coast. Pieces too heavy or unwieldy could simply not be taken to the river. The Mataldi–Leopoldville Railroad, completed in 1898, enabled explosive growth in the transportation of steamers from the coast to the river. Initially, the Belgians brought two thousand workers from Zanzibar and West Africa to work on the line, but nine hundred died in the first twenty-seven months of construction (another nine hundred would die before the railroad was finished). After the French and British forbade further recruiting in their African colonies, the Belgians imported workers from Barbados and Macao, both groups also facing catastrophic death rates, and rebelling in turn. The completed railroad carried rubber and later, copper.[24]

The first line on the Gold Coast, the Sekondi–Tarkwa line, began construction in 1899. The forty-mile line was built through dense forest on soft clay, difficult to drain and ballast, labor-intensive construction further hampered by ongoing Asante uprisings against imperial authority. The colonial governor had secured approval to import eight hundred indentured workers from the Malay Straits colony, but paucity of steamship service between the colonies stymied this plan. Instead, colonial officials began paying chiefs from coastal communities to supply workers, in gangs of 20–30 organized by village, with headmen appointed by the chiefs. Military police, ostensibly deployed to protect the railroad from Asante attack, prevented these workers from running away. The Germans had used a similar process to recruit labor for railroad construction between Swakopmund and Windhoek, paying Herero chiefs for workers organized into gangs, with headmen appointed by chiefs. The rail line was finished just four months after the Asante military defeat in March 1901, a defeat of Asante plans for industrialization. Ten years before, Asante administrators had incorporated the Ashanti and Prah Mining and Trading Company, seeking to finance and manage railroad construction, in order to strengthen Asante political and economic autonomy. A rail link to the gold fields was completed in 1904, cementing the British-chartered Ashanti Goldfields Corporation's land claims and mining operations. Asante leaders worked to destabilize railroad land claims until 1924, when the commissioner of Ashanti found no clear British title to the lands adjacent to the railroad tracks.[25]

INSURGENT LIFE

Beginning in 1897, railroads had become key sites of anticolonial uprisings, which would be defeated by the renewal of the war-finance nexus, deploying racial and tribal difference toward imperial governance. The resulting destabilization of China and the Ottoman Empire triggered a decline in British imperial preeminence, marked by the vulnerability of the sterling. As strike waves across Africa augured the organization of mass anticolonial nationalist movements, the dependency of Mexico on the United States facilitated the latter's rise in the global imperialist system. At the dawn of the so-called age of decolonization, railroad colonialism left its mark on the next era, through the violence of partition.

At the turn of the century, railroad construction in China and Africa had become a primary site of inter-imperialist competition, and of anticolonial struggle. Spurred by increasing rivalry with Japan, a Russian-controlled company broke ground on the Chinese Eastern Railway in August 1897, intended to link the Russian Trans-Siberian Railway with an ice-free port on the Pacific Coast. These kinds of railway concessions helped ignite the Boxer Rebellion. In May of 1899, French and Belgian railway engineers, and Cossacks sent to rescue them, engaged Boxers in battle. Rebels burned stations and wrecked bridges on the Beijing–Tianjin and Baoding railways. Concessionary railroads in China operated on the war-finance nexus. The Beijing-Hankou line was one of the largest French overseas investments, and French troops captured the railway in Hankou, continuing its construction under military occupation. As the Boxer Uprisings sputtered out in 1903, the Chinese government acceded to British demands for harsh terms for the Shanghai–Nanjing Railway, and to German demands for concessions in the Yangtze River valley, in exchange for evacuation of German soldiers from Shanghai.[26]

In 1904, the Herero rose up against German colonial power in southwest Africa. Colonial officials used railroads that had been built by forced Herero labor to rapidly move troops. Facing down a troop train armed with machine guns, insurgents sabotaged the tracks in several places after intense fighting, and the train was unable to lift the Herero siege on Okahandja. The fighting persisted for four years, until the Germans had destroyed the basis of independent Herero political leadership and Herero landholding, through mass executions and forced-labor concentration camps. Herero prisoners of war, regardless of gender, were forced to work on railroad construction from Lüderlitz to Aus. Upon completion of the Otavi railway line, surviving Hereros (including children) were then redistributed among settler farmers. In July of 1907, hundreds of Sudanese soldiers sent to suppress a Baganda and Ankole revolt mutinied against their British officers, causing alarm, a temporary breakdown in imperial control, and a renewed focus on the military utility of railroads. The British East Africa Company began issuing certificates of occupation to European settlers, contingent on completion of the Uganda Railway, requiring the cultivation of coffee, cotton, indigo, and rubber. Carrying settlers, suppressing revolts, and moving exports, railroads in British East Africa materialized the war-finance nexus.[27]

Colonial rail construction remade relations between bodies, as much as between places. In Bulawayo, a colonial town built over the ruins of the previous Ndebele capital, which became a railway terminus in 1897, an African community quickly developed on the segregated outskirts of the white town. A number of influential unmarried women held land and prestige, with the workforce divided around ethnic and geographic origins. In the North American Pacific Northwest, Indigenous, white, and Asian men and boys traveled a "circuit from train depot to bunkhouse," finding work in railroad construction. Colonial railroads were sites to improvise and elaborate new possibilities of intimacy and sociality, of new solidarities. In 1897, Indian railway workers began a wave of organized struggle that would continue until formal independence, their collective actions sometimes sparked by fury with miserable work conditions, sometimes by anticolonial rage. Within two years, nationalist organizations had begun collecting strike funds for rail workers, with strikes on the Great Indian Peninsula Railway accompanied by systematic train-wrecking in the North West Provinces. Building from their experience in trade union agitation, in the 1920s, Indian rail workers would join the currents of communist and nationalist struggle.[28]

At the turn of the century, the United States deployed railroads as key infrastructures of continental imperialism, splitting populations along the lines of race and tribe. Railroad construction influenced the politics of land allotment in the Creek Nation, beginning in April 1899. Recently arrived African Americans and whites had clustered around the tracks of the Missouri, Kansas, and Texas Railroad near Muskogee, many of them marrying citizens of the Creek Nation, others finding acceptance in Black Creek towns. In 1906, Black and other Creeks and African Americans joined in a series of community actions, called "riots" by railroad officials, to halt railroad construction through their communities. In the Creek Nation, railroad construction was a site to contest colonialist market integration and capitalization of land. In 1906–7, anti-Asian politics washing through British Columbia swept up the Grand Trunk Pacific Railway after talks with a Japanese labor contractor became public. Meanwhile, the railroad expropriated strips of land on several different First Nations reserves. Attempting to lay track through a gravesite of the Kitsumkalum band of the Tsimshian nation, the railroad met a blockade. The railway refused to comply with demands for a reburial process that respected Kitsumkalum protocols, calling on Department of Indian Affairs officials to enforce the priority of corporate land claims over Indigenous modes of relationship. In 1909, the DIA superintendent backed the railway's right to desecrate Kitsumkalum graves.[29]

Over the next decade, the imperial powers would destabilize the Chinese and Ottoman empires and accelerate competition to control African resources, thereby transforming the balance of imperial power. Imperialism, in Ronald Robinson's words, had become "a function of the railroad." Colonial railroads drained taxes and resources through guaranteed dividends, continuing to stunt the lives of millions of people across the colonized world. After repeated famines, colonial administrators in India downplayed the extent of Indian rice and wheat exports, and the transfer of agricultural acreage from foodstuffs to cotton, jute, salt, and opium, all enabled by railroad colonialism. Over £274 million, 80 percent of British industrial investment in India and the largest group of investments in British imperial history, had been allocated as capital for Indian railways, investments secured, in the final instance, by taxes levied on the Indian peasantry. In the Balkans and in Manchuria, railways carved out the Ottoman and Chinese empires, while in Africa, railways raced to connect the continental interior with imperial ports. With the Berlin Compromise of 1909, German, British, and French interests agreed to share the Hukuang Railways loan, which the British and French had understood as a destabilization of inter-imperial balance. Clemenceau, in Paris, ominously told a correspondent from the *London Times,* "There is a cleft in the *entente.*"[30]

Long-ripening relations of war and occupation with Mexico would provide a material basis for U. S. financial ascension during the First World War. By the beginning of the Mexican revolution, U. S. investors had funded construction of almost 11,000 miles of railroad track in Porfirian Mexico, steering the Mexican economy into export production, consolidating landholdings into fewer hands, amplifying internal dissent along the lines of region and class, and providing a context for the expansion of Mexican federal and state police forces. Northern mines exported zinc, lead, and copper, and southern plantations exported tropical products, during a period when Indigenous communities across the country lost effective control over their lands. In 1910, 56 percent of the gross revenues of all Mexican railroads leaked out of the country, mostly to the United States.[31]

In 1911, Ottoman leaders signed a new concession with the Baghdad Railway Company, providing for branch railway and harbor construction to facilitate deliveries of construction material. To assuage British fears of German encroachment on southern Asia, the Baghdad Railway renounced any rights to continue east of Baghdad. Months later, following the Italian invasion and occupation of Tripoli, skilled Italian masons left the Baghdad Railway. Seeking to stabilize their territorial authority, Italian firms rapidly laid down rails linking Tripoli and Benghazi. The 1912 outbreak of war in the Balkans, which substantially weakened the Ottoman state, led to the use of new railways to move large numbers of Muslim refugees to Istanbul.[32]

Territorial competition between Russian and Japanese concessionary railroads accelerated the unraveling of Ch'ing rule in Manchuria, the dynastic homeland. In 1915, the Japanese government demanded control and preemption rights over railroads in Manchuria. Three years later, the Chinese Eastern Railway's Russian general manager declared a counterrevolutionary government, backed by a force of five thousand troops, half of whom were Chinese. The Soviet government renounced direct control of the Chinese Eastern Railway, as the fruits of imperialism, although it later revised this to claim preferential rights. In 1924, after the British occupation of Kabul, concerns about Soviet support for an anticolonial uprising spurred the British to extend railroads, running trains with steel shutters that converted to nests for machine guns, even though rail-based warfare was already beginning to be superseded by occupation from the skies. Following the further collapse of Ch'ing and Ottoman rule, and anticolonial revolution in Russia, the British sterling stabilized through resource extraction and raw materials production, especially in Britain's West African colonies. In 1911 and 1912, the British finished two railroad lines in Nigeria, each connecting the coast with the northern interior, with the intention of developing the export of tin, rubber, and cotton. Rail lines in the Gold Coast stimulated growth of the cocoa industry. In early 1917, British geologists found large bauxite deposits in the Gold Coast, and colonial officials planned a rail extension into Kumasi, the former Asante capital, to capitalize on wartime restrictions on bauxite supplies. Raw materials exports, especially from West Africa, kept the sterling above water.[33]

Mass anticolonial struggle stormed the breach opened by inter-imperialist rivalries. In 1919, a wave of unrest hit Egyptian railways from two fronts, as rail workers organized successful mass strikes while peasants sabotaged rail and telegraph lines, constituent parts of an upsurge of radical struggle across the eastern Mediterranean. The strikes grew out of a long history of Egyptian workers' organization, centering on collective demands for shorter work hours and higher wages. Railways workers joined with gas, water, and electric company workers, drawing upon the support of the broader community. Military authorities responded by shooting and killing strikers, threatening to burn nearby villages to the ground. Strike-breaking blended with counterinsurgency as assertions of imperial control over Egyptians' lives, labor, and lands.[34]

Railroads had become the sites of mass, organized unrest across the African continent by the end of the First World War. After civil service staff received a war bonus to offset war inflation, Gold Coast rail workers went on strike in 1918 to achieve their own inflation offsets, inaugurating a three-year strike wave that spread from the rails to the docks. In 1923, when community leaders met colonial officials at conferences in Accra, Cape Coast, Saltpond, and Winneba to discuss new railroad construction, they consistently demanded that money allocated for railroad construction should instead be spent on urgent social needs. Over decades of mass struggle, Gold Coast workers had developed high levels of solidarity. Heavy-handed government response to a 1941 strike failed to break this organizational strength, and within a few years, rail workers' unions formed the core of organized mass support for Nkrumah and the nationalist movement. In Rhodesia, in October 1945, a strike in Bulawayo saw the rise of a new African leadership organized under the banner of African Trade Unions, and railway officials reacted by attempting to separate the workers' loyalties along tribal and ethnic lines. The heart of African workers' solidarity pulsed with the identities they had forged over the previous decades, and a concomitant sense of what they were owed by Rhodesia Railways.[35]

As infrastructures of colonial isolation, railroads have left a mark, even where formal decolonization has occurred, through the violent ruptures of partition. Between August and November 1947, over 1,250,000 people rode trains to cross the borders of newly independent Pakistan and India, most of them fleeing ancestral homes for newly declared nation-states that seemingly aligned with their religious or communal identities, thousands of people cramming onto trains built to carry hundreds. In South Asia, trains have become iconically associated with partition, markers of an incomplete process of decolonization, of new techniques of definition and division along the lines of religion and caste that would shape neocolonial territoriality at the precise moment of the colonialists' apparent departure.[36]

Against the lingering residues of partition, what Aileen Moreton-Robinson calls "the unfinished business of Indigenous sovereignty" constitutes core positions from which to further dismantle the new worlds of imperialism, to recapture the infrastructural basis of multiple, distinct, and interconnected futures. Dale Kerwin writes, "Aboriginal people have rights to cultural heritage; stock routes belong to this category and fall within the bundle of rights for native title. There is no legal provision within Australian jurisprudence to extinguish the stock routes from the ambit of native title."[37]

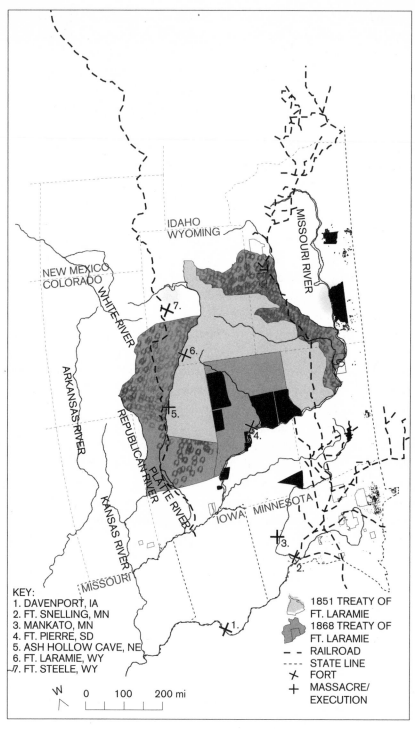

IDAHO
WYOMING

NEW MEXICO
COLORADO

MISSOURI RIVER

WHITE RIVER

ARKANSAS RIVER

REPUBLICAN RIVER

KANSAS RIVER

PLATTE RIVER

MISSOURI

IOWA MINNESOTA

×7.

×6.

×5.

×4.

+3.
×2.

×1.

KEY:
1. DAVENPORT, IA
2. FT. SNELLING, MN
3. MANKATO, MN
4. FT. PIERRE, SD
5. ASH HOLLOW CAVE, NE
6. FT. LARAMIE, WY
7. FT. STEELE, WY

W
N
0   100   200 mi

1851 TREATY OF
FT. LARAMIE
1868 TREATY OF
FT. LARAMIE
RAILROAD
STATE LINE
× FORT
+ MASSACRE/
  EXECUTION

MAPS 3 AND 4: Lakota Nation. Cartography by Elsa Matossian Hoover.

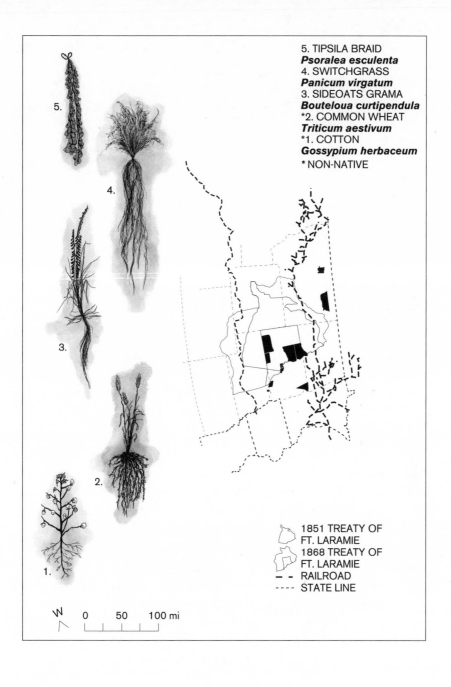

5. TIPSILA BRAID
Psoralea esculenta
4. SWITCHGRASS
Panicum virgatum
3. SIDEOATS GRAMA
Bouteloua curtipendula
*2. COMMON WHEAT
Triticum aestivum
*1. COTTON
Gossypium herbaceum
* NON-NATIVE

1851 TREATY OF FT. LARAMIE
1868 TREATY OF FT. LARAMIE
- - RAILROAD
---- STATE LINE

W

0   50   100 mi

FOUR

Lakota

LONG BEFORE THE TRANSCONTINENTAL RAILROAD, Lakotas sustained their collective lives through expansive relationships that they forged with each other, and with their homelands. Luther Standing Bear once wrote of this expansive relationship to place:

> No people ever loved their country or enjoyed it more than the Sioux. They loved the beautiful streams by which they camped, and the trees that shaded them and their tipis. They loved the green stretches of plains with its gardens here and there of sunflowers over which hovered and played myriads of yellow-winged birds. Moving day was just like traveling from one nice home to another.[1]

Standing Bear described a love based on a deep knowledge and appreciation of the complexity and variations of life in Lakota homelands, knowledge and appreciation that is the context of Lakota collective life, a form of possession *by* their homelands as much as a possession *of* those lands, a kind of reciprocal relationality. Lakota modes of relationship provided the strongest obstacle to the expansion of capitalism and U.S. sovereignty on the Plains in the second half of the nineteenth century, where machines of colonial expansion fueled by relationships of control met Indigenous modes of relationship between people, animals, plants, and places, shaped by an expansiveness that reflected the expansiveness of the place itself.[2] Focusing on Lakota historical geographies, and away from train tracks, highlights Indigenous relationships to place that are oriented to a different set of tracks: the tracks of massive, migratory buffalo herds.

Standing Bear described Lakotas' expansive relationship with place: "It was not like moving from one strange town to another, but wherever they settled it was home."[3] Where mobility has long been part of a sense of home among Lakotas, home, from a colonial perspective, can be, at best, a flickering mirage of security grounded in expropriation. For colonizers, who have taken what is not theirs, being expropriated, in turn, remains an ever-lurking possibility. Colonial sovereignty is counterinsurgency, what I call countersovereignty. This chapter analyzes the confrontation between expansive Lakota modes of relationship and the war-finance nexus.

BUFFALO NATION

The social foundations of expansive relationality reverberate in stories of Lakota origins. According to one Lakota creation story, Pte' Oyate' were humans who lived underground, and a few of them were enticed to the earth's surface by the aroma of freshly roasted buffalo meat. Anukite', who had been banished to the earth's surface, hunted a buffalo, roasting its meat, tanning and decorating its hide with porcupine quills, and then the trickster Iktomi left the robe and meat in a cave. Seven men and seven women followed the scent to the surface, where their descendants founded the seven councils that structure the Oceti Sakowin, which European invaders would come to call the "Great Sioux Nation." As the seasons turned, tormented by the cutting north wind, these fourteen people desperately and unsuccessfully searched for the cave that could return them to the underworld. Wazi and Wakanka, who were Anukite's parents, and who had also been banished, taught these fourteen how to live on the earth's surface. Movement, adaptation, and collective risk-taking have long shaped Lakota collective life, continuing to inform dynamic Lakota modes of relationship.[4]

The movement of buffalo herds defined the contours of Lakota society on the Plains. According to Delphine Red Shirt, "Always, they tried to stay near the buffalo—like the oyáte, the 'thatháka' were constantly on the move. They too migrated to better sources of food." Lakotas calibrated their calendar in proximity to the herds, from spring calving season through the major hunts in late autumn, when calves had matured. Lakota observations of buffalo also influenced the ways they organized community life. "They had common sense and we followed what they did. We learned to be like them because we depended upon them for everything." This was learning by observation, experiments leading to the development of new skills and new kinds of relationship, the way Wazi and Wakanka taught the fourteen people who first came to the earth's surface, skills that sustained reciprocity rather than dominion. Following buffalo herds, which adjusted their collective movements to find food, water, and shelter, Lakotas traced out a pattern of movements in relation to cycles of drought and rainfall, predatory pressure, and seasonal migrations. Theirs was an expansive relationship to place, emerging in dynamic relationship with the capacities for life on the lands where they lived.[5]

Delphine Red Shirt writes that Lakota winter counts record the first encounter with horses in the eighteenth century, and they soon "became as dependent on it as we were the buffalo." Lakota relationships with buffalo set the terms for incorporating horses into Lakota life, since horses enhanced Lakota abilities to follow the buffalo. Standing Bear described a time before horses, when buffalo sometimes wandered into villages to eat grass, and if there was a need for meat, the buffalo could be shared as a meal. A horse once followed a group of buffalo into a village, and as people gathered, watching it graze, a hunter was able to throw a rope on the animal's neck, and then a warrior was able to jump on its back. Lakota women's use of horses enhanced the mobility of their communities, broadening their communities' expansive relationships to their lands. While Standing Bear's story centers men in relation to horses, another story describes people's fear and bewilderment on seeing a strange, large animal, until an old woman manages to mount and subdue it. The age and gender of the rider are significant. Horses were useful not only as accouterments of hunting, but also for community mobility.[6]

Over time, Indigenous peoples adapted horses, so that their horses might loosely be understood as an Indigenous technology particularly suited to collective life in the region. A soldier in U.S. campaigns against Lakotas during the late 1870s noted, "The Indian ponies are accustomed to thrive upon grass or cottonwood bark and can travel untiringly upon such cheap fodder, while our cavalry horses break down unless they are provided with grain."[7] The ecological and social relationships emanating from horses and bison for Lakota society bear a relation to Marx's model of the two departments of capital. The first department, geared toward the means of production, mirrors the role of horses in the buffalo economy. The second department, revolving around production for consumption, mirrors the place of bison in the buffalo economy. The different temporalities of capital in the two departments necessitate reproduction on an expansive scale, in order for the total capital to reproduce itself over succeeding cycles.[8]

The growing fur trade on the central and northern Plains eclipsed a trading economy centered in Mandan and Hidatsa villages, and isolated fur trade posts became important trading sites. Initially established in 1832 or 1834, Fort Laramie, at the confluence of the Laramie and North Platte Rivers, at a place where the Plains begins to give way to the Rocky Mountains, was a significant site of this mercantile reorganization of space. Fur company employees and subcontractors trespassed on Indigenous hunting and trapping grounds, leading to an overproduction of furs and a corresponding drop in the value of beaver pelts in European markets. This augured a fuller development of a buffalo robe trade, further concentrating trading activity along the Missouri River, suffused with intense sexual and gendered violence.[9]

Toward the east, by the late 1840s, Dakota women had begun to participate directly in trade. The fur trade was structured around trading for goods on credit. Dakota women supplied furs for the trade, and they were primary consumers of trade goods. Credit, which underpinned the fur trade and its related economies, was a set of temporal relationships that enforced dependence. Credit was constitutive of the war-finance nexus, invoking personal relationships under the guise of "trust." But credit actually disrupted relationships, and accompanied sexual and gendered violence.[10]

The Lakota buffalo economy was not a capitalist one. A personal claim on bison was possible only after horses enabled individual Lakotas to ride into buffalo herds and make individual kills. According to Delphine Red Shirt, Lakota women "knew from the way the shaft was decorated whose arrow it was. Once they identified it, the carcass belonged to them. They could do with it as they wished."[11] Any claim on a buffalo, or on something harvested from a buffalo, only made sense through relationships with women, situated within larger communities.

Celane Not Help Him described how she works a deer hide "in old ways":

> Deer hide, you soak it and then pull out the hair as much as you could and then scrape the rest. Then stake it a little bit and when it dries up, you put oil on it, or grease. We always use bacon grease or that kidney fat, and you tend it. I got those side blades that you work it with, back and forth. Then you turn it over, all directions, and it spread out but you have to work it before it gets too dry. When you put it away you wet double layer of towel and wrap it around so it won't get dry, and then you work it again. So you learn things like that and always remember how to do it. What you learn, nobody can take away from you.[12]

Lakota women's skilled and creative work was a primary point of contestation between Indigenous expansiveness and the expansionist pressures of the global fur trade. In North America, capitalist relations of production do not supersede or eradicate Indigenous modes of relationship, but instead emerge in reaction to Indigenous modes of relationship. The persistence of Indigenous modes of relationship points to the imperative of decolonization, the possibility of unraveling colonial state formation as well as capital accumulation, as an imperative that is inherent within continental imperialism. On the Plains, the expanding reproduction of capital occurs, and can also be undone, in relation to expansive Indigenous relations rooted in place.[13]

Capitalism assimilated to Indigenous modes of relationship as it developed in the region. Leonard Crow Dog testified at the 1974 Sioux Treaty Hearing, "We are the nation. We are nation before even the government. Before we signed any treaties. We are nation."[14] In Lakota memory, the fact of Lakota existence continues to render Lakota nationhood inviolate on Lakota lands. "The government," like capitalism, imposes expansion over expansiveness, control over reciprocity, and imagines humans as separate and over the world. The war-finance nexus reacts to the expansiveness embedded in Lakota relationships.

TREATY AT HORSE CREEK

In 1851, nearly ten thousand Lakota, Cheyenne, Arapaho, Crow, Shoshone, Assiniboine, Mandan, Hidatsa, and Arikara people gathered for eighteen days at Horse Creek, a few miles away from Fort Laramie, visiting, exchanging gifts, feasting, and adopting children and siblings. These are Indigenous diplomatic protocols, and the United States was peripheral to them. The talks took place in a circular arbor that Lakota and Cheyenne women built out of lodge poles and tipi covers. Imperialist diplomatic protocols were more closely reflected in the written text of the 1851 Fort Laramie Treaty, which had been prepared beforehand, and which marked U.S. recognition of Lakota supremacy on the central and northern Plains, inaugurating a new round of confrontation. In the written treaty, representatives of the U.S. federal government imposed their own definitions of "nation" while imposing Cheyenne diplomatic practices on Lakota communities. The text declared an expanding United States as the sole power to negotiate on a basis of equality with Lakotas. The written treaty instituted a zone of intertribal peace on the Plains in a circumscribed area south of the Missouri River, east of the Rockies, and north of New Mexico and Texas, articulating a U.S. right to construct railroads, military forts, and other infrastructure in this area.

Territorialization proceeds through infrastructure planning and development. Imperialist peace proceeds through colonialist wars. What followed in ensuing years was a conflict between two armed camps, pitting Lakota expansiveness against U. S. expansionism. Countersovereignty, the U. S. pretension to legal authority over territory and bodies, revolves around an attempt to replace expansive Indigenous modes of relationship with expansionist modes of relationship, imagined through mystical conceptions of the unceasing expansion of capital, untethered from physical constraints. Expropriating Indigenous modes of relationship is a constituent element of financial imaginaries that project growth, profits, and progress in a way that disavows any material constraints, a core and ongoing element of the political economy of countersovereignty. As financial capital is fictitious capital, countersovereignty is fictitious sovereignty, sovereignty that follows the organization and functions of credit: a future claim that is backed by the full force of the state.[15]

Following Lakota understandings, however, Lakotas who "signed" the treaty agreed not to the written text, but to everything that had been spoken during the proceedings. Increasing settlement and the establishment of heavily traveled overland roads reshaped the patterns of buffalo migrations, and Lakotas understood that they won compensation for this damage in the treaty negotiations. Several of the Lakota negotiators at Horse Creek were incensed upon learning that the written treaty set the boundaries of their territory at the Platte River, pointing out that they hunted as far south of the river as the Republican Fork of the Kansas River, and the Arkansas River. Black Hawk, an Oglala leader, told David Mitchell, the superintendent of Indian affairs and lead U. S. negotiator, "You have split the country, and I don't like it." The 1851 Fort Laramie Treaty heralded a shift in the regional presence of the United States, with the U. S. federal government now claiming military authority over the region.[16]

After 1851, the United States began constructing new permanent trading posts and military forts across the region, diffusing imperialist authority over Indigenous space. Some of this new infrastructure, like Fort Kearny, had been established to protect, and to profit from, westward-bound traffic on overland trails. New trading posts and military forts quickly became points of distribution, where settlers and colonial officials attempted to dictate the terms of trade and enforce a colonialist peace. Bullets could not be grown or harvested. Guns did not reproduce. Intertribal relationships, however, were alive and organic. Communities most resistant to the United States moved northward, where, U.S. officials feared, they resupplied their arms through trade with Red River Métis. Scarcity continued to fail as a method for sustaining imperial control, unable to contain expansive Lakota modes of relationship.[17]

The 1851 treaty had carved the central and northern Plains into two opposing blocs. This stalemate exploded in August 1854 when a member of a group of Danish Mormons heading west filed a complaint at Fort Laramie that an Indian had stolen his property, killing and butchering a lame ox. Conquering Bear, a Brulé whom U.S. negotiators had named as head chief for all Lakotas during the treaty council at Horse Creek, reported the incident the same day, offering to help resolve the matter by paying the value of the ox. Absurdly, the commanding officer at Fort Laramie insisted that the person who killed the ox be turned over, and the next day, sent a force of twenty-nine infantry with a couple of howitzers to a large village eight miles away. On arriving, the soldiers quickly escalated their assault—soon after they started firing their guns, they fired off both cannons. The retribution against the outnumbered U.S. soldiers was swift and total. Among the casualties of the fighting was Conquering Bear himself. As soon as the violence subsided, the women of the village rapidly moved their homes and their children several miles away, seeking to defuse the violence, and seeking safety.[18]

A little over a year later, at daybreak on September 3, 1855, a retaliatory force of six hundred U.S. soldiers, led by Gen. William Harney, marched on a Brulé village camped about six miles off of a gorge in the North Platte River. Upon sighting the marching soldiers, the women villagers swiftly packed their belongings and began moving away. When Little Thunder, a village leader, attempted to speak with Harney, he was dumbstruck to learn that Harney assigned collective guilt to the entire village for the deaths of the U.S. soldiers from the previous year. At Blue Water Creek, the soldiers fired indiscriminately. One of the officers later rewrote history: "In the pursuit, women, if recognized, were generally passed by my men." We can see, here, colonial gallantry retroactively invoked to cover the reality of mass murder. After this day, Nick Estes writes, Lakotas call Harney "Woman Killer."[19]

The soldiers held all of the survivors as prisoners. A year after Blue Water Creek, at Fort Pierre, Woman Killer met with Lakota leaders to discuss the release of the prisoners and the restoration of annuities, insisting that Lakotas surrender individuals accused of crimes by the United States, and stay away from the overland trails, effectively ceding large swaths of territory through the heart of Lakota homelands. During these talks, he also demanded the selection of liaisons, "chiefs," who could then be deposed only by U. S. presidential fiat, attempting to replace expansive relations of leadership with expansionist practices of administration, for efficient domination. Severt Young Bear remembered this a century later:

> The government signed the treaty with some chiefs. They had a meeting there and they didn't have enough representatives of the Sioux bands. They made some agreements on this and they went back to Washington, revised it, the treaty, and they came back again to the same point, and they sent out to bring in the chiefs here.
>
> When they came back, the chiefs they expected were not there at that meeting, so the government got sore and appointed some chiefs, "Hey Chief, come here, you look like you make a good chief," so they signed some documents and according to my oral history they were politically appointed chiefs.

In Young Bear's telling, these men were selected to fulfill an imperial role through a racist gaze, in which any Indian could be interchangeable with another, so long as it suited U. S. negotiators. In a meeting with Lakota leaders on the southwest side of the Black Hills, these politically appointed chiefs were later exposed as lacking authority within Lakota frameworks.[20]

Indigenous land rights, enshrined through treaties, fundamentally contradicted land grants to the Union Pacific Railroad Company, as provided by the 1862 Pacific Railroad Act.[21] To honor the property claim is to abrogate treaty obligations: to honor the treaties would be to dissolve capital claims on territory and resources. U. S. countersovereignty suspends its unraveling through yet another round of expropriative violence. The Pacific Railroad Act named a set of property claims that failed to reflect reality. It was U. S. sovereignty as a provisional declaration, sovereignty on credit, a colonialist bond to be honored on future maturation. This is the war-finance nexus. The United States, as it appears in the Pacific Railway Act, was not a place, or a set of relationships in a place. It was, more precisely, a set of threats about what would be done in and to the places it described.

President Lincoln signed the act into law on July 1, 1862, incorporating the Union Pacific Railroad Company, to be financed by 100,000 shares, initially valued at $1,000. The future-orientation of the shares reflected the future orientation of Congress's sovereign claims over these lands. The law renamed Indigenous lands as "public lands," authorizing the Union Pacific to use dirt, stone, and timber for construction, granting 200 feet on each side of the line for stations, buildings, and other physical plant. The law was itself a speculative enterprise to remake Indigenous lands, and Indigenous modes of relationship in and with those lands. The capital relationship is inextricable from processes of invasion and occupation, but the capital claim actually preceded any functional colonial occupation of the region. This relationship between the state and the corporation provides a window into the dual faces of colonization and accumulation, the war-finance nexus. In the law, the imperial state chartered the corporation, while on the ground, the corporation would manifest the terms of imperial sovereignty. Capital accumulation and countersovereignty each constituted the other, seeking to expropriate Lakotas of their expansive relations.

The U.S. Congress bestowed land outside of its control upon the Union Pacific Railroad, granting alternating sections of land on either side of the track, explicitly for the purpose of securing "the safe and speedy transportation of the mails, troops, munitions of war, and public stores thereon." Security, here, can be understood in a dual sense: military control on the one hand, and on the other, managing the risks of financial capital, which, given the speculative nature of the law itself, were the risks of U.S. sovereignty claims. U.S. sovereignty over the Platte River country would be established through the war-finance nexus, blending military security with financial securities. The law defined terms for the maturation and repayment of railroad bonds in thirty years, legislatively annihilating Indigenous space through colonial time. Against the period of bond maturation, a period for the development of functional colonial sovereignty over the Platte River country, the law stipulated that failure to construct one hundred miles of track within two years of the law's passage, and one hundred miles each additional year, would result in the forfeiture of all Union Pacific assets. Indigenous nations' ongoing abilities to assert their distinct modes of relationship threatened the solvency of the Union Pacific Railroad and, in turn, threatened to unravel U.S. Congressional sovereignty by fiat.[22] The mythology of free market competition is unmasked here, as an alibi for underlying relations of invasion and occupation that are a point of origin for corporate profits.

A month after the Pacific Railway Act planted a legislative flag on Lakota lands, on August 17, 1862, Lakotas' eastern relatives rose up against famine and assault in Minnesota. After their surrender on September 26, the United States treated Dakotas as war criminals. Women, children, and elders were held in a concentration camp at Fort Snelling. At least three hundred people died in this camp. Most remaining Dakotas were imprisoned at Davenport,

Iowa. More than a third of these Dakota prisoners died in custody. Four months later, President Lincoln signed orders for the execution of thirty-eight Dakota men in Mankato, Minnesota, the largest public execution in U.S. history. In reaction to the uprising, the United States nullified Dakota treaty rights and removed Dakota people westward to Nebraska and South Dakota.[23]

Six days after the martyrdom of Dakota patriots, Lincoln signed the Emancipation Proclamation. This timing reflects more than a mere coincidence. A formal end to slavery occurred in a context of financialized territorial expansion. The dissolution of the slave property claim (with credit to former slaveholders, and a newly imposed moral economy of indebtedness for freedpeople), would pair with the expansion of real estate claims that originate in theft, occupation, and genocide. Relations of credit and real estate animated the expansion of continental imperialism, as the Union Pacific Railroad carried the violence and terror committed against their eastern relatives directly into Lakota homelands.

OCCUPIED TERRITORY

Two years after the Dakota Uprising, the military utility of the Union Pacific may already have been apparent to Maj. Gen. Grenville Dodge in the winter of 1864–65, when he led hostile campaigns against Lakotas. As Lakotas followed buffalo herds, the U.S. Army, according to Dodge's strategy, would follow Lakotas, but there was a difference. Where Lakotas followed the herds as a form of relationship, the U.S. Army would follow Lakotas to "pound" and "attack." Here we can see the difference between an expansive and an expansionist relationship to a place. Dodge had urged the army to prepare "to follow the Indians day and night, attacking them at every opportunity until they are worn out, disbanded or forced to surrender."[24] Nakedly indiscriminate, constant violence would be the means for establishing U.S. sovereignty and stabilizing U.S. property claims. In Dodge's memory, the justification for the Union Pacific, and techniques for expropriating Indigenous nations, merged onto the same tracks: counterinsurgency, a reaction to the renewal of Lakota modes of relationship. Counterinsurgency remains at the heart of U.S. pretensions to sovereign authority over Lakota homelands.

William T. Sherman, Dodge's commanding officer, would prove a staunch ally of Union Pacific construction. Sherman was primarily interested in the railroad as a means of military occupation. Settlement and troop movements, in his understanding, were constituent elements of a larger military strategy to enact some kind of functional control over Lakota homelands. Railroad surveying reflected an underlying imperative to transform specific places into extractive claims on credit. This is the orientation of U. S. countersovereignty over its supposedly "domestic" territory. James Evans, surveying the Black Hills in summer 1865 for the Union Pacific, reported that timber resources there could supply the railroad west of the North Platte River. Moreover, Evans reported, coal deposits at Bitter Creek and Black Buttes (where, decades later, a pogrom would drive Chinese miners from Rock Springs) made a case for routing the railroad in close proximity. The conditions of Evans's surveying work, however, were constrained by "Indian difficulties," which, over the course of the summer, had "rendered insecure" the entire Platte valley. In addition to timber and coal, Evans reported on U. S. military outposts, "but feebly garrisoned, and incapable of offering anything like a protracted defence." Fueled by a "feeling of insecurity," Evans assembled his report in much greater haste than he had initially planned. Indigenous presence constrained the production of empirical forms of colonial knowledge.[25] What could empirically be known or reported about the place was limited by the insecurity of invasion and occupation. Imperialism is a shaky ground for empiricism. Extraction and financialization are core elements of U. S. countersovereignty: the transformation of Indigenous places into capital claims that could be actualized at some future time, processes that were arrested (and which continue to be arrested) by the presence of Indigenous people, in an Indigenous present.

The perspective of a U. S. cavalryman is illuminating. Charles Springer kept a journal while serving on a campaign "in the country of the dreaded Sioux nation" over the summer of 1865. The place, itself, which the U. S. Congress had granted to the Union Pacific by legislative fiat, haunted Springer and his comrades. One of them cried out one July night, "The devil is shifting his headquarters. I can smell brimstone." In August, Springer and several of his comrades desecrated Lakota graves and then, as the weather turned sharply cold in early September, the company withstood three attacks, the harrowed soldiers speaking bitterly of surviving a brutal civil war only to be sent to suffer in Lakota country. "We swore mutually that this trip should be the last of our soldier life." As the north wind chilled their bones, the company's uniforms ran threadbare, and on the morning of September 9, "a horrid sight presented itself to our eyes." Two hundred and fifty horses and mules had either died, or had become so weak they had to be shot. "The rain and cold still continued, we took our breakfast in silence. Everybody thought, what will become of us, if this weather continues so?" Over the course of their ordeal, the company mapped sites of Lakota winter camps, which the U.S. Army would soon put to tactical and genocidal use. On October 18, Springer encountered two former comrades who had married Lakota women, earning money as interpreters. Rejecting their suggestions that he do the same, Springer yearned instead to return to the United States.[26] He recorded two options for white men in this country: assimilate to Indigenous modes of relationship, or leave.

That September, reports of "Indians" near the Julesburg area had made it difficult for Union Pacific management to station workers close to the end of the track, slowing down construction. The previous April, Dodge had received an intelligence report from Col. W. O. Collins detailing Lakota communities north of the Platte River, between Red Butte and the Powder River. Noting conflicts and alliances, Collins provided population estimates for Oglalas and Brulés, as well as information about community leaders. Surveying the land and the people, the Union Pacific and the army created an archive, assembled under conditions of invasion, mobilized toward industrialization as counterinsurgency. This archive would enable the deployment of credit within the secure precincts of colonial monopoly. In November 1865, officers at Fort Kearney transferred carbines, muskets, and rifles to a division engineer for the Union Pacific Railroad, on the understanding that the arms would be returned within fifteen days. Three months afterwards, the weapons had yet to be returned. In June 1866, an interpreter described a visit to Fort Laramie by Spotted Tail, Standing Elk, Red Cloud, and Man Afraid of His Horses, Brulé and Oglala leaders, who "spoke much about not having any roads made through their country," asserting the ongoing and functioning primacy of Lakota modes of relationship in their homelands.[27]

Expansive Lakota relationships, and Lakotas' actions to enforce these relationships, were central concerns for Union Pacific Railroad management. Dodge's 1867 *Report of the Chief Engineer of the Union Pacific* begins with accounts of multiple attacks on Union Pacific surveying teams, translating the death of surveyors into a profit loss for the Union Pacific, balancing the books of industrial occupation. Thomas O'Donnell, who worked on Union Pacific construction, wrote of struggles against the weather, and the North Platte River, in the effort to build a secure bridge, going on to write:

> There was then a squad of soldiers guarding the bridge, keeping the Indians
> from burning it. South of the Platte were three hundred hostile Indians. Jack
> Morrow, an Indian trader, told us they were getting ugly, not to trust them.
> We prepared to fight them.

The railroad workers, O'Donnell reminisced, were initially equipped with
muzzle-loading Springfield rifles, placing pickets in half circles at night, laying track at a rate of one to five miles a day. After reports that thousands of
fighters led by Red Cloud had been running away with graders' stock along
the South Platte, O'Donnell's group received a shipment of new breech-
loading rifles, which they then had to learn to use.[28] Breech-loaders, tele-
graphs, and other ancillary technologies arriving alongside trains aided
industrial warfare in the region.

In Dodge's recollection, Union Pacific construction was an extension of
the army, organized "purely upon a military basis." The ranks of the construction force were filled with Civil War veterans. The heads of most engineering
parties and all of the construction groups had been officers. John Casement,
who oversaw track-laying, had been a division commander. Military experience played an active role in railroad construction. "At any moment I could
call into the field a thousand men well officered." The true significance of this
military organization was not for the management of labor, or corporate
competition with the Central Pacific Railroad, but instead the colonization
of the lands through which the Union Pacific was being constructed. The
central fact, for the emergence of industrial capitalism in this place, was
expropriation. "There was no law in the country, and no court. We laid out
the towns, officered them, kept peace and everything went on smoothly and
in harmony." In Dodge's telling, the imperial state emerged in this place
through the functions of the railroad corporation. Where the U. S. Congress
had chartered the railroad corporation in the Pacific Railway Law, on the
ground, the corporation preceded the state, attempting to remake Lakota
lands as a space of capital accumulation. Labor on the Union Pacific Railroad
entailed soldiering, as much as construction work. Confederate veterans who
worked on Union Pacific construction, so-called "galvanized Yanks," played
a part in reconstituting the United States following the Civil War. The conditions of Southern white reentry into the United States were not reconstruction, carrying the promise of multiracial democracy; they were, rather, conditions of continental imperialism. According to Grenville Dodge, captured
Confederate soldiers preferred to fight Indians, rather than be returned to
their former commanders, and the army organized them into the Second and

Third Regiments of U. S. volunteers, known as "Reconstructed Rebs," which defended Union Pacific construction.[29] The abridgement of emancipation did not occur in isolation from the development of industrial capitalism on the Plains, and the extension of U. S. territorial claims on a continental scale.

In May 1867, Samuel Reed, chief engineer for the Union Pacific Railroad, complained repeatedly of Indian raids taking horses and mules along the line of construction, imploring Sherman to move additional forces to fight on behalf of the railroad. The army's direct involvement in Union Pacific construction flowed partly from justifications for the railroad as a tool to stabilize its occupation of the region. In 1867, Ulysses S. Grant, then acting secretary of war, reported to Congress that completion of the transcontinental railroad would significantly reduce the cost of maintaining troops between the Missouri River and the Pacific Coast. Moreover, railroad construction would "also go far toward a permanent settlement of our Indian difficulties," enabling the United States to negotiate treaties from a position of strength. Dodge and Sherman coordinated railroad construction with invasion and occupation. In early January 1867, Sherman informed Dodge, "The point where you cross the North Platte and Fort Laramie will become great military points, and you should make arrangements with cars to land there our troops and stores." The railroad would enable the military occupation of Lakota homelands. Eleven days later, Sherman pledged to "give you all the aid I possibly can, but the demand for soldiers everywhere and the slowness of enlistment, especially among the Blacks, limit our ability to respond." Military occupation would feed the chain of credit and debt that had financed the Civil War. Sherman expected Freedmen to consecrate their lives to imperial expansion, rather than forging multiracial democracy, let alone achieving some form of compensation or self-determination.[30]

Between these letters, Dodge had written directly to General Augur, requesting military escorts for work parties between Alkali Flats to Fort Sanders, from a perspective of labor management. "Any scare or attack . . . would be fatal to us, and almost impossible to obtain the necessary laborers." Dodge explained that he planned to post grading parties every fifteen to twenty miles, with parties of scouts moving north and south of the line, looking for signs of Indigenous people moving through their lands between Lodge Pole Creek, the South Platte, and Laramie Fork, "a country very little known until the last year, when we developed it by our different engineering parties." Dodge envisioned grading the Union Pacific as the wedge of invasion, with Union Pacific engineers as explorers of the unknown, mapping the land in order to reshape it, transforming the modes of relationship, the terms of life, on the land. This was encroachment, and it was the basis of capital accumulation, transpiring in a relationship of reaction to the ongoing relationships that Lakotas shared with their relatives, including their lands. A group of eleven engineers, with teamsters, cooks, a mail carrier, and a hunter, west of Laramie in February 1867, had a military escort of two companies, one infantry, one cavalry, because "the Indians were very bad . . . out there." The group did not encounter any Indigenous people, but the snow drove several of them blind, the others blackening their faces with charcoal "in order to soften the glare of light."[31]

While these intrepid explorers stumbled through the snow, Sherman implored Dodge, "I hope you will keep your men at work, spite of rumors, and even apparent dangers, for both General Augur and I will do all to cover the working parties that is possible." For 1867, Sherman explained, the army would concentrate its forces several hundred miles to the north, but he envisioned that by the following year, "by these railroads and the extension of your Great Road to the Black Hills (Sanders, if possible) and the Smoky Hill to the neighborhood of Cheyenne hills, we can act so energetically that both Sioux and Cheyennes must die, or submit to our dictation." Sherman imagined the Union Pacific as a weapon to finally enact a credible threat of genocide. He imagined countersovereignty (and countersovereignty, in the final instance, only exists in the imagination), mapping out a specific threat space, which we might think of as the "interior" of the United States.[32]

The Union Pacific Railroad, in Sherman's mind, was not an infrastructure for connection. The railroad was infrastructure to enforce a credible threat of total and catastrophic violence against Lakota communities. Three months later, Sherman reiterated that the army would soon be able to move more troops, especially cavalry, to the Plains, reposting them from "the reconstructed United States." That month, however, railroad work parties at Lodge Pole Creek, Rock Creek, Cooper Creek, and the Laramie plains faced attacks and had mules, horses, and cattle stock taken and tools destroyed. On May 27, Dodge escorted three U.S. peace commissioners to the end of track in Lodge Pole Creek valley, where they arrived just after noon, to witness "a large body of Indians" sweep down on grading parties, riding away with several horses and mules, before the graders could grab their guns. As attacks continued in Lodge Pole Creek valley in June, doubts began to creep in about the army's abilities to protect railroad construction. One person complained to Dodge, "I fear Sherman can fight Georgia crackers better than he can Indians." In early July, workers at the base of the Black Hills were attacked by a group of Lakotas, who killed several of them and rode off their stock animals before the cavalry escort could even begin pursuit. This particular attack was noteworthy only because it was witnessed by army officers. Despite Sherman's musings on the genocidal potential latent in the Union Pacific, in the summer of 1867, U.S. military protection remained insufficient to protect railroad work parties.[33]

On September 20, Sherman spoke at a treaty council with Brulés, Oglalas, and Cheyennes on the North Platte. Sherman described railroad construction as an elemental law of a new ecology that Lakotas could not overturn, speaking of white people in eastern North America, "They hardly think of what you call war out here, and if they make up their minds they will come to the plains as thick as the largest herd of buffalo and they will kill you all." The Americans, Sherman threatened, would replace the buffalo, and doing so, they would destroy the foundations of collective Lakota life. This desolation was the promise and fulfillment of countersovereignty. Sherman concluded, "This commission is not a peace commission only; it is also a war commission." As with the written text of the 1851 Fort Laramie Treaty, imperialist peace proceeds through conditions of colonialist war.[34]

While Union Pacific officials had been seeking protection from the U.S. Army for several years, the railroad itself now enabled the further penetration of military occupation over Indigenous lands and lives. Building the railroad occurred in tandem with building new military posts and supply lines. Fort Steele, for example, was erected in the summer of 1868 to protect the Union Pacific Railroad, at a summer and winter campsite, a central point for Indigenous movements. Restricting Indigenous mobility by enabling colonial mobility, the railroad provided a core infrastructure for continental imperialism.[35] The army's winter campaigns, a new and brutal tactic in which army units hunted and assaulted villages in the deep winter, were enabled by the ability to move troops and provisions over rails in subzero conditions. Winter campaigns struck communities in the precise time of year when food and heat were most scarce, conditions of scarcity that had been greatly exacerbated following several decades of colonial constriction. Winter campaigns occurred during the months that, for Lakotas, were times of storytelling, renewing relationships across generations. The U.S. Army's winter campaigns assaulted the renewal of Lakota relationships.

Vine Deloria Jr. explained how unilateral amendments that the United States made to the 1851 treaty shaped the context for 1868, after the Senate reduced the period of annuities from fifty to ten years. Lakotas had never been informed of these changes, let alone agreed to them. At a council in Fort Laramie in 1868, they began by discussing the failure of the United States to fulfill its treaty obligations: "So their intent, for the most part, was to reaffirm the provisions of the old treaty rather than to cede new rights and privileges to the United States under a new agreement."[36]

The tenor of the talks had already been set in preliminary conversations. On May 28, One Horn, an Oglala, spoke to the U.S. peace commissioners at Fort Laramie:

> This Indian country we all (the Sioux Nation) claim as ours. I have never lost the place from my view. It is our home to come back to. I like to be able to trade here, although I will not give away my land. I don't ever remember ceding any of my land to anyone . . . I see that the whites blamed the Indians, but it is you that acted wrong in the beginning. The Indians never went to your country and did wrong. This is our land, and yet you blame us for fighting for it.[37]

On the first day of the treaty council, April 28, Iron Shell, a Brulé leader, addressed Generals Harney and Sanborn, and other members of the Indian Peace Commission:

> You have come into my country without my consent and spread your soldiers all over it. I have looked around for the cause of the trouble and I cannot see that my young men were the cause of it. All the bad things that have been done you have made the road for it. That is the truth.

He continued with the core of his proposal, "We want you to take away the forts from the country," and he demanded that this be accomplished before winter. Swift Bear, a Brulé, spoke next, "You are making maps of our country and taking it away from us." Referring to the 1851 treaty, he continued, asking that the generals "repeat precisely" his words in Washington, "We want a reservation of land to be surveyed and have fenced off along the White River down to the Whetstone Creek along the Missouri River. We want that land respected by the whites. Protect us and keep the whites off it."[38]

When talks resumed the next day, American Horse said, "These whites that you have put in my buffalo country I despise, and I want to see them away." He and other Lakota speakers at the treaty council refused to accept treaty goods, asserting Lakota independence from colonial administration, asserting Lakota prerogatives of trade and diplomacy, against imperialist territorialization, refusing to constrain their self-determination under a contract logic. White Crane, a Brulé, continued, "You have no business to come and settle on this land. Go off it."[39]

A letter reporting to Fort Laramie of the signing of a treaty in November 1868 by Oglala leaders, described Red Cloud, "with a show of reluctance and tremulousness," washing his hands with the dust of the floor. Josephine Waggoner recalled that in old times, people used to throw dirt in the faces of someone who told a story that was too impossible or improbable to believe. Perhaps Red Cloud was commenting on the impossibility and improbability of U.S. stories about sovereign authority over Oglala lands. After the treaty was signed by the U.S. negotiators, Red Cloud voiced his hopes for a future in which, as in years past, "the country was filled with traders instead of military Posts," envisioning the restoration of relations of reciprocity, rather than domination.[40] Red Cloud's gesture provides a perspective on the Treaty of 1868 that sustained and enhanced Lakota independence and control over their lands, proceeding from the fact of ongoing Lakota modes of relationship.

Lakota oral histories remember the Treaty of 1868 in the breach. Edith Bull Bear testified "the government made a lot of promises it kept for only two years. After that, a lot of the promises were broken." The proof, Bull Bear argued, could be seen more than a century later.

> White people weren't supposed to come into our country but even with that in the Treaty they still came in anyway. Look at us, your people are sitting where our land is. The only purposes they came into our land was to take our land, and they are still coming in.

In Lakota memory, Lakotas negotiated the Treaty of 1868 from a position of strength. Severt Young Bear asserted that "the Sioux Nation never sat there with their hands out and said we want peace and friendship; it was the government that came to us and asked for peace and friendship." According to Gordon Spotted Horse, the treaty "is considered to be the final Treaty of the Lakota people," setting out "a boundary which the United States was not to enter under any circumstances." In Vine Deloria Jr.'s analysis of the oral history, Lakotas "didn't think they were surrendering any rights," and many of them were even resistant to the idea of signing a peace treaty, feeling that they had defeated the United States, and the U.S. was "suing for peace." Deloria concurred, "This was true in many respects; the Lakota were definitely negotiating from a position of strength."[41]

Lakota perspectives, from the recorded notes of treaty councils, provide essential context for reading the written text of the treaty. The treaty encoded the perpetual rights of Lakotas to hunt, rights which would be abridged by the mass slaughter of buffalo herds in ensuing years. Following this statement were seven subclauses recording the removal of "any pretense" of opposition to the Union Pacific Railroad, and to military posts built through their lands. Together, the railroad and the military infrastructure left no space for the buffalo, and for people who sustained their communities in relation to the buffalo. Delphine Red Shirt writes of her great-grandmother, "She learned how to make moccasins out of canvas instead of buffalo hide. The buffalo were our lifeline. Once that was cut, we could no longer survive on our own." As Red Cloud suggested at the treaty council, individuals would adhere to it only to the extent that the United States respected Lakota treaty protocols, and Lakota rights to place. As late as April 1869, just a month before the railroads joined at Promontory Point, Union Pacific workers faced attacks from Pine Bluffs to Willow Island, which continued to stall the progress of construction.[42]

The perspective on the treaty was different from the U.S. side. In the peace commissioners' report on the treaty negotiations, they recorded their initial charge, "If settlers and railroad men would treat Indians as they would treat whites under similar circumstances we apprehend but little trouble would exist."[43] If treaty commissioners had themselves treated Lakotas as they would treat whites whose country was under foreign military occupation, they would have gone much farther in addressing Lakota concerns. Those concerns centered on the next phases of imperial infrastructure. The railroad clauses of the 1868 treaty negotiations were especially contentious in a context of the construction of the Northern Pacific Railroad right through Lakota lands. Targeted attacks under Sitting Bull's leadership would lead to the halting of Northern Pacific progress. In the years after the failure of the Northern Pacific and defeat of the Seventh Cavalry, the United States would reassert power, policing reservation boundaries as a site of containment, flooding Oceti Sakowin lands with the world's largest system of river dams, through the present, authorizing pipelines to carry volatile toxic sludge from the Bakken tar fields to the Gulf of Mexico.[44]

In a pamphlet circulating among commanding officers in the Department of the Platte to share the details of the 1868 treaty, officers were instructed that "friendly Indians have withdrawn from that country, and you are instructed that hereafter, until further orders, all Indians found there are to be regarded as hostile, and treated accordingly." From a U.S. perspective, rather than institute a future of peace, the treaty forged a zone of war, a spatial perspective on U.S. sovereignty as a project of counterinsurgency. From a U.S. perspective, the rationalization of space along the Platte River, as it took shape through railroad construction, was simultaneously a racialization of space, folding the field of international engagement between Lakotas and the United States into a space of containment, imagined as part of the "national" interior. U.S. countersovereignty works by rendering Indigenous peoples collectively vulnerable to violence for remaining on their homelands. From a colonial perspective, industrialization developed in tandem with the transformation of the Platte River country in a shift from international to domestic law. U.S. interpretations of the 1868 treaty were part of the war-finance nexus that shaped the building of the transcontinental railroad, attempting to dress brute conquest in the finery of legality.[45]

George Gap testified at the Sioux Treaty Hearing in December 1974:

> From my understanding after the signing of the 1868 Treaty one of the promises that was made was the Union Pacific Railroad was to have only one side of the track right of way. The other side belongs to the Sioux people. The north side of the track, and the north side of the North Platte River will belong to the Sioux people. From my understanding the tract of that land where the track was on was leased out, but I don't know how long, or to whom.[46]

Gap's testimony, more than a century after the 1868 treaty, voices a consistent and living critique, an expansive Lakota mode of relationship that continues to profoundly destabilize U.S. sovereignty and property claims on Lakota lands. Lakota modes of relationship, in 1868, in 1974, and in the present, remain expansive enough to forge relationships with other modes of relationship, but the United States, rooted in expansion and control, can function with the possibility of only one future: liberty and justice, as they say, for all. This should be heard properly, as an imperialist threat.

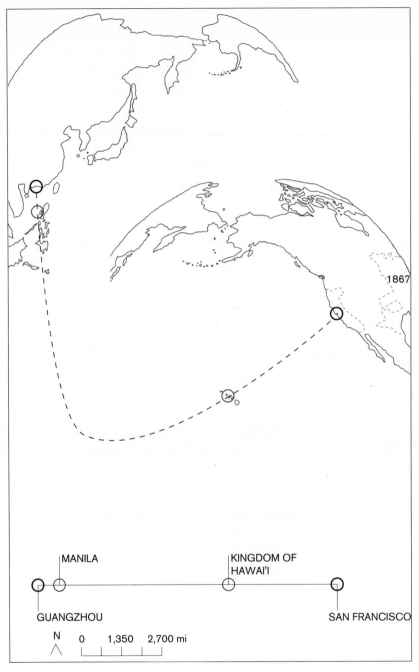

1867

MANILA

KINGDOM OF
HAWAI'I

GUANGZHOU

SAN FRANCISCO

N   0   1,350   2,700 mi

MAPS 5 AND 6: Chinese Workers. Cartography by Elsa Matossian Hoover.

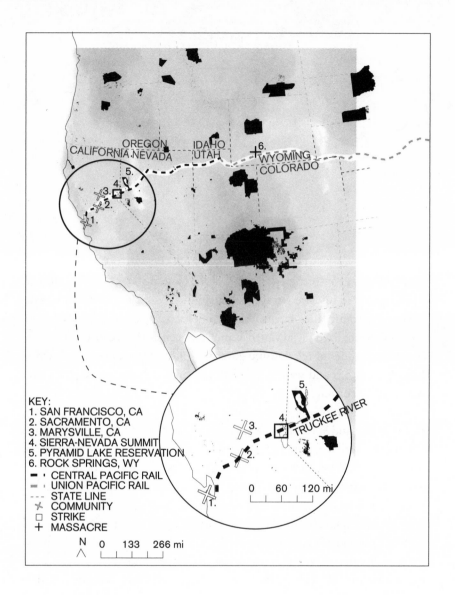

KEY:
1. SAN FRANCISCO, CA
2. SACRAMENTO, CA
3. MARYSVILLE, CA
4. SIERRA-NEVADA SUMMIT
5. PYRAMID LAKE RESERVATION
6. ROCK SPRINGS, WY

- • CENTRAL PACIFIC RAIL
▨ ▪ UNION PACIFIC RAIL
--- STATE LINE
⋇ COMMUNITY
☐ STRIKE
+ MASSACRE

N   0   133   266 mi
∧

OREGON
CALIFORNIA NEVADA   IDAHO   UTAH   WYOMING   COLORADO

TRUCKEE RIVER

0   60   120 mi

FIVE

Chinese

THE CENTRAL PACIFIC RAILROAD TRANSFORMED California from an overseas to a continental possession of the United States. Chinese railroad labor, organized under contract and disciplined by racial violence, was situated at the war-finance nexus. After completion of the railroad, Chinese exclusion formalized racial violence and labor control on a continental scale, evacuating modes of relationship governing the movement of people across Indigenous lands and waters. The railroad, and exclusion, were core infrastructures of continental imperialism.

Racial dimensions of the war-finance nexus manifested in the snarling rhetoric of Leland Stanford's 1862 inaugural speech as governor of California: "While the settlement of our State is of the first importance, the character of those who shall become settlers is worthy of scarcely less consideration." Stanford's fear of an Asian invasion grew out of racial and class anxieties, that California would act as an escape valve for the "dregs" of Asia. Racial, class, and cultural qualities of imagined future Asian migrations threatened Stanford's vision of California as a space of settler accumulation. He voiced a colonialist anxiety about dispossession, a racial paranoia centering on fears of invasion and divestment. The colonization of California, accomplished by constant, ongoing, and overwhelming violation of Indigenous life, proceeded through relationships with Asia's "numberless millions," threatening, in Stanford's perspective, to undermine the stability of the colonial order. Chinese labor was an instrument, not a subject, of colonialism. Stanford urged the California government to request land and credit from the U.S. federal government, to support the construction of a transcontinental railroad, to remake California as a site of continental imperialism. Stanford's rhetoric was not without precedent. In his 1851 inaugural speech as the first

U.S. civil governor of California, Peter Burnett had called for a "war of extermination" against Indigenous peoples in California. From the base of their "mountain fastness," Burnett argued, Natives engaged in irregular warfare that made settlers always vulnerable to random attack, and made it impossible for settlers to distinguish Indigenous combatants from noncombatants.[1] Colonialist race war fueled the fears for colonial futures.

Five weeks after Stanford gave his speech, the U.S. Congress approved "An Act to prohibit the 'Coolie Trade' by American Citizens in American Vessels." The act prohibited U.S. citizens and residents from transporting "the inhabitants, or subjects of China known as 'coolies,'" defined as individuals "disposed of, or sold, or transferred, for any term of years or for any time whatever, as servants or apprentices, or to be held to service or labor." U.S. law associated coolie status with indenture, a status marked in time, distinct from slavery. A distance from "freedom" was visible through categories of labor and relationships of exploitation rather than geographic origins, a suspicion of not quite being free. The act enumerated conditions for "free and voluntary emigration of any Chinese subject," requiring men arriving from China to carry a certificate of freedom, issued by a U.S. consular official at the port of emigration. Although the law made it illegal to bring Chinese people to the United States as "coolies," it would remain practically unenforced.[2]

Two months later, in April 1862, the California state legislature passed an Anti-Coolie Act, instituting a monthly tax on Chinese people working gold mines and owning businesses, a new cost for being identified as Chinese in California. Against the logic of the federal law, which presented "coolie" status as a condition of labor, California legislated in racial terms. "Coolie," in the logic of California law, meant "Chinese," a racial status, not a debt and labor structure. Where in the federal anti-coolie law, the U.S. government asserted territorial prerogatives to control borders, in the California law, the state distinguished Chinese people as a significant source of state revenue. The racial logics of California state revenue betrayed colonial origins, echoing an 1847 law mandating that Indigenous people's employers issue passes and certificates of employment for Indians who wished to trade in California towns.[3]

THE PRICE OF A TICKET

In an interview with the historian Hubert Bancroft, Kwong Ki-Chaou, a California-based representative of the Chinese government, described

Chinese migrations to the United States: "Chinese coming to this country are as free as European immigrants—they come here free." Kwong framed Chinese migrations (and freedom) in relation to the transformation of European provinciality into New World whiteness, distancing from the legacies of slavery on life in North America, claiming participant status in the creation of a New World. Contra Stanford, Kwong presented Chinese people not as alien invaders, but as constituents in the colonial pageant of California. Freedom was a claim to belong, a claim to possess, predicated on the ongoing occupation of Indigenous lands. Kwong continued, saying that Chinese people in North America "have no masters" with one exception: "Only those persons who came to work for the railroad came under contract but most of them ran away when they got here. Those who brought them lost money— but all others came free."[4] Were those who came from China to work for the railroad free?

U.S. authorities had inherited labor structures from Spanish colonial California. Toward the end of the 1840s, whites were organizing hunting parties that systematically attacked entire Indigenous communities, a particularly gendered form of violence that targeted Indigenous women. Amidst colonialist race war, with the high cost of labor during the Gold Rush, the California legislature passed one of its first laws, the 1850 Act for the Government and Protection of Indians, legalizing debt peonage to force Indigenous children and adults into compulsory labor for large-scale agricultural interests, under the guise of indenture. The U.S. military government in San Francisco had already begun enforcing compulsory Indigenous labor in 1847. The area north of San Francisco Bay was home to over 100,000 Indigenous people in 1846. Early U.S. military campaigns against communities branded as "horse-thief Indians" established U.S. authority over the region, a point of commensurability between the Mexican ranching elite, newly arrived settlers from the United States, and the U.S. military. Race war and overseas imperialism shaped the development of San Francisco. As a port of arrival, San Francisco was linked to Singapore and Penang, points of entry for Chinese workers to tin and gold mines in southeast Asia. En route to San Francisco, ships stopped in Manila, Guam, and Honolulu. Gold fields near Marysville, as well as Union Pacific construction, drew Chinese people, following Kānaka Maolis who had arrived to a place that was already deeply imbued with Oceanic histories and relationships.[5]

On arrival in California, most of the migrants from China found work through family or social connections, or through district associations, the huiguan. Known in San Francisco as the Six Companies, district associations functioned as mutual-aid societies where new and indigent arrivals could find shelter and basic amenities, following organizational models among Chinese communities in Southeast Asia. The huiguan entrenched the power of merchants in Chinatown communities, institutions to localize and delegate functions of community upkeep and policing, operating through solidarity and control, linking to a mercantile economy spanning southeast Asia, the Philippines, and Hawai'i.[6]

Sucheng Chan described Chinese merchants' main assets in California: working knowledge of English and ready access to laborers. Merchants developed businesses around arrivals to California and departures to China, situated strategically between Chinatown communities and major corporations. Chinese merchant capital in California could not shake off constraints on its reproduction and valorization. Its primary economic function was to provide and provision Chinese labor on demand. Labor contractors recruited and organized Chinese workers into gangs of twenty-five to thirty men. The Central Pacific kept accounts by gang, disbursing wages to a headman, who then divided the wages. Charles Crocker, who oversaw construction on the Central Pacific, told the U.S. Senate, "we cannot distinguish Chinamen by names very well." According to Crocker, the names of Chinese workers sounded too much alike for railroad authorities to distinguish between individuals, constituting instead a homogenous mass in the railroad company's wage accounts. "We could not know Ah Sin, Ah You, Kong Won, all such names. We cannot keep their names in the usual way, because it is a different language. You understand the difficulty. It is not done in that way because they are slaves." To be a Chinese worker on the Central Pacific was definitively not to be a slave, the property of another. It was, however, a reduction to the status of a tool for grading earth and drilling a mountain. It was to be expendable, interchangeable, replaceable. Chinese workers were instruments of labor, constant capital for the Central Pacific Railroad Company. The quality of their lives interfered with their essential function, as a quantity of labor.[7]

State and corporation supplied the organizational basis for colonialism in nineteenth-century California. Neither could be disentangled from the other. Leland Stanford was president of the Central Pacific Railroad while serving as the first Republican governor of California. The first locomotive in service for the Central Pacific was christened the "Governor Stanford." In 1863, Governor Stanford appointed Edwin Bryant Crocker, elder brother of

Charles (the superintendent of Central Pacific construction), as a justice of the California Supreme Court. A year later, E. B., "the Judge," as his associates hailed him, became chief counsel for the Central Pacific, joining the circle of directors including Stanford, Mark Hopkins, Collis Huntington, and Charles.[8]

Testifying later before the U.S. Senate, Charles Crocker would stress wages to argue that Chinese labor on the Central Pacific was free labor. "You cannot control a Chinaman except you pay him for it. You cannot make a contract with him, or his friend, or supposed master, and get his labor unless you pay for it, and pay him for it." The Central Pacific recruited Chinese labor through labor contractors, combining wages with coercion, resting on the power of contractors to control mobility and immobility at the same time. According to Crocker's Senate testimony, the Central Pacific procured Chinese workers through the services of Chinese and white labor contractors alike. One firm, Sisson, Wallace, & Co., eventually "furnished pretty much all of the Chinamen that we worked."[9] Clark Crocker, brother of Charles and E. B., was the "& Co." in question.

Leland Stanford, in his 1866 report of the president of the Central Pacific, assured investors there was no system similar to slavery among Chinese workers, whose wages and provisions were distributed by independent agents: "We have assurances from leading Chinese merchants, that under the just and liberal policy pursued by the Company, it will be able to produce during the next year, not less than fifteen thousand laborers." Employing Chinese workers as a racially distinct labor force, whose labor was cheaper than whites, was not inevitable for the Central Pacific. The directors arrived at these hiring strategies only after considering other sources of labor, such as Confederate prisoners working under guard. Across the South, African Americans competed with Confederate veterans for railroad jobs. In Virginia, in August 1865, such competition sparked a violent confrontation between Black workers and white workers (the latter backed by a Maryland militia sent to break up the fighting). That October, the Committee on Industrial Pursuits at the 1865 California State Convention of Colored Citizens forwarded a resolution to send three representatives to present to Central Pacific directors "the expediency of employing from twenty to forty thousand freedmen on the Great Pacific Railroad" and to petition members of the California state legislature and congressional representatives for aid.[10] The Central Pacific directors did not receive the message, or they chose to ignore it.

A few months earlier, in May 1865, at the outset of the summer construction season, Mark Hopkins had written to Collis Huntington, "We find a difficulty in getting laborers on the railroad work." According to Hopkins, workers would come and go as they pleased, like "tramping journeymen." Labor recruiting and labor control posed major obstacles for Central Pacific construction, and Hopkins saw Chinese workers as essential to managing both of these issues. "Without them," he worried, "it would be impossible to go on with the work. But China laborers are coming in slowly so that Charley thinks the force will steadily increase from this time on."[11] A report from the *Sacramento Daily Union* a little over a year later, in June 1866, provides a sense of the rapid increase of Chinese labor as Central Pacific construction proceeded. Between Colfax and the summit, the railroad employed 11,000 Chinese workers:

> Almost the entire work of digging is done by Chinamen, and the Directors of the road say it would be impossible to build it at present without them. They are found to be equally as good as white men, and less inclined to quarrels and strikes. They are paid $30 per month and boarded, and a cook is allowed for every twelve men. They do not accomplish so much in a given time as Irish laborers, but they are willing to work more hours per day, and are content with their lot so long as they are promptly paid.

The value of Chinese labor is accounted, here, in terms of racial comparison, involving a give and take between productivity and control, indispensable for making accurate predictions of the future. "If the work on this road continues to progress as fast as it has done during this season," the *Union* continued, "there is little doubt that the cars will be running from Sacramento to Salt Lake inside of three years."[12] Accurate predictions could stimulate investment. The ethereal relations of finance capital took flight from land grants, and the racial and gendered control of bodies in space.

Although celebrated for their supposed docility, news circulated in California of different modes of Chinese being. In December 1866, the *Sacramento Daily Union* reported that six Chinese miners working a placer on Bear River had defended themselves from four white men, killing two of their attackers, and causing the other two to flee for their lives. A second report, from Shasta County, relayed information about an attack on a group of miners near Rock Creek, which the *Daily Union* writer blamed on growing racist sentiment against Chinese miners. The attack at Rock Creek resulted in three wounded miners, and in the days afterwards, "the Chinese in the various camps around town have been purchasing arms to protect themselves with." Although mining life shaped the context for Chinese labor, it had already been superseded by the industrial transformation of the regional economy. As a *Daily Union* writer baldly stated a day after the reports of violence against Chinese miners, in an article entitled "Railroads and Capital": "This is emphatically an era of railroads."[13]

A few days later, on January 2, 1867, Stanford and Judge Crocker attended a banquet at the Occidental Hotel to celebrate the departure of the first steamship bound for China and Japan from San Francisco. In his remarks that evening, Stanford made no explicit mention of Chinese workers, but he had China on his mind. Projecting forward to an anticipated completion of the transcontinental in 1870, Stanford prattled:

> Then will the "ligament be perfect that binds the Eastern Eng and Western Chang together." Then, Mr. Chairman, behold the result! For America, the chief control of the developed trade of the better part of Asia with Europe and America. Our Pacific slope, and particularly California, filling rapidly with a hardy, enterprising and industrious people mostly of our brethren and sisters of our old Atlantic homes. [14]

Stanford had slightly revised his inaugural speech from eight years before, imagining a putatively national body assembled from distinct colonial parts, to enable the future development of California along desirable lines. For Stanford, Chinese people were not, themselves, part of the social body of continental imperialism. Instead, this social body acts on Chinese people in North America, and beyond.

Stanford's grandiose visions, however, were not borne out by the unfolding calculations among Central Pacific directors, to recruit and control a labor force at wages and work conditions that would maximize their profits. Just days after Stanford spoke, Judge Crocker and Collis Huntington debated how large of a workforce to maintain through the slower winter construction, Huntington favoring cutting the workforce down to seasonal size. Discharge experienced Chinese workers, Crocker worried, and they would move into mining, putting the Central Pacific at a decided disadvantage during the short summer season. The previous summer, construction managers had difficulty keeping workers at the grueling hard rock tunnel work. Those currently employed by the Central Pacific had already experienced the conditions at the summit, and the judge felt them to be "dependable." Crocker asked Huntington to test his own powers of forbearance and accept a relatively higher level of employment during the winter. "We hope you will strain every nerve bring every thing to bear to keep along, and not ask us to discharge a man."[15]

Huntington remained skeptical, or perhaps his nerves could not bear the strain, and he asked for an accounting of the cost of excavating one cubic yard at the summit tunnel. Judge Crocker obligingly explained that construction directors projected working three men on each drill, at the excruciating pace of a 1 3/4 inch hole one foot, per hour, organizing the work in day and night shifts of eight hours. Construction managers experimented with new tools, such as "gunpowder drills" and nitroglycerin, to speed up and cheapen construction. The tools met the rock, of course, through the application of the worker. And the worker was a category with distinctions. Closer to the status of tools, of drills, gunpowder, and nitroglycerin than white workers, Chinese railroad workers gave the directors of the Central Pacific a chance to squeeze more profit from a hard place. The judge calculated, "Each white man costs us in board and wages $2 1/2 each 8 hours, but Chinamen cost us $1.19 each 8 hours, and they drill nearly as fast." Chinese railroad labor was a quantity measuring time in relation to price, and the price was lower than that of white labor. Where the Central Pacific covered housing and food costs for white railroad labor, the reproduction of Chinese labor was free.[16] By the end of the month, the directors doubled down, printing and circulating a Chinese language recruiting notice throughout California and in China. The judge was not entirely sure what the notice said. "The Chinamen all understand it," he explained to Huntington, "but it is hard for them to translate it back into English."[17] Behind the bluster of corporate control lurked countersovereignty, a reactive dependence on others.

REPRODUCING RACIAL CONTROL

The shared culture of Chinese workers and merchants functioned simultaneously as a sphere of pleasure and sustenance and a sphere of constriction. Railroad workers' corporate wages supplanted the shared profits of miners in the goldfields. Chinese workers' isolation in temporary work camps, scattered along the line of railroad construction, bound them to relationships cementing their control. A separate system of disbursing wages and provisioning food and housing reflected these distinctions. Charles Nordhoff visited a Chinese railroad work camp on the San Joaquin River, where he found seven hundred Chinese men and one hundred white men. The Chinese workers were supposed to receive $28 for working twenty-six days each month, paying for food, tents, and utensils, with labor contractors paying the cooks. Several railroad cars at the end of track acted as a store for Chinese workers. According to Nordhoff, most of the items sold in this store were imported from China. Organizing and provisioning a male society, the Central Pacific took on a military structure. This was the organizational form of the war-finance nexus, in which class formation occurred through the structures of war. Merchants handled the distribution of food, and workers were captive to their supplies and profits. Collectively, Chinese railroad workers had no future. The success of their labor would ensure the obsolescence of their lives.[18]

Planning in relation to Chinese labor, Central Pacific directors balanced the temporality of seasonal work conditions with temporalities of Chinese laborers' lives. In early February 1867, recruiting delays during lunar New Year left the Central Pacific short of at least 1,500 workers for immediate work, threatening to jam up the progress of construction after the snow melted. In the howling winter, according to Judge Crocker's report, 1,500 Chinese men were already at work on the summit, and 1,000 on the approach.[19] The Chinese calendar, with its festivals and feasts, helped Chinese workers on the Central Pacific maintain a sense of connection to their homes and families and to their ancestors. It also ritualized their connection to the merchants and contractors who continued to profit from both their employment and their social reproduction. Calendar time blended into labor time for Chinese workers along the railroad's line of construction. The formation of a Chinese merchant class in North America, both provisioning and supplying labor, revolved around relationships to Chinese workers as both consumers and producers.[20]

As Judge Crocker explained to Huntington in mid-February 1867, nearly all of those drilling for the Central Pacific were Chinese men whose work was "fully equal to white men," but they were employed at a rate requiring them to work twenty-six days a month, covering the cost of their own food and housing, unlike their white counterparts.[21] Huntington remained unconvinced, and the judge emphasized the relative value of Chinese railroad labor two days later:

> we have had a chance to compass the merits of our Chinese laborers and
> Cornish miners, who are deemed the best underground workers in the world,
> and the Chinese beat them right straight all along, day in and day out. We
> have a large force of well trained Chinese tunnel workers, and they can't be

beat. They cost only about half what white men do, and are more regular in labor, and more peaceable. They are not men who get drunk and pick up rows, but can be relied upon for steady work.[22]

Empirical observation of racial competition settled the question. For Central Pacific Railroad Company directors, race was a calculus of profit maximization.

Mark Hopkins gave another perspective on this racial calculus, laying out three conditions whereby he and the other directors should "never be financially troubled hereafter," including an early spring melting off the Sierras, $250 per month of investments coming in from the eastern United States from June through November, and "increased numbers of Chinamen come into the work."[23] Weather, investments, and Chinese labor were the legs of a platform on which Hopkins and his associates planned to build their personal fortunes. For the first, they could pray. For the second, they could bluster and impress. For the third, they had to rely on others. How could anyone imagine this to be stable, to imagine that the men perched atop could be in control?

STRIKE

Late in May 1867, as the snow finally began melting between Cisco and the Truckee River, the Central Pacific directors prepared a full push on the summit. As the weather cooperated, and funds for equipment and wages flowed, it was suddenly difficult to find workers. Judge Crocker explained to Huntington,

> The truth is the Chinese are now exclusively employed in quartz mills and a thousand other employments new to them. Our use of them led hundreds of others to employ them, so that now when we want to gather them up for the spring and summer work, a large portion are permanently employed at work they like better. The snow & labor questions have our progress quite uncertain.

Five days later, the judge notified Huntington of plans to raise the Chinese workers' wages almost 13 percent, from $31 to $35 per month. Chinese workers were finding work in quartz mills, building roads and canals, and many were going to Idaho and Montana, looking for work. "Our supply," he cautioned, "will be short unless we do something." And so the Central Pacific directors responded, at a loss of "$100,000 in gold on this season's work." By early June, the judge was panicking, "Our force is not now increasing, and the season has come when it ought to increase." He understood the Central Pacific as a victim of its own innovation: "We have proved their value as laborers, and everybody is trying them, and now we can't get them."[24]

In late June, Mark Hopkins notified Huntington of "an unexpected feature." After the Central Pacific had raised Chinese workers' wages in the hopes of quickly increasing the drilling workforce for the summer construction season at the summit, news arrived that the Chinese workers had gone on strike, demanding $40 per month and a ten-hour day, instead of the current eleven-hour workdays. The strike demands would tip over the platform upon which the directors had imagined profit. As Hopkins put it, "if they are successful in this demand, then they *control,* and their demands will be increased." It was a war for control. It was not only a class war over the conditions of work. It was also a war to decide who would colonize California, and on what terms, echoing Stanford's gubernatorial address. Hopkins expressed hope in a Central Pacific "application for 5000 Freedmen from the Freedmen's Bureau." It was a lesson in political economy. "When any commodity is in demand beyond the natural supply, even Chinese labor, the price will tend to increase."[25]

The *Sacramento Daily Union* printed a telegram attributed to Huntington, dated June 28, stating, "There will be no trouble in getting all the laborers you want. How many thousand shall I send? Can contract for passage at low rates." He was bluffing.[26] The next day, Judge Crocker wrote with more honesty: "The truth is, they are getting smart." However, he doubted the workers' intelligence: "Who has stirred up the strike we don't know, but it was evidently planned and concerted." The strike was a bid for direct accountability between individual workers and the Central Pacific, directed against the railroad directors and construction supervisors. While it forced the Central Pacific directors to reckon with their workers as a unified group, it was also a bid to force the bosses to consider them as individuals.

The Central Pacific directors were inclined to reinvest in a racial division of labor. Judge Crocker notified Huntington of a man named Yates, a ship's steward who had met with Stanford in San Francisco. William Henry Yates had arrived in San Francisco in 1851 from Washington, DC, where he had been active in the Underground Railroad, and had worked as a steward on river steamers and ferry boats in California. Yates had played a leadership role in the 1865 Colored Citizens' convention. "His plan was to get a large number of freedmen to come to California under the Freedmen's Bureau, and under the aid of the government, that is a sort of military organization crossing the plains." The judge understood that Yates was then in Washington, trying to find support for the idea. The racial organization of labor, for the Central Pacific Railroad, was situated squarely at the nexus of war and finance. The social reproduction of continental imperialism is the social reproduction of war. The judge understood the strike as a skirmish in a deeper war.

> The only safe way for us is to inundate this state and Nevada with laborers. Freedmen, Chinese, Japanese, all kinds of labor, so that men come to us for work instead of our hunting them up. They will all find something to do, and a surplus will keep wages low. It is our only security for strikes.[27]

Racial importation was a means to control the price of labor. Hopkins reinforced Crocker's earlier message about Yates, whom he described as "a man of integrity and good abilities." According to the plan, the Central Pacific would be responsible for expenses to bring freedmen to San Francisco, but "a Negro labor force would tend to keep the Chinese steady, as the Chinese have kept the Irishmen quiet."[28] Hopkins saw this as a worthwhile investment in labor control. Judge Crocker fired off another note to Huntington that day. The strike was "the hardest blow we have here," he sighed, and Charles had informed leaders of the Chinese community that the Central Pacific would pay no more than $35. Chinese community leaders had sent messages to the work camps, advising the workers to return to work. Something is left unwritten in the judge's letter, which refers to more desperate measures, closing with the sentence, "It is the only way to deal with them."[29]

Three days later, Hopkins sent word of Capital triumphant. The strike was broken, the workers returning to their jobs at the same conditions as before the strike. Curiously, after their victory, Hopkins speculated that "the strike appears to have been instigated by Chinese gamblers and opium traders, who are prohibited from plying their vocation on the line of the work."[30] Hopkins imagined continuity between railroad workers' collective voice and the lurid visions of an underground Chinese vice economy, specters perhaps, of the English and American opium traders who had helped set trans-Pacific Chinese migration patterns into play, under the banner of free trade. If nothing else, his statement contradicts the image of docile, hardworking, and clean-cut pets that Hopkins and the judge had imagined these Chinese workers to fulfill, just months before. The lives of their workers threatened the security of their profits.

On July 2, Judge Crocker relayed details of how the associates broke the strike:

> Their agent stopped supplying them with goods and provisions and they really began to suffer. None of us went near them for a week. Did not want to exhibit anxiety. Then Charles went up, and they gathered around him, and he told them that he would not be dictated to, that he made the rules for them and not they for him.[31]

The destruction of the workers' solidarity brutally reinscribed a hierarchy of exploitation driving Central Pacific construction, proceeding with the active participation of Chinese merchants who stopped supplying food and provisions to the work camps. The participation of Chinese merchants and labor contractors in breaking the strike clarifies their investments in the organization and management of labor on Central Pacific construction. There was no mutual aid, no principle of racial solidarity here. The *Daily Union* printed a more detailed account of the strike action and demands, clarifying the demand for eight hours from those working the tunnels, and ten hours from those on open ground. The report conveyed core strike demands:

> We understand that a placard printed in the Chinese language was distributed along the line of the road a day or two before the strike occurred. This placard is said to have set forth the right of the workmen to higher wages and to a more moderate day's work, and to deny the right of the overseers of the company to either whip them or to restrain them from leaving the road when they desire to seek other employment.

The workers struck over wages and the length of the working day. But they also struck for an end to physical punishment, and for the right to leave employment when they wanted to. These are not the hallmarks of free labor.[32]

From the perspectives of the Central Pacific directors, the situation improved after the strike. On July 6, Judge Crocker surmised to Huntington of the Chinese workers' shame, predicting, "I don't think we will ever have any more difficulties with them."[33] Visions of worker docility had perhaps been reinforced with a confidence in racial hierarchies that had been reproduced by means of brute violence. A few weeks later, this turn coincided with workers, "arriving from China in large number," according to Judge Crocker, who projected that the Central Pacific would soon meet its labor target.[34]

Recruiting and controlling labor seemed to be resolved. While he imagined that the Chinese workers felt ashamed, the judge informed Huntington, "we feel a good deal encouraged."[35]

THE EXCLUSIONS OF COLONIALISM

On July 10, days after the strike was broken, the *San Francisco Commercial Herald and Market Review* reported on the state of shipping between China and Japan, and San Francisco. The cost of freight had dropped significantly, partly because of the introduction of new shipping companies. One steamship, the *Colorado,* carried about five hundred passengers, mostly Chinese, in steerage, and about $700,000 worth of freight, mostly arms and ammunition being shipped to Yokohama from New York and Liverpool. Guns and migrants: the *Colorado* carried raw materials for imperialism.

Meanwhile, if San Francisco was a thoroughly Pacific-oriented place, perhaps it could access whiteness by way of the Pacific. The report also touched on the arrival of a contingent of Australians to San Francisco, and the excitement some held at the possibility of fellow Anglo settlers supplanting Chinese migrations. The *Review* editors heralded Chinese work on the railroad, and "as reclaimers of the soil," looking to a future in which "thousands and tens of thousands of virgin acres are by these heathen to be reclaimed and made fruitful rice fields." The writers pointed to Chinese work on the Central Pacific, in agriculture, and in cotton and wool mills, as central to the development of industrial manufacturing in California, celebrating Chinese workers, whose labor remade the landscape, replacing Indigenous flora with commodity monocrops. The celebratory focus on Chinese labor obscured the role of Chinese merchants who supplied that labor, disciplined it, and kept it alive. Writing during the Chinese strike, the *Review* editors pointed out the one stopping point of continental imperialism: population. In order to replace the Indigenous order of these places, a settler population was necessary. While Chinese workers had been striking to raise the price of their labor, the *Review* editors argued the solution to labor control was also the solution to colonialism: "The only way to obtain required immigration is by cheapening the price of passage to the lowest possible figure, and granting good accommodations for families." The writers pointed to the railroad, with its potential to drop the price of travel from the eastern United States.[36] Chinese railroad labor could enable mass migration from the eastern United

States to California, thereby making Chinese labor obsolete in California. Fulfilling a structural function akin to animated tools, providing the muscle power and the consciousness to direct the application of metal and chemical to ground and rock, blasting, tunneling, and grading the landscape, Chinese workers were tools to establish some reproductive continuity to the capitalization of Miwok, Ohlone, and Paiute lands.

By September, Judge Crocker informed Huntington of preparations for the return of snow at the summit and the close of the construction season there. Now confident about labor, the Central Pacific directors raged against the weather. "We are taking time by the forelock this year," the judge asserted. Still, the supply of workers remained less than what the directors wished to have available. Crocker noted that a number of Chinese men had returned to China on a voyage of the *Great Republic*. The directors, however, had laid plans for the following year, working with several Chinese labor contractors who were on board the ship.

> They know all about the work and can explain it to their countrymen. I have no doubt they will be able to induce thousands to come over. We shall follow this up, and get others to go over to China to bring up immigration. We have those Chinese handbills to send to China. The Steamship Co. are willing to make favorable arrangements to bring them over. We want 100,000 Chinamen here so as to bring the price of labor down.

The judge expected 800–1,000 men to arrive from China on each monthly steamship voyage over the year, expecting, moreover, passengers from Pacific Mail ships to head straight to Central Pacific work. He hoped increasing migration would enable a smoothing of labor supply, further lowering the price, and the pliability, of Chinese labor.[37]

In these early January days, the prospects for labor supply looked salubrious to the Central Pacific directors on both flanks of the United States. Judge Crocker reported to Huntington, "Our force has not diminished at all this winter, but is rather increasing, and it will be doubled during the summer, in all probability. So the labor question seems to be all right." The judge was not describing a market in free labor, but instead a labor market designed through importation and policed by racial violence, operating under monopoly conditions. For his part, Huntington had placed articles in eastern newspapers reporting a high demand for "common and skilled labor" in California. He, too, felt optimistic about the labor supply in the coming months: "I am disposed to think that there will be a very large emigration to California this coming spring and summer." The directors had subcontracted grading on a section of the Western Pacific, and they "arranged it that they should get their supply of Chinamen from the same men we do, so as to prevent competition." Working conditions on the Central Pacific were absolutely brutal, "as low as 8 degrees below zero, but the Chinamen stand it."[38]

By March, the directors were focusing away from labor, on questions of resources. Judge Crocker informed Huntington about the Central Pacific's capture of land on the Pyramid Lake Reservation. The timber on the reservation was being cut and processed fast, "nearly all of it through for the C. P. R. R., for lumber, timber for bridges etc., and when we get our road completed the timber there will be pretty well used up." Whose timber was this? The Central Pacific certainly did not pay anyone for it. The judge pointed out the manifest absurdity of any impulse "to reserve *lumber* for the Indians." No, he insisted, this lumber was U. S. property, and cutting and using the lumber was an "improvement" provided for, in his judicious interpretation, by the 1862 Pacific Railway Act.[39]

By the end of May, Charles Crocker reported to Huntington, after returning from a trip through Humboldt Canyon, "among the Indians and the sage brush," in his words of picaresque racism. Moving further away from California as construction progressed posed challenges: "The Chinamen evince some reluctance to going out so far and fear of Indians, but we have no well founded fears of any great trouble—though it may occur." Crocker anticipated colonial anxiety as a sticking point for managerial control, and for him, control was a point of pride in comparison. "We have no men in our line with high sounding titles General, Colonel, etc., as we hear of on U. P.," he puffed, "but I think we can build R. R. as well and as fast as they." True, he had no military titles, but he had a racially stratified workforce, an army of laborers not exactly working under free labor conditions. Mark Hopkins weighed in a few days later, stating the problem in broad ethnographic terms: "Chinamen will not go so far away from their own people, and we could gather but few white laborers here for such an expedition." The recruiting and control of labor was, in his view, a matter of race, culture, and community cohesion. The directors lighted upon the possibility of recruiting among the Mormon community in Salt Lake as a solution to the perceived problem, debating the wisdom of sending Stanford off to communicate with "Mormon influences." Anxieties about labor recruiting and control remained unresolved by mid-June. Charles Crocker described "tremendous yarns" passing among the Chinese workers, and reported about a thousand workers had left out of fear. He was feeling the stress. "This is a critical period for us and my mind is constantly on the stretch to prevent a scattering of our laborers."[40]

On June 19, Collis Huntington informed Mark Hopkins that it would be difficult to fulfill a request for fifty masons from the eastern United States. Masons were on strike at the time, for $4.50 for an eight-hour day, and Huntington expected them to win. He anticipated the Central Pacific would have to advance fare for any masons to go to California, but on arrival, at least half would find other work. Still, he concluded, "if I can get some to go by advancing the fare I shall make the advance." Covering migration costs for skilled white labor from the United States entailed considerable risk to the Central Pacific. Where the Central Pacific exposed itself to risk by employing white labor, it inoculated itself from risk by employing Chinese labor. In the same letter about shipping skilled labor, Huntington shared news about an exclusive contract with the Pacific Mail to ship six thousand tons of iron at favorable rates. Labor and iron, alike, arrived in California by sea. In June 1868, California was still overseas territory of the United States. The Central Pacific, and California, were not just a continent away, they were an ocean away. This geographic fact shaped the temporality of production and profit on the Central Pacific. Huntington counseled that efforts to recruit Mormon workers would be for naught, because the Union Pacific could afford to outpay Mormon labor recruiters for the benefit of locking up their rivals' labor supply. No, it was Chinese workers, with whom the Union Pacific had no links and no means of influence, who would ensure the supply of labor for the Central Pacific, a kind of racial monopoly that secured profit and mitigated risk. California was not just overseas territory of the United States, but it was an overseas Pacific territory of the U.S. Employing a Chinese labor force to develop industrial infrastructure exploited this fact for corporate profits. In January, smallpox ran through Central Pacific work camps, afflicting foremen and white workers alike, while the thermometer read 10 below zero. Charles Crocker reported, "Men are running off scared out of their senses." In this scene of colonizing desolation, he proposed a familiar solution. "We are breaking in Chinamen and learning them as fast as possible." Chinese work camps, with superior hygiene, separated from the white camps, remained relatively unaffected.[41]

Chinese labor, in its price and its methods of control, had helped resolve crises of disease, weather, and supplies for the Central Pacific, smoothing the completion of the railroad. Less than a year after Promontory Point, the state senate of California passed an act "to Prevent the Importation of Chinese Criminals and to Prevent the Establishment of Coolie Slavery." The preamble of the act invoked police powers, charging that "criminals and malefactors" were "constantly imported" to California from Chinese ports, and these criminals' assaults on property caused great expense for the state. Moreover, "by the importation of such persons a species of slavery is established and maintained," degrading labor and contradicting "the spirit of the age." The act prohibited the entry of any "Chinese or Mongolian, born either in the Empire of China or Japan, or in any of the islands adjacent to the Empire of China," unless the migrant first obtained a license or permit from a commissioner of immigration. Having provided the labor to build colonial infrastructure, transforming California from an overseas to a continental possession, replacing Indigenous labor as the primary form of labor disciplined by racial violence, Chinese labor was now excluded. The act did not suppress the stench of slavery associated with Chinese migration. Instead, it formalized it from a corporate to a state function. With the immigration license or permit, a forerunner of the visa, the state, itself, would now manage the importation, selection, and oversight of labor, a sea change that continues unabated to the present.[42]

In 1877, amidst debate over Chinese exclusion, the Chinese Six Companies published a memorial addressed to the U.S. Congress, presenting Chinese in the United States as an important bridge between the U.S. and Chinese economies. Their arguments against exclusion reflected their class position as merchants. The authors of the memorial invoked a mutual agreement between the U.S. and Chinese governments to recognize "the inherent and inalienable right" of people from the United States, or from China, to migrate "for the purposes of residence, trade or commerce." Merchants, the memorial authors argued, played a crucial role in expanding trade relationships between the countries, and exclusion would put an end to this pattern. The authors set forth a comparison, in size of population, and "greatness," between China and the United States, presenting both as continental empires rooted in expansion. They counterposed the benefits of expansion with the ills of exclusion, which, they argued, had its roots in "an agrarian mob," consisting of a "lawless element . . . led by aliens." If working-class advocates for Chinese exclusion misplaced the direction of their ire against corporate exploitation, merchant critics of Chinese exclusion misplaced their critique of white supremacy by focusing on the criminalized immigrant poor. Neither side took a consistent stand against capital and white supremacy, because both sides appealed to belonging and participation in continental imperialism.[43]

Chinese labor, so long as it was mobile, was an integral part of projections for colonialist futures in California. The underside of this utopian vision was a harrowing projection of future Chinese dominance. The racial and gendered fear of Chinese labor, the seed of the exclusion movement, revolved around an equation of Chinese labor with slave labor, and its impact on white labor. Fear of competition with laboring lives that were racially defined as servile, the spur for Chinese exclusion, was fundamentally about the ability to shape, control, and claim subjecthood, to empty the land of Indigenous modes of relationship and make space for the profit motive. The California senate, advocating Chinese exclusion in 1878, asserted, "If cheap labor means servile labor, it is a burlesque on the policy of emancipation." Notions of freedom articulated with colonial power to produce racial exclusions. The politics of Chinese exclusion were voiced in the language of anticorporate critique, but at the core, exclusion was about the future of continental imperialism. Behind the threat of alien races, or alien classes, lay Indigenous modes of relationship, predefined as criminal, if not unthinkable. Arguments for and against Chinese exclusion took place on the ideological terrain of countersovereignty.[44]

Frederick Low, who was governor of California during the years of Central Pacific construction, envisioned a future for Chinese people in California as a servant class. Their presence, in contained numbers, he argued, allowed for the possibility of an upwardly mobile lifestyle among white skilled labor. According to Low, "you go along any of these streets any day and you will see 3/4 of the servants are Chinamen—washing and scraping around the house." In rural areas, he described Chinese laborers as "an absolute necessity." Still, this only worked within prescribed limits. "When you bring them over here in shiploads that's different." Chinese people had a role to play, providing the service and unskilled labor to colonize and occupy California. Chinese merchants played a role in supplying that labor. Too many Chinese people, however, would upset the balance, destabilizing countersovereignty. Belonging entailed a constituency of continental imperialism, and it articulated racially. Chinese railroad workers, in this view, were the constant capital of a colonial mode of relationship.[45]

The U. S. Congress passed the Chinese Exclusion Act on May 6, 1882. The law suspended the migration of Chinese workers. Where the 1862 law against coolie importation sanctioned U. S. shippers involved in indentured migrations under the coolie trade, exclusion sanctioned U. S. shippers from involvement in any migration of Chinese laborers. Chinese workers who were in the United States before exclusion was passed could receive certificates allowing them to return if they chose to depart North America. The 1862 federal law had legislated a condition of "free" migration to Chinese people, but exclusion removed this option. Free migration, in the earlier sense, was no longer a recognized legal category for Chinese workers going to U.S. territory. The federal government, in 1882, moved in the direction of the California state legislature from earlier decades, defining "Chinese," in law and policy, as "unfree," and therefore, as excluded.[46]

During its construction phase, the Union Pacific Railroad began to exploit rich bituminous coal fields in southern Wyoming on captured Shoshone lands, opening two mines, including one at Rock Springs, in 1868. The coal industry developed rapidly in southern Wyoming, and the Union Pacific Coal Company, a subsidiary of the UPRR, enjoyed extensive mineral rights as a result of land grants, controlling 64.4 percent of the total production in the southern coalfields. The workforce in these mines included a large number of Chinese men. In the wake of the Panic of 1873, in 1875, one hundred and fifty Chinese workers were brought to Rock Springs to help break a strike. Over the next decade, racial tensions between Chinese and white miners simmered, until in 1883, the year after the Chinese Exclusion Act, a whites-only Knights of Labor local organized around the slogan "The Chinese must go!" Two years later, Chinese miners outnumbered white miners at Rock Springs by more than two to one. After enduring years of racist violence and harassment, Chinese miners refused an invitation from the Knights of Labor to join a strike. In response, on September 2, 1885, a mob of white men attacked Chinese people in Rock Springs, burning their houses and hunting them down in the surrounding hills. At least twenty-eight Chinese people died in the violence, while the police stood idly by. Twenty-two years later, in 1907, southern Wyoming, which included Rock Springs, became a site of multiracial solidarity, including Japanese and Chinese coal miners. Union organizers in southern Wyoming had learned that dividing the workforce by nationality was a deeply entrenched management tactic to forestall solidarity, which had made Rock Springs itself, in the aftermath of the Chinese massacre, a center of anti-union efforts. In 1914, in Ludlow, Colorado, the Colorado National Guard and private security forces opened fire on striking UMW members and their families, killing over two dozen people, in a historic assault on working-class organization.[47] Colonialism and racial violence were the powder that ignited this assault on working people's collective aspirations for lives of greater dignity.

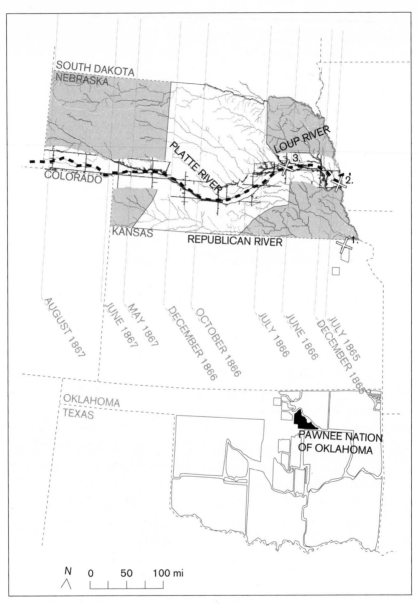

MAPS 7 AND 8: Pawnee Nation. Cartography by Elsa Matossian Hoover. Map 7 based on data from Charles C. Royce, ed., "Schedule of Indian Land Cessions," *Eighteenth Annual Report of the Bureau of American Ethnology to the Secretary of the Smithsonian Institution, 1896–1897*, as printed in H. R. Doc. No. 736, 56th Cong., 1st Sess. (1899–1900).

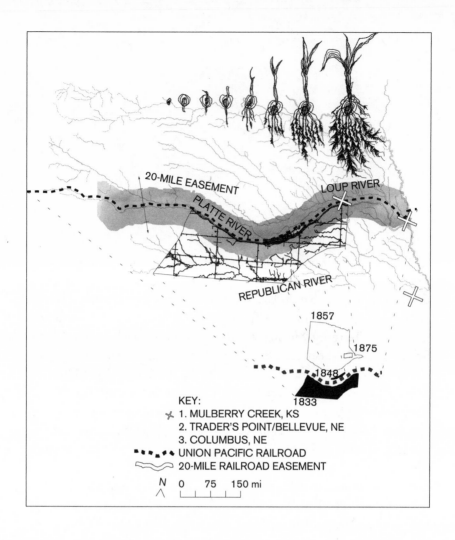

20-MILE EASEMENT

LOUP RIVER

PLATTE RIVER

REPUBLICAN RIVER

1857

1875

1848

1833

KEY:
✕ 1. MULBERRY CREEK, KS
2. TRADER'S POINT/BELLEVUE, NE
3. COLUMBUS, NE
▪▪▪ UNION PACIFIC RAILROAD
〰 20-MILE RAILROAD EASEMENT

N   0   75   150 mi
∧

SIX

Pawnee

IN JULY OF 1868, a group of fifty Pawnee men rode south from a station at Wood River to the Republican River. They belonged to a battalion of scouts that had been organized the past February to patrol a hundred-mile section of Union Pacific Railroad track from Wood River station to Willow Island, in Nebraska Territory. Moving southward, the men joined a group of about five thousand Pawnees and Omaha, Winnebago, and Ponca allies, "a great city of canvas and thousands of ponies," in the words of an embedded journalist from the *Omaha Weekly Herald*. They were out on their summer buffalo hunt, a regular part of Pawnee life in earlier years, becoming increasingly rare after the establishment of the Pawnee reservation in 1857. After a successful hunt, netting almost a thousand kills, the women were busy at work, cutting and drying the meat. The scouts rode out from camp early the next morning, making a buffalo surround about four miles from Mud Creek to bring fresh meat back to their compatriots who had remained along the railroad line. As the hunters scattered, pursuing individual buffalo they had wounded in the initial surround, they saw groups of Lakotas approaching, perhaps a hundred total. They began to fight, continuing for about three hours, the scouts running low on ammunition. Eventually, the larger body of Pawnees arrived, repulsing the Lakota attack. Two of the scouts, and four other Pawnee men, died in the fighting.[1]

This episode provides a glimpse into capitalism, as it actually existed on the central Plains in the late 1860s. The reporter who traveled with the scouts described "beautiful and fertile lands," where he saw farmhouses, barns, and bountiful wheat, oat, and corn crops—"the ground seemed almost overburdened with its production." Pawnee men's experiences as U. S. Army scouts did not result in their subsumption into the domain of unmarked, abstract Capital. To the contrary, Pawnees exploited gaps and fissures in reservation control to sustain a Pawnee mode of relationship, while staring in the face of imperial incorporation. Continental imperialism proceeds through a series of alibis, which include improvement through the market, peace through security, and integration into larger social worlds. In actuality, the war-finance nexus reproduces ecological and social destruction through the market, constant war, and isolation from existing relationships, which are confined into the normative straightjacket of imperial monopoly. This chapter contextualizes Pawnee scouts in relation to the imposition of commercial farming by white men on Pawnee communities, and the imposition of compulsory English education on Pawnee children, which attempted to displace Pawnee women's ongoing relationships of cultivation, whether in agricultural fields, or in intergenerational relationships between Pawnee grandmothers and their grandchildren.

CACHES

For generations, Pawnee women had kept gardens, storing their harvest in underground caches. Pawnees recognized the food stored in these caches as belonging to particular households, and in a broader sense, to particular villages. Unlike market conceptions of alienable property, however, other Pawnees, or even members of neighboring communities, could draw on this food in times of need. Robert Campbell remembered that in 1825, he and a company of fellow fur traders dug up corn from caches in a Pawnee village on the southern side of the Republican River, fifty miles north of Grand Island, and later repaid these Pawnees for the corn.[2] In Pawnee country, the fur trade was predicated on engaging and participating in Pawnee modes of relationship. This is one way to understand countersovereignty.

Pawnees negotiated their second treaty with the United States in 1825. In the treaty's written text, the United States promised protection and trade regulation. Pawnees agreed to "apprehend and deliver any foreigner or other person, not legally authorized by the United States," who came to their country "for the purpose of trade or other views." Early diplomacy between Pawnees and the United States revolved around the colonial administration of trade and defense. Diplomatic relationships between the Pawnee nation and the United States, in the text of the treaty, emerge through a twinned monopoly on trade, and monopoly on foreign relations. Over the following decades, Pawnee treaties with the United States elaborated twinned colonial policies of defense and development, a combination that would later shape twentieth-century doctrines of counterinsurgency warfare. In mid-nineteenth-century U.S. diplomacy with the Pawnee nation, we can see a historical precursor to the modus operandi of imperialist war a century afterwards.[3]

WORK AND LABOR

In October 1833, in a Pawnee village on the Platte River, H. L. Ellsworth, a U.S. negotiator, addressed a Pawnee assembly. Ellsworth apologized for removing the Delaware nation to Pawnee lands. As recompense, the United States offered agricultural aid and goods in exchange for land on the southern banks of the Platte River. "You have land enough that is good without this," Ellsworth said. He promised funding for "farmers to assist you," as well as cattle and hogs, if Pawnees would agree to stop ranging across their land to hunt. On offer was a dual constriction outlawing hunting, and ignoring the reality that Pawnee women already farmed their lands. The treaty's written text begins with Pawnees ceding all of their territory south of the Platte River, which would "remain a common hunting ground" for Pawnees and others, under the permission of the U.S. president. In exchange, the United States promised to provide agricultural implements, and to fund a school and a workshop staffed by two blacksmiths and assistants, as well as four horse-mills for grinding corn. In addition, the treaty allocated funds to "furnish each of said four tribes with a farmer," as well as oxen and other stock animals. The United States would not consider itself bound by these provisions, the treaty continued, until the Pawnee bands would reestablish their villages "in convenient agricultural districts" where they would remain throughout the year, so that the teachers, the farmers, the stock, and the mill could be protected. The treaty's text invoked protection, including the protection of property, as a reason to restrict Pawnee life in place. In 1825 the United States had pledged to protect Pawnees. In 1833, U.S. negotiators expected that Pawnees would protect U.S. property. This protection would be enabled by U.S. disbursement of guns and ammunition, placed in the hands of the farmers, and not in Pawnees' own control. The written text of the treaty effectively attempted to hold Pawnees hostage to alien property relations. U.S. negotiators, proclaiming their country's desire "to show Pawnees the advantages of

agriculture," ignored the generations-long agricultural knowledge and practices of Pawnee women on their lands, knowledge and practice that was the
historical precondition for the imposition of market-oriented farming by
white men. Pawnees assert that this treaty was fraudulent.[4]

Treaty farms marked the reservation as a pedagogical space. Complemen-
ting these farms, the treaty imposed religious-vocational schools on Pawnees.
The agency schools and farms received funding through annuities from the
1833 treaty, in effect diverting a portion of Pawnee annuities under control of
the Indian agent. Agency schools were structured to rupture Pawnee modes
of relationship. Through schools, Pawnee children could be drafted into new
gendered logics of labor, new relations of ownership, on a strictly binary and
hierarchical basis. Boys would be taught to farm for the market (some would
be taken out of school and apprenticed with a blacksmith) and girls would be
taught to tend the nuclear domicile. Once established, the schools were
administered, and classes taught, by members of Protestant missions sent out
to Pawnee territory in the preceding decades. These schools were intended to
remake intergenerational relationships among Pawnees, especially relationships between grandmothers and their grandchildren.[5] Where previously,
caches had oriented relationships of sustenance, schools were intended to
hack away at these roots, replacing them with a new set of relations revolving
around capitalized land. The decades-long failure of agency schools to
actually achieve these kinds of fundamental changes in the lives of Pawnee
children and their families signals, among other things, the continuation of
Pawnee modes of relationship.

In 1835, John Dunbar, a Presbyterian missionary, commented on Pawnee
gender relations: "The Pawnee women are very laborious . . . It is rare, they are
seen idle. When a Pawnee woman has nothing to do, she seems to be out of
her element. Their women are mere slaves . . . The men are abominably lazy."
Dunbar metaphorically invoked slavery as a moral justification for continental imperialism. He was incapable of understanding that Pawnee women's
hard and constant work sustained interrelationships across households, villages, and nations, a fact that had been clear to Robert Campbell a decade
earlier.[6] Pawnee women's constant, hard work could proliferate and sustain
life, as well as relationships. Their work was at the heart of Pawnee modes of
relationship.

Despite the language of the 1833 treaty urging Pawnees to isolate themselves in their villages throughout the year, they continued to go on communal hunts, sustaining and renewing their distinct modes of relationship.

Charles Murray, traveling through the Plains in 1836, described a hunt on a mid-July day that was "beautiful for buffalo hunting." Before the community hunted, they selected "soldiers," who managed the hunt, watching the buffalo herd and preventing anyone from hunting without their permission.[7] These hunts asserted ongoing Pawnee control over their collective relations with their homelands. Decades later, Pawnee men enlisted as scouts for the U.S. Army would watch over Union Pacific Railroad workers as they graded and laid track, actively shaping railroad construction by enacting earlier roles among Pawnees.

In 1843, the U.S. government purchased fourteen yokes of oxen, to supplement four yokes bought the previous year. The government appointed four agency farmers and built two blacksmith shops, each staffed by a blacksmith and an assistant. The infrastructure and technology of the agency connected Pawnees to a broader colonial geography. Saws for the mills were transported from Pittsburgh and St. Louis. Pressures to increase labor productivity with new machines permeated the reservation and preceded the railroad. Efficiencies of labor, energy, and government expenditures all seemingly freed Pawnee women from their endless drudgery. There was a demographic aspect of this gendered expropriation. David Wishart found that during the initial decades of colonization and occupation, the majority of Pawnees were women. In 1840, he argued, only about 41 percent of Pawnees over ten years old were men.[8]

The farming theory of the 1833 treaty did not actualize in practice. By the fall of 1844, the Pawnee Agency had hired G.B. Gaston, George W. Woodcock, and James and Carolan Mathers, a father and son, to work on the agency farms. Pawnees disliked these men, who murderously asserted control over "their" land and property. John Dunbar reported back to Boston that the agency farmers whipped Pawnees, and that one of them shot a man in the back, likely killing him, after he had taken some corn. This Pawnee man paid with his life for an imposed shift in conceptions of property on Pawnee territory. Corn, even if grown on Pawnee lands, ostensibly for Pawnee benefit, was no longer available for use and consumption by Pawnees. Agency farmers expected Pawnees to assimilate to their own notions of property and ownership. Caches held food grown by Pawnee women, available to anyone who needed it, provided they replaced it later. Agency farmers, on the other hand, grew their crop on Pawnee land, made available to them under treaty, and they hoarded it according to their own calculations of optimal sale price.

Pawnees took matters into their own hands. A group of Skidi men armed themselves and went to the field that James Mathers cultivated, digging potatoes while challenging Mathers to come out and fight, taunting him while he hid in his house. The funds diverted from Pawnee annuities for this half-hearted pedagogy of civilization were intended to further break down Pawnee relations with land, hardly masking the naked imperatives of expansion and settlement, of refashioning people and land, alike, as property relations. Through the 1860s, the United States continued to redirect agency funds toward the support of two manual labor schools, two teachers, two blacksmiths and strikers, farmers, farming tools and stock, a miller, an engineer, and mill apprentices: funds that joined neatly with the intrusion of industrial capitalism into Pawnee modes of relationship.[9]

In an 1848 treaty with the United States, Pawnees ceded a band of territory running along the north side of the Platte River, as well as rights to timber along the Wood River, north of the ceded lands. Pawnees pledged "not to molest or injure the property or person of any white citizen of the United States, wherever found," and to refer any intertribal disputes to the arbitration of the U.S. president. The 1833 and 1848 treaties ceded the Platte River bottomlands, where rich soil and water were cultivable with Pawnee farming tools, which had long been the places of Pawnee women's agriculture, and of their villages. By this time, due to changing pressures of settlement, resulting in increasing population density in Pawnee villages, Pawnee women worked agricultural fields located at progressively increasing distances from villages. As part of an 1851 Moravian missionary effort, Gottlieb Oehler reported that Pawnee women farmed fields five to eight miles away from their villages, a distance that left them exposed to attacks when they were working the fields.[10] Pawnee women continued to develop and maintain their agricultural lands, and their harvest was especially crucial in years of poor communal buffalo hunts, such as the one that Oehler recorded that year. The United States did not make Pawnees any safer on their lands, and Pawnee women continued to work on their own terms.

Oehler also recorded his impressions of a Pawnee gendered division of labor in a commentary on civilization, faith, and ethics of work. For Oehler, this division of labor took bodily form in distinctions between Pawnee men, "almost feminine in their features," and Pawnee women, whom he saw as filthy with overwork, deformed by their constant toil, justifying colonialism as a civilizing influence, projecting the liberation of Pawnee women through continental imperialism. Oehler's perspective, like those of other colonial critics of Pawnee gender relations, was limited to a perspective on village life. Bodies, comportment, and labor are all read as evidence of Pawnee distance from, and potential receptivity to, the saving graces of a Protestant work ethic, from which to follow the conquering lamb of individual self-interest to liberal norms of gendered labor. Lost to this perspective, Pawnee women's incredible hard work materialized the strength of their bonds with each other, with their communities, and with the places where they made their lives. Pawnee women's work marked their independence from the values of capitalism and this, not any distance from bourgeois gender norms, is what drove Oehler's seeming concern for Pawnee women, as it had driven Dunbar's perspective a few decades earlier. Pawnee women's work, by bringing concrete, living form to Pawnee modes of relationship, continued to arrest the grasping, acquisitive fingers of continental imperialism. The development of labor exploitation on Pawnee lands was predicated on the expropriation of Pawnee women's relationships with each other, and with their lands.[11]

PEDAGOGIES OF CONTAINMENT

Oehler reported from Traders' Point, later renamed Bellevue, where he visited a government school that Samuel Allis operated for Pawnee children. The school was near the Pawnee, Otoe, and Omaha agent's office, two trading posts, and blacksmith shops, a mile upriver from a missionary station. Eighteen years after the United States had pledged to establish and fund schools for Pawnee children, Oehler reported that "the provisions, for the accommodation of Mr. Allis' family and Pawnee children, are wretched . . . The dwelling which is occupied by them . . . is almost in ruins." Oehler found ten to twelve Pawnee children attending the school, alongside some white children, all living together in a small room, about eighteen square feet. Colonial pedagogy reflected colonial property relations. Frank North, who would later hold the position of commanding officer of the Pawnee scouts, and his brother Luther, who led one of the scout companies, had long participated in multiple aspects of Pawnee Agency life. The North family came to Nebraska Territory in 1856 from New York by way of Ohio, settling in the growing town of Columbus, close to a Pawnee village. Their mother Jane, and a sister, worked as teachers at the agency school. Their elder brother James volunteered in the so-called 1858 Pawnee War, and later started a trading business at the Pawnee Agency, supplying Pawnees with goods in the constricted atmosphere of colonial occupation.[12]

Rapidly escalating colonialism pushed the establishment of a Pawnee reservation in the treaty of 1857 and the resulting confinement of Pawnees to the space of the reservation and the authority of the Indian Office. In this treaty, Pawnees ceded even more territory, establishing a reservation on the land remaining under their control. "In order to improve the condition of the Pawnees, and teach them the arts of civilized life," the United States agreed to found two manual labor schools, and would potentially open an additional two schools if it found them necessary. The curriculum at these schools would be directed by the U. S. federal government, and would include "the various branches of a common-school education," as well as "the arts of agriculture, the most useful mechanical arts," as if Pawnees, themselves, had no agriculture and technology of their own. All Pawnee children between seven and eighteen years old "shall be kept constantly at these schools for, at least, nine months in each year," and parents or guardians would have their annuities deducted in "an amount equal to the value, in time, of the tuition thus lost." The treaty sought to impose controls over Pawnee children, and their parents and guardians. By sundering intergenerational ties, it was intended to break Pawnee children's relationships with their grandmothers. Pawnee children would be unable to participate in at least one of the communal hunts, nor would they be able to participate in the harvest, thereby losing crucial opportunities to learn and develop Pawnee practices of agriculture, mechanical arts, and community life.

In addition to mandating that all Pawnee children live at reservation schools, the treaty provided for Pawnee men to apprentice in blacksmith, gunsmith, and tinsmith shops, as well as at a grain and lumber mill. The means of setting the wage was unaddressed in the treaty. Wages subsidized colonial occupation and administration on the Pawnee Agency. The United States agreed to build workshops and a mill, and to fund reservation farms, infrastructure that would benefit adjacent settler communities. Moreover, the treaty stated, "Pawnees agree to prevent the members of their tribe from injuring or destroying the houses, shops, machinery, stock farming utensils, and all other things furnished by the Government, and if any such shall be carried away, injured, or destroyed, by any of the members of their tribe, the value of the same shall be deducted from the tribal annuities." Policing agency property was tied to the development of infrastructures of occupation. Pawnee laborers hired to work on the reservation would answer to the

Pawnee agent, not to their own leaders. The eleventh article of the treaty provided for payment in money and horses, to four Pawnees who had guided U.S. troops on an expedition against Cheyennes, presaging the fuller development of Pawnee scouts in coming years.[13]

Pawnee women, however, asserted their own interests, sustaining their own modes of relationship in the face of colonial restrictions. By 1859, Pawnee women had begun farming upland areas close to their villages, where Mormon settlers who settled there the previous decade had broken hundreds of acres of sod with their plows. These fields, closer to Pawnee villages, and higher than the surrounding grounds, made women less vulnerable to attacks while they worked in their fields. Lists of annuity goods show the interests of Pawnee women. An 1859 bill of trade included "brass kettles, short pans, half axes, hoes, butcher knives, flint, awls, combs, mirrors, needles, shears, flat files, 4&6 quart pans, tin cups, and kettles."[14] These goods were implements for Pawnee women's work, and, once distributed, would belong to Pawnee women. If we look closely at the annuity process, we can see underlying continuities with Pawnee relations of ownership and use revolving around Pawnee women's labor.

MONOPOLY CAPITALISM

In 1860, Pawnee agent James Gillis reported to the commissioner of Indian affairs that since 1857, settlers had stolen twenty horses from Pawnees, who had been met with violence when attempting to recover their horses. Gillis noted that settlers had filed claims amounting to more than twenty thousand dollars with the commissioner against Pawnees, claims which can be understood as a constituent element of a colonial economy on occupied Pawnee lands. Justice blended with policing and military authority to garner value in market terms, deepening Pawnee expropriation through indebtedness.[15] This was the war-finance nexus. Colonialists claimed money through producing and policing colonial borders. Pawnees bore the risks and vulnerabilities of this kind of value production. This was not any kind of free market. It was a set of value relations grounded in colonial occupation.

The reservation imposed a new political order on Pawnees. In the words of Lawrie Tatum, an Indian agent on the Kiowa reservation, the Indian agent served as governor, legislature, judge, sheriff, and treasury:

First, the agent is governor. It was his duty to see that the laws and regulations of the United States Government applicable to Indian reservations were executed . . .

Second, the agent constitutes the legislature. An order published by an Indian agent became a law for that agency unless a superior officer countermanded it.

Third, the Indian agent is judge. Controversies between white men and Indians were heard and decided upon by the Indian agent. The decision was generally final.

A fourth office of an Indian agent was that of sheriff. Whiskey smugglers or other violators of the law were to be arrested by order of the Indian agent.

The fifth office of an Indian agent was that of accounting officer. All moneys to pay employees, also for buildings and other improvements, also for provisions for the Indians, annuity goods, medicine, iron, lumber, and for other property belonging to the Government was to be recounted for on cash and property rolls, and every three months the agent reported to the Government at Washington what had been expended, for what purpose, and the balance on hand.[16]

This authority, stemming from a single outsider over an entire community, could be understood as an imperial dictatorship, or proconsul, whose powers stemmed from authority over Indigenous lands, and a corresponding deterioration of Indigenous peoples' collective and individual status. The colonization of Pawnee lands took place through the suspension of self-rule, the abridgment of democracy—what Hobson called an "expansion of autocracy." In Indigenous contexts, among others, the United States suffocates actually existing democracy. The agent's control over the Pawnee economy, especially over annuity goods, checked Pawnee political power. For example, Pawnee agents consistently distributed annuity goods in late spring or early summer, but held annuity blankets until the weather turned cold, justifying this practice on the grounds that destitute and struggling Pawnees sold their blankets and winter goods below value before the winter. Controlling the distribution of annuity goods, in this logic, exemplified relationships of benevolence toward wards who had not yet developed capabilities of rational action in a market economy.[17]

Reservation authority played a role in financializing the space of Pawnee life. In 1860, Agent Gillis noted his reluctance to hold large amounts of cash on the reservation. "I have now on deposit here over sixteen thousand dollars and do not consider it, at this time, safe to take that amount of money on the reservation, on account of the unsettled state of the Indians, and surrounded as their reservation is, by a reckless set of desperadoes." Agent Gillis described an intended sequence, where annuities lead to credit, which leads to security (in a military sense) and securities (in a financial sense). Successive Pawnee agents requested weapons, under their control. In June 1860, Agent Gillis argued that defense was the rightful work of the U.S. federal government, and not of Pawnees themselves. Defense would deepen colonial power over Pawnee lands, transforming the motive of Pawnee self-defense into U.S. colonial aggression: "If the Government will furnish me with one six Pounder, thirty Sharps, or Harpers Ferry rifles, and the necessary ammunition, I will render a good account of these hostile attacks." Gillis reported a group of Pawnee men chasing down an attack that September, after a company of Army Dragoons failed to overtake the attackers. Less than two weeks later, Capt. Alfred Sully reported that a group of twenty-two Pawnee men had organized a war party and departed for Lakota territory.[18] These were precisely the kinds of mobility that agency authorities sought to constrain.

Despite attempts at administrative and financial control, we can glimpse, at a granular level, the ongoing and adaptive presence of Pawnee modes of relationship. For example, in June 1861, a Skidi leader bought a horse from a settler for forty dollars, deducted from the upcoming cash annuity. This exchange moved from the cash and annuity systems to Pawnee relations of value and distribution. There are other windows, as well, powerfully attesting to the ongoing primacy of Pawnee women's work and relationships at the core of Pawnee life. In July 1861, Agent DePuy estimated that a thousand acres were being cultivated: 825 by Pawnee women, and 175 by agency farmers, and that one hundred of these acres had been broken by agency teams, and another hundred by Pawnee women themselves. Colonial terms of labor, value, property, and gender were unable to fully assert themselves over Pawnee modes of relationship.[19]

In December 1861, Agent DePuy reported that he bought eight rifles and three revolvers to arm white agency employees, acknowledging that "these arms I had neither money nor authority from the Department to purchase." DePuy went on to request the purchase of an additional pair of four pounders, twenty Sharp's rifles, and remounted cannon brought from Fort Kearney. These arms, ostensibly to defend Pawnees, could be turned against Pawnees themselves in the service of maintaining colonial administration of agency farms and schools. Defending the Pawnee Agency blended with occupying Pawnee lands. At the end of that month, Agent DePuy hired Frank and

Luther North to haul wood to the agency sawmill. The following year, Benjamin Lushbaugh would replace DePuy, appointing a son-in-law of the commissioner of Indian affairs, who lived in Illinois and only came to the agency for the spring and fall annuities disbursement, as trader for the Pawnees. The new trader hired Frank North to oversee his business.[20]

Agent DePuy had imposed a different type of credit through the annuity system, when he reported the failure of the winter hunt:

> They are consequently now consuming the food which should be preserved for their sustenance at the time of planting corn. Many are entirely without food, and I have been compelled to authorize the trader to bring me a quantity of flour and sell to them on credit . . . I urge upon the chiefs to have as little purchased as possible, as it is deducting so much from their annuity—that the less they consume now the more they will have to support themselves throughout the hardest part of the winter, which is yet before them. If the money were here now, their very need would make it injudicious to pay them before the 1st of February, as there would be a greater likelihood that it would be exhausted before the coming of spring.[21]

DePuy utilized Pawnee credit, controlling its terms himself, teaching financial literacy at the precipice of starvation. In contrast to caches, Pawnee credit preempted Pawnee futures, imposing relations of scarcity, isolation, and dependency through the war-finance nexus.

By 1862, the federal government had established the Pawnee Manual Labor School. The initial class comprised sixteen students, and over one hundred students enrolled over the next year, although they did not all attend at once. Elvira Platt, who worked as a teacher, and eventually as principal at the school for a decade, reminisced:

> To learn to speak and read the English language was the first object to be required, and teach industrial habits and learn civilized ways. Being in close proximity to their village, they were tempted to speak the Pawnee language instead of the English. The boys were detailed for farm labor and also to work in the smitheys and flouring mill. One, an assistant engineer, became quite skillful in that department and another, an assistant miller. Others were distributed around in different shops to learn trades, etc.[22]

Platt's reminiscences provide a glimpse into the colonial pedagogy that Pawnee children faced, spanning culture, ideology, and bodily comportment. Teachers worked at the school to transform the bodily realities of Pawnee girls and women that missionaries had observed a few decades earlier. While her letter made no mention of girls at the school, her attention focused on those boys who were able to learn skilled trades that would enfranchise them as wage laborers under the reservation's production regime. Their education itself was a form of colonial infrastructure, along with fenced fields, workshops and mills, and surveyed plots of land. Expropriation and exploitation together shaped the lives of these Pawnee children.

Wages also carried pedagogical implications for some Pawnee men. In June of 1862, former agent DePuy recorded a certificate of indebtedness for back wages due to Frank North, as well as James Murie and Baptiste Bayhylle (a Pawnee man), for labor and interpreting services. Like North, Murie and Bayhylle would play important roles with the Pawnee scouts. Joseph McFadden, a white man who had married a Pawnee woman, worked as an agency interpreter in 1862. He would later serve as the initial commanding officer for the Pawnee scouts.[23] That September, Agent Lushbaugh requested authority to organize four to five hundred Pawnees, "properly equipped and officered by whites," who would scout for one or two infantry regiments in order to defend reservation communities. A few months later, Lushbaugh requested a set of complete cavalry equipment for use by agency employees and "such of the Pawnee Indians as may have adopted the habit of civilized life," laying bare the contention that reservation defense should result in further control over Pawnee life. In a deposition that December, related to a charge against Agent DePuy, Frank North was listed as a laborer on the school farm on the reservation.

Agent Lushbaugh conceived of Pawnee defense on behalf of colonial expansion. In January 1863, Lushbaugh justified a request for guns and ammunition for Pawnees on the logic that "The whites in the vicinity derive what protection they have from the Pawnees and of course would not object to an increase of facilities being afforded the Pawnees for this purpose." Defense at the Pawnee reservation, Lushbaugh suggested, could be turned toward settlement and occupation. Six months later, he reported that an attack had resulted in the deaths of "a number" of Pawnee women. According to Lushbaugh, members of the Second Nebraska Cavalry, which had arrived at the agency a few days earlier, assisted Pawnees in fighting, but only after their captain was attacked and wounded. No defense of Pawnees (no treaty obligations), just revenge. Behind this "avowed repudiation of treaty obligations" lurked "earth hunger and the scramble for markets."[24] U. S. authority operated in reaction to Indigenous presence, through the logic and relations of countersovereignty.

Pawnee women faced new weeds brought by settlers and their cows and horses, necessitating more intensive and regular attention to their fields. Ultimately, a combination of drought and grasshoppers brought repeated crop failures over several years in the 1860s, leading Pawnees to the brink. In September 1864, agency farmer Charles Whaley recorded the failure of the corn crop. Agent Lushbaugh corroborated this, later that month: "The loss of their crops is a severe blow upon the Pawnees, and leaves them in a destitute condition." This was compounded by the failure of that year's summer hunt, due to attacks on Pawnee villages while hunting. "Having neither corn or meat," Lushbaugh concluded, "their only remaining resource is their annuity." The following March, Lushbaugh invoking crop failure, requested ten thousand dollars of the annuity fund to be disbursed directly into his hands.[25] Crop failures deepened assertions of colonial power over Pawnees.

THE PROPERTIES OF REACTION

In 1864, a group of Pawnee men graded four miles of the Union Pacific Railroad for a local contractor who was finding it difficult to recruit workers. Agent Lushbaugh, in a fit of excitement, imagining a harvest of liberalism emerging from the loam of colonialism, wrote to the commissioner of Indian affairs, "If the presumption is not too broad I would respectfully suggest that Congress change the name of the road referred to, to that of the *Pawnee and Pacific Rail Road*." In June 1864, he relayed a request for one hundred rifles for summer and winter hunts, conveying continuities of Pawnee collective relationships with their lands, decades after this kind of mobility was to be constrained by the United States. On their first scout campaign, in 1864, Pawnee men provided their own horses. Their wages were supposed to be supplemented by an additional payment to cover care and upkeep of their horses. They never received either. Pawnee men chose to fight, uninterested in general scout service. The initial group recruited to serve as scouts that year decided instead to go on their winter hunt, after hearing rumors that the army planned to deploy them south to fight in the Civil War.[26]

Measles and diphtheria spread among Pawnee children at school, leading to children's deaths, teacher J. B. Whitfield reported in October 1864. As for the school itself, "The health of the school at this time is good. I would in the connection urge the importance of not taking very small children and the necessity of exercising the utmost care in selecting only those of good constitutions of sound physical health." Whitfield understood deeper control of the children, and not remaking the school itself, as a productive way to deal with these illnesses and deaths. Whitfield noted that students had been taken on the summer hunt by their parents, and argued for school authority to supersede family authority:

> I would respectfully suggest that it be distinctly impressed in the minds of these parents that upon their entrance into the school all control over the child by the parent ceases to exist, as the meddling and interference of these persons creates discontent and insubordination among the children, and causes no small amount of trouble for the teachers.

Fantasies of control, attempting to rupture intergenerational relationships, underlay the colonial functions of Whitfield's pedagogical work with Pawnee children, just as they marked the operations of agency farms and reservation administration.[27] Whitfield's remarks exemplified the unevenness of colonial control, and its ongoing failure to rupture Pawnee relationships, to impose a new calendar and relationship to space, and to stamp out the Pawnee language itself.

Illness at the school continued to present a problem in 1865, when Whitfield relayed information on the deaths of two students, "a period of health beyond anything heretofore realized in the history of this school." By now, Whitfield acknowledged that mortality among the students was structural, tracing it to cramped, poorly ventilated sleeping quarters. Thirteen boys and nine girls attended the school that year. "The girls are taught the arts of housewifery while the boys perform all kinds of outdoor work capable of being performed by boys of their age." Toward this end, Whitfield requested the purchase of a team of horses, wagon, and farming tools, a stable for horses and cattle, as well as fencing. "The reasonableness of these appropriations will at once be perceived when we reflect that it is the peculiar design of the enterprise to teach them to labor and to fit them by an efficient course of practical training to provide for themselves in life." Pawnee children, coerced into living at the school, labored for nothing, a pedagogy in an imperialist division of labor and its gendered and racial expectations.[28]

Pawnee scouts had perhaps sought a measure of independence from the attempted restrictions of reservation life, but like Pawnee children at school, they also suffered illness and exposure. Scout units were dispatched by officers, such as the commanding officer of Fort Kearny, who sent them out on foot during a blizzard in the winter of 1865. Grenville Dodge remembered ordering two companies of Pawnee scouts on an attack on the north side of the South Platte River that same winter. Caught in the worst storm in memory, with temperatures at thirty degrees below zero, the scouts lost half of their horses, and many of them struggled with severe frostbite. Scouts' wages supplemented an annuity void, with the U.S. federal government repeatedly providing inferior annuities, sometimes failing to provide any at all. In 1865, for example, after receiving orders to relieve a company of Seventh Cavalry at the Pawnee reservation, scouts continued to draw wages and rations. In an 1865 request for two hundred rifles and ammunition, Lushbaugh invoked the military service of almost a hundred Pawnee men as justification for the disbursement of arms.[29]

Reservation life among Pawnees entailed uneven incorporation into the regime of private property. The property regime emanating from the establishment of the Pawnee reservation reflected war and dependency, rather than the exchange of commodities of equal value. Acts of exchange across Pawnee and U.S. lines, though incorporative on their face, enacted expulsion on deeper levels. Pawnee capital was stamped, through its core, with the trauma of conquest, not as dead scar tissue, but as a festering wound, reopened in each moment of the production process. Here, in economic terms, was incorporation through difference, private property as the fruit of the tree of imperialism. Instead of property becoming visible and active through community, community, in the space of the reservation, became active and visible through property. Pawnee relations of distribution were the basis for the development of a colonial economy. The capitalization of the Platte River lands reflected the relations of occupation. In spring of 1866, James North contracted with the Union Pacific Railroad Company to provide piling for a bridge being built across the Loup River, and Luther North worked for him on this contract. After finishing this work, Luther contracted on a grading job about twenty miles from the end of track. That October, President Andrew Johnson appointed Frank North as trader at the Pawnee Agency.[30] While profiting from industrial development, the North brothers continued to make money through the reservation economy. Territorial authorities and local traders continued to press for the circulation of coin, a precondition for wages and credit in the colonial economy.

In January 1867, John Becker, a new Pawnee agent, reported that the Union Pacific Railroad had driven the buffalo from the Platte River valley, which had "convinced the Pawnees that they have either to look up some location not so remote from their hunting ground or to pay more attention to tilling the soil." Pawnee women were written out of his perspective, but their work and relationships set the terms for the changes that he suggested. When Becker wrote his report, Pawnees were still undertaking winter and summer buffalo hunts. Pawnee women continued to farm near their villages, establishing productive fields in new lands, growing far more than reservation farmers. Becker's report described a future wish in the language of present reality, the administration of countersovereignty as the preemption of Indigenous futures. A month after Becker's report, Maj. Gen. Christopher Augur requested the services of Frank North to organize a scout battalion. Those Pawnee men who signed up to serve as scouts would be able to move across the region, living in the company of other Pawnee men, contrasting with the experiences of children at the reservation schools. Central to the pedagogical thrust of reservation schools was replacing the relationships that shaped the lives of Pawnee children, and in 1867, Elvira Platt began enforcing a rule isolating Pawnee schoolchildren from their families, which she justified as a way to teach English.[31] The overriding impulse of agency farms and schools pushed to make Pawnee women's work and relationships valueless: illogical and illegible in the face of capitalist production.

COLONIAL REACTION

Union Pacific workers depended on Pawnees for protection. An engineer wrote to Grenville Dodge from the Black Hills in July of 1867, "My escort of twenty Pawnee warriors left me rather unceremoniously about six miles east of here, and I have not seen them since." Just days after this, a group of scouts guarding a Union Pacific wagon train en route to the Black Hills abruptly vanished.[32] Railroad workers, from the perspectives of Pawnee scouts, may themselves have been "drudges," poor souls mired in filth, stooped under the weight of the rails they carried and the ground they moved, not unlike missionary perspectives on Pawnee women a few decades earlier.

Pawnee scout service allowed Pawnee men to renew their modes of relationship with each other, and with their homelands. During a winter campaign, a Pawnee man named Kuruksuwadi led the scouts to a canyon with wood, grass, and shelter for their horses. He instructed the men to cut poles and stood them up, took the covers off the wagons and stretched them around the poles. Once the tent was up, others cut grass and spread it on the floor, and he built a fire to dry out their robes and blankets. Kuruksuwadi gave orders, while Luther North, the ranking officer, watched and participated. Younger men tended horses, struck camp, and cooked, traveling with the scouts. In 1836, Charles Murray had described younger Pawnee men who attended older men's horses while out ranging.[33] Scout service enabled Pawnee men to maintain such intergenerational relationships, renewing Pawnee pedagogical practices, decades after the establishment of the reservation.

In December 1867, after the scouts mustered out, Luther North returned to the Pawnee Agency and worked for his brother James as a clerk in the trading post. Luther recalled that over the winter, he and his brother traded for about five hundred buffalo robes, as well as beaver skins and other furs. The North brothers also bought ponies during the winter season. Luther described their strategy:

> When on their winter hunt they had to ride their best horses pretty hard, and they always came home very thin. As the Indians never made any provisions for wintering their horses, they sold those that were so thin that they thought them likely to die before spring. There was much hay put up by the settlers near the reservation, and we could buy it cheaply, and if the ponies lived through until spring, the Indians would buy them back. The thinnest ones were usually the fastest and best buffalo horses, and as the Indians got an annual money payment of forty thousand dollars from the Government, they had something to buy with.[34]

The North brothers found ways to profit from the full cycle of Pawnee colonization: industrialization, militarization, and the annuity economy. They accumulated capital by exploiting the specific kinds of risk and vulnerabilities that individual Pawnees faced over the course of a year, risk and vulnerability emanating from colonialism.

At the end of January 1869, while Frank North was enlisting a new company of scouts at the Pawnee Agency, a group of Pawnee men, who had recently been discharged from scout service for the U.S. Army, were attacked by U.S. soldiers who had been egged into the attack by local settlers, near Mulberry Creek. Pawnees said that these men had set out to trade with southern nations, traveling along old trade routes. The U.S. soldiers murdered nine of the Pawnee veterans. A few days later, an army surgeon dug up their graves, decapitated their corpses, and sent their skulls to the Army Medical Museum, where they remained until 1995.[35]

Some Pawnee women found work as domestics for reservation staff, settlers, and army officers. Earlier missionary denunciations of Pawnee women's status as "slaves" resonated with historical memories of Indian enslavement in the region. Various forms of coercive and unpaid labor, of taxation and administrative control, shaped agency authority. By September 1869, measles still presented a problem at the school. Two students had died of it in the previous year. The number of students attending had grown considerably, to fifty-six. Five of the enrolled students were serving as Pawnee scouts that year.[36] Four months after the completion of the transcontinental railroad seemingly finalized continental enclosure, Pawnee children continued to die at school, or to serve in the U.S. Army.

Pawnee scout service can be understood as a form of wage labor, but it cannot be isolated from the realities of occupation, from the colonial context. An 1869 clothing voucher for Company A, Pawnee Scouts, gives an impression of some of this context. Each of the men received a pair of trousers, a flannel shirt, a pair of stockings, and a pair of boots. Some of them also received flannel underwear, a coat, and blankets.[37] At first glance, this appears to be standard requisitions for U.S. military personnel on the Plains, but for Pawnee men, the experience of these disbursements aligned with the distribution of annuities in their communities, annuities which were often withheld by reservation authorities and administrators. U.S. recognition of Pawnee relationships with land was a precondition of federal and corporate claims on the land of the Union Pacific Railroad. Without a relationship to Pawnee collective life, the claims of settlers and corporations alike would have been enacted over tenuous ground. Without Pawnee modes of relationship, distinct from, but integrally involved with the emerging capitalist economy, continental imperialism could have turned inward and cannibalized the community of settlers. Countersovereignty inoculated the Union Pacific Railroad from the violence that was its founding condition.

An 1870 guide to Union Pacific land described the Platte River valley:

widely celebrated for its picturesque scenery, rich productive soil, and mild and healthful climate . . . Persons settling in this valley will not find it a "new country." Neighbors are nowhere distant, towns and villages are springing up and rapidly growing in size and importance, extensive and well-cultivated farms and thriving communities are found throughout the entire tract.[38]

Pawnees had been erased from this speculative landscape, but it was Pawnee women's work across generations that made the soil so rich and productive.

It was Pawnee villages and the Pawnee reservation that facilitated the development of towns and villages, and the rapid growth of a settler population. Pawnees were erased from the landscape of speculation, but their work and their relationships were invoked as easing the risks involved in land purchase.

The brochure touted these lands as a "good investment," marshaling a theory of financial capital firmly tied to imperialism:

> To the capitalist, the lands of this Company offer a safe and paying investment. A rapid enhancement in their value is inevitable, and large profits are certain to be realized. The credit system gives the man of limited means an equal chance with the capitalist to avail himself of the present low prices, and by the payment of a small annual sum to become in five years the owner of a farm and the possessor of a competence and independence for all future time.

The combination of land purchase and credit provided a general investment in the reproduction of continental imperialism. Railroad colonialism made land purchase on credit a rational investment for a skilled worker. The ghost of Jeffersonian agrarianism stalked the grounds of the war-finance nexus on the Plains. A mirage of individual self-sufficiency belied the fact of concentration of power. Dreams of self-sufficient yeomen farmers, of European immigrants remade as Americans, remaking liberty and democracy in the process, spun centrifugally around the ether of credit and the muck of colonial occupation. Children taken from their families, often to die from illness; colonial administrators engaging in brazen graft; promises of defense resulting in heightened vulnerabilities to violent attacks; random, murderous violence from settlers who showed up and acted as if they owned the place. In the Platte River valley, these were some of the concrete preconditions for finance capital. Continental imperialism made Pawnee women's work even more central to supporting the entire community. Pawnee scouts were rendered hypervisible, a condition that continued as scout veterans performed in Wild West shows in later years.[39] Pawnee women, whose relationships materialized collective life, in its manifold manifestations in Pawnee lands, were rendered invisible by the same process of railroad construction, seemingly sequestered and confined to reservation space.

After the scouts mustered out in 1877, Frank North wrote to Gen. Phil Sheridan about their horses and transportation allowances. In the previous winter's campaign, the scouts had captured about one hundred horses, in addition to the hundred they started with, and fifty horses they had since purchased.

What I desire to ascertain from you is this: Are not my men—the same as other regularly enlisted and honorably discharged soldiers—entitled to "travel pay" and rations or commutation of rations, from here to their home and also will they not be entitled to the 40c/per day each for their ponies during the time they shall be on the march home?

Scout service offered Pawnee men opportunities to move over their territory free of the constraints of reservation authority. North informed Sheridan, "they came up here with the expectation and hope of remaining in their old country for some time, and they are very much disappointed indeed that they are so soon to go back." When not immediately in the service of the army, the Pawnee men who worked as scouts found themselves vulnerable to everyday colonial violence. North continued, "My men desire, when they are sent home, that I and my 1st Lieut.—my brother—accompany them, as the country through which they must travel is quite thickly settled all the way and they wish us to be with them, and for the protection of their interests on the road I think it necessary that we go."[40] North's discourse of protection was a colonialist pantomime, providing a pretense of security through proximity to whiteness, scripting Pawnee men as his dependents. North's logic mirrored, at an interpersonal scale, the alibis of peace and protection offered by the United States to the Pawnee nation. Continental imperialism manifested on Pawnee lands as gendered expropriation. Attempting to impose constraints on farming and on self-defense, through wage labor and schools, colonial authorities repeatedly failed to replace Pawnee modes of relationship. These attempts are what I am referring to as countersovereignty. The transformation of the Platte River country into "domestic" space of the United States was yet to be accomplished.

In 2009, Pawnee eagle corn grew within a field of sunflowers along the Platte River. The corn had been grown from seed preserved by a Pawnee woman named Deb Echo-Hawk. After removal, many of the traditional corn varieties Pawnee women brought with them did not grow in the heavy clay and the hotter climate of Oklahoma. This eagle corn, which thrived on the rich alluvial Platte River soil, was a reassertion of a distinctly Pawnee mode of relationship, of relationships between Pawnee women, the corn that they cultivated, and the soil that they tended. The eagle corn, as well as several other Pawnee corn and watermelon varieties, grew in fields surrounded by miles and miles of monocrop corn grown under the aegis of monopoly agribusiness. These fields replenished the bank of Pawnee seeds that had been carried, and carefully preserved, after removal.[41] Against the war-finance nexus, here is a very different practice of loans and credit, revolving around renewing distinctly Pawnee modes of relationship with their Platte River homelands, and with the many forms of life on those lands. These are seeds of a decolonized future.

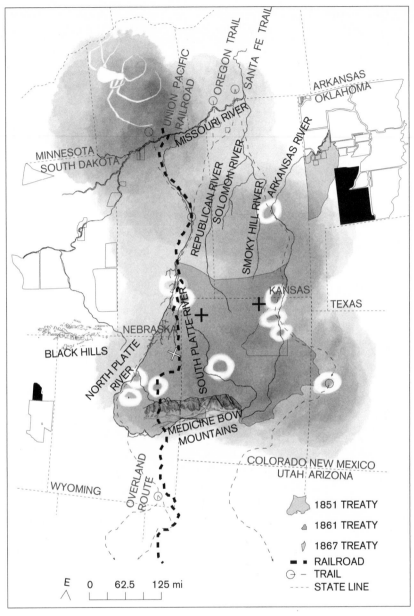

MAPS 9 AND 10: Cheyenne Nation. Cartography by Elsa Matossian Hoover.

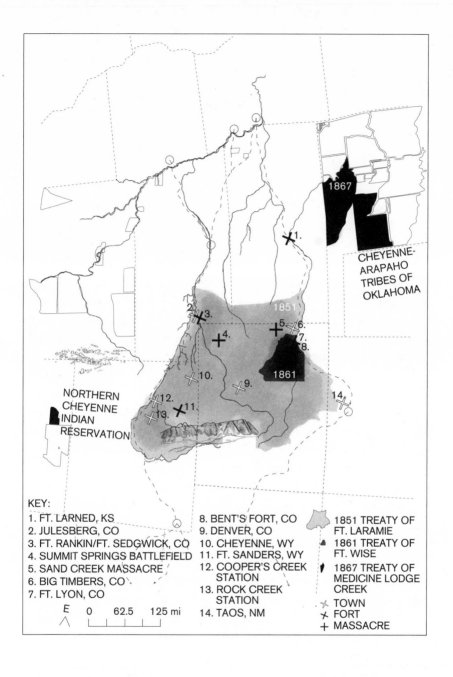

CHEYENNE-
ARAPAHO
TRIBES OF
OKLAHOMA

1867

1851

1861

NORTHERN
CHEYENNE
INDIAN
RESERVATION

KEY:
1. FT. LARNED, KS
2. JULESBERG, CO
3. FT. RANKIN/FT. SEDGWICK, CO
4. SUMMIT SPRINGS BATTLEFIELD
5. SAND CREEK MASSACRE
6. BIG TIMBERS, CO
7. FT. LYON, CO

8. BENT'S FORT, CO
9. DENVER, CO
10. CHEYENNE, WY
11. FT. SANDERS, WY
12. COOPER'S CREEK
    STATION
13. ROCK CREEK
    STATION
14. TAOS, NM

1851 TREATY OF
FT. LARAMIE
1861 TREATY OF
FT. WISE
1867 TREATY OF
MEDICINE LODGE
CREEK

TOWN
FORT
MASSACRE

E   0   62.5   125 mi

SEVEN

Cheyenne

IN THE EARLY DAYS OF AUGUST 1867, a group of Cheyenne men returning from Pawnee country crossed the Union Pacific tracks, near what is now Cheyenne, Wyoming. They saw a railroad work crew approaching slowly with a handcar, and decided to wreck the car, laying logs across the tracks, some of them riding back and frightening the work crew into accelerating the handcar until the logs tipped it over from the tracks. After this experience, one of the men, Sleeping Rabbit, suggested that they try to derail a train.

They set about cutting the telegraph line, pulling out railroad ties, somehow managing to dislodge the track itself. While the sun was setting, a Union Pacific train hurtling along at full speed, with no foreknowledge of the damage, derailed spectacularly. Under lantern light joining the quarter moon and early August stars, the group began moving through the boxcars, rummaging through the cargo, finding food and cloth, taking what they wanted, and what they could carry. They returned the next morning to take more, finding some bread and sweet foods, which they ate for lunch. Some boys who came along that morning had fun tying bolts of calico to horse's tails, watching the horses stamp about with ribbons of bright cloth unfurling behind. Soon, a group of Pawnee scouts organized by the U. S. Army arrived on another train and began searching for them.[1] This train-derailing frequently appears in histories of the transcontinental railroad, as an anecdote of random savagery. To the contrary, Cheyennes derailed this train at the nexus of war and finance.

To understand Cheyenne responses to the war-finance nexus, we need to understand the development of Cheyenne relationships with horses. According to one story, horses came into Cheyenne life from the south, when a group of Cheyennes observed Mexicans riding ponies, soon afterwards catching a gentle pony, realizing its potential as a pack animal superior to dogs. A group that ventured south into Mexico returned with the first Cheyenne herd. Cheyennes found the new animals useful for hunting and for moving their villages, and they also found that sharing, giving, and trading horses helped build relationships across their families and communities. The pony soon became, according to the person who recorded this story, "the standard of value," altering gendered and generational relationships among Cheyennes, transforming relations with neighboring nations and with non-human animals. In a profound transformation, for example, Cheyennes used horses to develop new ways of hunting collectively. Long-standing Cheyenne practices, such as older Cheyenne women continuing to use dogs as pack animals, endured alongside novelty and experimentation, reminders that Cheyennes had transformed their mode of relationship as they crossed the Missouri River.[2]

Cheyennes placed the most value on horses trained by a "gentling" process, a relationship of reciprocity rather than domination. Iron Teeth remembered an earlier period of her life: "When I became a woman I never asked any man to tame my horses for me. My sister and I used to take the wild animals to a sandy place beside the river before trying to ride them." She recalled, "One time, after my marriage, when I was riding with my baby strapped to my back, I saw some wild horses. I put the baby in its board cradle down upon the prairie and got after the herd. That day I caught two horses." Mules and other stock animals were distinctly valuable to Cheyenne women, carrying burdens when villages were moving. Horses circulated through Indigenous communities through both trading and raiding, enhancing Indigenous modes of relationship.[3] By the 1860s, imperialist value relations revolving around labor, real estate, and credit would be forcibly refracted through prior and ongoing Indigenous relations of value in horses.

As Cheyennes moved onto the Plains, reshaping the boundaries of their nation, they traded in villages along the Missouri, and on the North Platte. After 1815, Cheyennes were centrally positioned in the major sites of intertribal trade that connected the Plains to regions beyond. Cheyennes distinguished between Mexicans, with whom they had long-standing relationships, and U. S. whites, newcomers with a different culture. An elder remembered these kinds of observations:

> Two different kinds of white men were known to the Cheyennes when I was a boy. At the far South were people we called Español, who lived in Mexico.

We traded there with them, and sometimes they came into our country for trading with us . . . The other kind of white men we met first in our own Black Hills country. These were United States people. We called them vihio, our word for the crawling spider.

The end game of continental imperialism was isolation, rupturing the interrelationships that had long shaped Indigenous life on the Plains. The Santa Fe Trail, the first of the major overland trails from the United States, followed the Arkansas River. In the early 1820s, the trail connected Missouri and New Mexico, and by the mid-1830s, traffic along the trail had increased considerably. Caravans on the Santa Fe Trail moved through Cheyenne lands between the Missouri and Cimarron Rivers, before passing into Kiowa territory. Major routes of Indigenous movement over the plains coursed on a north–south axis, for example, from the Black Hills, across the headwaters of the Platte and Arkansas Rivers, across the Canadian and Red Rivers, and southward into Mexico. Indigenous movements tracked the cycle of seasons on the Plains, the flowering of plants, and the related movements of animals, reflecting a deep and abiding commitment to the place itself. Colonial pathways crossed the region on a journey elsewhere. Overland trails materialized isolation, cutting off the existing regional trade that centered on relationships between Indigenous communities. Continental imperialism partitioned Cheyenne life from densely interconnected geographies of trade and interrelationship.[4]

In 1826, news spread from the Blackfoot of massive buffalo herds and large horse herds between the Arkansas and Platte Rivers, the farthest north that wild horses had been reported, and soon after, a group of Cheyennes and Arapahos moved south to the Platte from the Black Hills. That year, a party led by Yellow Wolf near the north fork of the Red River returned with an enormous herd. Intertribal trade in these years was tied to the development of the fur trade in the region. Bent's Fort, built between 1828 and 1832, on the Arkansas River, was an important location for a mercantile conquest of New Mexico, throwing hooks deep into Mexican territory from St. Louis. U.S. colonization of New Mexico, which was predicated on a class alliance between New Mexico elites and merchants from the United States, against Pueblo and village unity, was a historical predicate for the U.S. occupation of the central and southern Plains. The fort was a key site for the burgeoning U.S. colonial conflict with Mexico, a stopping point for the U.S. military invasion of Santa Fe. Bent's Fort enabled the centralization of trade in the region, resulting in an increasingly militarized traffic on the Santa Fe Trail, with the direct support of the U.S. Army. Trade at the fort encouraged violence against buffalo hunters and traders from New Mexico (many of Indigenous descent) who had long moved through Indigenous communities in an independent trade. Bent's Fort was vital infrastructure for the colonization of the Plains, a major stop along the Santa Fe Trail, and an important station on mail expresses, encouraging the raising of smaller trading outposts.[5]

By the 1830s, Cheyennes controlled the broad swath of intertribal horse-centered trade on the Plains, which made Cheyennes central conduits between the Indigenous-centered horse trade and the colonial fur trade, enjoying material success beyond their relatively small demographic numbers. Cheyenne modes of relationship shaped this material abundance. Manhastoz, districts of Cheyenne villages comprising groups of sisters and their children, were the social core of Cheyenne community life in the years that Cheyennes established themselves as a preeminent trading community on the Plains. A drawing by the Cheyenne artist Howling Wolf provides a glimpse into this social relationship. In the image, two Cheyenne women, each wearing a distinct dress, face away from the viewer, while a Cheyenne man, facing the viewer, stands to their right. The women, at the center of the image, sharing a blanket yet individually distinct, are the core of the image, and the man is legible in relation to them. By the 1830s, each manhastoz had begun specializing in a specific form of trade, attuned to its geographic location, organized under the leadership of selected men within each community. Hevhaitaneos were renowned horse handlers. Oivimanas, toward the north, specialized in the buffalo trade, and Hevikisnipahis, living nearest to the Missouri River, continued to be involved in the beaver trade.[6]

A SWARM OF SPIDERS

As the California Gold Rush commenced, the ecological destruction of Cheyenne lands accelerated. Continental imperialism is a mode of relationship that fosters mass destruction and impoverishment. By 1849, the Oregon Trail along the Platte River had been fairly denuded of grass for settlers' stock, wood for their fires, and game for their meat. Those headed to California moved along the Arkansas River. The trails pinned southern Cheyennes between settler routes. Buffalo herds in the area dwindled rapidly and cottonwoods, which were important for feeding horses through winter, disappeared "in a single season." The desolation stretched for miles along the course of the rivers. In addition to this rapid destruction, migrants brought cholera in 1849, and while the epidemic spread northward, it was Cheyennes, Arapahos, and Lakotas who suffered the greatest catastrophe. The epidemic hit the manhastoz, comparatively dense living arrangements of sisters and their relatives, particularly hard.[7]

As the epidemic subsided and a new reality snapped into painful focus for surviving Cheyennes, Dog Soldiers began to transform into a new kind of stable, large-scale Cheyenne community, especially after they merged with the Masikotas, one of the older manhastoz. The manhastoz economy, organized around a stable core of groups of sisters, was oriented primarily toward trade. The Dog Soldier economy was oriented less toward trade. They established themselves east of the other Cheyenne communities, between the Platte and the Arkansas, on the Republican and Smoky Hill headwaters. This was not a stark separation, and people continued to visit and move between camps and villages. William Bent and his Cheyenne relatives and allies fled the cholera zone, eventually building a new fort on the Arkansas River, which the United States later purchased and renamed Fort Lyon, a significant army post on the Plains during the 1860s.[8] More than a decade after it was built, Black Kettle's village was at nearby Sand Creek, seeking the safety of Fort Lyon, when the Colorado Volunteers massacred them.

Following the U.S. war with Mexico and the development of overland trails, the pace of colonialism on the central Plains accelerated. Mormons attempted to establish a claim to the basin of the Colorado River in the early 1850s, but were unable to gain federal recognition; unlike the Arapaho, Arikara, Assiniboine, Cheyenne, Crow, Hidatsa, Lakota, and Mandan nations, all of which the U.S. government recognized in the 1851 Fort Laramie Treaty. In the years that followed, Cheyennes scrupulously upheld the terms of peace, refraining from attacks on any community that had signed the treaty, agreeing to reparations or reduced annuities on occasions when tribal members took cattle following unsuccessful buffalo hunts. Amidst this peace, they and their allies viewed the increased U.S. military presence with unease, which flared after U.S. troops violated the 1851 treaty, in an attack on their Lakota allies near Fort Laramie.[9]

By the end of the decade, a series of localized gold rushes triggered explosive settlement in the region. In 1859, the publicization of gold near Denver spurred a massive, rapid gold rush in 1860. Swarms of settlers rampaged through southern Cheyenne territory in a collective delirium. The U.S. federal government established Colorado Territory in 1861. Colorado settlers imported food and other subsistence items, relying on overland routes to transport these goods. With an infrastructure and economy oriented around gold strikes, local agricultural production was insufficient to feed the population. Rapid boomlets followed isolated gold strikes, fueling spending sprees and binge consumption of luxury items.[10]

In 1861, a small group of men representing some of the manhastoz leadership negotiated the Treaty of Fort Wise with U. S. negotiators, who pressed the cession of 12 / 13ths of 1851 treaty lands. The new treaty provided for annuities, and also contained provisions that granted the U. S. rights-of-way for "roads and highways, laid out by authority of law." Only six Cheyenne men signed the treaty, and Cheyennes widely considered it illegitimate. Here is an instance of a pattern that Hilferding described, in which "diplomacy serves directly the interests of investment-seeking capital." The treaty sought to cement the peripheral status of Cheyenne communities on their lands.[11]

Annuities were a point of interface between Indigenous and colonial economies, resulting in the transformation of long-standing practices of distribution and gendered ownership. Iron Teeth described an annuity made to Cheyennes when she was fifteen:

> We were given beef, but we did not care for this kind of meat. Great piles of bacon were stacked upon the prairie and distributed to us, but we used it only to make fires or to grease robes for tanning. We got soda, but we did not know what to do with it. Green coffee was distributed among us. We supposed the grains were some new kind of berries. We boiled them as they were, green, but they did not taste good. We liked the sugar presented to us. They gave us plenty of it, some of it light brown and some of it dark brown. We got brass kettles, coffee-pots, curve-bladed butcher knives and sharp pointed sewing awls which were better than ours that were of bone. There were boxfuls of black and white thread for us. The thread was in skeins, not on spools. All of the women got black goods, colored goods and bed ticking material. We made the cloth into summer clothing for children and into draperies for the interiors of the lodges. We were given plenty of colored beads, brass buttons, brass finger-rings, and red and blue face paints. Blankets were issued out to everybody, all of them solid colors—red, blue, yellow, green, white.[12]

Her memories foreground the wastefulness of annuities, stacking meat in piles on the ground, goods and items with no practical use for Cheyennes, that pushed Cheyennes into dependent positions of consumption in the colonial economy. On the other hand, the annuity economy potentially shored up Cheyenne women's economic roles within their communities. Annuities allowed for a change in the role of the manhastoz in Cheyenne economic and social life, from distribution between communities, as had been the case in previous decades, to distribution within communities. Annuities potentially sustained women's centrality to the circulation of goods in Cheyenne life.

In the summer of 1863, Colorado Volunteers commenced a series of attacks on Cheyenne villages, and on small groups of Cheyennes moving through their own lands, who continued to participate in intertribal trade, diplomacy, and ceremonies. These attacks flared up as symptoms of everyday, quotidian colonial violence that attempted to impose Colorado claims over the changed geography that followed the Treaty of Fort Wise, to which many Cheyennes had never assented. Settlers used force "to secure new markets by annexing fresh tracts of territory," which Hobson would later describe as a core function of imperialism. The attacks culminated in the assassination of Lean Bear, who had taken a central role in diplomacy with the United States, one of the six Cheyenne signatories at Fort Wise. As Lean Bear approached a company of soldiers on foot to shake hands with the commanding officer, the soldiers opened fire on him, and the artillery opened fire on his relatives. Widespread shock at this escalation of colonial violence spurred Dog Soldiers and their allies to scale up and formalize their raids. Doing so, Dog Soldiers asserted control over Cheyenne lands, in a context of attacks on the manhastoz-centered trading economy.[13]

In May, Dog Soldiers undertook sporadic raids, and by July, they turned their attention toward ranches, farms, and trading posts within their territory, from the Platte River to the vicinity of the Santa Fe Trail. Raiding parties attacked the Overland Stage Line, which had stations every ten or twelve miles, and coaches carrying the daily mail. This was a major freight route. Wagon trains continued to lumber along, enabling raiding parties to engage in lightning strikes, seemingly appearing from nowhere, only to vanish into the surroundings. Dog Soldiers and their allies systematically bore pressure down on the stations, and on the coaches, expropriating stock and goods, egging settlers and freighters on into battle. George Bent described the scene at a village on the Solomon Fork that summer, with an abundance of food, including sides of bacon, bags of coffee and sugar, boxes of crackers, and other goods, such as boots, shoes, and bolts of brightly colored and patterned silk. Old men in the village wore fine cloaks. Women wore silk dresses, and young men wore silk shirts. The circulation and consumption of luxury goods and food signals the proximity of the Dog Soldier's raiding economy to both the annuity economy and the Colorado economy, suggesting deep interrelations between raiding and annuity economies. These interrelations materialized in the experiences of individual Cheyennes who moved between villages, consuming and sharing the same goods in different contexts. Drinking coffee, eating bacon, enjoying new cloth and new shoes, there was no clear line of division separating Cheyenne communities accessing these goods through raids, and communities accessing them through annuities.[14]

By August 15, raiding parties succeeded in completely suspending travel along the Platte route, halting overland shipments of mail and food. Supplies to Denver slowed to a trickle, at the same time that swarms of locusts devoured crops in the agricultural hinterlands of the city. One hundred pounds of flour jumped in cost from $9 to $25. Dog Soldiers tore open the spider's web for a time, and overland traffic stopped completely. Mail was redirected between the Atlantic and Pacific coasts via Panama, and then eastward from California toward Denver. The raiding economy made U. S. sovereignty untenable in the Plains, and the façade of continental control was replaced with a reversion: the infrastructure of overseas imperialism connected Denver with the United States.[15]

EXPROPRIATE THE EXPROPRIATORS!

A Cheyenne elder recalled a historical shift in Cheyenne experiences of war following colonialism: "Wars were quite common when I was young; but these wars were not the same as the wars of the white people; they were mere skirmishes."[16] In contrast, Americans practiced a totally destructive form of warfare. The Colorado Territory elite, in particular, attempted to impose their interests over Cheyenne modes of relationship, most brutally enacted on November 29, 1864, when eight hundred Colorado Volunteers under the command of John Chivington attacked one of the largest Cheyenne villages at dawn. The victims were almost entirely women, children, and elders, and included leading advocates of peaceful coexistence with the United States, all of whom had gone to Sand Creek under a white flag. The violence at Sand Creek was a catastrophic attack on community life centering around Cheyenne sisters, an index of colonialism as gendered replacement.[17]

Compelled to swift action by their anguish, relatives of Sand Creek survivors began organizing an armed response on the headwaters of the Smoky Hill River, in the dark of winter. In the first days of 1865, the joint villages overwhelmed the garrison at Fort Rankin, burning ranches and stations within eighty miles of the fort, and then moved along the South Platte toward Julesburg. Cheyennes did not later portray these raids as easy, or as foregone conclusions. An image from the Dog Soldier ledger book shows a Dog Soldier on horseback charging a wounded cavalryman who is on foot, riding into the fire of two howitzers and fourteen rifles. George Bent, who participated in this raid, recalled that the raiders took their time rummaging through the supplies at the fort. Still, they left a lot of corn, flour, bacon, molasses, and canned goods, such as sardines, oysters, and tomatoes. The leaders decided not to destroy the buildings, because they planned to return and take more. During an attack on a stagecoach at Julesburg, raiders captured "a lot of greenbacks, paper money," and plundered a store, while U.S. soldiers in a stockade, half a mile west, fired on them with a cannon. The raids took the occupiers by surprise. "It was early in the morning as we found a table set with breakfast, ready for men to eat." Several of them sat down and enjoyed the meal, relishing the butter.[18]

In the following days, the massive raiding village moved up and down the South Platte River. In one fight, a fleeing soldier dropped a saddlebag filled with mail, so that his horse could run faster. Recovering the bag, the raiders found military correspondence, which included orders, plans for troop movements, and faulty counterintelligence. In the coming weeks, they destroyed almost eighty miles of telegraph line, burning or chopping up the poles, pulling out the wire, disrupting colonial communications. During these fights, Cheyennes and allies tracked down discharged Colorado Volunteers, recovering the mementos of mass murder that the killers of Sand Creek carried with them. By February, settler communities in the area were deserted, and the massive village was comfortably supplied with food and other provisions. As George Bent later described it, "In this camp we had everything good to eat. Plenty of fat beef, lots of sugar, coffee, and flour." With raiding at this scale, commodities moved through Cheyenne communities in new ways, enabling Cheyennes to savor tangible possibilities of renewing their collective livelihoods in their homelands.[19]

In late May, small groups made short raids in different directions as they made their way toward the Platte River for a planned attack. The river was high, and raiders captured a large number of government mules, leading them across with a captured mare. After the river went down, the groups crossed, raiding wagon trains and ranches. The raiders traveled in a large group, which included about two hundred women, mostly Cheyenne women. Traffic along the Santa Fe Trail came to a standstill, and long-established ranchers and traders fled. The supply trains for military forts, and the forts themselves, also provided targets for Cheyenne raids, such as the raids on Fort Larned in June 1865. In an image from the Dog Soldier ledger book depicting this kind of raid, White Bird dismounts from his horse to claim a mule team and a loaded freight wagon. Cheyenne raiding villages asserted their place within a broader regional economy not on the basis of their control over intertribal trade, but instead on the basis of their control over points of distribution for the colonial economy. This was a transformation of Cheyenne economic roles in the region where they lived, and its effects were felt as far as Denver, where food prices had jumped to famine rates in the winter. Imperialist incursions into their territory had the paradoxical effect of providing enhanced opportunities for raiding. By exploiting access to horses and commodities made available through colonial economies, Dog Soldiers experimented with new ways to sustain and foster collective life in a colonial context.[20]

Although their tactical position in relation to the colonial economy was new, individuals living in Dog Solder villages experienced underlying continuities with the earlier trading and annuity economies. As they raided ranches and other isolated trade locations, they were flush with foods, such as coffee, flour, and sugar, familiar items from the annuity economy. In addition, raiding also provided access to calico and other cloth. The Dog Soldier ledger book gives a glimpse of this, with an image of a dismounted Cheyenne man counting coup on a wounded U.S. soldier. The Cheyenne man wears a modified U.S. military coat, striped leggings likely made out of trade cloth, and a stroud-cloth breechclout. Other images show Dog Soldiers with red trade cloth braided into their hair, or tipping the ends of eagle feathers. A marked increase in the consumption and display of luxury goods corresponded with the raiding economy, and people living in the raiding camps improvised new fashions and new tools.[21]

Raiding, for these Cheyennes and their allies and relatives, was a dynamic solution to a changing geography of trade and distribution, one that could potentially take advantage of weak points of colonial infrastructure over Cheyenne lands. The success of the raiding economy, however, contained its demise. By shutting down the overland trade routes, they endangered the future of those food and supply sources, as the colonial geography reshaped in response to the raids. Cheyennes had learned to herd horses in earlier years; they now learned to herd settlers. Their raids expropriated the colonizers, a combination of tax, toll, and rent levied by Cheyennes on the trespassers. In the coming years, dissipation of the raiding economy allowed for the resumption of the colonial economy, and raids acted as control valves over distribution. This dissipation was possible, among Dog Soldier communities, through ongoing interrelation with trade and annuities centered on the manhastoz. By 1866, we can glimpse the Dog Soldier economy in relief through the railroad.

THE WEB RECONSTITUTED

By this time, U. S. military command on the central and northern Plains was closely yoked to industrial management. Occupation and industrialization proceeded in reaction to the perceived presence, the perceived threat, of Cheyenne communities on their land. Union Pacific chief engineer Grenville Dodge was useful to the Union Pacific, not only for his railroad, management, and engineering expertise, but perhaps especially because of his experience overseeing U. S. military operations in the very place the railroad sought to pass through. The railroad was an actively militarized economy, organized hierarchically, made up almost entirely of men with no prior relationships to the place of the railroad, or to anyone or anything they might find in its path. The very organization of the Union Pacific Railroad instituted colonialism as a form of gendered expropriation.

In the fall of 1866, an army detachment proceeded from Fort Sanders, Wyoming Territory, escorting a Union Pacific engineering party. On Dodge's request, the escort was then supplemented with twenty additional cavalry to join the engineers in building and maintaining their winter quarters in the Black Hills. In addition to military escorts, Union Pacific engineering parties made use of army stock and lumber that was processed and stored at military posts. Federal funding for soldiers' wages and equipment subsidized corporate development. These were scarce resources for a military occupation that was stretched to threadbare limits.[22]

As the U. S. Army and Union Pacific deployed these resources in a joint effort to capitalize Cheyenne territory, industrial and military capital was exposed to Cheyenne relations of value. In its strategic deployment of overstretched resources toward industrial occupation, the Union Pacific Railroad helps us see countersovereignty as more of a sieve than a siege. In an image from the Dog Soldier ledger book, Red Lance claims a pair of army mules, braving the fire of seven U. S. soldiers. Mules were particularly valuable to Cheyenne women as stock animals. This image, which seemingly represents a conflict between men across the colonial line, also represents a deeper and underlying set of relationships with Cheyenne women. In another image, a Dog Soldier captures a U. S. Army horse, drawn with clearly detailed saddle, stirrups, bridle, reins, horseshoes, and even a brand. This level of detail, recorded and remembered afterwards, underscores the keen eyes that Dog Soldiers brought to their raids. Far from merciless attacks with no governing logic, these raids were a means to acquire wanted and needed things. Raiding overland stages and army personnel had become a new means for Cheyennes to increase their horse herds, buttressing Cheyenne horse wealth, renewing and reinforcing Cheyenne modes of relationship.[23]

Against the fearful reactions and impetuous fantasies of countersovereignty that pose as empirical reality, Dog Soldiers and their allies developed their own strategies. Pages of the Dog Soldier ledger book portray the details of what Cheyennes wore and carried while attacking U. S. soldiers. An image shows Red Lance charging a dismounted U. S. cavalry soldier on horse, bearing down while wearing a war bonnet, carrying a shield, and dressed in a red tunic with a trailing sash. Other images depict Cheyenne men riding into battle wearing their own individualized regalia. If the U. S. soldiers, in their army-issue uniforms and weapons, held confidence in the principles of homogeneity, hierarchy, division of labor, and implicitly, financialization, Dog Soldiers and their allies took confidence in their knowledge of their homelands, in their collectively recognized honors, and in their personal visions. This is what gave Red Lance the confidence to ride down a soldier armed with a rifle, himself armed only with a saber.[24]

On May 9, 1867, Capt. Henry Mizner, commanding at Fort Sanders, recalled twenty cavalry men who were escorting a Union Pacific engineering party, only to countermand his order on the following day after receiving news of "Indians reported by Stage Company, this side of North Platte." Both military and industrial resources were marshaled in reaction to the mere presence of "Indians" on their own lands. An image from the Dog Soldier ledger book shows Big Crow in an attack on a wagon train, in which the wagons are circled, and the teamsters engaged in defensive fire. Another image shows the capture of an Overland Stage Company coach. Attacks on railroad work and engineering parties, on infantry and cavalry details, on army posts, and on wagon trains, give us glimpses of Dog Soldier herding tactics.[25]

Two days after his letter, Mizner informed Gen. Christopher Augur, who commanded the army's Platte department, "Indians have run off stock, and have burnt Rock Creek Station, also run off stock from Cooper's Creek

Station, thirty miles from here. Stages have ceased running." Later that day, Mizner requested a cavalry replacement for a company that was with Union Pacific engineers. "My infantry force," Mizner informed Augur, "is weak from details with Engineer party." Two members of the escort and engineering party had been taken as prisoners. The next day, Mizner resorted to arming the settler and corporate population in the vicinity, supplying arms and ammunition to stage stations, telegraph and geological parties, Union Pacific employees, "as well as other citizens in the vicinity." This section of the spider's web was stretched taut.[26]

From providing military resources toward industrial development, the army swung in the opposite direction, calling on the industrial workforce and settlers to buttress the military occupation. In countersovereignty, the feeble claim to control over the relations and terms of value on Cheyenne lands, the state and the corporation constitute each other at the nexus of war and finance. Mizner mobilized the personnel and resources of the corporation, and of settler society, as a kind of citizens' militia against Cheyenne raiding parties, extending the role of Colorado Volunteers at Sand Creek. Mizner justified this drastic measure because his own command was heavily depleted from escorting Union Pacific engineers, leaving him "unable to maintain a chain of sentinels." Military escort was a fixture of the U. S. industrial invasion of Cheyenne homelands in these years, and Cheyennes responded accordingly. On one page of the Dog Soldier ledger book, Brave Bear, charging on horseback with a lance, bears down on a mounted soldier who is retreating toward the rest of his small party in a stage or telegraph station. On another page, White Bird counts coup on a ranch hand fleeing a station. On May 17, Augur notified Mizner that Dodge had requested a military escort of fifty men for yet another engineering party. This was the war-finance nexus on the ground, frantic attempts to tie knots with threads that Cheyennes were constantly unraveling. Cheyenne eyes clearly distinguished between civilians and military personnel involved in the colonization of their lands, and saw both groups as legitimate targets for raids. In the Dog Soldier ledger book, Big Crow counts coup on a teamster before moving on to a dazed, wounded soldier, who has fallen from his horse. Both men had been riding together, but in this moment of violence the teamster flees the scene, leaving the wounded soldier alone with Big Crow.[27]

That May, Samuel Reed, then engineer of construction and superintendent of operations for the Union Pacific, begged Dodge for more military protection, but Dodge responded "that the men defending themselves were of far more benefit than the troops that could be gotten there." Many of the Union Pacific workers were war veterans, and Dodge insisted that they should protect themselves. The armed industrial incursion into Indigenous homelands was part of Union Pacific labor control, requiring of the lowest-paid workers the most direct involvement, and the greatest exposure, to violence. Labor exploitation, in a context of countersovereignty, entails a set of pressures toward participation in murder, massacre, and everyday colonialist violence, the true birthright of the aristocracy of labor. Dodge tried to shame a group of graders into fighting Indigenous people who came within the line of their work. Recalling this conversation, he remarked, "they knew the condition of the country when they made the contract." Colonial violence and military occupation were part of the work on the Union Pacific Railroad. For Union Pacific workers, contract discipline was conscription to colonial violence, conscription to genocide. They would bear the toll of this conscription, and their bosses would reap the profits. In the rarefied swagger of finance and self-proclaimed "national" politics, genocide could be flippantly invoked in the interests of social progress and corporate profit. The Union Pacific Railroad and the U.S. Army manifested as relationships of invasion in the service of both countersovereignty and capital accumulation. This was the war-finance nexus.[28]

In this buffer zone between industrialization and occupation, U.S. soldiers and Union Pacific workers reacted in concert to Dog Soldiers, moving slowly as a lumbering herd, or chaotically stampeding in panic. U.S. countersovereignty feints the originary position, on theological grounds, but the United States is always reacting to Indigenous modes of relationship, which already exist (and continue to persist) in the "homeland" of continental imperialism. Dodge sought to maximize army resources on behalf of Union Pacific construction. On May 20, 1867, he expressed concern to Sherman about the army's strategy and ability to protect railroad construction. He urged that infrastructure be prioritized over retaliation, suggesting that infrastructure might be understood as a deeper form of retaliation.

In the previous two weeks alone, Union Pacific subcontractors near Fort Sedgwick had been met by a party of raiders who took everything they had, leaving the workers so terrified that they refused to return to work. An engineering party on Lodge Pole Creek had a mule taken from them, and were told to leave the area, as raiders pulled up the stakes they had put in the ground. Groups of men making railroad ties in the Black Hills were forced out of the area, and their tools destroyed. Another engineering party suffered two deaths and its stock was taken, along with stock from its military escort. As Dodge explained to Sherman, this caused a basic crisis in the workability of the Union Pacific. According to Dodge, Union Pacific employees were simply too terrified to work within the existing corporate-colonial infrastructure. Their terror was one concrete boundary for the limits of functioning U.S. claims over land and resources. Industrialization could proceed as far as colonial occupation could be established and sustained. "Our station men will not stay at the tanks and stations, some 20 miles apart, unprotected." Dodge implored Sherman to funnel army resources toward railroad protection until the next season, when additional cavalry could be moved to the Plains from the southern United States. He identified two primary threats that Dog Soldiers and their allies posed to the railroad. First was sabotage, which could do "irreparable damage" to the railroad. Second was terror. If Augur stationed his troops westward along the North Platte, Dodge suggested, it would "give confidence to the workmen." Confidence to investors was important too. Without military protection, Dodge emphasized, Union Pacific construction would stall for at least a year. This confidence was fragile, its trust a spider's web. "They are working," Dodge declared, "in the worst Indian country you have got."[29]

Whatever Dodge called it, this was not the United States. In June 1867, Henry Parry sent letters from Fort Sedgwick, Colorado Territory, reporting that all of the ranches between the vicinity of the Platte and Julesburg were cleared out. There were daily reports of skirmishes, and the Overland Stage Company would only run three stages at a time. He wrote of Cheyennes, "I am told that they are much like the Bedouin Arabs in the mode of fighting," underscoring the foreignness of Cheyenne territory to emigrants from the United States. From his perspective, this was a vacant, vast surrounding. Parry described the first train approaching the fort: "Every cloud of its white smoke seemed to bring with it peace and civilization over the plains of the far West." Parry's reflections give us a glimpse of the disorientation that people from the United States experienced in the Platte River country in these years, the fragility of functioning U.S. claims to this place, and the ways that the corporation and the state co-constituted colonial claims to place.[30]

By this time, military occupation had itself become dependent on the further progress of railroad construction. A telegram to Augur, in July 1867, requested information about when Dodge would direct Union Pacific resources to complete the North Platte crossing. Augur clarified a few days later:

I wish you to go with all your command except one company . . . and give effi-cient protection to Rail Road surveying parties and the stage and telegraph lines between Sanders and Bridger. You may suspend temporarily all orders I have given for movement of troops in that vicinity. If you find you cannot do all this and build the new post too inform me immediately and I will report the fact to General Sherman for his authority to postpone the latter until Spring.[31]

The railroad was first priority for the army, as part of its own strategic encir-clement of the central Plains. For the moment, the corporation would pre-cede the state in attempting to stake control over this place.

Disease continued to travel over railroad tracks, military posts, and over-land trails. In early August 1867, days before the Cheyenne men derailed a Union Pacific train, cholera was reported at Fort Lyons, Ellsworth, and Harker. The reporting officer had no doubt that travelers from the United States were spreading the disease westward. A month later, a group escorting a military work party reported one of their members stricken with symp-toms. The occupation of Cheyenne territory proceeded, not only through financialization and military strategy, but also as disease, disturbing the rela-tionship between the land and its people, its memories and embodied knowl-edge, leaving behind nameless, lifeless material for capital accumulation.[32]

In October 1867, southern Cheyenne and Arapaho leaders negotiated their assent to the Treaty of Medicine Lodge Creek, which diminished rec-ognized territorial boundaries by half. Manhastoz were no longer suppliers of a range of trade goods. Rather, they negotiated over territory, an incredible risk, since any attempt to maintain peace followed massacres, encroach-ments, and the ongoing, everyday indignities and catastrophes of occupation and settlement. At the same time, annuities could ensure a material funda-ment for community survival, opportunities to sustain and extend Cheyenne modes of relationship, to guarantee Cheyenne control over land that colonial authorities recognized. At its outset, the reservation regime offered a possibil-ity of maintaining continuity amidst the traumatic disruptions of railroad colonialism. The treaty contained a clause stating that

tribes party to the agreement . . . withdraw all pretense of opposition to the construction of the railroad now being built along the Platte River, and westward to the Pacific Ocean; and they will not in future object to the con-struction of railroads, wagon-roads, mail-stations, or other works of utility or necessity, which may be ordered or permitted by the laws of the United States.

The Treaty of Medicine Lodge Creek asserted U.S. jurisdiction over Cheyenne places, and also over Cheyenne futures. This preemption was continental in scope.[33]

As Union Pacific construction progressed, army officers reoriented their tactics around the railroad itself. No longer working solely in defense of railroad construction, they now began to employ the railroad as a weapon. The infrastructure of continental imperialism remakes Indigenous places as spaces of capital accumulation, spaces which are thereby reimagined as the "national" interior. It does this by enhancing and enabling concrete capacities for mass murder. In his December 1867 monthly report from Fort Sanders, for example, Col. John Gibbon anticipated: "Early in the spring it is expected that the track of the U. P. R. R. will be laid to this point, the track passing directly alongside the garrison, and this will afford a quick and easy method of supplying the fort with all necessary stores not to be had in the country." The struggle over technology, in colonial situations, is a struggle over modes of relationship, a struggle over the capacities to sustain or destroy life in a particular place.[34] Grenville Dodge sent a detailed request for the upcoming year in January 1868, beginning with escorts for railroad parties working between Fort Sanders and Green River. According to Dodge, Union Pacific construction crews working Little Laramie to Bitter Creek necessitated a fanned-out escort covering a distance of about two hundred miles. To facilitate this, Dodge suggested that the army establish nine temporary posts through the region. Tie gangs employed along the Medicine Bow Mountains from Little Laramie to the North Platte also required military protection. Dodge's suggestion would mean a rapid suffusion of military occupation across the area, hundreds of spiders bursting out from an egg sac.

This escalation, though, was defensive, protecting supplies to feed railroad construction, supplies that also fed the Dog Soldier economy. Dodge proposed establishing three supply bases, which alongside the three depot points the Union Pacific was planning to erect, would sustain the occupation after the snow melted and construction began again. Speed was the goal, and it was not spurred by competition with the Central Pacific Railroad, but instead by the prerogatives of railroad colonialism. "I hope this season will place us virtually beyond the hostile tribes, and we will have only to guard the rear." Ideally, in Dodge's telling, railroad construction would pass swiftly through Cheyenne, Lakota, and allied territories, after which the U. S. Army could exploit the new technology in its mission of instituting U. S. sovereignty at the smoking end of a gun barrel.[35]

Railroad construction and military occupation continued to develop as a joint project, co-constituent elements of reactive U.S. claims to control Cheyenne homelands. In February 1868, Col. Gibbon notified superiors of plans for the upcoming months at Fort Sanders. Gibbon disagreed with the efficacy of Dodge's requests, suggesting instead that the railroad workers should themselves be armed, with support from four or five cavalry companies. This rapidly woven skein put the strategic flexibility of the Dog Soldiers' expropriative strategies to the test. Cheyennes had already experienced the seemingly solid, seemingly permanent built environment of colonialism as fundamentally impermanent, with large buildings falling into disrepair and abandonment, and colonial routes of traffic pulled taut to the snapping point.[36]

The mutative face of occupation and industrialization shared overlapping jurisdiction. In February 1868, General Augur telegraphed Gibbon to allow the Union Pacific to build a station at Fort Sanders, pending approval from the Department of War. In April, Gibbon reported to a Union Pacific agent that the railroad had been permitted to "occupy and settle" part of the military reservation of Fort Sanders. Dodge reiterated his request for the establishment of new military posts to station military escorts for railroad work parties, suggesting that, with limited military resources available, the Union Pacific could "change the troops with our graders" as it progressed west. Industrialization proceeded as occupation, occupation as industrialization.[37]

In April, Gibbon sent detailed orders to Col. Richard Dodge. "The primary object is the protection of the road, by giving the necessary confidence to the workmen employed along it to prevent their being stampeded by Indian scares." Work of protection, this was also work of extraction. Colonel Dodge was instructed to send reports, after establishing a post on the Platte, of timber, coal, limestone, and other resources in the vicinity. His orders mirrored another order that Augur had sent the previous April to Mizner, instructing him to select the most desirable timber for the construction of Fort Sanders, and then to give the balance of the timber to the Union Pacific Railroad. Desacralization of Cheyenne lands, which bore their own names and stories, was part of the invasion. The alienation of the land from itself fed the tumorous growth of Denver. Two days later, following an attack on railroad workers, Gibbon instructed Colonel Dodge to amplify the rule of war in the area. "It is strongly suspected that the party of Indians making this attack have white men amongst them. If this is so and you are fortunate enough to catch any of them shoot them at once." How the Americans should distinguish white from Indian men is unclear. What should be done to Indian people in the vicinity of the railroad line was left unwritten in this command.[38]

In orders to Capt. Ed Ball, Second Cavalry, the railroad and the stage line provided geographical coordinates. Ball was instructed to move along and across both lines, fortifying and reporting on stations on the way. Brown's summit, for example, was named for a Union Pacific engineer who had been killed in a skirmish. It was as if the history of the land itself began with colonialism. Everything preceding this history was geology, information to be mined for profit. Ball's unit was given a mission of propaganda:

> Assure the people at the different stations on the stage road of protection that different parties are out in pursuit of the Indians. Impress upon them the necessity of keeping their arms about them and of defending their stations as long as possible to enable troops to come to their assistance. And do the same with all working parties on the railroad.[39]

The upshot was a generally armed settler, corporate, and military population, waiting in tense fear of the next appearance of Native people moving through their homes.

Gibbon, in correspondence with General Dyer, commented in more depth on this development. Noting frequent requests for arms and ammunition by settlers near Fort Sanders, Gibbon requested the right to sell ammunition and to disburse outdated weapons. The U.S. Army was an intermediary between a military economy and the developing industrial economy along the North Platte River that together constituted capitalism in the Platte River country, supplanting the earlier role of Cheyennes in the intertribal trade in this very place. White men with guns replaced communities of Cheyenne sisters and their relatives.[40]

Nothing prevented further circulation of arms and ammunition to Indigenous insurgents through trade with settlers, and the occupation remained porous and incomplete, containing the loose threads of its own unraveling. From afar, though, military logic blended smoothly with corporate management into fantasies of genocide. Oliver Ames, one of the principal investors and political backers of the Union Pacific, reveried to Grenville Dodge in April of 1868, "I see nothing but extermination to the Indians as the result of their thieving disposition, and we shall probably have to come to this before we can run the road safely." Ames invoked a logic of capital accumulation through genocide, the logic of the war-finance nexus.[41]

Against a combined military and railroad infrastructure, which depleted buffalo herds and rerouted economic activity, Dog Soldiers were pushed in the spring of 1869, out of the central Plains, and into the foothills of the Rockies, as the transcontinental railroad neared completion. Meeting the U.S. Army at Summit Springs, they lost their leader, as well as the bulk of their horse herd and wealth, making it nearly impossible to sustain their independence from the annuity economy. In the coming years, strategies for the sustenance of collective Cheyenne life narrowed into the annuity form. The geography of anticolonial insurgency moved northward.[42]

ALIVE IN A DEATH-STALKED LAND

Some years later, after hearing about Wovoka's prophetic vision, a group of five Cheyenne elders decided they wanted to learn more. Having fitted themselves with food and equipment for the journey, they set out on horseback, following the railroad tracks westward, in the direction where Wovoka lived, eventually deciding to board a train. They left their horses at a ranch near the railroad, walking to the next railroad stop, boarding the next train that arrived, on the basis of agreements with the Union Pacific that allowed Cheyennes restricted access to ride in cattle car sand on top of trains. When the train conductor approached and asked them their destination, one of them, replied, "Seanno," meaning "Land of the Dead." The conductor may have heard this as "Seattle," but whatever he understood, he took them between cars, signaled for the engineer to slow down, and pushed them out of the train, one at a time. The profound violence of the conductor's act is a window into the violence of countersovereignty, which needs to be constantly reproduced and enacted, which is, at heart, a refusal of relationship.[43]

For these elders, clearly, the land of the dead was a place different from the place where they lived. They were willing to seek out information from this foreign place that could potentially be useful to their people, and they were willing to rely on technologies of colonialism and capitalism, whether riding trains, or using them in other ways, such as following railroad tracks as they went west. Even though it was not armed resistance, theirs was a militant commitment to self-determination, insisting upon their own power to be (to remain, and to become) as they wished, through an enactment and renewal of their relationships with their lands, and with each other. These elders moved and traveled in relation to the women in their lives, the Ghost Dance, like so many other prophetic movements among colonized peoples, cohering through the shared knowledge and practice of women participants.[44]

What might they have thought or felt after being pushed out of the train? Perhaps a sense of being pushed out of their own place, a palpable feeling of the colonial society that was built over their place in the world. If they took this as a communication from the conductor, perhaps there was a sense that, for the train conductor, a personification of railroad colonialism, Cheyennes were already living in the Land of the Dead, their home bereft of comfort, covered with foul spider webs. There was, perhaps, nothing living, nothing valuable, nothing generative, left for Cheyennes to give, from that other perspective. Or, perhaps they had a sense of the limitations of capitalism, of industrial technology. The elders set out, after all, to learn more information about a prophecy of the return of Indigenous nations' control over their homelands, and the return of their martyred relatives. Perhaps, after being pushed out of the train, the Cheyenne elders felt that the train was not a useful vehicle. This train would not take them where they wanted to go.

EIGHT

Shareholder Whiteness

THE YEAR 1869, DURING WHICH THE TRANSCONTINENTAL railroad was completed, also saw the publication of *Scenes in the Life of Harriet Tubman,* which provided an account of Tubman's involvement in the fight against slavery, and also helped Tubman pay pressing debts on her house.[1] In 1886, amidst a counterrevolution against Black people's experiments to realize freedom, amidst widespread and active forgetting of her living legacy, Tubman was struggling to cover the costs for housing and feeding poor Black people in Auburn, New York. She asked her collaborator, Sarah Bradford, to update the original book, resulting in a new edition entitled *Harriet, the Moses of Her People.* While the first book was published the year of the transcontinental railroad's completion, the second book was published the year that the U.S. Supreme Court found that corporations enjoyed the rights of persons, as granted under the Fourteenth Amendment. In short, Harriet Tubman's ongoing insurgent practices of Black mutuality took place under and against structures of debt and property. Her struggle continues. This chapter traces out emancipation as an incomplete breach of the estate, an emancipation of capital resulting in the development of shareholder whiteness.

Shareholder whiteness developed through the nexus of war and finance. In the last quarter of the nineteenth century, the standardization of a division of authority among the actors involved in corporations transformed the social nature of property. This was a fundamental transformation in the terms of whiteness, a historical process that was central to what Du Bois referred to as the "counter-revolution of property." Racism is an effect, not a cause, of imperialism. Whiteness, for example, is not a biological truth that can be traced genealogically, or on the skin. Whiteness is a fiction, but it has material impacts on the world. In this way, whiteness is like finance capital, which Marx analyzed as fictitious capital. Marx explained that banking arises from the concentration of money capital, so that bankers "become the general managers of money capital," taking the place of individual lenders. We can trace this shift in what I call the incomplete breach of the estate under emancipation, which eradicated the possibility of an individual slaveholder's claims of property in slaves, but sustained the underlying claims of property in real estate.[2] Finance capital and whiteness ripened through a historical elaboration of relationships between imperial corporations and colonial states, forging and sustaining continental imperialism. I call this shareholder whiteness.

Fictitious capital develops in order to overcome barriers to the circulation of money capital, driving to preserve its flexibility and liquidity, as titles to capital carry their own value, becoming sites of accumulation, forms of capital, in their own right. The forms that capital took after emancipation had origins in the contradictory circulation and valorization of money, land, and slave forms of capital. As investors became increasingly disconnected from the sources of their revenue, financial profits seemed to arise through agreements between individuals, seemingly separated from, even independent of, the sweat of specific bodies in specific places. With the maturation of the modern corporation in the wake of emancipation, investors imagined financial accumulation as autonomous from labor, whiteness as autonomous from blackness and indigeneity.[3]

STATE AND CORPORATION

A close interrelationship between state and corporation has shaped the invasion and occupation of the Americas. In the early years of the invasion, emergent monarchies in Europe stabilized governance by granting corporate charters, relying on corporations to assume risks, particularly risks involving territorial expansion. Monarchies elaborated new, interlinked principles of sovereignty and property, combining security and improvement as prescriptions for colonialism. Over time, the law of corporations would blur distinctions between personal rights and rights in property. Corporate ownership would come to confer rights without responsibilities.[4]

In North America, corporate power is inextricable from countersovereignty. A critique of the state without a critique of the corporation is a sanctimonious hope. The relationship between sovereignty and property provided foundational legal justifications for modern colonialism. Grotius, for example, sought to legitimize Dutch East India Company sovereignty, justifying the right of the United Provinces to engage in naval war on a preemptive basis. Not "natural" persons, but also more than a reflection of group identities, the state and corporation have each been interpreted as the apex of social hierarchy. In North America, as elsewhere in the colonized world, there is no clear and definitive way to assert priority between state and corporation, where imperial states granted charters but corporations established the terms of actual colonial power. Sovereignty and property emerged in reaction to Indigenous modes of relationship.[5]

Territorialization occurred through corporate charters. The rights of corporations served the interests of imperial sovereigns. Corporate charters delineated protocols for relations with Indigenous nations and colonial subjects, ranging from diplomacy to war, providing for the organization and maintenance of standing armies, predefining places as empty of political and economic claims. The charters of colonial corporations, such as the East India Company and Royal Africa Company, instituted the structures of colonial government, including powers to suspend the law and engage in war. In North America, by the 1600s, chartered corporations participated in land purchases that would later become the basis for colonial sovereignty claims, administered and regulated the terms of trade, and waged war. Corporate directors claimed state titles.[6]

In North America, the corporate share remains a core vehicle of continental imperialism. Joint-stock or chartered companies founded European colonies, mobilizing resources drawn from multiple investors, raising capital while leavening individual exposure to risk. Pooling risks for colonialism and slavery led to the development of very particular rationalities, empirical knowledge about the strategic immiseration of human life in the interests of maximizing returns on investment. In the United States, impulses of regulation and control lurk behind a thin veil of radical democracy, the succession of imperial sovereignty from the Crown to "the people," citizens as shareholders of a colonial corporation. The sovereignty of the colonial state, in the form of legal exemptions for the discipline of individuals and populations, displays a fundamentally corporate nature. Fabricating an order to govern property claims in both Indigenous lands and Black lives was a project of counterinsurgent reaction. Federal and state governments chartered and capitalized corporations, outlining their rights and responsibilities. The infrastructure of colonialism in North America has been built, in the main, by corporations, with the oversight and planning of infrastructure leading to the growth of state administrative capacities, especially around taxation. Corporations assume core functions of state power in continental imperialism.[7]

Countersovereignty is at once an assertion of the property of the colonial state, *and* an assertion of the sovereignty of capital. In the 1810 decision *Fletcher v. Peck,* the first Supreme Court decision under the leadership of John Marshall, the court upheld the contract relation between individuals by ignoring the treaty rights of the Cherokee nation, emphasizing the sovereignty of the state of Georgia, and shifting the contract clause from a foundation in diplomacy, toward the direction of corporate interests. Marshall sought to replace diplomacy with contracts, as a means to capture Indigenous futures. Marshall's decision revolved around the territorial boundaries of the Proclamation of 1763, and whether the dissolution of those boundaries folded into the control of the U. S. federal government, or of the individual states. In Marshall's analysis, Native title was transitory and colonization was inevitable. Control of "vacant" lands, whether as a joint property of the United States, or as the property of separate states, was central to U.S. state formation, threatening, Marshall quaked, "to shake the American confederacy to its foundation." In the end, Marshall found that Indian title can potentially be seized under seisin in fee, a legal category representing a feudal fiefdom, on the part of individual states. From the perspective of the Cherokee nation in 1810, by Marshall's logic, the state of Georgia was a feudal overlord.[8]

Marshall's 1819 decision in *Trustees of Dartmouth College v. Woodward* restricted the rights of states from invalidating contracts on buying and selling land that was recognized, by treaty, as under tribal control. Marshall defined a corporation as "an artificial being, invisible, intangible, and existing only in contemplation of law." This "mere creature of law . . . possesses only those properties which the charter of its creation confers upon it." These properties, the sole possessions of the corporation, are immortality and individuality, "a perpetual succession of many persons are considered as the same, and may act as a single individual . . . a perpetual succession of individuals are capable of acting for the promotion of the particular object, like one immortal being." The corporation, in Marshall's logic, is predicated on a "perpetual succession" for colonizers. The futures of corporate ownership assert the futures of countersovereignty. The citizen-shareholder is the agent and beneficiary of the war-finance nexus. As we will see, policing racial and territorial borders, as they shift over time, is at the heart of maintaining this perpetual succession. Inheritance and heritability become key questions for defining the terms of legibility for this immortal individual. The future of the corporation presupposes the future of the colonial state, and the law of the corporation colonizes the future. Shareholding profits arise from capturing a claim, a share, of future surplus. The value of shares is future-oriented, as with the preemption dimensions of countersovereignty, like the rents arising from real estate claims.[9] In North America, a corporate share is a means to claim both ownership *and* sovereignty, in reaction to Black and Indigenous modes of relationship.

Justice Washington's concurring argument distinguished between corporations for public government and those for private charity. Government, in his analysis, arises in the first instance from property interests in land. The distinction between government and charity can further be split into a distinction between a sovereign, who grants a charter, and a patron, who is a founder. Washington described the private corporation as "a franchise, or incorporeal hereditament, founded upon private property." "Incorporeal hereditament" is a kind of property, real property, which can be passed to an heir. At its core, countersovereignty emerges through claims in real estate, claims that can be inherited in a perpetual succession. While seemingly sequestering rent in the realm of the patron and investor, Washington invoked Blackstone, seeking to outline the precise character of corporations. "The founder of all corporations . . . in the strictest and original sense, is the king alone, for he only can incorporate a society." The U.S. corporation clothes itself in robes inherited from monarchy. What is central to the corporation is the capitalization of land, the basis for rent, which Marx described as "the form in which landed property is economically realized, valorized." Rent captures the futures of a place.[10]

Whose land is this? In the 1823 *Johnson v. M'Intosh* decision, the Supreme Court nullified tribal land ownership within U.S. law, restricting "aboriginal title" to the use and occupation of lands, by regulating trade within and beyond tribal territories. The relationship between property and sovereignty was at the heart of the *Johnson* decision. Marshall noted that the social right to prescribe rules for the acquisition and preservation of property claims, such as land titles, rests entirely "on the law of the nation in which they lie." In a context where Indigenous nations and colonial states lay claim to the same territory, this raises a question on which law supersedes the other. At no point can Indigenous nationhood simply be ignored and evacuated in a property and political order rooted in conquest. This is why I refer to U.S. sovereignty as countersovereignty. It is inherently reactive to Indigenous modes of relationship. Relations between colonizers and Indigenous nations "were to be regulated by themselves," and no other power could interfere in these regulations, a chilling assertion of the rule of conquest that seeks to trap Indigenous politics within a colonial mode of relationship. A specter is haunting North America—the specter of anticolonial internationalism. *Johnson v. M'Intosh* hinges on a real estate transaction. Marshall theorized what he called "the original fundamental principle": the exclusionary, exclusive underpinnings of property in land and sovereignty alike. In North America, the two constitute each other. Countersovereignty "necessarily diminished" tribal nations' rights to self-governance, as well as "their power to dispose of the soil." Countersovereignty, as an assertion of "ultimate dominion," is exercised as "a power to grant the soil, while yet in possession of the natives." Countersovereignty is, at heart, an assertion of the power to destroy Indigenous nations' ongoing modes of relationship, to wipe away ongoing Indigenous collective presence on Indigenous lands. Countersovereignty works by diminishing the possibilities of Indigenous-centered diplomacy, backed by the threat of catastrophic violence.[11]

At stake is the alienation of the earth itself into the capital relation. Countersovereignty rests on this dual process of police power and capitalization. The sovereign is bound by the stipulations of the colonial grant. Colonial charters combine powers of government with powers "expressly granting the land, the soil, and the waters," and the state asserts its sovereignty by granting charters. The states initially forming the United States inherited their relations with Indigenous communities from the colonial corporations that preceded them. Marshall argued that, in joining the United States, these states ceded "the soil as well as the jurisdiction" of tribal lands to the U.S., "and that in doing so, they granted a productive fund to the government of the Union." Colonialism in North America has proceeded through the interrelationship of state *and* corporation.[12]

EMPTINESS

Filius nullius, the bastard child, joins *terra nullius,* the empty place, as constituent elements of countersovereignty. A colonial sleight-of-hand, "the use of a commercial principle to vitiate a social relationship," defines land and bodies as empty of human relationships, clearing the way for a property order that refuses relationships and produces death at ever-expanding scales. The category of *filius nullius* marks a legal refusal of recognition. Legal personhood rested on a claim to inheritance rights, rights to participate in the reproduction of social relations of ownership, rights of inheritance to the "perpetual succession" of Marshall's corporate jurisprudence. The enslaved person, excluded from the bounds of state-sanctioned marriage, excluded from functional claims to the capacities of binary gender, and excluded from the prerogatives of holding wealth, constituting instead the basis of wealth, was, definitively, not *filius*. Rather than inheriting property, slaves constituted the inheritance of others, denied any recognition of familial or other collective identity. Enslaved women gave birth to property, while white women could give birth to potential owners of property.[13]

A dead body that has not been buried is *res nullius,* gaining legal recognition only after a living person has worked on it, recognition arising from the labor of another. There is an echo here with the alibi of "improvement," an alibi of perpetual deferral (it never seems to be finished), which is used to justify racism and colonialism on civilizational grounds. From a colonialist perspective, the dividing line between civilization and savagery is a dividing line between animate bodies and unburied corpses. The law of slavery disfigured the personhood of people claimed as property. The depersonification of the slave posed a contradiction for the possibility of manumission under the law of slavery. How could a thing become a person, without irrevocably disrupting the property relation, which is constituted by the legal boundaries between things and persons? How could a thing become a person? There is a deep, contradictory relationship between the legal status of a corporation and the legal status of a slave.[14]

The gap between the slave and the corporate share might be one place to glimpse the gap between blackness and whiteness, the first predefined as criminal, the second receiving the full protection of, and immunity from, the law. Whiteness entails membership in a colonial succession, conceived of as having everlasting life.[15] This membership is predicated on the restriction of white women's sexuality, to cohere and protect the heritability of white racial purity. Ownership of shares originally implied ownership of a share of a company's assets, viewed as equitable interests in the property of a company. Shares could consist of either real or personal estate, depending on the nature of a company's assets. Under this theory of the share, the corporation was not an entity that could be considered separately from the people who constituted it. Beginning in the 1830s, a separation began to be elaborated between the shareholder and the corporation, separating corporate shares (intangible forms of property: rights to revenue, rights of property) from corporate property (concrete, material goods or services). According to the logic of slave law, slaves, who had no civil capacities of their own, could commit criminal acts, but not civil acts. The agency of slaves, where it was legally recognized as such, was predefined as a criminal agency, and this predefinition underwrote the slave, itself, as a legal category. The legal recognition of the slave was elaborated alongside the legal recognition of the corporation, enshrining the power of the owner, providing impunity for the violence of property claims over Black people and Indigenous land. The gap between the slave and the corporate share might be one place to glimpse the gap between blackness and whiteness.[16]

The relationship between sovereignty and property outlines the war-finance nexus. In the 1832 case *Worcester v. Georgia,* the Supreme Court found that tribal governments engage with the United States at the federal level, not the state level, following priorities that Congress asserted in the Trade and Intercourse Acts. Marshall noted that the British crown granted corporate charters in order to establish American colonies, before the fact of possession. This was, Marshall argued, restricted to "the exclusive right of purchasing such lands as the natives were willing to sell." Colonial corporations in North America have the right to engage in war to defend their real estate. These war powers inform Marshall's understanding of the relationship between the Cherokee nation and the United States, which "receive the Cherokee nation into their favor and protection." The federal relationship with tribal nations is a protection racket over capitalized tribal lands and resources.[17]

Fugitive slave law and Indian removals outlined a space for the circulation of a national currency, a space where property claims on Black people, and on Indigenous lands, would be backed by the authority and force of the state. This was the "domestic territory" of the United States. The National Banking Act, passed on February 25, 1863, provided for the issue and regulation of a uniform national currency, in order to standardize the multiple forms of bank notes circulating through the U.S. economy. The banking act was a significant infrastructural development to produce a territorially bounded political economy, a counterpart to the Pacific Railway Act, which Lincoln had signed into law six months earlier, enabling the development of hundreds of new banks, the concentration of the banking sector in New York City, and a diffusion of smaller-scale investment across the United States. The act placed limits on the liabilities of individuals, companies, and firms holding shares in banking corporations. The perpetual succession of the corporation included an inheritance in limited liability. In the United States, a market in small shares developed in efforts to raise capital to fund the U.S. military effort in the Civil War. New York's financial and merchant elites had risen to prominence through close interrelationship and investment in the cotton plantocracy, leading them to oppose Republican Party policies. The response from the Treasury Department helped inaugurate a transformation of financial institutions into their current form, with the introduction of a standard paper currency. In 1869, the year of transcontinental railroad completion, the Open Board of Stock Brokers merged with the New York Stock Exchange, spatially extending the stock market through the telegraph, enabling an exponential growth in securities trading. In the United States, the basic infrastructure for financial capitalism was constructed in a context of war over slavery's futures.[18]

Almost $2.8 billion in war debts to finance the Civil War, at a moment of collapse in the cotton trade, provided immediate incentive for U.S. merchants to forge modern financial corporations, giving rise, by the time of the defeat of the Confederacy, to widespread shareholder interests in westward expansion, diffused throughout the population of Midwestern farmers and small business owners. Innovations resulted in the growth of a mass market of small investors in war bonds, a new market in securities, and the incorporation of new investment houses, including Lehman Brothers and Goldman Sachs. These banking firms developed new techniques, particularly ways to maintain price levels on securities, which would become standard techniques in railroad finance. Railroads provided early opportunities for investing capital in securities, ultimately tied to land grants. Railroad land grants served to further concentrate the control of land and capital, with fourteen railroads receiving nearly all of the 180 million acres of land granted by the U.S. federal and state governments. Continental imperialism proceeds through the centralization of capital, and the railroad corporation was a core vehicle for the war-finance nexus.[19]

THE EMANCIPATION OF CAPITAL

Emancipation marked the most fundamental breach, to date, for the U.S. property order, opening the capital claim to transformation, perhaps even eradication. Emancipation fundamentally ruptured the practice of owner-ship in the United States. Property, in the U.S., shows its face at the cross-roads of racialization and territorialization. Racial differentiation is materi-ally linked to the control of specific places. The threat and actuality of racist violence suffuses a certain space as a threat space, a space of terror. This, too, was the "domestic territory" of the United States. While emancipation for-mally ended chattel slavery as a property system, it failed to disturb real estate as a property system. There is yet to be a breach with a basic presupposition of U.S. colonial power: the willful misreading of international treaties with tribal nations as real estate contracts.[20] In the generation after emancipation, this incomplete breach in the estate authorized the continued organization of collective life around alienated, exclusionary, and possessive claims on space.

Control over space provided a basis for instituting Black indebtedness and criminalization after emancipation. After emancipation, racial indebtedness was inflected twice over: Black freedom rescripted as a condition of indebted-ness to white progress, and Black criminality as a condition of indebtedness to white law. Black indebtedness was linked to Black criminalization on a spatial basis, the crime of loitering, the indolence of Black mobility after slavery's end. This can be contrasted to compensation for slaveowners, the corresponding development of a lingering mythology of national whiteness as creditor to African Americans and tribal nations, and the invention of southern white male nobility to perfume over the stench of high treason.

By the late nineteenth century, as corporation law inhered the person-hood of corporations, the legal personhood of felons was moving in a com-pletely contrary trajectory of depersonalization. During the historical period when corporations gained legal recognition as persons, felons lost legal rec-ognition as persons. Human nonpersons, juridically designated as felons, overwhelmingly Black people, worked for corporations under forced labor conditions, providing the core labor to rebuild the transportation infrastruc-ture of the southern United States, a massive corporate subsidy. Even when Black people leased out as convicts did not labor directly for corporations, the fruits of their labor, organized with a complete disregard for their own survival, rebuilt an infrastructure for capital accumulation across the region. In Atlanta, the elaboration of the meanings of emancipation took place within the context of rebuilding the infrastructure of the city, as novice employers engaged freedwomen's demands for control over their own labor, in the space of the white household.[21]

Emancipation threw the interrelationships of sovereignty and property into question. The historical emergence of the legal personhood of the corporation would be predicated on a conception of personhood as self-possession. Self-ownership was a predicate for understanding the corporation as a distinct and separate entity from its shareholders and creditors. This transformed the meaning of ownership, distinguishing tangible corporate capital from intangible corporate shares, making ownership itself more fungible and alienable. Whiteness, as a form of property, can be understood as the capacity to be an owner, a capacity that increasingly separated tangible from intangible claims, so that whiteness, as property, could be progressively abstracted from the possibility of owning slaves, to a more generalized share in the dividends arising from Black suffering. Whiteness is a reactionary formation, an inheritance in countersovereignty. A share can be understood as "a claim to a part of the profit." Shareholder whiteness is a claim to what W. E. B. Du Bois referred to as the "dividends of whiteness," not merely psychological, but also material. In the aftermath of emancipation, whiteness began to take a shareholding form, the passive ownership of functionless investors in racial capitalism.[22]

Was this the emancipation of the enslaved, or was it the emancipation of capital? Shareholder whiteness is a cover for law-breaking, an enfranchisement of whiteness over Indigenous and Black modes of relationship. Corporations slithered between legal conceptions of "real" person and "collective aggregate" in ways that allowed them to capture legal and political rights while shirking responsibilities and obligations. The context for these maneuvers was a historical transformation of the concept of personhood and the emergence of the singular individual, harnessing the idea of free labor to the idea of free trade as constituent elements of liberal imperialism.[23]

By delinking from claims on actual existing assets, which represent the capital of a corporation, and instead organizing around future claims on corporate assets, the share, in the present moment, multiplies the capital in circulation for a given set of tangible assets, such as land, resources, or labor. As these fictitious capitals developed, they were reified and fetishized as things in their own right, and capital itself began to be understood as equally productive as labor. In the United States, this "fetishization of money capital," the basis of the dominance of market ideologies beginning in the mid-nineteenth century, grew out of interactions with fetishized whiteness, and the corresponding dominance of nationalist myths of frontier and lost-cause masculinities. Once slave property claims were removed from the balance sheet, property claims in future revenues became depersonalized and increasingly immaterial, seeming to take on a personality of their own. The withdrawal of capitalists from the production process, henceforth to be supervised by managers, facilitated the development of shares and other forms of credit, but it also reflected the large-plantation model of management by overseers. The modern corporation bears traces of the antebellum plantation.[24]

Against an emerging ideal of "shareholder democracy," corporate power increasingly emphasized managers and directors, technocrats and experts, over a democracy of property owners. Shifting accountability from public governance to the structures of corporate capitalism, shareholder democracy involved a concentration of economic and political power, transforming relationships within and beyond whiteness, splitting the ownership of industrial capital from money capital, multiplying the actual assets of a corporation. A divide between those with rights in the corporation, and those who "are merely 'owed'," reflects a divide in whiteness, between the technocratic administrators of racial and colonial capital, and the beneficiaries of imperialist futures. Capturing and controlling corporate assets as common property would fail to resolve the colonial and racial contradictions that shape corporate assets. Railroad unions that actively excluded Black workers from membership and employment, sometimes striking to demand the elimination of Black workers, fulfilled shareholder whiteness.[25]

In the post-emancipation era, corporate property was defined through legislation and judicial reasoning, rated and regulated by state institutions, the sanctity of individual property claims upheld, in the final instance, by the police and the army. Compulsory Black labor, justified by notions of Black indebtedness to the United States, shaped a transition to a new racial regime. This transition took place in a context of mass white terrorism under state sanction; Ida B. Wells pointed to the legal impunities of racist violence as a constituent feature of the law itself. Expansion of police powers informed the Indian Appropriations Act, passed by Congress in March 1871, in which Congress declared that it would unilaterally suspend the treaty process with tribal nations, thereby evacuating the international diplomatic protocols governing the U.S. "national" interior. While the United States continued to acknowledge the presence of "independent tribes, nations, or powers" it would not recognize these as distinct political actors "within the territory of the United States," expanding the scope and claims of the federal government.[26]

While the United States was suspending diplomatic relations with Indigenous nations, a debate over the legal status of corporations was shaped, in part, by relations of debt. Amidst land grants to railroad corporations, and a growing international market in railroad securities, U. S. courts began to reconceive the corporation as an entity apart from its shareholders, focusing on the terms of contract between the corporation and its shareholders. If the corporation was a person, it was indentured to its shareholders. This was a very different form of debt than the racial and civilizational debt invoked to valuate Indigenous and Black modes of relationship. Corporate debt was, instead, an enabling sort of debt.[27]

EXCLUSION AND POSSESSION

The Chinese Exclusion Act, passed in 1882, like the Indian Appropriations Act, legislated territorial and racial boundaries for the putative interior of the United States. Chinese exclusion was about U. S. control over the circulation of Chinese bodies in space, rendering individual Chinese bodies vulnerable to forced expulsion. The exclusion act, like the Fugitive Slave Law, legislated the infrastructure for controlling this circulation, including offices, papers, and procedures. I want to suggest a linkage between control over the circulation of Chinese bodies and the circulation of corporate debts and shares, constituent elements of what I am calling shareholder whiteness.[28]

The core of private property is the "right to exclude others." Chinese exclusion, following both the Indian Appropriations Act and the Fugitive Slave Law, could be understood as territorialization through the property right, excluding racial aliens and Indigenous nations from the territorial space the law has designated for white citizens, and those who could become white citizens. In his foundational 1886 treatise on police power in the United States, Christopher Tiedeman wrote,

> when an altogether dissimilar race seeks admission to the country ... the State may properly refuse them the privilege of immigration. And this is the course adopted by the American government towards the Chinese who threaten to invade and take complete possession of the Pacific coast ... It was even feared that the white population, not being able to subsist on the diet of the Chinese, and consequently being unable to work for as low wages, would be forced to leave the country, and as they moved eastward, the Chinese would take their place, until finally the whole country would swarm with the almond-eyed Asiatic.

Continental imperialism, across the breach in property that we call emancipation, is conditioned on racial exclusions from humanity, from politics, and from places, exclusions which cannot be neatly divorced from territorial power.[29]

As corporations grew in size, beginning to gain recognition as autonomous legal actors, they began to compete with the sovereignty of the states that had originally chartered them. In 1882, the year of Chinese exclusion, the first major trust, Standard Oil, was formed. Individual shareholders exchanged their stock for trust certificates, enabling the trust to claim immunity from legal prohibitions against one corporation holding the stock of another, prohibitions that had been designated to prevent monopoly formation. From the 1880s to the first years of the twentieth century, one of the shifts in corporate law was a removal of requirements of unanimous shareholder approval for corporate mergers, calcifying a sense of the corporation as a distinct entity in its own right, and not the representation of collective shareholder rights and interests. The emergence of trusts was a mark of the centralization of financial and industrial capital, the consolidation of monopoly power, and the development of cartels.[30]

In 1883, the year that the U. S. Supreme Court found the 1875 Civil Rights Act to be unconstitutional, Ida B. Wells boarded the Chesapeake & Ohio Railway, of which Collis Huntington was an owner, in Memphis, after purchasing a first-class ticket. The conductor refused to honor her ticket, demanding that she sit in the smoking car. Wells later recalled, "I thought if he didn't want the ticket I wouldn't bother about it so went on reading." The conductor attacked her, tearing her dress, and Wells defended herself until two passengers assisted the conductor to forcibly remove her from the car. Standing between the cars, Wells decided to disembark at the next stop, to the loud cheers of white passengers. She sued, and won damages from the railroad. Her experience and her case were part of a wave of resistance by Black women against the enforced vulnerabilities of racial segregation on trains. Railroads, Wells demonstrated, were infrastructures for producing the practical meanings of gender through the racial control of bodies in space. The railroad corporation appealed the ruling, which was overturned in April 1887, by the Tennessee Supreme Court.[31]

The abridgement of Black freedom concretized through the practice of corporate freedom. We can see this in *Yick Wo v. Hopkins,* a case which is seemingly about neither Black nor corporate freedom. A series of cases in the Ninth Circuit, grouped as Chinese equal protection cases, emphasized corporations' right to be free from state interference. The court's decision revolved around contract relations and economic rights. A decision, seemingly about the civil rights of Chinese noncitizens, shows its true import, defining competence, qualification of legal persons in relation to public interests, and constraints on government action. The court invoked the Fourteenth Amendment in its decision, not to uphold the legal rights of "strangers and aliens," but instead to uphold U.S. territorial authority. The crux of the decision is that vesting the powers of sovereignty, "author and source of law," in the hands of an individual, would undo "the victorious progress of the race in securing to men the blessings of civilization" and represent "the essence of slavery itself." Emancipation necessitated the end of sovereignty in the individual slaveholder, and *Yick Wo* was part of a process that cohered sovereignty, instead, in shareholder whiteness. Corporate freedom authorized the counterrevolution of property.[32]

On the same day that it submitted its decision on *Yick Wo v. Hopkins,* six days after the firestorm at Haymarket Square that continues to be commemorated every May 1 by workers around the world, the U.S. Supreme Court submitted its decision on *Santa Clara v. Southern Pacific,* a case revolving around a branch of the Central Pacific Railroad's parent company. In the headnotes for the decision, the clerk recorded, "The court does not wish to hear the argument on the question whether the provision in the Fourteenth Amendment to the Constitution, which forbids a State to deny to any person within its jurisdiction the equal protection of the laws, applies to these corporations. We are all of the opinion that it does." The decision further evacuated collective Indigenous territorial rights from U.S. federal law, failing to consider Indigenous territorial rights against both the Southern Pacific Railroad and Santa Clara County, enshrining the Fourteenth Amendment as the "chief refuge and bulwark of corporations."[33]

The case revolved around taxes levied, in fiscal year 1882, the year of the Chinese Exclusion Act, on fences bordering the tracks. The decision locates the birth of this particular corporate person in the Pacific Railway Act, in which "every part of it was declared to be a post route and military road." This particular corporate person was part of the infrastructure of military occupation. The decision moves to find that the Southern Pacific Railroad Company is not the property of its shareholders. It is, instead, a "person" who owns the fences, tracks, and materials of the railroad, and as a "person" who owns things, the Southern Pacific cannot be owned by others. That would make it a slave. Instead, the Southern Pacific relates to others on the basis of ownership. Corporations transformed, from extensions of state power for establishing sovereignty, into sanctuaries from state power for the accumulation of capital. The court moves on to define the relationship between "foundation" and "superstructure," finding that the roadbed is the foundation, and the rails are the superstructure. The foundation, the court argues, can be taxed as part of the roadway. Corporate personhood was first articulated in relation to a railroad corporation, through the constitutional amendment guaranteeing citizenship, due process, and equal protection to formerly enslaved people and their descendants. Corporate personhood was articulated around a principle of freedom from taxation, articulated around fences, a mechanism of exclusion. The concept of corporate personhood defined the corporation as a legal entity with its own independent existence, separating the company from its shareholders. Where racial exclusions functioned to enhance vulnerabilities to violence, exclusions in capital functions enriched shareholders, limiting exposure to liability and risk. Shareholder whiteness can be understood as a creation of the state and a liberty against the state, as a form of property, a legal embodiment of capital.[34]

LIMITING THE LIABILITIES OF WHITENESS

The Interstate Commerce Act, passed on February 4, 1887, was intended to regulate railroads "engaged in the transportation of passengers or property" across state lines. The act declared "unjust discrimination" in fees, rates, and rebates, whether direct or indirect, to be unlawful, stating that all railroad carriers were responsible for providing "reasonable, proper, and equal facilities for the interchange of traffic between their respective lines." The act instituted an Interstate Commerce Commission, housed in the Interior Department, which would regulate the movement of people and goods across state lines. This involved administrative innovations that echoed the administrative structure of Chinese exclusion. Both laws legislatively outlined a certain geographic space as the "interior" of the United States, to administratively establish its control over territory, key mechanisms of continental imperialism.[35]

Congress passed the Dawes Act four days after President Cleveland signed the Interstate Commerce Act into law. The two laws can be read together as acts of imperial state formation, controlling and regulating bodies in relation to places. Under the guise of enfranchising individual Indigenous people through ownership of land deeds, allotment attempted to splinter collective landholdings, and to shatter distinct tribal protocols of use and ownership. Allotment policy, administered through colonialist conceptions of marriage, family, and household, further diminished U. S. recognition of tribal landholdings and tribal membership. Presented as reform through the empowerment of individual Indigenous people, allotment resulted in a loss of the great majority of reservation land into nonnative control. The elaboration of corporate personhood emerged in relation to the destruction of the collective personality of Indigenous communities, enabling a further centralization of capital. The war-finance nexus was predicated on individual property rights over tribal lands and resources, asserted through the decimation of Indigenous collective territorial rights. The decades-long practice of granting Indian lands to railroad corporations joined allotments, attempting to dissipate Indigenous modes of relationship. Corporate personhood inoculated railroads and other corporations from accountability for the expropriation of Indian lands, and the resources on them. The explosion of corporate activity in the second half of the nineteenth century was located, primarily, in Indian country, building and maintaining colonial infrastructure for the extraction of resources from tribal lands. Allotment was a mechanism for this corporation explosion, a seemingly bloodless dispossession through the capital relation, proceeding through its own definitions of personhood. Those deemed "incompetent," often along racial and gendered lines, were given title in trust, and those deemed "competent" were given title in fee simple, imposing both U. S. citizenship and property taxes on their land. Almost 60 percent of the lands allotted under fee simple were lost within a decade, overwhelmingly to state tax foreclosure.[36]

By the 1880s and 1890s, the Supreme Court further removed restrictions and limitations on the recognized powers of corporations. New Jersey's 1888 and 1889 general incorporation laws provided virtually unrestricted legal rights to corporations, allowing corporations to own stock in other corporations, ultimately funding the entire expenses of New Jersey state government. While recognizing the personhood of railroad corporations, the federal government limited the scope of its recognition of Black personhood. The removal of protection for Black citizens is linked to the establishment of protection for corporations. Railroad corporations, and their employees and customers, enforced the removal of legal and social protections for Black people. The railroad was a vehicle for the counterrevolution of property.[37]

In *Plessy v. Ferguson,* the Supreme Court was to find that corporate capital trumped Black personhood. The court's decision cited Ida B. Wells's overturned decision in the Tennessee Supreme Court. The *Plessy* decision limited the liability of railroad corporations, and of shareholders in whiteness. Limited liability has the function of transferring risk from investors to creditors, shifting from industrial forms, involving the exercise of authority over production and distribution, to a financial form, involving collective investments for nominal title, without the authority of management or responsibility for debt. Limited liability facilitated a transformation in the capital relationship, by which those who invested their capital no longer expected to have control over the administration of that capital. Shifting from an active relationship of ownership to a more passive relationship of credit is a key aspect of the formation of shareholder whiteness.[38]

Plessy responded to a Louisiana statute instituting exclusionary racial borders within railroads operating in the state, empowering and requiring railroad employees to uphold and enforce state power. The majority decision agreed with these core principles, reading race as "a distinction which is founded in the color of the two races, and which must always exist so long as white men are distinguished from the other race by color." The incoherence of this stance is famously clear just a few paragraphs earlier, when the court described Homer Plessy as "seven eighths Caucasian and one eighth African blood; that the mixture of colored blood was not discernible in him." Color, in this logic, is not visible on the skin, but is instead an infrastructural function of bodies moving through space, and race was made legible through the administration and operation of the railroad itself. "The power to assign to a particular coach obviously implies the power to determine to which race the passenger belongs, as well as the power to determine who, under the laws of a particular State, is to be deemed a white, and who a colored person." From theorizing race, the court moved to theorize the enforcement of racial segregation in schools, and prohibitions on interracial marriages by state governments as "the exercise of their police power." Race and police power, in *Plessy,* are clarified as infrastructures of territorialization, the control over the relationships between bodies in place. Justice Harlan's dissenting opinion pointed to the example of Chinese people, racially excluded from the "nation," who were, nevertheless, not prohibited from white train cars under Louisiana law. His arguments raise not only the question of racial aliens, but also Native peoples, citizens of tribal nations, who were not, at the time of the decision, recognized as citizens of the United States.[39]

The United States renewed a federal bankruptcy statute in 1898, months after launching a war with Spain, over control of its Caribbean and Southeast

Asian colonies. This was a foreign policy that primarily functioned as "a struggle for profitable markets of investment," for "a nation living upon tribute from abroad." Continental imperialism involved an overaccumulation of investments on railroads, collapse of functioning railroads due to mismanagement, and ongoing gaps between capitalization and colonial sovereignty in the vast territories that railroads connected or passed through. Land grants to the Union Pacific Railroad, alone, covered an area the size of New England. In 1898, the Interstate Commerce Commission, examining massive railroad trusts, flatly stated that the railroad "is essentially a monopoly," and hence it must be regulated. As "non-individualistic" or "collectivist legal institutions," corporate persons paradoxically matured during the high season of liberal individualism, baring contradictions of the rule of individuals through racial and colonial monopolies, contradictions tending toward the promotion of oligarchic control of state and corporation alike. Shareholding whiteness is one name we could use to refer to these oligarchic tendencies. The perpetually deferred premise of liberal individualism functions as an alibi for ongoing vulnerabilities to overwhelming violence along racial and colonial lines, the underbelly of Frederick Jackson Turner's frontier.[40]

NINE

Continental Imperialism

IN 1833, THE U.S. FEDERAL GOVERNMENT established an Office of Indian Affairs, administered under the War Department. Sixteen years later, in 1849, in a new bureaucratic arrangement, U. S. Indian policy moved from the War Department to the Department of the Interior, a signal moment in the history of U. S. imperial state formation, administratively reimagining U. S. territory, from a space of international war to a space of domestic policing. Focusing on the construction of the first transcontinental railroad, *Empire's Tracks* demonstrates how the production of the U. S. "interior" proceeded through the development of industrial and financial capitalism in the mid-nineteenth century, through an imperial process materializing as military occupation. This is the war-finance nexus. The frontier dynamic is at the heart of U. S. political economy, involving suspensions of law by individual colonialists, by corporations, and by representatives and institutions of the colonial state itself, in acts of overwhelming, often random violence, targeted along colonial, gendered, and racial lines. The "domestic" space of the United States, the "nation's interior," is governed on the principle of extraterritoriality, of legal impunity for colonizers and their economic and political institutions.[1]

Frederick Jackson Turner called this the frontier, the central fact of American history, "the outer edge of the wave—the meeting point between savagery and civilization." While Turner described a dividing line in geographic and temporal terms, he also inscribed it in racial and colonial terms, a division between savage and civilized humans, savage and civilized modes of relationship.[2] In this chapter, I read Lenin's theory of imperialism alongside Turner's frontier thesis, and W. E. B. Du Bois's arguments about imperialism in Africa, to theorize continental imperialism.

168

Turner conceived of U. S. national space, and capitalism, as closed structures. The frontier is not simply a place; like capital, it can be understood as a process and a relationship. A sense of the completion of the "colonization of the Great West" prompted Turner's anxious, melancholy triumphalism. Colonialism, proceeding in relation to a continuously receding area of free land, pulling "the advance of American settlement westward," explains "American development" for Turner.[3] The frontier marks a refusal or failure of relationship, a structure of desire for "free land," and the process of consummating that desire, which, in Turner's terms, is core to the "national" character of the United States.

There is something elemental about the frontier, involving a suspension of morals and ethics, in which the individual American crosses the line from civilization to savagery. "For a moment, at the frontier, the bonds of custom are broken and unrestraint is triumphant." Crossing the line, the individual colonist rejuvenates a distinctly American mode of relationship. The apparent unavailability of further free land, in Turner's mind, did not necessarily indicate that this structure of desire, this ethical and moral suspension, "the expansive character of American life," would cease. "Movement has been its dominant fact," he wrote, "and, unless this training has no effect upon a people, the American energy will continually demand a wider field for its exercise." The supposed closing of the frontier potentially marked a hinge between continental and overseas imperialism.[4]

In Turner's conception, a dynamic excitement joins a melancholy about the frontier process, where Americans gleefully throw off the fetters of civilization to renew themselves, only to find that the place has already been civilized, simply by their arrival in it. This melancholy fuels the repetition of the process, which Turner shaded with a wistfulness about the supposed closure of the frontier process in North America. "And now, four centuries from the discovery of America, at the end of a hundred years of life under the Constitution, the frontier has gone, and with its going has closed the first period of American history." While empires competed to monopolize relations with Indigenous nations and their lands, Indigenous nations are themselves, in Turner's telling, irrelevant to state formation in North America. Imperial states act upon Indigenous nations, as they act upon the land.[5]

We can turn to W. E. B. Du Bois's 1915 article, "The African Roots of War," for particular insights on the process of continental imperialism. Du

Bois's prescient analysis, which preceded Lenin's pamphlet on imperialism, anticipated many of Lenin's themes, but also included an analysis of the centrality of white supremacy and racism to modern imperialism, modes of relationship present in Turner's model of the frontier. Du Bois listed the prime methods, "contemptible and dishonest beyond expression," employed in the conquest of Africa: "lying, treaties, rivers of rum, murder, assassination, mutilation, rape, and torture," a sordid reality, sustained only with the world "deliberately stopping its ears and changing the subject of conversation while the devilry went on." Continental imperialism proceeds through an active production of ignorance. Imperialism in the Americas and Africa shares techniques, as well as a sense of historical closure. Imperialists coveted Africa, Du Bois wrote, not only because of "the well-known and traditional products," but also "boundless chances in a hundred different directions." Imperialism is itself a site of entrepreneurial activity, where risks find shelter under monopolies. In addition to access and control over key raw materials, such as gold and copper, Africa attracted imperialists with its "throng of human beings who, could they once be reduced to the docility and steadiness of Chinese coolies or of seventeenth- and eighteenth-century European laborers, would furnish their masters a spoil exceeding the gold-haunted dreams of the most modern of imperialists."[6] In Du Bois's analysis, a voracious appetite for both land *and* labor drives continental imperialism.

Territorialization proceeds on racial and gendered grounds, which Du Bois described as "the brutal truth": "a white man is privileged to go to any land where advantage beckons and behave as he pleases; the black or colored [person] is being more and more confined to those parts of the world where life for climatic, historical, economic, and political reasons is most difficult to live and most easily dominated by Europe for Europe's gain." Continental imperialism inscribes racial and gendered borders, restricting and controlling bodies. Dislocation and deterritorialization are key aspects of this mode of relationship. The frontier, an imperialist creation story, narrates a process and a relationship that produces both a mature, liberal colonial individual, and a national space where that individual can enact their agency. The rights-bearing citizen of the settler state inhabits a colonial relation to the space of the putative nation. In North America, to speak of the nation-state is to invoke imperialism.[7]

Turner's frontier is a disappearing act, averting attention from Indigenous and Black presence. "In the settlement of America we have to observe how European life entered the continent"—a model of colonial invasion that continues to inflect the mythology of "America" as a nation. The historical development of capitalism in England, and elsewhere in Europe, was predicated on the mass expulsion of rural, agrarian communities from their land. The history of capitalism in Europe cannot be divorced from the mass migration of the dispossessed of Europe to the Americas, in the service of reproducing the capital relationship in the "home country." This historical process cannot be separated from the unprecedented violence that enabled the military invasion and civil occupation of an entire hemisphere.[8]

Invasion is inherently reactive to Indigenous modes of relationship preceding it, persisting despite its violations. The theft of Indigenous lands, and the attempt to replace Indigenous relationships to land, is facilitated by conceiving the territorial, legal, political, and economic unit of the settler "nation" as the only rightful unit to govern collective life on the continent. Turner emplotted a naturalist account of urban industrial life, with trading posts, built "on the sites of Indian villages," growing into Midwestern cities. Against theft, Turner offered an image of fetal maturation for the colonial state, "the steady growth of a complex nervous system for the originally simple, inert continent." In North America, the change of railroads from short lines connecting cities, to long paths connecting remote places, played a central role in the growth of Turner's nervous system, almost as if biological and social relations alike begin with the fact of invasion, as if a European seed somehow inseminated an inert continental mass, a colonialist, if not immaculate, conception.[9]

Du Bois unmasked these theories of evolution, not only as racist fictions, but in a deeper sense, as transformations in class rule, moving along a trajectory that sees "the dipping of more and grimier hands into the wealth-bag of the nation." The "dream of exploitation abroad" itself became socialized, from the individual merchant to trading monopolies, to the merchant class, until in the early twentieth century, "the laborer at home is demanding and beginning to receive a part of his share." Following Du Bois, the dividends of imperialism, the capture of wealth "from the darker nations of the world—Asia and Africa, South and Central America, the West Indies and the islands of the South Seas," enable the possibility of the nation as a space for a stunted socialism. I would add the Indigenous nations of North America, whose lands and relationships continued to provide a "home space" for capital accumulation across these centuries of transformation, through the present. Reading Du Bois in relation to Turner can help further unmask the profoundly racist and antidemocratic dimensions of the frontier as evolutionary process. The stakes of the color line, Du Bois argued, are that the "darker folk . . . are by common consent for governance by white folk and economic subjection to them." All of the resources of scientific rationalism and Christian theology alike have been mobilized to reinforce this "highly profitable economic dictum," arriving at "the astonishing doctrine of the natural inferiority of most . . . to the few." This astonishing doctrine fuels the frontier perspective, and any distinctly "American" character arising in relation to it.[10]

Turner presented the frontier as a site for "the formation of composite nationality for the American people," where "the immigrants were Americanized, liberated, and fused into a mixed race, English in neither nationality nor characteristics." What are some of the characteristics of this "composite nationality," this fused race that is a product of the frontier experience? With finance capitalism, Lenin argued, "production becomes social, but appropriation remains private," which might be another way to understand the wages of whiteness in its shareholder form, fostering and sustaining the power of a financial oligarchy. In its shareholding form, "monopolies, oligarchy, the striving for domination instead of the striving for liberty, the exploitation of an increasing number of small or weak nations by an extremely small group of the richest or most powerful nations" shape and inform Turner's "composite nationality."[11]

Continental imperialism, as a reactive and reactionary mode of relationship, has an essentially parasitic character, a parasitism that infects whatever genuine democratic progress is achieved within the confines of the settler "nation." A focus on continental imperialism can help put the lie of U.S. exceptionalism to rest. The frontier does not distinguish the United States from other nations. Rather it situates the United States in a context of imperialism. As Lenin suggested, "a comparison of, say, the republican American bourgeoisie with the monarchist Japanese or German bourgeoisie shows that the most pronounced political distinctions diminish to an extreme degree in the epoch of imperialism—not because they are unimportant in general, but because in all these cases we are discussing a bourgeoisie which has definite features of parasitism." Du Bois describes a similar process, capturing financial profits through racist violence on a world scale, through which "the world began to invest in color prejudice. The 'color line' began to pay dividends," resulting in a "new democratic despotism," democratic for those enfranchised by the "nation," despotic for the many who are variously excluded, expelled, and dispossessed by the same "nation." Racism within the nation and imperialism abroad are core mechanisms for deflecting demands for higher wages, shorter work hours, and workplace democracy arising from workers' organization, through an emergent "aristocracy of labor" identifying with the prerogatives of whiteness, finding incidental pleasures in racial despotism. The "domestic" peace thus won, Du Bois argued, remains an unstable mechanism of power, because "the ignorant, unskilled, and restless still form a large, threatening, and, to a growing extent, revolutionary group in advanced countries."[12]

The capture and transformation of putatively free land into a space of liberal imperialist freedoms occurs through infrastructure. Turner described the frontier army post as "a wedge to open the Indian country" and "a nucleus for settlement." Ostensibly created in order to serve and protect colonizers from Indigenous people, the infrastructure of war and occupation actually establishes preconditions for settlement. Lenin analyzed the role of infrastructure in imperialism, by which, alongside the monopolization of skilled and technical labor, "the means of transport are captured: railways in America, shipping companies in Europe and America," with the concentrated control of labor, expertise, and infrastructure dragging capitalists "into a new social order," reshaping the conditions of production from competition to socialization. The transcontinental railroad constituted a core infrastructure of continental imperialism.[13]

Sounding a note that recapitulates Turner's frontier thesis on a global scale, Lenin wrote, "For the first time the world is completely divided up, so that in the future only redivision is possible; territories can only pass from one 'owner' to another, instead of passing as unowned territory to an 'owner.'" Born in war over territory, imperialism leads to war at ever-greater scales. The redefinition of ownership, especially in its territorial dimensions, is implicit within Lenin's observation. Decolonization is imperative in order to dismantle the imperial war machine. Turner's sense of the end of the frontier process shaped his understanding that wars with Indigenous nations were over, and that the United States was victorious. Despite the administrative transfer of federal Indian policy from the Department of War to the Department of the Interior, however, wars against Indigenous communities have not ceased. They have changed form. The idea of the nation, of the closure of the frontier process, provides a cover for the continuation of war by other agencies, and by other uniforms. Sarah Winnemucca, for example, described the economic basis of war on Paiute lands: "The only way the cattlemen and farmers get to make money is to start an Indian war, so that the troops may come and buy their beef, cattle, horses, and grain. The settlers get fat by it."[14] War was, and remains, inextricable from the capitalization of Indigenous lands.

Du Bois argued that imperialist competition over Africa was a primary cause for the First World War, pointing to "war today" and "the menace of wars tomorrow" as a "terrible overturning of civilization which we have lived to see." War, the lifeblood of the frontier process, is not a fleeting element of an evolutionary transition from savagery to civilization. War had been a central function of the emergent capitalist state, flourishing over the high period of liberal imperialism. Imperialist wars ripen the fruits of civilization, producing the most irrational destructiveness through the most rational outlooks. The "nation," in this context, provides an alibi for imperialism, and, following Du Bois, can more specifically be described as "armed national associations of labor and capital whose aim is the exploitation of the wealth of the world mainly outside the European circle of nations."[15] Throughout this book, I have invoked "the United States" with this definition in mind.

CAPITALISM

In Turner's conception—westward leaning, looking away from the Atlantic, centered squarely within the precincts of whiteness—the question of the frontier in American life trivializes slavery to "an incident" in American history, thereby truncating North America from the rest of the world. To invoke the words of Du Bois, the first true world commerce, the driving conditions for territorial and economic expansion, was "a commerce mainly in the bodies and souls of men." Slavery, Du Bois continued, was a facet of continental imperialism, a "sinister traffic, on which the British Empire and the American Republic were largely built," wrecking existing modes of relationship in order to produce the continent (Africa as well as North and South America) as a space inviting "aggression and exploitation," Turner's dividing line on the scale of continents. Contra Turner, Du Bois can help us understand the frontier process as thoroughly imbued with the dynamics of slavery: "the ownership of materials and men in the darker world is the real prize that is setting the nations of Europe at each other's throats today." Racism is a material force, permeating the social structures emergent from capitalism.[16]

The idea of *terra nullius* lurks behind Turner's understanding of the frontier, informing a very particular conception of freedom. "The most significant thing about the American frontier is that it lies at the hither edge of free land"—free, according to Turner, for the taking, free of claims, free of relationships. His mind empties the land of Indigenous modes of relationship, through which the land is not free, but is instead richly known and richly claimed. Slavery and colonialism are distinct but deeply interrelated modes of power. Both can be traced to property claims in real estate. Together, these property claims outline the specific kinds of freedom traveling under the documents of the imperialist "nation." For Turner, the existence and availability of land provides the opportunity for economic power, and "economic power secures political power." Turner conceives of the frontier in mercantilist terms, considering trade with Indigenous nations as "coeval with discovery." Trade, for Turner, propels the evolutionary trajectories of the frontier, from "the trader's frontier, the rancher's frontier, or the miner's frontier, and the farmer's frontier," propelling, also, westward expansionist trajectories, from the Alleghenies to the Great Lakes to the Rockies. The frontier, for Turner, is a space of merchant capitalism, itself imbued with a kind of liberal economic agency, the ability to create "demand for merchants." Reading Turner next to Lenin, we can see that what is called the frontier process might index a circular, not a linear progression, as Lenin noted. "Capitalism, which began its development with petty usury capital, ends its development with gigantic usury capital."[17]

For Lenin, finance and monopoly drive imperialism, not trade and discovery, with the appearance of monopolies exacerbating disparities between agriculture and industry, and correspondingly, between the country and the city. Lenin pointed to an underlying centralization beneath the appearance of decentralized production and consumption, a centralization that masks the growing consolidation of what he called "monopolist giants." The activities of the major financial institutions foster monopoly formation, increasing the concentration of production in industries like coal and iron, while these banks are themselves able to monopolize the financial sector. "In America," Lenin wrote, "there are not nine, but *two* big banks, those of the billionaires Rockefeller and Morgan." Among the few banks left solvent after the process of centralization, Lenin noted a tendency toward the consolidation of banking trusts, in which independent firms, nominally competing with each other, coordinate their operations and their political demands.

Banking monopolies developed in, and shaped, the historical process Turner named "the frontier." Against Turner's picturesque of fur traders and birch bark canoes, Lenin's described "the concentration of production; the monopoly arising therefrom; the merging or coalescence of banking with industry—this is the history of the rise of finance capital and what gives the term 'finance capital' its content." Finance capital, Lenin argued, has the capacity to rapidly accelerate the pace of technological change, and to subordinate politically independent states to its own interests in economic policy and international relations. Reading Lenin in relation to Turner can help us better understand how the specific dynamics that Lenin described as "imperialism," particularly the domination of finance capital, were already shaping life in North America by the mid-nineteenth century. When we understand North America as a space of imperialism, an international space of hundreds of colonized Indigenous nations, rather than of settler "nations," we can see that in many ways, North America has been a staging ground for imperialist techniques and processes that would reoccur elsewhere in the world. Turner portrayed this as "the disintegrating forces of civilization," a profoundly violent process in which the land itself "became a fissure in Indian society," and Indigenous social life, like Indigenous landholdings, "became honeycombed." There is a certain wistfulness here, a salvage perspective on irrecoverable Indigenous precolonial pasts, but also a profound anxiety on the part of colonizers, pioneers who have "met Indians armed with guns," as colonial trade provides a means for collective armed resistance to land grabs.[18]

Lenin periodized the evolution of capitalism into imperialism in three phases. The first, from 1860–70, the period of the building of the transcontinental railroad, he described as the height of free competition. Following the financial crisis of 1873, which was triggered by Lakota resistance to incursions on their homelands by the Northern Pacific Railroad, Lenin argued that we begin to see the emergence of cartels. In the third stage, which proceeded through the boom conditions at the end of the nineteenth century, culminating in the economic crisis at the turn of the century, "cartels become one of the foundations of the whole of economic life. Capitalism has been transformed into imperialism." The colonization of North America, and of the Plains in particular, anticipated and triggered many of the global dynamics that Lenin analyzed, suggesting that, even within Lenin's model of imperialism, the imperative to decolonize North America holds a central position of importance. Across North America, the union of financial and industrial capitalism, in the form of cartels that impelled state and military policy, was already in place by the end of the 1860s. In other words, viewed from Indigenous places, capitalism actually began in an imperial mode—capitalism *is* imperialism.[19]

For Lenin, imperialism structures and propels the dividing line between capitalism and socialism, proceeding through an extremely rapid concentration of industrial forces, conditions which are made possible by the ability of financial capital to control and dominate practically all economic activity around the world. With these developments, the ethos of the United States, which Turner had identified as the frontier process, is not exceptional, but instead exemplifies core imperialist values: "'American ethics,' which the European professors and well-meaning bourgeois so hypocritically deplore, have, in the age of finance capital, become the ethics of literally every large city, no matter what country it is in." One of the key characteristics of imperialism is not a supposed division between civilization and savagery, but partition, the breaking of relationships, the planetary completion of the colonial policy of territorial seizure. Partition is, itself, an ongoing process, both a structure and an event. Lenin echoed Turner on the close of the frontier: "For the first time the world is completely divided up, so that in the future only redivision is possible; territories can only pass from one 'owner' to another, instead of passing as unowned territory to an 'owner.'"[20]

Territorialization, he argued, is a core aspect of imperialism, partition manifesting as a structural feature of imperialism, after capitalism has arrived at a degree of concentration that forces capitalists to divide the world "in proportion to 'capital,' in proportion to 'strength,' because there cannot be any other system of division under commodity production and capitalism." In Lenin's analysis, imperialism arises through the interrelationship of state and corporation, the division of the world proceeding in a figurative sense from capital exporting countries, and in actual fact from finance capital. As large trusts with monopolizing tendencies expanded alongside the increasing export of capital, agreements among the major trusts led toward "the formation of international cartels." Read in relation to Turner's frontier thesis, this may provide us with a working description for U.S. state formation: not a national entity, but an imperial one, an international cartel that supplies a framework for coordination among major monopolist trusts, in a way that coheres racist and masculinist expectations of future returns on current property claims. Lenin foregrounded two characteristic features of capitalism: the growth of industry and the concentration of production. Large-scale financial capitalism, he argued, enables concentration, transforming competition into monopoly, resulting in "immense progress in the socialization of production." A century after his writing, we might counterpose Lenin's understandings of technological organization against the resurgence of Indigenous modes of relationship, including Indigenous technologies, as a practical means to dismantle imperialism in a context of flexible accumulation.[21]

For Lenin, financialization is central to capitalist imperialism, achieved, in part, through the circulation of small shares in corporations. The sale of small shares, backed by congressional land grants of unceded Indigenous territories, financed the building of the Central Pacific and Union Pacific railroads. With the supremacy of finance capitalism, "the big profits go to the 'geniuses' of financial manipulation," who, through "swindles and manipulations," are able to capture the results of the immense socialization of production through an essentially parasitic relationship to the broader economy. In the process, the state itself splits into usurer and debtor functions, sustaining the circulation of finance capital across national and imperial boundaries. Imperialism results in the suspensions of competition, democracy, and liability, exemplified in the "holding system" of large corporations, such as the Contract & Finance Company, or the Credit Mobilier, employed by the directors of the Central Pacific and Union Pacific Railroad companies to slough off accountability, "for the directors of the parent company are not legally responsible for the subsidiary companies, which are supposed to be 'independent,' and *through the medium* of which they can 'pull off' *anything.*"[22]

Finance capital, Lenin argued in conversation with Hilferding, "stimulates the striving for colonial conquest," seeking domination, not liberty. In Du Bois's analysis, the vehicle for colonial conquest is no longer the monarch, nor the ruling classes, but the nation, "a new democratic nation composed of united capital and labor," organized and acting on racial lines, a nation held together by more than "sentimental patriotism, loyalty, or ancestor worship," but also by "increased wealth, power, and luxury for all classes on a scale the world never saw before." These bonds are the result of Turner's frontier process, investments in possession on a colonialist basis. Against Turner's model of the frontier as a space of renewal and rebirth, Lenin identified the transformation of competition into monopoly, enabling agreements and coordination across and between giant corporations, as a core impulse of imperialism. Monopoly, manifesting through both the corporation and the state, he argued, is a product of finance capital, utilizing "connections" for profitable transactions in lieu of market competition, in order to displace or lessen risk and vulnerability. The struggle over the division of the world is a struggle between the major monopolists. Arising out of the concentration of production, taking life from banks, accelerating the capture of sources of raw materials, monopoly, according to Lenin "has grown out of colonial policy." This is the essence of imperialism, "the monopoly stage of capitalism," which, in

North America, grew out of what Turner named as the frontier process, with its tendencies toward "stagnation and decay."[23]

Lenin noted that England and France possessed the most colonies in the world, while the United States and Germany had achieved rapid economic development and concentration of industrial production, together controlling nearly 80 percent of the financial capital in the world. "Thus," he wrote, "in one way or another, nearly the whole world is more or less the debtor to and tributary of these four international banker countries, the four 'pillars' of world finance capital." At this point, imperialism provided a dual function. First, it almost completely mitigated risk, guaranteeing success against competitors, partly through close coordination with the policies of colonial governments. Second, imperialism supplied access and control over raw materials, a category in which we might include the labor power of the colonized. With the diminishing landmass to be claimed, imperialism leads to struggle and conflict between the imperial powers. Lenin argued that interimperial concentration and control was predicated on the concentration and control of industrial production, proceeding under systems of alliance and combination, and as a result, meaningful competition transformed into monopoly relations, leading to the socialization of production. Imperialism is "capitalism in transition," or "moribund capitalism."[24]

Lenin argued, "The supremacy of financial capital over all other forms of capital means the predominance of the rentier and of the financial oligarchy; it means the crystallization of a small number of financially 'powerful' states from among all the rest." The assertion of financial power, which at the time of Lenin's writing, the United States manifested by funding the First World War, was predicated on a certain set of claims in land as real estate. Land grants, and the willful misreading of treaties as real estate transactions, to paraphrase Vine Deloria, were central to the growth of the United States as a continental, and then a global imperial power, central to waging war at ever-greater scales. Lenin noted: "The capital exporting countries have divided the world among themselves in the figurative sense of the term. But finance capital has also led to the *actual* division of the world." Before this could happen, in North America, finance capital led to the division of the continent itself, and the transcontinental railroad was a key instrument of this division.[25]

The transcontinental railroad occupied a prominent place in Turner's understanding of the frontier. "The frontier reached by the Pacific Railroad, surveyed into rectangles, guarded by the United States Army, and recruited by the daily immigrant ship, moves forward at a swifter pace and in a different way than the frontier reached by the birch canoe or the pack horse." Lenin widened the geographic frame, pointing out that railroad construction in Africa, the Americas, and Asia, "two hundred thousand kilometres of new railways in the colonies and in the other countries of Asia and America," was most rapid, with about 80 percent of the total existing railways concentrated under the control of the Great Powers. "The concentration of ownership of these railways, of finance capital," he noted, "is much greater still." The construction and control of railroads, through investments on "particularly advantageous terms," often with guaranteed returns, also increased the production of steel and iron, necessitating the expansion of coal mining, enabling the extraction and circulation of resources and agricultural exports. Among the imperialist powers, Lenin argued, there is a structural disparity between the development of productive capacities and the control of colonial territories, and under capitalism, the only way to resolve this disparity is war, on a global scale.[26]

COUNTERSOVEREIGNTY

In Turner's conception, the frontier names a linear process of westward continental expansion, a linearity that has shaped the narrative form of stories about the settler "nation." Along this line, Turner suggested, an ongoing process of reversion and maturation took place. "American social development has been continually beginning over again on the frontier." In the frontier, Turner found "perennial rebirth," a fluidity of life, new opportunities, and a certain proximity to simple life, interacting elements that delineate "the forces dominating American character." For Turner, the frame to understand something called "American life" is not the Atlantic world, but rather the heart of the continent, so as the frontier moved west, it became increasingly American. As Turner presented it, the frontier is not a purely abstract process that is replicated in different places. It reflects the distinct features of the land, taking different forms along rivers, on plains, in deserts, and in mountains. It also reacts to already existing, distinct, living Indigenous modes of relationship.[27]

The "Indian question" is central to Turner's frontier—how this process of recursion and development, the capitalization of lands, the construction of economic and political infrastructure, the maturation of social life, and the resultant modes of relationship, all attempt to usurp and replace the already existing, highly complex relationships and forms of knowledge shaping distinct Indigenous collective ways of living in specific places. The frontier is reactive to Indigenous modes of relationship, perpetually failing to remake and replace these modes of relationship. Turner's notion of closure, with its implication that history begins with colonialism (a history that is spatialized, in a strange way, at the point of invasion), also feeds perspectives of Indigenous nations as frozen (or vanished) in some timeless, authentically precolonial past.[28]

The linearity of the frontier, for Turner, is not only spatial, but also social, teleologically developmentalist, reflecting a distinctly Midwestern flavor of white supremacy. "Line by line, as we read this continental page from West to East we find the record of social evolution," moving from Indigenous peoples to commodity hunters, to traders, ranching, small family farms, large-scale monocrop agriculture, and culminating in cities and industrial production. As evolutionist models of social life do, Turner's story severely misrepresents the actual history of the colonization of North America, in which the frontier often manifested in the dual and overlapping forms of corporation and plantation. The visions of evolution that Turner presents mask profoundly distinct modes of relation to land. According to Turner, "The buffalo trail became the Indian trail, and this became the trader's 'trace'; the trails widened into roads, and the roads into turnpikes, and these in turn were transformed into railroads."[29] However, as we have seen, the overland trails and railroads of colonization, situated on an east–west axis, materialize a very different relationship to place than the circular trails of buffalo and other migratory animals, and of the human communities living in relation to them, which reflected the cycle of seasons and a deep commitment to, and knowledge of, place. These circular orientations were not superseded with the arrival of the frontier, with all of its isolating tendencies, but to the contrary, these orientations to movement and change persist through the present.

Turner argued that "the peculiarity of American institutions is the fact that they have been compelled to adapt themselves to the changes of an expanding people," but his framing isolates institutions from their colonial context. The question is about more than simply taking up too much space. To focus on expansion is to focus on adaptation to prior and ongoing modes of relationship. The peculiarity of American institutions is the fact of adaptation and reaction to Indigenous modes of relationship. This adaptation and reaction is what I am referring to as "countersovereignty."[30]

Turner began his essay, quoting the superintendent for the 1890 census, on the end of the frontier as a meaningful category in census reports after 1880. The apparent close of the frontier follows the formation of "isolated bodies of settlement," isolation understood here both in terms of geographic space, and in terms of social relationships, which might give us a sense of the actual form of U. S. countersovereignty, past and present, across North America. Turner described the frontier as "the line of most rapid and effective Americanization," where "The wilderness masters the colonist." In the frontier process, colonialists assimilate to Indigenous modes of life and relationship with the lands of settlement, which might help us understand the anachronistic lie of the notion of discovery. Trying to go "back to nature," the colonialist finds himself tacking along the paths of Indigenous society. "At the frontier the environment is at first too strong for the man. He must accept the conditions which it furnishes, or perish, and so he fits himself into the Indian clearings and follows the Indian trails." Countersovereignty, through a suspension or evacuation of both Indigenous and imperial legal norms, involves crossing the line from civilization to savagery, not in racial terms, but in legal and spatial terms. Crossing, for example, the line of the Proclamation of 1763. As the frontier consolidated, and as the colonialists sought to reestablish legal norms, "the management" of Indigenous communities "became an object of political concern." This reaction and reactiveness to Indigenous life, which I am calling countersovereignty, is a "consolidating agent" that outlines and defines the United States. Turner described Indigenous people as "a common danger, demanding united action." In this feeling of invasive vulnerability, and in the range of responses to that feeling, we can locate countersovereignty, an origin point for "American," as a functional identity, a distinct way of being in the world.[31]

Turner cautioned on the dangers accompanying the supposed benefits of "the democracy born of free land, strong in selfishness and individualism, intolerant of administrative experience and education, and pressing individual liberty beyond its proper bounds."[32] These are clearly not dangers for Indigenous people, who are relegated to the savage side of the frontier line. Nor is Turner concerned about Black life. Instead, Turner is pointing out the root instability, the fragility and weakness of countersovereignty, as a reactive mode of relationship, one that perpetually threatens to turn in and cannibalize itself. If the frontier would ever close, then what could protect the war-finance nexus from its own constitutive violence? What could protect imperialists from themselves?

In North America, what we are looking at is the transfer of European feudal relations, and their reaction to Indigenous tribal and intertribal relations. Logics and practices of containment are central to the war-finance nexus. Lenin assessed revolutionary possibilities in Russia, where "modern capitalist imperialism is enmeshed, so to speak, in a particularly close network of pre-capitalist relations," a diagnosis that could also relate to Indigenous life in North America. Countersovereignty is a chain made out of weak links, entailing possibilities of anti-imperialist, anticapitalist transformations of collective life. Imperialism, for Lenin, strives for annexations, strives "towards violence and reaction." Annexation, violence, reaction: these are core modes through which the United States manifests, as countersovereignty. To conceive of the United States in national terms is to concede the grounds of imperialism. At the heart of countersovereignty is a profound anxiety about the future, about the rational response of the teeming millions who have been subjected to its yoke. In the words of Du Bois, "All over the world there leaps to articulate speech and ready action that singular assumption that if white men do not throttle colored men, then China, India, and Africa will do to Europe what Europe has done and seeks to do to them." Countersovereignty consists of anxious and reactive attempts to control bodies in space, to prevent or preempt nightmare visions of future retribution spilling over the borders dividing civilization from savagery.[33]

At stake are colonial and racial relations of control. Upon the maturation of finance capitalism, Lenin noted, "a handful of monopolists control all the operations, both commercial and industrial, of the whole of capitalist society," control that enables them to ascertain, influence, and determine outcomes for individuals and institutions. This is why Lenin described U.S. anti-imperialism against the occupation of the Philippines as a "pious wish," so far as the anti-imperialist movement "shrank from recognising the indissoluble bond between imperialism and the trusts, and, therefore, between imperialism and the very foundations of capitalism." Imperialism calls for a critique of state *and* corporation.[34]

For Du Bois, racism is a refusal of relationship, a paradox at the core of U.S. claims to civilized status. "It is this paradox which allows in America the most rapid advance of democracy to go hand in hand in its very centers with increased aristocracy and hatred toward darker races, and which excuses and defends an inhumanity that does not shrink from the public burning of human beings." Lynch law provides a foundation for countersovereignty, under the alibi of securing the domestic space: defending the white family.

Decolonization, the basis for "real peace," is the restoration and renewal of relations, an extension of "the democratic weapons of self-defense." What are these weapons? To follow from Indigenous critique, we might begin with Indigenous-centered diplomacy. To continue, with Du Bois, we might include land, education, and self-determination. Du Bois's insight about the color line is a warning to the imperialists. "These nations and races, composing as they do a vast majority of humanity, are going to endure this treatment just as long as they must and not a moment longer. Then they are going to fight and the War of the Color Line will outdo in savage inhumanity any war this world has yet seen. For colored folks have much to remember and they will not forget." This is the bind of imperialism, another way to think about the significance of the frontier in American history: a failure and refusal to enter into relationship; a fear of what might result from that failure; barbaric and random imperialist violence intended to momentarily assuage that fear; at which point, the cycle starts anew, with the failure and refusal to enter into relationship.[35]

Taking Indigenous modes of relationship as the point of departure for a critique of political economy, we might understand decolonization in a way that centers Indigenous nationhood, compelling us to rethink the very conception of the "nation" that constitutes the international arena. The international unites the human race, at least in part by drawing upon Indigenous practices of interrelation. In North America, the call to honor the treaties can bear anti-imperialist valences, in a way that prioritizes Indigenous life and knowledge. We might take this as an opening to reconsider what we mean by capitalism, and what we might mean by anticapitalism, perhaps focusing less on modes of production than on modes of relationship.[36]

Epilogue

THE SIGNIFICANCE OF DECOLONIZATION
IN NORTH AMERICA

HOW TO PRACTICE A GENUINE ANTI-IMPERIALISM in North America, in the twenty-first century? The major breakthroughs against imperialism in the twentieth century revolved around coordinated mass action of workers and peasants in the peripheries of global capitalism. Peasant-worker alliances animated the core of the century's great revolutions. Imperialism, in reaction, reconsolidated its deathly grip on land and life, a process that has accelerated greatly after the dissolution of the Soviet Union in 1991. In the interregnum, imperialism has reinstituted uneven geographies of human suffering with a vengeance, unleashing new contradictions.

Empire's Tracks has argued that the history of capitalism is the history of imperialism. The book demonstrates that U.S. imperialism predates 1898, when the United States apparently leapt its continental boundaries.[1] To take 1898 as a moment of origin for U.S. imperialism would be to naturalize U.S. claims to control over its "homeland." Continental imperialism, I have argued, proceeds through the nexus of war and finance. A consistent anti-imperialist critique necessitates a sustained critique of state *and* corporation. Contradictions in the war-finance nexus are sites for the renewal of imperialism, but they are also points of possibility for a genuine rupture with imperialist modes of relationship. Countersovereignty, the reactive mode of U.S. power, is one such contradiction, an inflexion point for both imperialist and anti-imperialist futures. Imperialism, in North America, is a chain built out of weak links.

Across North America, the union of financial and industrial capitalism in the form of cartels that impelled state and military policy was already in place by the end of the 1860s. Viewed from Indigenous places, capitalism actually began in an imperial mode. Capitalism *is* imperialism. A clear perspective on continental imperialism, the nexus of war and finance that shapes capitalism in North America, can help us understand the centrality of Indigenous decolonization to anticapitalist struggle on this continent. North America is simultaneously the homeland of contemporary imperialism and occupied territory. Indigenous struggles for self-determination are significant anti-imperialist struggles. In an age of international finance capital, Indigenous struggles for self-determination hold the possibility of seriously disrupting the rentier class, which monopolizes capital through financial and real estate assets, by disrupting a land grab of continental scope.

In this epilogue, I read key documents of U.S. military, energy, and financial policy that have framed the war on terrorism. I focus on continental imperialism, as it manifests in a plan to "rebuild America's defenses" proposed by key architects of Bush administration foreign policy, and on energy infrastructure in North America. I then consider countersovereignty, arising through a kind of "imperial sovereignty" in the aftermath of the U.S. Congress's Authorization to Use Military Force, passed days after 9 / 11. I conclude with an argument for the centrality of Indigenous modes of relationship to the vision and practice of anticolonial internationalism.

THE WAR-FINANCE NEXUS

In September 2000, two months before the fateful "election," the Project for the New American Century released a report, *Rebuilding America's Defenses*, spurred by a sense of declining U.S. military strength. Following an apparent victory against communism, this was a program to maintain a unipolar world order organized under U.S. control. While the beginning of the new century offered an "unprecedented strategic opportunity," the report warned of "a future that promises to be very different and potentially much more dangerous," involving a proliferation of threats, including "potential rivals like China" and "adversaries like Iran, Iraq and North Korea." The Project advocated a U.S. foreign policy revolving around preserving a favorable balance of power in Europe, the Middle East and the oil and natural gas lands surrounding it, and East Asia, as well as stabilizing the international system of nation-states against nonstate actors, including "terrorists."[2]

"Homeland security" was key to this military strategy. This would necessitate repairing a "frayed and torn" military social fabric, which saddled the U.S. military with poor enlistment and retention rates, arising from a "degraded quality of life," separating military life from the "middle-class expectations" seen as vital to maintaining a volunteer army. The authors urged efforts to improve the quality of life for service personnel, strengthening a culture of civilian support and aggrandizement of the military. In tandem with efforts to improve the quality of military life, the Project argued that the costs of "social entitlement programs" like Social Security and Medicare will limit discretionary funds for the military, thereby endangering the "American peace." There are at least two threads to draw from this strategy. First, the apparent victory against communism obviated any need to offer a pretense to concessions won by mass working-class struggle during the previous phase of imperialism. Second, the widespread suffering unleashed by dismantling the social wage acts as a further incentive for poor people to join a "volunteer" army. Imperialism is a project of class rule.[3]

The nature of war in a unipolar age, the authors argued, would shift to policing, or "constabulary operations." Unipolarity entails an expansion of U.S. countersovereignty on a global scale, in which U.S. military forces engage missions "requiring forces configured for combat but capable of long-term, independent constabulary operations," to respond to "smaller scale contingencies." Such missions would extend already existing practices, such as no-fly zones over Iraq following the withdrawal of U.S. land forces in 1991, or operations ostensibly against drug trafficking in Latin America and the Caribbean. This required an expansion of the "American security perimeter," through the development of a "worldwide archipelago of U.S. military installations." A proliferation of forward operating bases around the world allows the United States to more easily skirt political, economic, and practical constraints, and to facilitate political as well as military operations. The continental United States remains significant in this vision, as a reserve site for rapid reinforcements. Still, the essential fact of U.S. foreign policy, after the closing of the Cold War, was "the American security frontier." The U.S. armed forces, the authors wrote, "are the cavalry on the new American frontier." U.S. foreign policy in the twenty-first century remains grounded in a long tradition of war against Indigenous nations, through the lived experience of continental imperialism.[4]

Through constabulary missions, the United States would assert political control over the people of the world. While the authors urged that the United States cannot assume "a UN-like stance of neutrality," the real point of contention is not neutrality, but the possibility of international democracy. U.S. troops could forestall European assertions of independence from U.S. imperial policies. In Saudi Arabia, nominally rotational forces, and deeper reliance on private contractors, could assuage "domestic sensibilities." In Korea, reunification would not involve the end of U.S. military occupation, but a change in the occupation forces' mission. In Latin America, the military would expand its use of airfields, nominally for "counterdrug operations." In the short term, this expansion was necessitated by the need to defend against regimes deemed "hostile to America": North Korea, Iraq, Iran, Libya, and Syria.[5]

In warfare with primarily political ends, land power is essential. "Regimes are difficult to change based upon punishment alone." The authors anticipated that urban warfare will be fundamental to the operations of future land forces. Land power will be complemented by the "global reach, global dominance" of U.S. air power, including drones to extend aerial strike and surveillance capacities. In addition to land and air power, the authors of the report anticipated U.S. military control of space. Back on earth, they looked forward to new kinds of biological weapons that can target "specific genotypes," which could "transform biological warfare from the realm of terror to a politically useful tool." Most thoroughly, the authors urged the necessity for the United States to "maintain nuclear strategic superiority," as an essential element of homeland defense. This would involve "safer and more effective nuclear weapons," including nuclear weapons that could be deployed in battlefield situations. Such weapons of mass destruction, the authors argued, would provide "the final guarantee of security, democratic freedoms and individual political rights." Writing in September 2000, the authors were sanguine about the possibility of quickly achieving their objectives: "the process of transformation, even if it brings revolutionary change, is likely to be a long one, absent some catastrophic and catalyzing event—like a new Pearl Harbor."[6]

In May 2001, the National Energy Policy Development Group released a report on the future of U.S. energy, under the signature of Vice President Dick Cheney. U.S. energy use had increased by 17 percent over the course of the 1990s. In 2001, the United States consumed over 25 percent of the oil produced worldwide. The report projected that U.S. energy consumption will increase a further 32 percent by 2020. To address these needs, the report focused on a mix of energy sources, key among them, coal, natural gas, and oil. Coal could supply the United States far into the future, and was becoming cheaper as a result of expanding low-cost coal production, such as in the Powder River basin, in and adjacent to the Crow and Northern Cheyenne reservations. Energy production includes the majority cost for industrial fertilizers and pesticides, potentially affecting monopoly beef, pork, corn, wheat, and soy production. The report noted that the U.S. federal government controls "about 31 percent of the nation's land," mostly unceded Indigenous lands, which were already providing almost 30 percent of U.S. energy production. Pointing to a deteriorating energy infrastructure, the report advocated expedited permits for pipeline construction, such as a natural gas pipeline connecting Alaska to the lower 48 states. In addition to land use and infrastructure within U.S. territory, the report argued that "energy security" must be a priority of U.S. foreign policy, including financing and training in U.S. energy technologies.[7]

Energy security, as described in the report, entails controlling the production and distribution of cheap energy, a twofold strategy of imperialist and class rule. The ability to control energy distribution, especially to Western Europe and Japan, has enabled the United States to steer inter-imperialist competition. Within the United States, cheap energy was the cornerstone of an industrial and regional shift to nonunion, nonmetropolitan manufacturing from the late 1970s onward. The further encroachment of Indigenous nations' lands and water lurks behind these two approaches to U.S. energy security. Six months after the release of the energy policy report, the energy corporation Enron declared bankruptcy after a decline in investor confidence, SEC investigation, and ratings downgrade. Enron strategy, the functioning mechanisms of "energy security," revolved around a combination of accounting fraud and close relationships with politicians and government regulators. In the Gulf of Mexico, a region spanning Houston, Texas, to Alabama, including thirty thousand offshore acres, made up the world's "largest oil plantation," producing oceanic dead zones, cancer zones, and widespread social devastation. "On the eve of Hurricane Katrina," Clyde Woods wrote, "the double curse of plantation and oil economics had already created a major social disaster." Enron and the Gulf oil complex are models for the newer Bakken shale complex on the northern Plains that began to boom after 2000.[8]

In 2010, Energy Transfer Equity was focusing on the distribution of natural gas. Finance is core to the company's operations. Future growth necessitated new pipeline construction. The company held existing right-of-way agreements with the Navajo Nation, Southern Ute, Laguna Pueblo, and Fort Mojave tribes, but it needed to obtain new rights-of-way on tribal lands. Such new rights-of-way, the company informed its shareholders, were "critical" to its financial position. Over the next few years, a series of mergers resulted in a renewed centralization of energy infrastructure in North America. In 2012,

Energy Transfer Partners acquired Sunoco, diversifying into oil and retail, thereby becoming party to a number of outstanding legal proceedings for MTBE groundwater contamination in nineteen sites in New Jersey and Puerto Rico. In 2012, a pipeline overseen by ETP leaked in Ohio, and pump stations in Texas and Oklahoma leaked. In 2013, Vermont filed a groundwater contamination suit, and the U.S. Department of Transportation proposed penalties on alleged safety violations relating to a 2012 spill in Baton Rouge, Louisiana. The company was also fined by Pennsylvania for violating safety regulations, and received notices of violations of environmental regulations. Centralization made ETP profits newly vulnerable to a moratorium on offshore oil production in the wake of the 2012 Deepwater Horizon oil spill (involving an oil rig operated by British Petroleum), and vulnerable to collective action, as well as pension obligations, from unionized employees of Sunoco.[9]

By 2015, the company viewed the brand recognition of Sunoco as an asset in its operations, and drew significant parts of its cash flow from retail operations at gas station convenience stores. It warned shareholders that climate change legislation "could result in increasing operating costs and reduced demand for the services we provide." That year, Sunoco acquired a controlling stake in the Dakota Access pipeline, to build a pipeline system connecting the Bakken shale field with the Gulf Coast. The company expected that DAPL would begin commercial operations in the fourth quarter of 2016. In August 2016, Sunoco Logistics announced that it had raised $2.5 billion to finance Bakken pipeline construction. That summer, Energy Transfer Equity notified its shareholders, "individuals affiliated with, or sympathetic to, the Standing Rock Sioux Tribe began gathering near a construction site on the Dakota Access pipeline project in North Dakota to protest the development of the pipeline project." The company reported that the dispute centered around permits granted by the Army Corps of Engineers to cross over and near the Missouri River. The company expected to complete the pipeline in March or April 2017. Delays, the company noted, were delaying the receipt of revenues from the project.[10]

The Canadian energy corporation Enbridge owns the largest pipeline infrastructure in the Bakken oilfield, which spans southeastern Saskatchewan and North Dakota, one of the largest oil producing regions in North America following the introduction of hydraulic fracturing and horizontal drilling. In its shareholder documents, Enbridge takes care to present "trusting relationships," between the corporation and First Nations. In 2016, the corporation announced an "Indigenous Peoples Policy" that "sets out principles governing the Company's relationships with Indigenous peoples and makes commitments to work with Indigenous peoples so they may realize benefits from the Company's projects and operations." In 2012, Enbridge identified political uncertainty in Libya and Iraq as making North America "one of the most secure supply sources of crude oil." In August 2016, Enbridge announced that it had acquired a 49 percent stake in the holding company that controlled the Bakken Pipeline System, including the Dakota Access Pipeline, agreeing to provide a $1.5 billion bridge loan for the project. Listing risks to its shareholders in 2017, Enbridge listed "changes in our reputation." Under the banner of "sustainability," the corporation announced agreements with fifty-six Indigenous communities in Canada, and the delivery of almost $74 million "in social-economic opportunities to Indigenous contractors or partners," deploying the language of "Indigenous consultation and inclusion." The company warned of "increased environmental activism against pipeline construction and operation," which could result in work delays, reduced demands, increased regulations and denials of permits, adversely affecting financial results.[11]

Starting in at least September 2016, as Alleen Brown, Will Parrish, and Alice Sperri reported for *The Intercept,* Energy Transfer Partners contracted with TigerSwan, a mercenary company founded by a former commander of a U.S. Army special operations unit, during the U.S. occupation of Iraq. TigerSwan produced a counterintelligence archive, drawing on the logic and language of counterinsurgency operations in Afghanistan, coordinating with over seventy-five law enforcement agencies, as well as campus police from the University of Illinois and Lincoln Land College. Major energy corporations, federal, state, and local law enforcement agencies, and private military contractors all coordinated "constabulary duties." This included aerial surveillance by drone and helicopter, and "nonlethal" weapons. TigerSwan requested permission to use infrared and night vision technologies, employing operational logics from counterinsurgency efforts in Iraq and Afghanistan, including the structure of targeted assassination programs. TigerSwan operated without a license in North Dakota, continuing its operations after its application was denied by the state's licensing board. The war-finance nexus functions through legal impunity. Part of TigerSwan's work was propagandistic, "tactical and strategic messaging... that drives the message that we are the good guys ... address the negative messaging with counter-messaging." Counter-messaging is the historiographical mode of countersovereignty.[12]

Imperialism, Samir Amin suggests, is capitalism in its actually existing form. Capitalism does not instantiate homogenous historical trajectories of development. Instead, polarization is a basic and permanent characteristic of capitalism. The struggle at Standing Rock should be understood within the current imperialist conjuncture, which emerged out of a structural crisis of overaccumulation that hit the capitalist world in the 1970s, a process that had a historical parallel with the close of railroad colonialism in the early twentieth century, and a corresponding decline of British global hegemony. Neoliberalism has redistributed income upwards. Globalization has driven down production costs, and in so doing, has exacerbated overaccumulation. Financialization has resulted in extreme volatility, spurring at least fourteen major financial crises since the 1980s. Since the 1991 dissolution of the USSR, the U.S. economy has projected growth through an explosion of its financial sector, which has cannibalized its real economy. Consumption levels for the U.S. population rely on massive external credit inflows, resulting in ballooning trade deficits. Enforcing the dollar as the global reserve currency has enabled U.S. policymakers to maintain an artificially high level of consumption for the U.S. population, assuaging political unrest amidst deindustrialization and the dismantling of the social wage, while also maintaining record levels of military spending. Whatever growth the U.S. economy has shown since the 1990s has been of a highly parasitic character, making the United States highly vulnerable, both socially and economically.[13]

The immediate effect of the 2008–09 financial crisis was a catastrophic food and agricultural crisis ranging across the global South. The reconsolidation of creditor solvency in the wake of the financial crisis is projected to produce large drops in per capita incomes across the global South. The immiseration of peasant producers in the global South, over 3 billion human beings who constitute almost half of humanity, has reversed gains made over the previous half century, by the policies of newly decolonized nations. In 2006, the food deficit in African countries was close to $9.6 billion, diverting currency resources away from investments in agricultural productivity or the social wage, sharply increasing dependency on food aid from wealthy nations. Amidst these social catastrophes, African nations have been net exporters of capital. Capital flight almost doubled between the 1970s and 1990s, with forty percent of privately held wealth invested outside of Africa in 1990. IMF and World Bank programs have encouraged logging and mining for export, leading to a small number of dangerous jobs, exacerbating deforestation and desertification. Financialization and export-oriented agriculture have intensified mass hunger across the continent. Enforced state divestment produced a social catastrophe of global scale, eroding the legitimacy of newly decolonized states, weakening public sector employment, exacerbating a drain of technical and skilled labor from the South to the North, and from the public to the corporate sectors. This global catastrophe is a corollary of the current regime of international finance capital and its war component.[14]

The internationalization of finance has devastated the countries of the Tricontinent. In Latin America, "the cradle and the experimental laboratory of neoliberalism," successive economic crises led to the deepest continental crisis since the 1930s. Following trade liberalization on the Indian economy in the mid-1990s, a collapse of rural employment affected 70 percent of the Indian population, particularly rural women. Corporations captured land and water through the language of "development." Wages cratered, and with them, average daily calorie intake. The lowest ranks of the rural poor have headed off starvation only by asset liquidation, including land sales. This is the context for mass suicide among Indian farmers. In Africa over the past decade, a renewed process of large-scale land expropriation had resulted in the seizure of a landmass the size of Sweden, to supply food to wealthy consumers.[15]

WEAK LINKS IN THE CHAIN

Two decades after the advent of the so-called "War on Terror," life on earth persists under the shadow of radioactive, chemical, and biological weapons. The United States, Aijaz Ahmad has argued, now operates through a principle of imperial sovereignty, declaring a unilateral right to engage in police action in any part of the world, against any person in the world. On September 18, 2001, the U. S. Congress passed an authorization for the use of military force, with the sole dissenting vote coming from Rep. Barbara Lee, of Oakland. Imperial sovereignty is reactive and reactionary. Warning that the 9 / 11 attacks "continue to pose an unusual and extraordinary threat to the national security and foreign policy of the United States," the law authorized the U.S. president "to use all necessary and appropriate force" against nations, organizations, and individuals deemed to have been involved with the 9 / 11 attacks, as well as to prevent "any future acts of international terrorism against the United States by such nations, organizations, or persons." As Ahmad argued, this all-but-unanimous vote enshrined three principles in a new doctrine of U.S. international relations. First, the U.S. Congress ceded its war powers to the president, who could authorize war against entire nations for attacks committed by individuals or organizations. Second, this potentially includes any nation in the world. Third, this war could be preemptive. The authorization of force solidified collective punishment as a basic article of U.S. imperial policy. It centered the twin motives of quelling local insurgencies and instituting control over the extraction and distribution of critical resources, especially oil and labor. The name for this new global policy: regime replacement.[16]

This is a preemptive mode of power, reacting to ongoing, independent modes of relationship. It manifests in the world, primarily, as a threat of mass destruction. This is the essence of the United States in the world. In 2003, L. Paul Bremer, civilian U.S. proconsul in Iraq, announced, "We are going to fight them and impose our will on them and we will capture or . . . kill them until we have imposed law and order on this country. We dominate the scene and we will continue imposing our will on this country." Bremer spoke of Iraq, but his words reverberate in North America. Imperial sovereignty projects U.S. military control over the planet, while compensating for the relative deficiencies of the real economy in the United States.[17]

The years since the end of World War II are years of major U.S. military defeats. Stalemate on the Korean peninsula. Defeat in Vietnam. More recently, defeat in Afghanistan, where the Taliban currently controls more territory than the U.S. client-state. In Iraq, five months after a hastily announced "victory," U.S. occupation forces faced an average of thirty-five daily attacks, with estimates of U.S. casualties at 7 percent of the total occupation force. By that time, occupation forces could not move freely throughout the country, and their bases of power—including the offices of the U.S. high command—had been hit by major attacks. The political bloc led by Muqtada al-Sadr, who led the insurgency against occupation forces, won the May 2018 Iraqi elections. This military record of defeat, no matter the perennial fascistic squeals about national honor, is no blemish to the historical record of imperial sovereignty. Instead, the motive and method is to disrupt independent modes of relationship. Where the so-called Cold War was a period of imperialist assault against progressive nation-building projects across Africa, Asia, and Latin America, the current phase of "war on terrorism" is a result of an apparent victory. Believing that they have murdered their common enemy, the erstwhile allies of anticommunist reaction are now at each other's throats. Their logic, "with us or against us," poses all democratic and progressive opposition to imperialism as terrorist by definition. Such logic takes spatial form, "apartheid at a global scale," carving the world into green zones and red zones.[18]

The United States and its allies have dismantled the national projects of Afghanistan, Iraq, Sudan, and Libya. Syria and Yemen may be next, and maybe Iran? Each of these countries had a vibrant communist or socialist movement in earlier years. Activists in Latin America speak of the "neoliberalism of war," a deepening of the repressive and authoritarian power of police forces, alongside the criminalization of poverty, and of social movements. Imperial sovereignty involves the transformation of the entire world into Indian country, where the hand of the market is backed by the fist of military power. In the twenty-first-century United States, the real economy is a war economy. More dangerous than defeat to the future of U.S. imperial sovereignty is mutiny and discontent in its vaunted "volunteer" army, with large, multiracial contingents of working class and poor people, including large noncitizen contingents. Such cracks in the armor had already appeared by fall 2004 in Iraq.[19]

In his 2016 letter to shareholders, JP Morgan Chase & Co. CEO Jamie Dimon named deglobalization as one of the corporation's biggest risks. Against intellectual property rights and agricultural subsidies, people's movements seek crucial space to reorient national economies away from commodity exports, to production for the local market, alongside a pluralistic system of international trade regulation, with precedents in the multilateral institutions of the Third World project. Collectively, developing nations have been running an accounts surplus in the major reserve currencies. This is what Julius Nyerere, back in 1990, referred to as "aid from the South." Institutions for circulating surpluses within developing countries, at regional and international levels, could skirt the financial control of the wealthier nations. Moving away from the U.S. dollar as a reserve currency could open space to prioritize investment and growth in poorer countries, rather than consumption in the wealthier ones.[20]

Neoliberal globalization has significantly degraded the food sovereignty of underdeveloped nations. The poorest farmers in Africa, Asia, and Latin America are competing with the largest agricultural corporations in the world, which are in turn backed by enormous state subsidies. Peasant women, who constitute the majority of rural populations around the world, are excluded from the financial sector. In Uganda, for example, women form the majority of those without access to credit, 70 percent of the rural population, and 7 percent of rural landowners. Banks explicitly label poor rural women as "risky borrowers." International lenders tout programs like microfinance, but evidence suggests that such programs often increase poor women's dependence on and vulnerability to male relatives. Samir Amin emphasized that contemporary imperialism manifests through monopolies on natural resources, monopolies of technology (enforced through intellectual property law), and monopolies on weapons of mass destruction. Anti-imperialist struggle in the current moment entails breaking these monopolies. Struggles for Indigenous modes of relationship have a central role to play in this process, breaking the hold of imperialist rent. Imperialism has uprooted millions of peasants and agricultural workers, many of them Indigenous people, from their lands in the South. Cities across the world are primary receiving areas for millions of people expelled from their lands. Indigenous struggles for self-determination in the global North and peasant struggles in the global South both revolve around land relations. Indigenous-led struggles against industrial agriculture, ranching, and extraction articulate alongside the struggles of the urban poor, who are themselves largely constituted of displaced Indigenous people and peasants.[21]

Historically speaking, pure conceptions of bourgeois freedom articulate through hostility to the state, and to organization. Antistatism aligns with the current ruling bloc strategy of deregulation, reducing the role of the state to police functions. This does not suppress the state at all. Instead, it serves to violently suppress mass democratic struggle. In a related way, critiques of "the nation" can encourage "acceptance of the role of the United States as a military superpower and world policeman." Antistatism is the governing logic of imperial sovereignty, providing the tip of the spear for a proto-fascist appeal that dips into statism in moments of historical fascism. A culturalist mode of politics, aligning with the democratic management of diversity, cannot break with the governing logic of imperialist war. Imperialism in the present, as during the high point of nineteenth-century liberalism, rules through defining cultural difference. The U.S. occupation achieved the destruction of the Iraqi national project through calcification of religious, sectarian, and tribal identities.[22]

In Iraq, U.S. occupation rapidly dismantled the institutional and legal structures of the Iraqi state: nationalized oil, state-owned enterprises, key industrial and infrastructure enterprises, an extensive welfare system including education and health subsidies, and workers' rights. It was, Ahmad wrote at the time, "a counterrevolution of private property against state property."

Across the global South, the neoliberal era has been marked by a retreat of the state from rural infrastructure development, for example, on irrigation systems, power supply, roads, bridges, schools, and health clinics. The governing logic assumes that private investments will fulfill these needs more efficiently, but private investments have largely ignored social development infrastructure, and have proliferated privately held kinds of infrastructure, such as tube wells, that have further depleted collective resources and exacerbated scarcity.[23]

TURN THE IMPERIALIST WAR INTO AN ANTICOLONIAL FRONT

Indigenous struggles for self-determination and other contemporary anti-imperialist struggles offer insight into infrastructures that align with and through biological and geological processes, centered on relationships with specific places. Consider, for example, the restoration of taro farms in Hawai'i, of milpas among Mayan farmers in Central America, of rice cultivation in the backwaters of Kerala, and the great advances in urban farming in Cuba. By centering the imperative to decolonize Indigenous places in North America and elsewhere, we might renew the revolutionary slogan "Peace, Land, and Bread" as an urgent infrastructural challenge for collective well-being. Calls and programs of Indigenous self-determination address a related set of circumstances that programs of delinking seek to address in the global South, except these Indigenous nations are surrounded by core states of contemporary imperialism. Ongoing encroachment of Indigenous lands and resources is a historical and structural condition for the renewal of capitalist accumulation. Consider continental imperialism in North America in relationship to continental imperialism in Africa, where countries are being depleted of petroleum, minerals, timber, and rare metals, which have left the continent poorer than it would have been without this emphasis on primary commodity exports. African countries are more marginalized in world trade after globalization and financialization—not because they are insufficiently integrated with the global economy, but because their industrial manufacturing capacities have been steadily dismantled through international aid policies designed to stabilize consumption levels in the North. Vulnerability to the short-term interests of international finance has exacerbated instabilities in these economies.[24]

In the global South, this is a politics of re-enlivening mass popular democracy, and re-enlivening regional linkages, pursued from below. U.S. overconsumption is sustained by maintaining the U.S. dollar as the reserve currency for key international commodities, especially oil. Attempts to assert independence from this regime have spurred economic and military reaction. Saddam Hussein's regime, for example, had increasingly traded Iraq's oil in the euro, enhancing its value as an international currency competing with the U.S. dollar. Muammar Qaddafi had floated the possibility of a common currency in the African Union. Both ended their lives tortured and executed by clients of the United States. The value of money, not any newfound respect for human rights, can better explain the swift transformation of allies into tyrants in what passes for respectable discourse within the echo chambers of U.S. "foreign policy." Such efforts as the Bank of the South and the Bolivarian Alternative potentially represent major advances in recapturing the relations of credit and securitization toward social ends, rather than toward the enrichment and empowerment of a cosmopolitan rentier class, whose power rests on "a great superstructure of nonproductive income claims." Efforts toward regional diplomacy offer the only hope toward drawing down the horrific spread of civilian-targeted war through the eastern Mediterranean, the Great Lakes region of Africa, and Yemen.[25]

We have seen, in North America, a tactical convergence in Indigenous struggles, and Black-led urban struggles of the poor and working class. International finance capital maintains liquidity through flexible accumulation, which it achieves through control over infrastructures of logistics and circulation. In North America, timber, oil, coal, diamonds, and other resources are extracted from Indigenous lands as core contemporary sites of accumulation by encroachment. Major highways and rail lines pass through Indigenous territories. Control over extraction, and over infrastructures of circulation, is at the heart of continental imperialism today. For decades, Indigenous communities in North America have been deploying blockades at strategic sites of extraction and distribution on their lands, to assert their autonomy and self-determination from the settler states that surround them. Blockades have become central tactics to oppose the occupation and capitalization of Indigenous places across the Americas. Since the rise of the Black Lives Matter movement, urban infrastructure has also become a site of tactical blockades, whether key thoroughfares or tourist sites, or airports and highways. These blockades potentially arrest the liquidity, and hence the value, of finance capital.[26]

At the heart of W.E.B. Du Bois's argument in his magisterial *Black Reconstruction,* the coordinated action of enslaved people in the U.S. South pushed the first experiment in world history with a genuine multiracial workers' democracy. This was the world historical achievement of a general strike of the enslaved. A synthesis between urban and rural struggles in North America might build toward a general strike of Indigenous peoples and the urban poor and working class, to transform the war into a multi-front movement towards liberation. This involves renewing basic principles of anticolonial solidarity, a united front of the dispossessed of the North with the working classes, peasants, and Indigenous peoples of the poorer nations, a renewal of organizational principles driven by clear perspectives of distinct classes in coordinated struggle over the means of social reproduction, including peace, bread, and land. At stake is the economic independence, sovereignty, and well-being of the majority of the world's people, the unfinished business of the long struggle for decolonization. What kinds of coordination can develop between Indigenous nations that are reasserting their self-determination, building a base of their flourishing, and the struggles of peasants, workers, and the urban poor, for lives of dignity? What forms of organization can enhance modes of relationship with nonhuman forms of life? What economic models will rapidly address the specific burdens on peasant and poor women's time, land access, health, and social reproductive labor?[27]

At the height of the Second International, Karl Kautsky and other leading figures of the Social Democratic Party of Germany (SPD) developed a thesis of ultra-imperialism, contending that the centralization of capitalism offered the possibility of further development under conditions of peace. Imperialism was the historical precondition for a putative European "peace" hailed by the leading intellects of the Second International. This was a period, Eqbal Ahmad reminds us, when "an estimated 120 million people were killed in the process of colonial expansion and ensuring the safety of the capitalist market." Lenin sharpened his pen against this thesis, drawing out the competition between national financial cartels that did not augur peace, but war on a hitherto unimaginable scale of destructiveness. Hindsight shows that his analysis would prove more accurate than that of Kautsky. The key task for the Left, he argued with Zinoviev, was to turn the imperialist war into a civil war. Turn the war between empires, fielding peasant armies fed at the trough of nationalism, into a civil war between classes, offering workers and peasants a road to self-emancipation.[28]

A half-millennium after the European invasion of the Americas, more than a half-century after the advent of the counterrevolution against anticolonial internationalism, three decades after the transition to the current phase of imperialist war, we are living amidst: runaway climate crisis, the sixth major extinction of species in planetary history, the recurrence of mass famine, the spread of war that deliberately targets civilians, and recrudescent racial, gendered, and religious authoritarianisms. A leading voice on foreign policy from the U. S. ruling party speaks casually about the deaths of tens of millions of people on the Korean peninsula as a price worth paying for the prolongation of an "American way of life." U. S. foreign policy has ramped up the logic of "mutually assured destruction" (first asserted in 1968, amidst global revolutionary upsurge and Soviet nuclear parity), and successive U. S. administrations have prioritized the development of smaller-scale nuclear weapons for first-strike, battlefield capacities. The United States has already littered Fallujah with depleted uranium munitions and novel weaponry, resulting in catastrophic rates of cancer and birth defects. We are living, in other words, in the throes of barbarism. At the start of the First World War, Rosa Luxemburg posed the alternatives for humanity: socialism or barbarism. A century later, decades after the apparent defeat of communism, the choice has seemingly been made.[29]

The rapid growth of a global mass movement against the U. S.-led invasion of Iraq was a historical turning point in the practice of anti-imperialist solidarity. On February 15, 2003, between eight and fifteen million people poured into the streets, following the course of the sun across the earth, to protest a war that had not yet started. At the time, the fear in reigning political circles outside of the United States was that the movement against the war would link with the movement against globalization. It was not to be. In 2018, with many key players in that earlier rush to war back in power, the antiwar movement remains dormant. In the international arena, the record of U. S. military loss, and the limits on its ability to sustain global police operations, alongside increasing inability of the global economy to sustain growth, amidst accelerating financial crises with devastating impacts on the lives of the global majority, open space for strengthening and building more genuinely internationalist institutions. In this moment, Samir Amin argued, "To bring the militarist project of the United States to defeat has become the primary task, the major responsibility, for everyone." The task at hand, in the Americas, Africa, and Asia, is to "abolish the still-present heritage of . . . historic conquest."[30] As Ella Deloria, Sarah Winnemucca, Winona LaDuke, and other anticolonial Indigenous feminists have been warning for several generations: There is no alternative. Decolonization, or mass extinction.

ACKNOWLEDGMENTS

The best things I know of are the result of collective effort. So it is with whatever is good in this book.

I presented portions of this book at the Massachusetts Historical Society, the Humanities Center at Haverford College, the Radcliffe Center at Harvard University, and the annual meetings of the American Studies Association, the Association for Asian American Studies, the Native American and Indigenous Studies Association, and the Organization of American Historians. The engagement of my ideas and arguments shaped their ongoing revision.

In more ways than one, I am an alien in the space of the U.S. academy. Lisa Duggan and Walter Johnson were rigorously defiant graduate school mentors, who continue to influence the ways I teach and write. Vijay Prashad's work is a beacon that orients my understanding of the world. Gary Okihiro has helped me glimpse the future, and anchored me within intellectual lineages that I am proud to claim. Moon-Ho Jung has been a generous mentor since my undergraduate days. A years-long collaboration with Alyosha Goldstein and Juliana Hu Pegues has shaped the trajectory of my work. During a crucial fellowship year in the American Indian Studies program at the University of Illinois, Urbana-Champaign, I found an intellectual home. I continue to grieve the administrative destruction of that home.

Elisabeth Armstrong, Vivek Bald, Sylvia Chan-Malik, Sohail Daulatzai, Iyko Day, Elizabeth Esch, Andrew Friedman, Christina Hanhardt, David Hernandez, Fred Hoxie, Scott Kurashige, Heijin Lee, Danika Medak-Saltzman, Junaid Rana, Chandan Reddy, Neal Salisbury, Dean Saranillio, Naoko Shibusawa, Nikhil Singh, Robert Warrior, and Adam Waterman have provided crucial mentorship, support, and fellowship. Laura Briggs and Lisa Lowe have been particularly generous with their time and support. Sujani Reddy has consistently introduced me to the right idea, at the right time. Paul Bjerk, Jennie Hill, Karlos Hill, Jeffrey Mosher, Emily Skidmore, and above all, Saad abi-Hamad helped me move through a difficult time and place.

I am happy to work at Barnard College. Tina Campt, Elizabeth Castelli, Yvette Christianse, Severin Fowles, Abosede George, Elizabeth Hutchinson, Karl Jacoby, Janet Jakobsen, Rebecca Jordan-Young, Jennie Kassanoff, Brian Larkin, Kathryn McLean, Monica Miller, Premilla Nadasen, Celia Naylor, Mark Nomadiou, Elliot Paul, Alex Pittman, Michelle Rowland, Audra Simpson, and Neferti Tadiar have been generous mentors and colleagues.

Joanne Barker, Jordan Camp, Nick Estes, Severin Fowles, Mishuana Goeman, Christina Heatherton, Moon-Ho Jung, Nikhil Singh, and Neferti Tadiar read and provided comments on the entire manuscript. David Roediger and K-Sue Park read and commented on sections of the manuscript. Roxanne Dunbar-Ortiz read sections of the manuscript, and generously provided time and critique that oriented the direction of the book's overall argument.

I am grateful to Elsa Hoover for her maps, which are brilliant visual narratives that complement the chapters they accompany, and which also contain critiques of those chapters. An attentive reader will not read this book as a closed text, but instead one that propels a critique of itself.

The books in the *American Crossroads* series have shaped my understanding of American Studies and Ethnic Studies. I am proud that this book joins that list. Niels Hooper has been an ideal editor, supporting and facilitating the further development of the argument and visions of this project. Bradley Depew, Emilia Thiuri, and the production team have been excellent to work with.

I have been preparing for decades to work in collaboration with Christina Heatherton and Jordan Camp. Jordan has been my primary sounding board in the last stages of this book. I hope that our collaboration will have a long and impactful future.

Jodi Byrd has been a friend in the deepest sense of that word. The Bae, Kocherry, and Vimalassery families give me an embodied awareness of the intimacies of five continents. I would be lost without the love and support of my parents, as well as Priya, Anand, Amir, Omony, Cristina, Stephan, and Wilson. Diana Yoon knows what it comes down to, better than anyone else I know. Biko: born under a harvest moon, take and enjoy the abundance that is yours. Revel, rebel!

NOTES

PREFACE

1. Cited in H. Craig Miner, *The Corporation and the Indian: Tribal Sovereignty and Industrial Civilization in Indian Territory, 1865–1907* (Norman: University of Oklahoma Press, 1976), 47–48.

2. "Celebration: Completion of the Transcontinental Railroad," *San Francisco Chronicle,* May 9, 1869; "Rivet the Last Pacific Rail!" *New York Tribune,* May 10, 1869; "The Pacific Railroad: Interesting Ceremonies at Promontory Point," *New York Tribune,* May 12, 1869; "East and West: Completion of the Great Line Spanning the Continent," *New York Times,* May 11, 1869; Robert Spude, *Promontory Summit,* May 10, 1869 (National Park Service, 2005).

3. Richard White, *Railroaded: The Transcontinentals and the Making of Modern America* (New York: W. W. Norton, 2011), 37, 227.

4. Elizabeth Cook-Lynn: "my core is, historically speaking, there are no two sides to this history of the United States and its relationship to people who have lived here for thousands of years. There are no two sides to that story. You have no right to displace people, to steal their resources, and steal their lives. No human right, no human being has the right to do that to another human being. That's my core resistance": Nick Estes, "'There Are No Two Sides to This Story': An Interview with Elizabeth Cook-Lynn," *Wicazo Sa Review* 31, no. 1 (2016): 40. Bonita Lawrence, "Rewriting Histories of the Land: Colonization and Indigenous Resistance in Eastern Canada," in *Race, Space, and the Law: Unmapping a White Settler Society,* ed. Sherene Razack (Toronto: Between the Lines, 2002), 26.

5. This is what Joanne Barker refers to as "the polity of the Indigenous," which "is reflected by attention to the unique yet related ethics and responsibilities of gendered and sexed land-based epistemologies, cultural protocols and practices, governance histories and laws, and sociocultural relationships": Joanne Barker, *Critically Sovereign: Indigenous Gender, Sexuality, and Feminist Studies* (Durham, NC: Duke University Press, 2017), Introduction, 5, 7. My framing of "countersovereignty" is meant to displace the United States and Canada as the originary location

of sovereignty. I am mindful of the robust conversation within Native studies on the usefulness and applicability of "sovereignty" to Indigenous decolonization, self-determination, and autonomy. My invocations of "countersovereignty" and "modes of relationship" are in no way meant to question the usefulness and importance of sovereignty discourse for Indigenous peoples to wrest concrete concessions from the colonial states that surround them. "In Indigenous epistemologies, sovereignty means access to well-being for all our citizens. It means being assured of safety (and we cannot ever be sure we are safe)": Patricia Monture, "Women's Words: Power, Identity, and Indigenous Sovereignty," *Canadian Women's Studies* 26, nos. 3–4 (2008): 158. Joanne Barker, *Sovereignty Matters: Locations of Contestation and Possibility in Indigenous Struggles for Self-Determination* (Lincoln: University of Nebraska Press, 2005); Brian Klopotek, *Recognition Odysseys: Indigeneity, Race, and Federal Tribal Recognition Policy in Three Louisiana Communities* (Durham, NC: Duke University Press, 2011); Jean Dennison, *Colonial Entanglement: Constituting a Twenty-First-Century Osage Nation* (Chapel Hill: University of North Carolina Press, 2012); Circe Sturm, "Reflections on the Anthropology of Sovereignty and Settler Colonialism: Lessons from Native North America," *Cultural Anthropology* 32, no. 3 (2017): 340–48. Discussions of Indigenous sovereignty are resonant with calls for renewing national sovereignty in the global South, as a means to extend the unfinished project of decolonization; Sam Moyo and Paris Yeros, "The Fall and Rise of the National Question," in *Reclaiming the Nation: The Return of the National Question in Africa, Asia, and Latin America*, ed. Sam Moyo and Paris Yeros (London: Pluto Press, 2011), 5–6, 19–20. This is also related to what Vijay Prashad defines as "internationalist nationalism," or the Third World form of nationalism; Vijay Prashad, *The Darker Nations: A People's History of the Third World* (New York: New Press, 2007), 12.

6. W. E. B. Du Bois, *Black Reconstruction in America* (New York: Free Press, 1998), 48; Chandan Reddy, *Freedom with Violence: Race, Sexuality, and the U. S. State* (Durham, NC: Duke University Press, 2011), 225; Colleen Bell, *The Freedom of Security: Governing Canada in the Age of Counter-Terrorism* (Vancouver: UBC Press, 2011); Laleh Khalili, *Time in the Shadows: Confinement in Counterinsurgencies* (Stanford, CA: Stanford University Press, 2013); Gerald Horne, *The Counter-Revolution of 1776: Slave Resistance and the Origins of the United States of America* (New York: NYU Press, 2014); Jordan T. Camp, *Incarcerating the Crisis: Freedom Struggles and the Rise of the Neoliberal State* (Oakland: University of California Press, 2016); Patrick Wolfe, *Traces of History: Elementary Structures of Race* (New York: Verso, 2016), 15.

7. Karl Marx, *Grundrisse: Foundations of the Critique of Political Economy* (New York: Penguin, 1973), 99–100; Stuart Hall, "A 'Reading' of Marx's 1857 Introduction to *The Grundrisse*" (Centre for Cultural Studies, University of Birmingham, November / December 1973). Here, I critique understandings of capitalism that toggle between structural abstraction and phenomenological richness, as predefined, separate categories. In a long period of resurgent fascist mass movements and right-wing authoritarian governments, which make revanchist claims about the

richness and specificity of local contexts against the supposedly deracinating (and emasculating) abstractions of the structure, I find such approaches, at best, to offer inept and dull critical tools, and at worst, potential weapons in the hands of fascists. My understanding of modes of relationship proceeds from core insights of materialist feminism and queer critique. As Laura Briggs writes, "we're all engaged in the reproduction of things we value." Laura Briggs, *How All Politics Became Reproductive Politics: From Welfare Reform to Foreclosure to Trump* (Oakland: University of California Press, 2017), 2. See also Macarena Gómez-Barris, *The Extractive Zone: Social Ecologies and Decolonial Perspectives* (Durham, NC: Duke University Press, 2017).

8. Ronald Takaki, *Iron Cages: Race and Culture in Nineteenth-Century America* (New York: Knopf, 1979); Gary Okihiro, *Cane Fires: The Anti-Japanese Movement in Hawaii, 1865–1945* (Philadelphia: Temple University Press, 1991); D. W. Meinig, *The Shaping of America: A Geographical Perspective on 500 Years of History*, vol. 2, *Continental America, 1800–1876* (New Haven, CT: Yale University Press, 1993); Amy Kaplan and Donald Pease, eds., *Cultures of United States Imperialism* (Durham, NC: Duke University Press, 1993); Lisa Lowe, *Immigrant Acts: On Asian American Cultural Politics* (Durham, NC: Duke University Press, 1996); Penny von Eschen, *Race against Empire: Black Americans and Anticolonialism, 1937–1957* (Ithaca, NY: Cornell University Press, 1997); David Palumbo-Liu, *Asian / American: Historical Crossings of a Racial Frontier* (Stanford, CA: Stanford University Press, 1999); Matthew Frye Jacobson, *Barbarian Virtues: The United States Encounters Foreign Peoples at Home and Abroad, 1876–1917* (New York: Hill and Wang, 2000); Julian Go, "Chains of Empire, Projects of State: Political Education and U. S. Colonial Rule in Puerto Rico and the Philippines," *Comparative Studies in Society and History* 42 (2000): 333–62; Peter Onuf, *Jefferson's Empire: The Language of American Nationhood* (Charlottesville: University of Virginia Press, 2000); Amy Kaplan, *The Anarchy of Empire in the Making of U. S. Culture* (Cambridge, MA: Harvard University Press, 2002); Nadia Kim, *Imperial Citizens: Koreans and Race from Seoul to LA* (Stanford, CA: Stanford University Press, 2008); Walter Johnson, *River of Dark Dreams: Slavery and Empire in the Cotton* Kingdom (Cambridge, MA: Harvard University Press, 2013); Nerissa Balce, *Body Parts of Empire: Visual Abjection, Filipino Imagines, and the American Archive* (Ann Arbor: University of Michigan Press, 2016); Sarita See, *The Filipino Primitive: Accumulation and Resistance in the American Museum* (New York: NYU Press, 2017).

9. I am working with a definition of imperialism provided by Amiya Kumar Bagchi: "the persistent tendency of mature capitalist state systems to generate violent conflicts"; Amiya Kumar Bagchi, "Towards a Correct Reading of Lenin's Theory of Imperialism," in *Lenin and Imperialism: An Appraisal of Theories and Contemporary Reality*, ed. Prabhat Patnaik (New Delhi: Orient Longman, 1986), 27. On recovery and the colonial archive, see Saidiya Hartman, "Venus in Two Acts," *small axe* 26 (June 2008); Jodi A. Byrd, "In the City of Blinding Lights," *Cultural Studies Review* 15, no. 2 (2009): 15; Lisa Lowe, "History Hesitant," *Social Text* 13, no. 4 (2015); Reddy, *Freedom with Violence*, 17, 223.

10. "The tendency of European civilization through capitalism was thus not to homogenize but to differentiate—to exaggerate regional, subcultural, and dialectical differences into 'racial' ones": Cedric Robinson, *Black Marxism: The Making of the Black Radical Tradition* (Chapel Hill: University of North Carolina Press, 2000), 26.

11. Hortense Spillers, "Mama's Baby, Papa's Maybe: An American Grammar Book," *diacritics* (Summer 1987): 70.

12. Lisa Lowe, *The Intimacies of Four Continents* (Durham, NC: Duke University Press, 2015), 21; Jodi A. Byrd, " 'Do They Not Have Rational Souls?': Consolidation and Sovereignty in Digital New Worlds," *Settler Colonial Studies* 6, no. 4 (2016): 426.

CHAPTER ONE

1. Charles Crocker to Collis Huntington, June 15, 1868, *Collis Huntington Papers*.

2. J. P. Usher to William Fessenden, February 11, 1865, *Letters Sent by the Land and Railroad Division of the Office of the Secretary of the Interior, 1849–1904*, NARA Record Group 48.

3. Lalla Scott, *Karnee: A Paiute Narrative* (Reno: University of Nevada Press, 1966), 34.

4. Ranajit Guha, "The Prose of Counter-Insurgency," in *Selected Subaltern Studies*, ed. Ranajit Guha and Gayatri Chakravorty Spivak (New York: Oxford University Press, 1988), 69.

5. Luise White, *Speaking with Vampires: Rumor and History in Colonial Africa* (Berkeley: University of California Press, 2000), 210.

6. Ibid., 5–6, 10.

7. Ibid., 70–86.

8. For example, see Laurent DuBois, *A Colony of Citizens: Revolution and Slave Emancipation in the French Caribbean, 1787–1804* (Chapel Hill: University of North Carolina Press, 2004), 88–92, 105.

9. Colonialism was a significant factor in the history of rumors in imperial epicenters, as well; Arlette Farge and Jacques Revel, *The Vanishing Children of Paris: Rumor and Politics before the French Revolution* (Cambridge, MA: Harvard University Press, 1991), 30–33, 95.

10. Guha, "Prose of Counter-Insurgency," 69.

11. Ibid., 48.

12. John M. Coward, *The Newspaper Indian: Native American Identity in the Press, 1820–90* (Urbana: University of Illinois Press, 1999), 45–62.

13. Terry Ann Knopf, *Rumors, Race and Riots* (New Brunswick, NJ: Transaction Books, 1975), 81–82.

14. Ibid., 161.

15. Ibid., 164.

16. Tamotsu Shibutani, *Improvised News: A Sociological Study of Rumor* (Indianapolis: Bobbs-Merrill, 1966), 13–14.

17. Guha, "Prose of Counter-Insurgency," 61.

18. Gary Fine and Patricia Turner, *Whispers on the Color Line: Rumor and Race in America* (Berkeley: University of California Press, 2001), 57.

19. Ralph Rosnow and Gary Fine, *Rumor and Gossip: The Social Psychology of Hearsay* (New York: Elsevier, 1976), 4.

20. Shibutani, *Improvised News*, 17.

21. Knopf, *Rumors, Race and Riots*, 108.

22. Ibid., 8.

23. Rosnow and Fine, *Rumor and Gossip*, 24–29.

24. Knopf, *Rumors, Race and Riots*, 159–60.

25. Shibutani, *Improvised News*, 21–22.

26. On rumor and standards of evidence, see Knopf, *Rumors, Race and Riots*, 2–3.

27. Guha, "Prose of Counter-Insurgency," 51.

28. Rosnow and Fine, *Rumor and Gossip*, 11.

29. Shibutani, *Improvised News*, 73.

30. Rosnow and Fine, *Rumor and Gossip*, 1, 77–78. On the role of rumor in the rapid development of extractive economies, see Anna Tsing, *Friction: An Ethnography of Global Connection* (Princeton, NJ: Princeton University Press, 2005).

31. Martha C. Knack and Omer C. Stewart, *As Long as the River Shall Run* (Berkeley: University of California Press, 1984), 45.

32. Ibid., 46.

33. Ibid., 46–47.

34. Isabel T. Kelly, *Southern Paiute Ethnography,* Anthropological Papers, Department of Anthropology, University of Utah, Number 69 (Glen Canyon Series Number 21), May 1964, pp. 22, 43.

35. *Records of the Nevada Superintendency of Indian Affairs, 1869–1870,* NARA Record Group 75.

36. Knack and Stewart, *River Shall Run*, 90.

37. On these types of agreements, and their questionable legality, see Vine Deloria, Jr., and Raymond J. DeMallie, *Documents of American Indian Diplomacy: Treaties, Agreements, and Conventions, 1775–1979,* vol. 1 (Norman: University of Oklahoma Press, 1999), 514–17.

38. Knack and Stewart, *River Shall Run*, 103; *Numa: A Northern Paiute History* (Reno: Inter-Tribal Council of Nevada, 1976), 70.

39. C. A. Bateman to F. A. Walker, Wadsworth, Nevada, February 17, 1872, March 28, 1872, *Letters Received by the Office of Indian Affairs, 1824–1880,* NARA Record Group 75.

40. Alexander Saxton, "The Army of Canton in the High Sierra," *Pacific Historical Review* 35, no. 2 (1966): 141–52; William F. Chew, *Nameless Builders of the Transcontinental Railroad: The Chinese Workers of the Central Pacific Railroad* (Victoria: Trafford, 2004).

41. In her book, Winnemucca also recorded a story of a conflict between Paiutes and a neighboring tribe of cannibals, in distant memory; Sarah Winnemucca, *Life among the Piutes: Their Wrongs and Claims* (New York: Putnam, 1883), 12, 73–75. James Downs, *Two Worlds of the Washo* (New York: Holt, Rinehart, and Winston, 1966), 73; Knack and Stewart, *River Shall Run*, 42.

42. These types of rumors may have arisen from a familiar cultural repertoire. Barend Ter Haar analyzed rumors and prophecies that circulated in nineteenth-century southern China that described cannibalism; Barend J. Ter Haar, *Telling Stories: Witchcraft and Scapegoating in Chinese History* (Leiden: Brill, 2006), 92–93, 157.

43. Brooke S. Arkush, *The Archaeology of CA-Mno-2122: A Study of Pre-Contact and Post-Contact Lifeways among the Mono Basin Paiute* (Berkeley: University of California Press, 1995), 41.

44. Michael Givens, *The Archaeology of the Colonized* (London: Routledge, 2004).

45. H. Martin Wobst, "Power to the (Indigenous) Past and Present! Or: The Theory and Method behind Archaeological Theory and Method," in *Indigenous Archaeologies: Decolonizing Theory and Practice,* ed. Claire Smith and H . Martin Wobst (New York: Routledge, 2005), 18–23.

46. Ranajit Guha, *History at the Limits of World-History* (New York: Columbia University Press, 2002), 12.

47. *Numa,* 54. See also Edward C. Johnson, *Walker River Paiutes: A Tribal History* (Schurz, NV: Walker River Paiute Tribe, 1975), 89–93. Johnson discussed interactions between Walker River Paiutes and the Chinese merchants who followed the Carson and Colorado Railroad and sold opium and alcohol.

48. Pat and Bob Ferraro, *The Past in Glass* (Sparks, NV: Western Printing, 1964), 71.

49. On Chinese medicine in the United States, see Stewart Culin, "The Chinese Drug Stores in America," *American Journal of Pharmacy* 59 (1887). On Paiute medicine, see Beatrice Blyth Whiting, *Paiute Sorcery* (New York: Viking Fund Publications in Anthropology, No. 15, 1950), 27.

50. Knack and Stewart, *River Shall Run*, 101–2.

51. *Numa,* 52.

52. Mary McNair Mathews, *Ten Years in Nevada or Life on the Pacific Coast* (Lincoln: University of Nebraska Press, [1880] 1985), 291.

53. John Taylor Waldorf, *A Kid on the Comstock* (Berkeley: Friends of the Bancroft Library, 1968), 37.

54. Lalla Scott provides an account of this type of story, from the perspective of a Paiute girl, who joins a group of white children in eating food from a Chinese gravesite. In her telling, this episode highlights examples of racial differences between the Paiute girl and her white companions. Scott, *Karnee*, 48–50.

55. Vincent Brown, *The Reaper's Garden: Death and Power in the World of Atlantic Slavery* (Cambridge, MA: Harvard University Press, 2008), 59, 69–70.

56. *Numa,* 41.

57. Dan De Quille, *The Big Bonanza: An Authentic Account of the Discovery, History, and Working of the World-Renowned Comstock Lode of Nevada* (New York: Thomas Crowell, 1947), 11, 40.

58. Kalpana Shesadri-Crooks, *Desiring Whiteness: A Lacanian Analysis of Race* (London: Routledge, 2000), 101–2.

59. Russell M. Maghnaghi, "Virginia City's Chinese Community, 1860–1880," in *Chinese on the American Frontier,* ed. Arif Dirlik (Lanham: Rowman & Littlefield, 2001), 142.

60. *Numa,* 69.

61. For example, see John How, R. E. Trowbridge, Western Shoshone Agency, Elko, Nevada, May 26, 1880, NARA Record Group 75.

62. Waldorf, *Kid on the Comstock,* 35.

63. James Nye to J. P. Usher, Carson City, Territory of Nevada, August 22, 1863, *Selected Classes of Letters Received by the Indian Division of the Office of the Secretary of the Interior, 1849–1880,* NARA Record Group 48.

64. Amos Dallam, letter to Mark Hopkins, December 14, 1869, *Mark Hopkins Papers.*

65. Emil Billeb, *Mining Camp Days* (Berkeley: Howell-North Books, 1968), 128; De Quille, *Big Bonanza,* 179, 196.

66. T. T. Dwight to S. F. Bogy, Carson City, Nevada, January 9, 1866, *Letters Received by the Office of Indian Affairs, 1824–1880,* NARA Record Group 75.

67. Joseph Wilson to N. G. Taylor, June 16, 1868, *Letters Received by the Office of Indian Affairs, 1824–1880,* NARA Record Group 75.

68. U.S. Indian Inspector Report to Commissioner of Indian Affairs, San Francisco, June 11, 1875, *Letters Received by the Office of Indian Affairs, 1824–1880,* NARA Record Group 75.

69. E. H. Derby, *The Overland Route to the Pacific: A Report on the Condition, Capacity and Resources of the Union Pacific and Central Pacific Railways* (Boston: Lee & Shepard, 1869), 74.

70. John Kincaid to Carl Schurz, February 2, 1880, *Letters Received by the Office of Indian Affairs, 1824–1880,* NARA Record Group 75.

71. James Spencer to R. E. Trowbridge, Nevada Agency, Pyramid Lake Reservation, July 13, 1880, *Letters Received by the Office of Indian Affairs, 1824–1880,* NARA Record Group 75.

72. James Spencer to R. E. Trowbridge, Nevada Agency, Pyramid Lake Reservation, May 26, 1880, *Letters Received by the Office of Indian Affairs, 1824–1880,* NARA Record Group 75.

73. De Quille, *Big Bonanza,* 291; Waldorf, *Kid on the Comstock,* 22; Mathews, *Ten Years in Nevada,* 224–25.

74. Billeb, *Mining Camp Days,* 119–20, 131.

75. H. G. Parker to D. W. Cooley, Carson City, Nevada, April 10, 1866, *Letters Received by the Office of Indian Affairs, 1824–1880,* NARA Record Group 75.

76. Knack and Stewart, *River Shall Run,* 47.

77. Mathews, *Ten Years in Nevada,* 287.

78. De Quille, *Big Bonanza*, 291.

79. Emil Billeb relays the story of one Chinese cook who fed himself and his "Indian friends" the steaks, roasts, and varieties of meats sent to the boardinghouse where he worked, and fed the boarders stews supplemented with chipmunk meat; Billeb, *Mining Camp Days*, 123. Mary Mathews complained of the "filthy China cooks" in most restaurants in Virginia City; Mathews, *Ten Years in Nevada*, 171, 251.

80. Mathews, *Ten Years in Nevada*, 54, 252–55.

81. Ibid., 180.

82. John Higham, *Strangers in the Land: Patterns of American Nativism, 1860–1925* (New York: Atheneum, 1963), 9.

83. See *Collis Huntington Papers*, Series 4.

84. Billeb, *Mining Camp Days*, 205–6.

85. Sharon Holland, *Raising the Dead: Readings of Death and (Black) Subjectivity* (Durham, NC: Duke University Press, 2000), 74.

CHAPTER TWO

1. "... capital is not a thing, it is a definite social relation of production pertaining to a particular historical social formation, which simply takes the form of a thing and gives this thing a specific social character": Karl Marx, *Capital, Vol. 3* (New York: Penguin, 1993), 953; Karl Marx, *Capital, Vol. 1* (New York: Penguin, 1992), 932.

2. Karl Marx, *The Poverty of Philosophy* (New York: International, 1963), 78, 80–81; Karl Marx, *A Contribution to the Critique of Political Economy* (New York: International, 1970); Marx, *Capital, Vol. 3*, 953–54. See also E. Richard Atleo, *Principles of Tsawalk: An Indigenous Approach to Global Crisis* (Vancouver: UBC Press, 2011).

3. Ella Deloria, *Waterlily* (Omaha: University of Nebraska Press, 2009), 6, 9; Paula Gunn Allen, *The Sacred Hoop: Recovering the Feminine in American Indian Traditions* (Boston: Beacon Press, 1986), 119; Simon Ortiz, "Introduction: Wah Nuhtyuh-yuu Dyu Neetah Tyahstih (Now It Is My Turn to Stand)," in *Speaking for the Generations: Native Writers on Writing*, ed. Simon Ortiz (Tucson: University of Arizona Press, 1998), xii–xiii, xvii–xviii; Mishuana Goeman, "From Place to Territories and Back Again: Centering Storied Land in the Discussion of Indigenous Nation-Building," *International Journal of Critical Indigenous Studies* 1, no. 1 (2008): 24; Mishuana Goeman, *Mark My Words: Native Women Mapping Our Nations* (Minneapolis: University of Minnesota Press, 2013), 28; Soren C. Larsen and Jay T. Johnson, *Being Together in Place: Indigenous Coexistence in a More Than Human World* (Minneapolis: University of Minnesota Press, 2017); Shiri Pasternak, *Grounded Authority: The Algonquins of Barriere Lake against the State* (Minneapolis: University of Minnesota Press, 2017), 81–88. "Property moves in this fluid direction, through water, through people, through animals, through relationships produced not by the flows of capital, but by responsibility": Audra Simpson, " 'Tell

Me Why, Why, Why': A Critical Commentary on the Visuality of Settler Expectation," *Visual Anthropology Review* 34, no. 1 (2018): 62.

4. Deloria, *Waterlily*, 54–57, 200; Goeman, *Mark My Words*, 84.

5. Deloria, *Waterlily*, 5; Allen, *Sacred Hoop*, 24.

6. Deloria, *Waterlily*, 8, 11; Ella Deloria, *Buffalo People* (Albuquerque: University of New Mexico Press, 1994), 47–49; Jodi A. Byrd, *The Transit of Empire: Indigenous Critiques of Colonialism* (Minneapolis: University of Minnesota Press, 2011), chap. 3.

7. Deloria, *Waterlily*, 20, 158; Ella Deloria, *Iron Hawk* (Albuquerque: University of New Mexico Press, 1993), 122, 139; Allen, *Sacred Hoop*, 49–50; María Eugenia Cotera, *Native Speakers: Ella Deloria, Zora Neale Hurston, Jovita González, and the Poetics of Culture* (Austin: University of Texas Press, 2008), 161–62.

8. Deloria, *Waterlily*, 6–7, 11, 60, 162. On Deloria's "kinship" as a critique of "domesticity," which drove allotment policy, see Mark Rifkin, *When Did Indians Become Straight?: Kinship, the History of Sexuality, and Native Sovereignty* (New York: Oxford University Press, 2011), chap. 4. For the centrality of kinship to Deloria's ethnographic method, and ethnographic critique, see Cotera, *Native Speakers*, 59.

9. Deloria, *Waterlily*, 190. "Ella Deloria was one of those people, instead of, 'I never met a man that I didn't like,' well, she never met a person she wasn't related to, related to her in some way!" Joyzelle Gingway Godfrey and Susan Gardner, "Speaking of Ella Deloria: Conversations with Joyzelle Gingway Godfrey, 1998–2000, Lower Brule Community College, South Dakota," *American Indian Quarterly* 24, no. 3 (Summer 2000): 458–59.

10. Deloria, *Iron Hawk*, 108; Deloria, *Waterlily*, 61–62, 128, 166; Sarah Hunt, "Ontologies of Indigeneity: The Politics of Embodying a Concept," *Cultural Geographies* 21 (2014): 27; Leanne Simpson, *As We Have Always Done: Indigenous Freedom through Radical Resurgence* (Minneapolis: University of Minnesota Press, 2017), 3, 29–30, 33.

11. Deloria, *Waterlily*, 14, 36, 70–73.

12. Ibid., 52, 64, 79–80, 142, 192–94.

13. On labor as "creative process," see Deloria, *Iron Hawk*, 110–11; Deloria, *Waterlily*, 222–23, 226; Patrick Wolfe, *Traces of History: Elementary Structures of Race* (New York: Verso, 2016), 22–23; Carol Williams, ed., *Indigenous Women and Work: From Labor to Activism* (Urbana: University of Illinois Press, 2012).

14. Deloria, *Waterlily*, 103–4, 189; Allen, *Sacred Hoop*, 39–40, 216–17; C. L. R. James, *Modern Politics* (Oakland: PM Press, 2013), 52–54.

15. Deloria, *Waterlily*, 168.

16. Winnemucca, *Life among the Piutes*, 13, 43–44, 59.

17. Ibid., 10–11, 15; Leslie Marmon Silko, "Interior and Exterior Landscapes," in Ortiz, *Speaking for the Generations*, 16; Margo Lukens, "Her 'Wrongs and Claims': Sarah Winnemucca's Strategic Narratives of Abuse," *Wicazo Sa Review* 13, no. 1 (Spring 1998): 101.

18. Winnemucca, *Life among the Piutes*, 12, 14, 34, 37; Sarah Deer, *The Beginning and End of Race: Confronting Sexual Violence in Native America* (Minneapolis: University of Minnesota Press, 2015), 112.

19. Winnemucca, *Life among the Piutes*, 41.

20. Ibid., 18, 28, 77–78.

21. Ibid., 133–34; David Harvey, *The Limits to Capital* (New York: Verso, 1999), chap. 13; Goeman, *Mark My Words*, 30–31; Audra Simpson, "Consent's Revenge," *Cultural Anthropology* 31, no. 3 (2016): 330; Robert Nichols, "Theft Is Property! The Recursive Logic of Dispossession," *Political Theory* 46, no. 1 (2018): 3–28.

22. Winnemucca, *Life among the Piutes*, 10, 15, 137, 214.

23. Ibid., 9, 21, 27, 48, 76–77; William J. Bauer Jr., *We Were All Like Migrant Workers Here: Work, Community, and Memory on California's Round Valley Reservation, 1850–1941* (Chapel Hill: University of North Carolina Press, 2009).

24. Winnemucca, *Life among the Piutes*, 38–40, 213.

25. Ibid., 86–88, 94–99.

26. Ibid., 11–12, 244; Aileen Moreton-Robinson, *The White Possessive: Property, Power, and Indigenous Sovereignty* (Minneapolis: University of Minnesota Press, 2015), 11–15; Dian Million, "Felt Theory: An Indigenous Feminist Approach to Affect and History," *Wicazo Sa Review* 24, no. 2 (2009): 54; Sarah Hunt and Cindy Holmes, "Everyday Decolonization: Living a Decolonizing Queer Politics," *Journal of Lesbian Studies* (2015): 154–72.

27. Winona LaDuke, *All Our Relations: Native Struggles for Land and Life* (Chicago: Haymarket Books, 2015), 2, 11, 140; Allen, *Sacred Hoop*, 59–60; Jack D. Forbes, "Indigenous Americans: Spirituality and Ecos," *Daedalus* 130, no. 4 (2001): 283–300; Neferti X. M. Tadiar, *Things Fall Away: Philippine Historical Experience and the Makings of Globalization* (Durham, NC: Duke University Press, 2009), 13–14; Jonathan Goldberg-Hiller and Noenoe K. Silva, "Sharks and Pigs: Animating Hawaiian Sovereignty against the Anthropological Machine," *South Atlantic Quarterly* 110, no. 2 (2011): 431, 435–37, 439, 441; Jennifer Nez Denetdale, "Planting Seeds of Ideas and Raising Doubts about What We Believe: An Interview with Vine Deloria, Jr.," *Journal of Social Archaeology* 42, no. 2 (2004): 142–43; Robert Allen Warrior, "Canaanites, Cowboys, and Indians: Deliverance, Conquest, and Liberation Theology Today," *Christianity and Crisis* 49, no. 12 (1989): 261–65.

28. LaDuke, *All Our Relations*, 148, 159; Stephen C. Torbit and Louis LaRose, "A Commentary on Bison and Cultural Restoration: Partnership between the National Wildlife Federation and the Intertribal Bison Cooperative," *Great Plains Research* 11, no. 1 (2001): 175–82.

29. LaDuke, *All Our Relations*, 1, 143, 154.

30. Ibid., 146.

31. Ibid., 49, 140, 151–52; Goeman, "Ongoing Storms and Struggles: Gendered Violence and Resource Exploitation," in *Critically Sovereign*, ed. Barker, 100; Goeman, *Mark My Words*, 32–34; Ken Zontek, *Buffalo Nation: American Indian Efforts to Restore the Bison* (Lincoln: University of Nebraska Press, 2007); María Josefina Saldaña-Portillo, *Indian Given: Racial Geographies across Mexico and the United*

States (Durham, NC: Duke University Press, 2016), 114. Kancha Ilaiah centered relations with water buffalo as a core of a Dalit mode of relationship; Kancha Ilaiah, *Buffalo Nationalism: A Critique of Spiritual Fascism* (Kolkata: Samya, 2004); Henri Lefebvre, *The Production of Space* (Malden, MA: Blackwell, 1991); William Connolly, "Tocqueville, Territory, and Violence," *Theory, Culture, and Society* 11, no. 1 (1994): 24; Saskia Sassen, "Territory and Territoriality in the Global Economy," *International Sociology* 15, no. 2 (2000): 372–93; Mark Neocleous, "Off the Map: On Violence and Cartography," *European Journal of Social Theory* 6, no. 4 (2003): 409–25; Audra Simpson, "From Place to Territories and Back Again: Centering Storied Land in the Discussion of Indigenous Nation-Building," *International Journal of Critical Indigenous Studies* 1, no. 1 (2008): 23; Stuart Elden, *Terror and Territory: The Spatial Extent of Sovereignty* (Minneapolis: University of Minnesota Press, 2009), xxviii–xxix; Saskia Sassen, "When Territory Deborders Territoriality," *Territory, Politics, Governance* 1, no. 1 (2013): 21–45; Alyosha Goldstein, "Introduction," in *Formations of United States Colonialism,* ed. Alyosha Goldstein (Durham, NC: Duke University Press, 2014), 17; Joanne Barker, "Territory as Analytic: The Dispossession of Lenapehoking and the Subprime Crisis," *Social Text* 36, no. 2 (2018): 19–39.

32. Brian Larkin, *Signal and Noise: Media, Infrastructure, and Urban Culture in Nigeria* (Durham, NC: Duke University Press, 2008), 6; Andre Lakoff and Stephen J. Collier, "Infrastructure and Event: The Political Technology of Preparedness," in *Political Matter: Technoscience, Democracy, and Public Life,* ed. Bruce Braun and Sarah Whatmore (Minneapolis: University of Minnesota Press, 2010); Patrick Carroll, *Science, Culture, and Modern State Formation* (Berkeley: University of California Press, 2006), 25, chap. 6; Stephen Graham, ed., *Disrupted Cities: When Infrastructure Fails* (New York: Routledge Press, 2010); Michelle Murphy, *The Economization of Life* (Durham, NC: Duke University Press, 2017).

33. LaDuke, *All Our Relations,* 3, 61, 65, 66.

34. Ibid., 88, 97, 189. Brent Ashabranner, *Morning Star, Black Sun: The Northern Cheyenne Indians and America's Energy Crisis* (New York: Dodd, Mead, 1982); Gregory R. Campbell, "Northern Cheyenne Ethnicity, Religion, and Coal Development," *Plains Anthropologist* 32, no. 118 (1987): 378–88; Rosemary Brown, "The Exploitation of the Oil and Gas Frontier: Its Impact on Lubicon Lake Cree Women," in *Women of the First Nations: Power, Wisdom, and Strength,* ed. Christine Miller and Patricia Chuchryk (Winnipeg: University of Manitoba Press, 1996); Danielle Endres, "Animist Intersubjectivity as Argumentation: Western Shoshone and Southern Paiute Arguments against a Nuclear Waste Site at Yucca Mountain," *Argumentation* 27, no. 2 (2013): 183–200; Andrew Needham, *Power Lines: Phoenix and the Making of the Modern Southwest* (Princeton, NJ: Princeton University Press, 2014); Traci Brynne Voiles, *Wastelanding: Legacies of Uranium Mining in Navajo Country* (Minneapolis: University of Minnesota Press, 2015).

35. LaDuke, *All Our Relations,* 147; Elizabeth Woody, "Voice of the Land," in Ortiz, *Speaking for the Generations,* 167; John Opie, *Ogallala: Water for a Dry Land* (Lincoln: University of Nebraska Press, 2000); Peter J. Longo and David W.

Yoskowitz, eds., *Water on the Great Plains: Issues and Resources* (Lubbock: Texas Tech University Press, 2002); "Ogallala Aquifer Depleted by Drought," *Water Technology News,* March 1, 2003; Jadwiga R. Ziolkowska, "Shadow Price of Water for Irrigation: A Case of the High Plains," *Agricultural Water Management* 153, no. 1 (2015): 20–31.

36. LaDuke, *All Our Relations,* 2, 141; David D. Smits, "The Frontier Army and the Destruction of the Buffalo, 1865–1883," *Western Historical Quarterly* 25, no. 3 (1994): 312–38.

37. LaDuke, *All Our Relations,* 119–21; Woody, "Voice of the Land," 160–61; Melissa L. Meyer, *The White Earth Tragedy: Ethnicity and Dispossession at a Minnesota Anishinaabe Reservation, 1889–1920* (Lincoln: University of Nebraska Press, 1994); Judith A. Boughter, *Betraying the Omaha Nation, 1790–1916* (Norman: University of Oklahoma Press, 1998), chap. 6; K-Sue Park, "Money, Mortgages, and the Conquest of America," *Law & Social Inquiry* 41, no. 4 (Fall 2016).

38. LaDuke, *All Our Relations,* 142; Shaun Milton, "The Transvaal Beef Frontier: Environment, Markets, and the Ideology of Development 1902–1942," in *Ecology and Empire: Environmental History of Settler Societies,* ed. Tom Griffiths and Libby Ronin (Seattle: University of Washington Press, 1997); Ian MacLachlan, *Kill and Chill: Restructuring Canada's Beef Commodity Chain* (Toronto: University of Toronto Press, 2001); Nathan B. Sanderson, "We Were All Trespassers: George Edward Lemmon, Anglo-American Cattle Ranching, and the Great Sioux Reservation," *Agricultural History* 85, no. 1 (2011): 50–71.

39. LaDuke, *All Our Relations,* 5, 11–12, 54–55, 57, 78, 81, 190, 197–99; Robert A. Williams, *The American Indian in Western Legal Thought: The Discourses of Conquest* (New York: Oxford University Press, 1990); Robert Nichols, "Disaggregating Primitive Accumulation," *Radical Philosophy* 194 (2015): 23.

40. The struggle in Nitassinan subsequently turned to damming and hydropower. Annette Lutterman, "Draining Energy from the Innu of Nitassinan," *Cultural Survival Quarterly* 24, no. 2 (2000): 34; Stephen Loring, Moira T. McCaffrey, Peter Armitage, and Daniel Ashini, "The Archaeology and Ethnohistory of a Drowned Land: Innu Nation Research along the Former Michikamits Lake Shore in Nitassinan (Interior Labrador)," *Archaeology of Eastern North America* 31 (2003): 45–72; Winona LaDuke, *The Militarization of Indian Country* (East Lansing: Michigan State University Press, 2013); Glen Coulthard, *Red Skin, White Masks: Rejecting the Colonial Politics of Recognition* (Minneapolis: University of Minnesota Press, 2014), 117–67.

41. LaDuke, *All Our Relations,* 21, 63, 70. Leanne Simpson presented Indigenous internationalism as a series of relationships not only between human communities, but also including nonhuman forms and processes of life; Simpson, *As We Have Always Done,* 35, 56–70.

42. LaDuke, *All Our Relations,* 127–30, 139, 190; Allen, *Sacred Hoop,* 190, 214; Jennifer Nez Denetdale, "Chairmen, Presidents, and Princesses: The Navajo Nation, Gender, and the Politics of Tradition," *Wicazo Sa Review* 21, no. 1 (2006): 10; Katsi Cook, "Powerful Like a River: Reweaving the Web of Our Lives in Defense

of Environmental and Reproductive Justice," in *Original Instructions: Indigenous Teaching for a Sustainable Future,* ed. Melissa K. Nelson (Rochester: Bear, 2008); Rauna Kuokkanen, "Indigenous Economies, Theories of Subsistence, and Women: Exploring the Social Economy Model for Indigenous Governance," *American Indian Quarterly* 35, no. 2 (2011): 232–33; Amanda Morris, "Twenty-First-Century Debt Collectors: Idle No More Combats a Five-Hundred-Year-Old Debt," *Women's Studies Quarterly* 42, nos. 1–2 (2014): 245; Roxanne Dunbar-Ortiz, *An Indigenous Peoples' History of the United States* (Boston: Beacon Press, 2014), 10; Nefert X. M. Tadiar, "Decolonization, 'Race,' and Remaindered Life under Empire," *Qui Parle* 23, no. 2 (2015): 151; Elizabeth Hoover, *The River Is in Us: Fighting Toxics in a Mohawk Community* (Minneapolis: University of Minnesota Press, 2017); Simpson, *As We Have Always Done,* 72–73.

CHAPTER THREE

1. "The revolution in transport is a milestone in the history of capital exports." Rudolph Hilferding, *Finance Capital: A Study in the Latest Phase of Capitalist Development* (London: Routledge, 2006), 323; Daniel Headrick, *The Tentacles of Progress: Technology Transfer in the Age of Imperialism, 1850–1940* (New York: Oxford University Press, 1988), 4; Laura Bear, *Lines of the Nation: Indian Railway Workers, Bureaucracy, and the Intimate Historical Self* (New York: Columbia University Press, 2007), 3; Marian Aguiar, *Tracking Modernity: India's Railway and the Culture of Mobility* (Minneapolis: University of Minnesota Press, 2011), 11.

2. Donald Fraser, *"Katy": Pioneer Railroad of the Southwest!: 1865* (New York: Newcomen Society, 1953), 10; L. H. Gann and Peter Duignan, *The Rulers of British Africa: 1870–1914* (Stanford, CA: Stanford University Press, 1978), 286–87; Marc Linder, *Projecting Capitalism: A History of the Internationalization of the Construction Industry* (Westport, CT: Greenwood Press, 1994), 48–49, 62; Headrick, *Tentacles of Progress,* 259; Amarjit Kaur, *Bridge and Barrier: Transport and Communications in Colonial Malaya, 1870–1957* (New York: Oxford University Press, 1975); Kenneth Pomeranz, *The Great Divergence: China, Europe, and the Making of the Modern World Economy* (Princeton, NJ: Princeton University Press, 2000), 182–83.

3. Lowe, *The Intimacies of Four Continents,* 107; Linder, *Projecting Capitalism,* 47, 51, 84, 96–97; Daniel Headrick, *The Tools of Empire: Technology and European Imperialism in the Nineteenth Century* (New York: Oxford University Press, 1981), 186–87.

4. Walter Rodney, *How Europe Underdeveloped Africa* (Baltimore: Black Classic Press, 1972), 166–67; Crawford Young, *The African Colonial State in Comparative Perspective* (New Haven, CT: Yale University Press, 1994), 174; Headrick, *Tentacles of Progress,* 323–25; Linder, *Projecting Capitalism,* 15–17, 31, 61.

5. Linder, *Projecting Capitalism,* 61; Werner Biermann, *Tanganyika Railways—Carrier of Colonialism: An Account of Economic Indicators and Social Fragments* (Münster: Lit Verlag, 1995), 3, 6–7; Gann and Duignan, *Rulers of British Africa,*

283; David Roediger and Elizabeth Esch, *The Production of Difference: Race and the Management of Labor in U. S. History* (New York: Oxford University Press, 2012).

6. Ronald E. Robinson, "Introduction: Railway Imperialism," in *Railway Imperialism,* ed. Clarence B. Davis and Kenneth E. Wilburn, Jr. (New York: Greenwood Press, 1991), 3.

7. John Stover, *American Railroads* (Chicago: University of Chicago Press, 1961), 2, 61–62.

8. Charles O'Connell, Jr., "The Corps of Engineers and the Rise of Modern Management, 1827–1856," in *Military Enterprise and Technological Change: Perspectives on the American Experience,* ed. Merrit Roe Smith (London: MIT Press, 1985); James A. Ward, *Railroads and the Character of America, 1820–1887* (Knoxville: University of Tennessee Press, 1986), 41–42, 81–82; Robert G. Angevine, *The Railroad and the State: War, Politics, and Technology in Nineteenth-Century America* (Stanford, CA: Stanford University Press, 2004), xiv, 41–42, 64–67, 89, 91, 111–12; Aaron W. Marrs, *Railroads in the Old South: Pursuing Progress in a Slave Society* (Baltimore: Johns Hopkins University Press, 2009), 31–32. I have written about preemption in Manu Karuka [as Manu Vimalassery], "Counter-Sovereignty," *J19* 2, no. 1 (2014): 142–48.

9. Aruna Awasthi, *History and Development of Railways in India* (New Delhi: Deep & Deep, 1994), 17–18, 48, 58, 121–23, 156–57; M. A. Rao, *Indian Railways* (New Delhi: National Book Trust, 1975), 21–22, 45–46; J. A. Hobson, *Imperialism: A Study* (Ann Arbor: University of Michigan Press, 1965), 49; Manu Goswami, *Producing India: From Colonial Economy to National Space* (Chicago: University of Chicago Press, 2004), 47–49; Damien Bailey and John McGuire, "Railways, Exchange Banks and the World Economy: Capitalist Development in India, 1850–1873," in *27 Down: New Departures in Indian Railway Studies,* ed. Ian J. Kerr (New Delhi: Orient Longman, 2007), 108, 129; Stuart Sweeney, *Financing India's Imperial Railways, 1875–1914* (London: Pickering & Chatto, 2011), 13, 23–24, 42, 180; Zach Sell, "Worst Conceivable Form: Race, Global Capital, and the Making of the English Working Class," *Historical Reflections* 41, no. 1 (2015): 54–69; Marrs, *Railroads in the Old South,* 7.

10. Robert Lee, *The Greatest Public Work: The New South Wales Railways, 1848–1889* (Sydney: Hale & Iremonger, 1988), 14–15; Frank Dobbin, *Forging Industrial Policy: The United States, Britain, and France in the Railway Age* (New York: Cambridge University Press, 1994), 49; A. A. den Otter, *The Philosophy of Railways: The Transcontinental Railway Idea in British North America* (Toronto: University of Toronto Press, 1997), 97–98; Robert Lee, *Colonial Engineer: John Whitton: 1818–1899 and the Building of Australia's Railways* (Sydney: University of New South Wales Press, 2000), 74, 76; Moreton-Robinson, *The White Possessive,* xix; Stover, *American Railroads,* 30, 36–37, 42; Headrick, *Tools of Empire,* 194; Linder, *Projecting Capitalism,* 43; Angevine, *Railroad and the State,* 119–24.

11. Marrs, *Railroads in the Old South,* 53, 55–66, 110–11; Walter Johnson, *River of Dark Dreams: Slavery and Empire in the Cotton Kingdom* (Cambridge, MA: Harvard University Press, 2013), 125, 293–99; Linder, *Projecting Capitalism,* 44; Robert

C. Black III, *The Railroads of the Confederacy* (Chapel Hill: University of North Carolina Press, 1952), 29–30; William G. Thomas, *The Iron Way: Railroads, the Civil War, and the Making of Modern America* (New Haven, CT: Yale University Press, 2011), 21–36.

12. For trains as sites of racial and gendered segregation in the United States, see Amy C. Richter, *Home on the Rails: Women, the Railroad, and the Rise of Public Domesticity* (Chapel Hill: University of North Carolina Press, 2005), 100; Mahmood Mamdani, *Define and Rule: Native as Political Identity* (Cambridge, MA: Harvard University Press, 2012); Awasthi, *Railways in India*, 145; Bear, *Lines of the Nation*, 26–27, 37, 41–42, 49–50; Linder, *Projecting Capitalism*, 39–42; Goswami, *Producing India*, 117–19, 121–27; W. E. B. Du Bois, *Dusk of Dawn: An Essay toward and Autobiography of a Race Concept* (New York: Oxford University Press, 2007), 63.

13. Du Bois, *Black Reconstruction*, 589; Stover, *American Railroads*, 52–59; Thomas Weber, *The Northern Railroads in the Civil War, 1861–1865* (Westport, CT: Greenwood Press, 1972), 220–28; John E. Clark, Jr., *Railroads in the Civil War: The Impact of Management on Victory and Defeat* (Baton Rouge: Louisiana State University Press, 2001).

14. Marrs, *Railroads in the Old South*, 193; Ward, *Railroads and the Character of America*, 156–58; Angevine, *Railroad and the State*, 164–71; Stover, *American Railroads*, 62–82; Linder, *Projecting Capitalism*, 55–56.

15. Rao, *Indian Railways*, 19; Augustus J. Veenendaal, Jr., *Slow Train to Paradise: How Dutch Investment Helped Build American Railroads* (Stanford, CA: Stanford University Press, 1996), 44–45; María Montoya, *Translating Property: The Maxwell Land Grant and the Conflict over Land in the American West* (Lawrence: University of Kansas Press, 2002), 129; Sweeney, *Financing India's Imperial Railways*, 6, 67, 69, 73–75; Awasthi, *Railways in India*, 53.

16. Clarence B. Davis, "Railway Imperialism in China, 1895–1939," in Davis and Wilburn, *Railway Imperialism*, 159; James Gao, *Meeting Technology's Advance: Social Change in China and Zimbabwe in the Railroad Age* (Westport, CT: Greenwood Press, 1997), 15; Ellis Oberholtzer, *Jay Cooke: Financier of the Civil War, Vol. 2* (Philadelphia: George W. Jacobs, 1907), 401–39; Watt Stewart, *Henry Meiggs: Yankee Pizarro* (Durham, NC: Duke University Press, 1946), 112–15, 120–23, 158, 160–64, 199–200; Watt Stewart, *Chinese Bondage in Peru: A History of the Chinese Coolie in Peru, 1849–1874* (Durham, NC: Duke University Press, 1951), 80–84, 93–95, 214–16; Leslie E. Decker, *Railroads, Lands, and Politics: The Taxation of the Railroad Land Grants, 1864–1897* (Providence: Brown University Press, 1964), 6–7; James Reed Golden, *Investment Behavior by United States Railroads, 1870–1914* (New York: Arno Press, 1975), 20–21; Eric Hobsbawm, *The Age of Empire: 1875–1914* (New York: Vintage, 1989), 66; William Robbins, *Colony and Empire: The Capitalist Transformation of the American West* (Lawrence: University of Kansas Press, 1994), 87; José R. Deustua, *The Bewitchment of Silver: The Social Economy of Mining in Nineteenth-Century Peru* (Athens: Ohio University Press, 2000); Stover, *American Railroads*, 82–83.

17. Matthew Hale Smith, *Bulls and Bears of New York* (Hartford: J. B. Burr, 1875), 568–69; Mark W. Summer, *Railroads, Reconstruction, and the Gospel of*

Prosperity (Princeton, NJ: Princeton University Press, 1984), 275; Elmus Wicker, *Banking Panics of the Gilded Age* (New York: Cambridge University Press, 2000), 19–33; Angevine, *Railroad and the State*, 194–98.

18. William R. Summerhill, *Order against Progress: Government, Foreign Investment, and Railroads in Brazil, 1854–1913* (Stanford, CA: Stanford University Press, 2003), 38–39, 44–45, 51–53, 193–94; William J. Fleming, "Profits and Visions: British Capital and Railway Construction in Argentina, 1854–1886," in Davis and Wilburn, *Railway Imperialism*, 81; I. D. Derbyshire, "The Building of India's Railways: The Application of Western Technology in the Colonial Periphery 1850–1920," in Kerr, *Railways in Modern India*, 279–89. Awasthi, *Railways in India*, 128; Rao, *Indian Railways*, 24–25; Sweeney, *Financing India's Imperial Railways*, 3, 25, 62, 64–65; Mike Davis, *Late Victorian Holocausts: El Niño Famines and the Making of the Third World* (New York: Verso, 2002), 26–27, 332.

19. Thomas E. Ennis, *French Policy and Developments in Indochina* (New York: Russell & Russell, 1936), 122–24. The French conquest spurred alarm in London, and renewed British investments on border territories in Burma. E-tu Zen Sun, *Chinese Railways and British Interests, 1898–1911* (New York: King's Crown Press, 1954), 30; Robert Lee, *France and the Exploitation of China, 1885–1901* (Oxford: Oxford University Press, 1989), 1, 141–42, 144–46, 155–56; Christian Tsey, "Gold Coast Railways: The Making of a Colonial Economy," PhD dissertation, University of Glasgow, Faculty of Social Sciences, 1986, 11–13, 103; Komla Tsey, *From Head-Loading to the Iron Horse: Railway Building in Colonial Ghana and the Origins of Tropical Development* (Bamenda, Cameroon: Langaa Research, 2013), 4–5; Gao, *Meeting Technology's Advance*, 17, 27–28; Linder, *Projecting Capitalism*, 58–59, 63.

20. Philip S. Foner, *The Great Labor Uprising of 1877* (New York: Monad Press, 1977); John Coatsworth, *Growth against Development: The Economic Impact of Railroads in Porfirian Mexico* (DeKalb: Northern Illinois University Press, 1981), 154–56, 163–65, 171–72, 185; "'La vie en rose?' Métis Women at Batoche, 1870 to 1920," in Christine Miller and Patricia Chuchryk, *Women of the First Nations: Power, Wisdom, and Strength* (Winnipeg: University of Manitoba Press, 1996); David O. Stowell, *Streets, Railroads, and the Great Strike of 1877* (Chicago: University of Chicago Press, 1999); Thomas Flanagan, *Riel and the Rebellion: 1885 Reconsidered* (Toronto: University of Toronto Press, 2000), 24–28, 85; Ahmad Alawad Sikainga, "*City of Steel and Fire*": *A Social History of Atbara, Sudan's Railway Town, 1906–1984* (Portsmouth: Heinemann, 2002), 26–30, 44–45, 50, 57–59; Samuel Truett, *Fugitive Landscapes: The Forgotten History of the U.S.-Mexico Borderlands* (New Haven, CT: Yale University Press, 2006), 58; Otter, *Philosophy of Railways*, 171–72, 212–13.

21. W. Travis Hanes III, "Railway Politics and Imperialism in Central Africa, 1889–1953," in Davis and Wilburn, *Railway Imperialism*, 41; Gao, *Meeting Technology's Advance*, 22, 26–27, 45–46, 49–50; T. O. Ranger, *Revolt in Southern Rhodesia, 1896–7* (London: Heinemann, 1967), 89–90.

22. "Slave Trade in Africa," September 22, 1890, 51st Cong., 1st Sess., Serial Set vol. no. 2816, Session vol. no. 10; M. F. Hill, *Permanent Way: The Story of the Kenya and Uganda Railway* (Nairobi: East African Railways and Harbours, 1961), 46–47;

Tsey, *From Head-Loading to the Iron Horse*, 6–7; Tsey, "Gold Coast Railways," 17, 32–33; Veenendaal, *Slow Train to Paradise*, 31; Kenneth E. Wilburn, Jr., "Engines of Empire and Independence: Railways in South Africa, 1836–1916," in Davis and Wilburn, *Railway Imperialism*, 25–30. Railway development in Central Africa played a major role in the efforts of Southern Rhodesia to absorb Northern Rhodesia, and in the white settler politics that ensued in the mid-1950s. Hanes, "Railway Politics," 41, 44, 59–65; Gao, *Meeting Technology's Advance*, 40–44, 72, 96–97, 142–43; Biermann, *Tanganyika Railways*, 10–11, 16.

23. Ernest P. Liang, *China: Railways and Agricultural Development, 1875–1935* (Chicago: Department of Geography, 1982), 47–53; Davis, "Railway Imperialism in China," in Davis and Wilburn, *Railway Imperialism*, 159–60; Gao, *Meeting Technology's Advance*, 28–29, 86, 97–99; Ralph William Huenemann, *The Dragon and the Iron Horse: The Economics of Railroads in China, 1876–1937* (Cambridge, MA: Harvard University Press, 1984), 48–57, 59–60; Jonathan S. McMurray, *Distant Ties: Germany, the Ottoman Empire, and the Construction of the Baghdad Railway* (Westport, CT: Praeger, 2001), 32, 61.

24. Neera Kapila, *Race, Rail and Society: Roots of Modern Kenya* (Nairobi: Kenway, 2009), 18, 20–21, 64; Hill, *Permanent Way*, 86; Biermann, *Tanganyika Railways*, 24–26; Headrick, *Tools of Empire*, 196–99.

25. Ivor Wilks, *Asante in the Nineteenth Century: The Structure and Evolution of a Political Order* (New York: Cambridge University Press, 1975), 636–37; Tsey, *From Head-Loading to the Iron Horse*, 18–22, 66–68, 81; Tsey, "Gold Coast Railways," 38–39, 44–46, 104, 106, 110, 114, 150–51; Jan-Bart Gewald, *Herero Heroes: A Socio-Political History of the Herero of Namibia, 1890–1923* (Athens: Ohio University Press, 1999), 128–29, 132–33.

26. Chun-lin Tan, "The Boxer Catastrophe," PhD dissertation, Political Science, Columbia University, 1952, 90–93, 98, 123–24, 229–36; Paul A. Cohen, *History in Three Keys: The Boxers as Event, Experience, and Myth* (New York: Columbia University Press, 1997), 47–48, 127; R. Edward Glatfelter, "Russia, the Soviet Union, and the Chinese Eastern Railway," in Davis and Wilburn, *Railway Imperialism*, 137–42; Lee, *France and the Exploitation of China*, 102–8; Sun, *Chinese Railways and British Interests*, 50–51, 69–71.

27. David Olusoga, *The Kaiser's Holocaust: Germany's Forgotten Genocide and the Colonial Roots of Nazism* (London: Faber and Faber, 2010); Linder, *Projecting Capitalism*, 81; Gewald, *Herero Heroes*, 150, 154, 190, 216–17; Hill, *Permanent Way*, 158–59, 161–71, 250–51; Gann and Duignan, *Rulers of British Africa*, 272.

28. Terrence Ranger, *Bulawayo Burning: The Social History of a Southern African City, 1893–1960* (Rochester: Boydell & Brewer, 2010), 25–30, 38–39; Nayan Shah, *Stranger Intimacy: Contesting Race, Sexuality, and the Law in the North American West* (Berkeley: University of California Press, 2011), 79; Peter Boag, *Same-Sex Affairs: Constructing and Controlling Homosexuality in the Pacific Northwest* (Berkeley: University of California Press, 2003), 42–44; Bear, *Lines of the Nation*, 91–93, 98–99.

29. Frank Leonard, *A Thousand Blunders: The Grand Trunk Pacific Railway and Northern British Columbia* (Vancouver: UBC Press, 1996), 104–8, 177–83; David

Chang, *The Color of the Land: Race, Nation, and the Politics of Landownership in Oklahoma, 1832–1929* (Chapel Hill: University of North Carolina Press, 2010), 90, 103.

30. Sweeney, *Financing India's Imperial Railways*, 1, 42; Robinson, "Railway Imperialism," 1–4; Kenneth E. Wilburn, Jr., "Engines of Empire and Independence: Railways in South Africa, 1836–1916," in Davis and Wilburn, *Railway Imperialism*, 37. A claim by U.S. financial interests for participation in the Hukuang Loan delayed its ratification by the Chinese government; Sun, *Chinese Railways and British Interests*, 105–7, 110–11.

31. Coatsworth, *Growth against Development*, 79, 134, 146; William E. French, "In the Path of Progress: Railroads and Moral Reform in Porfirian Mexico," in Davis and Wilburn, *Railway Imperialism*, 89–90, 94–95; Michael Matthews, *The Civilizing Machine: A Cultural History of Mexican Railroads, 1876–1910* (Lincoln: University of Nebraska Press, 2013).

32. McMurray, *Distant Ties*, 84, 88, 92–94.

33. Davis, "Railway Imperialism in China," in Davis and Wilburn, *Railway Imperialism*, 165; R. Edward Glatfelter, "Russia, the Soviet Union, and the Chinese Eastern Railway," in Davis and Wilburn, *Railway Imperialism*, 144–46; Sweeney, *Financing India's Imperial Railways*, 90; Susan Strange, *Sterling and British Policy: A Political Study of an International Currency in Decline* (London: Oxford University Press, 1971); Christopher Prior, *Exporting Empire: Africa, Colonial Officials and the Construction of the British Imperial State, c. 1900–1939* (Manchester: Manchester University Press, 2013), 124–25; Tsey, *From Head-Loading to the Iron Horse*, 36, 157–61; Tsey, "Gold Coast Railways," 62, 64–65, 71.

34. For radicalism in a regional context, see Ilham Khuri-Makdisi, *The Eastern Mediterranean and the Making of Global Radicalism, 1860–1914* (Berkeley: University of California Press, 2010), chap. 5; On Barak, *On Time: Technology and Temporality in Modern Egypt* (Berkeley: University of California Press, 2013), 176–79, 190–91.

35. Tsey, *From Head-Loading to the Iron Horse*, 114–15; Tsey, "Gold Coast Railways," 96; Richard Jeffries, *Class, Power and Ideology in Ghana: The Railwaymen of Sekondi* (London: Cambridge University Press, 1978), 28–29, 31, 38–39. On Communist internationalism and West African rail workers' leaders, see Jeffries, *Class, Power and Ideology*, 46–47; Ranger, *Bulawayo Burning*, 152–58; Eric Arnesen, *Brotherhoods of Color: Black Railroad Workers and the Struggle for Equality* (Cambridge, MA: Harvard University Press, 2001).

36. Aguiar, *Tracking Modernity*, 74, 84, 87.

37. Dale Kerwin, *Aboriginal Dreaming Paths and Trading Routes: The Colonisation of the Australian Landscape* (Brighton: Sussex Academic Press, 2010), 170; Moreton-Robinson, *White Possessive*, 140–41.

CHAPTER FOUR

1. Luther Standing Bear, *Stories of the Sioux* (Lincoln: University of Nebraska Press, 1988), 54.

2. In drawing a distinction between Lakota expansiveness and U.S. expansion, and between Lakota modes of relationship and U.S. imperialism, I draw distinctions where Pekka Hämäläinen has read similarity. See Pekka Hämäläinen, "Reconstructing the Great Plains: The Long Struggle for Sovereignty and Dominance in the Heart of the Continent," *Journal of the Civil War Era* 6, no. 4 (2016): 498.

3. Standing Bear, *Stories of the Sioux*, 3–4.

4. Waziyatawin framed this as a "dramatic loss of subsistence" marked by a move away from wild rice and maple harvesting, pushed under conditions of duress and survival; Waziyatawin, *What Does Justice Look Like?: The Struggle for Liberation in Dakota Homeland* (St. Paul: Living Justice Press, 2008), 25–27. Mark St. Pierre and Tilda Long Soldier, *Walking in the Sacred Manner: Healers, Dreamers, and Pipe Carriers—Medicine Women of the Plains Indians* (New York: Touchstone, 1995), 36–38.

5. Douglas B. Bamforth, *Ecology and Human Organization on the Great Plains* (New York: Plenum Press, 1988), 49–52, 79–80; Delphine Red Shirt, *Turtle Lung Woman's Granddaughter* (Lincoln: University of Nebraska Press, 2002), 16–18; Kevin Gallo and Eric Wood, "Historical Drought Events of the Great Plains Recorded by Native Americans," *Great Plains Research* 25, no. 2 (2015): 157.

6. Standing Bear, *Stories of the Sioux*, 71–74; John C. Ewers, *Indian Life on the Upper Missouri* (Norman: University of Oklahoma Press, 1968), 13. Oral histories recall a continuity in the use of horses, and the use of dogs, for community mobility, both innovations of women; Virginia Driving Hawk Sneve, *Completing the Circle* (Lincoln: University of Nebraska Press, 1995), 10.

7. Robert E. Strahorn, *The Handbook of Wyoming and Guide to the Black Hills and Big Horn Regions, for Citizen, Emigrant, and Tourist, Cheyenne, Wyoming* (Robert E. Strahorn, 1877), 64.

8. Karl Marx, *Capital, Vol. 2* (New York: Penguin, 1978), 471–74.

9. David Wishart, *The Fur Trade of the American West, 1807–1840: A Geographical Synthesis* (Lincoln: University of Nebraska Press, 1992), 33, 54, 62–64, 72–73; Jeffrey Ostler, *The Plains Sioux and U.S. Colonialism from Lewis and Clark to Wounded Knee* (New York: Cambridge University Press, 2004), 28–32; Douglas McChristian, *Fort Laramie: Military Bastion of the High Plains* (Norman: Arthur H. Clark, 2008), 26–29; Sneve, *Completing the Circle*, 25; Nick Estes, *Our History Is the Future: #NoDAPL, Standing Rock, and the Long Tradition of Indigenous Resistance* (New York: Verso, forthcoming).

10. "...the barriers to capitalist production—private property—seem to have fallen, and the entire productive power of society appears to be placed at the disposal of the individual. The prospect intoxicates him, and in turn he intoxicates and swindles others": Hilferding, *Finance Capital,* 180. Andrea Bear Nicholas, "Colonialism and the Struggle for Liberation: The Experience of Maliseet Women," *University of New Brunswick Law Journal* 223 (1994): 231; Colette Hyman, *Dakota Women's Work: Creativity, Culture, and Exile* (St. Paul: Minnesota Historical Society Press, 2012), 40–41, 43–44, 49–51; Estes, *Our History Is the Future.*

11. Delphine Red Shirt, *Turtle Lung Woman's Granddaughter*, 17; Sneve, *Completing the Circle*, 11.

12. Sarah Penman, ed., *Honor the Grandmothers: Dakota and Lakota Women Tell Their Stories* (St. Paul: Minnesota Historical Society Press, 2000), 39.

13. Wishart, *Fur Trade of the American West*, 29; Alan Klein, "The Political-Economy of Gender," in *The Hidden Half: Studies of Plains Indian Women*, ed. Patricia Albers and Beatrice Medicine Woman (Washington, DC: University Press of America, 1983).

14. Roxanne Dunbar-Ortiz, *The Great Sioux Nation: Sitting in Judgement of America* (Lincoln: University of Nebraska Press, 2013), 41. As Rosa Luxemburg wrote, "capitalism needs non-capitalist social organizations as the setting for its development . . . it proceeds by assimilating the very conditions which alone can ensure its own existence": Rosa Luxemburg, *The Accumulation of Capital* (New York: Routledge, 2003), 346.

15. *Treaty of Fort Laramie with the Sioux, etc., 1851*, September 17, 1851, 11 Stats., p. 749. Hiram Chittenden and Alfred Talbot Richardson, *Life, Letters, and Travels of Father De Smet*, vol. 2 (New York: Arno Press, 1969), 675. For Cherokee women's central roles in diplomacy with the United States, see Theda Perdue, *Cherokee Women: Gender and Culture Change, 1700–1835* (Lincoln: University of Nebraska Press, 1998), 100–105; Raymond J. DeMallie, "The Great Treaty Council at Horse Creek," in *Nation to Nation: Treaties between the United States and American Indian Nations*, ed. Suzan Shown Harjo (Washington, DC: Smithsonian, 2014), 97; Richard White, "The Winning of the West: The Expansion of the Western Sioux in the Eighteenth and Nineteenth Centuries," *Journal of American History* 65, no. 2 (September 1978), 340–42; Catherine Price, *The Oglala People, 1841–1879: A Political History* (Lincoln: University of Nebraska Press, 1996), 33–36; Hilferding, *Finance Capital*, 66.

16. Ostler, *Plains Sioux and U.S. Colonialism*, 36–38; DeMallie, "Great Treaty Council at Horse Creek," 101, 105–7.

17. *Letter from the Secretary of the Interior, information in relation to the late massacre of United States troops by Indians at or near Fort Phil. Kearney, in Dakota Territory*, 39th Cong., Ex. Doc. No. 16 (1867) at 16; Wishart, *Fur Trade of the American West*, 54–64, 211–12; David G. McCrady, *Living with Strangers: The Nineteenth-Century Sioux and the Canadian-American Borderlands* (Lincoln: University of Nebraska Press, 2006), 25–26.

18. R. Eli Paul, *Blue Water Creek and the First Sioux War, 1854–1856* (Norman: University of Oklahoma Press, 2004), 18–24.

19. A young man who would later be called Crazy Horse returned to the village from a hunting trip, to find his relatives mutilated and murdered, a moment that is remembered as solidifying his hatred of colonialism and colonialists: Joseph M. Marshall III, *The Journey of Crazy Horse: A Lakota History* (New York: Viking, 2004), 63–69. Paul, *Blue Water Creek*, chap. 6; Estes, *Our History Is the Future*; Ostler, *Plains Sioux and U.S. Colonialism*, 39–42; Susan Bordeaux Bettelyoun and Josephine Waggoner, *With My Own Eyes: A Lakota Woman Tells Her People's History* (Lincoln: University of Nebraska Press, 1998), chap. 8.

20. Dunbar-Ortiz, *Great Sioux Nation,* 129; Charles A. Eastman, *Indian Heroes and Great Chieftains* (Lincoln: University of Nebraska Press, 1991), 3–4; Paul, *Blue Water Creek,* 146–47.

21. On Congressional land allotments and Union Pacific corporate strategy, see J. B. Crawford, *The Credit Mobilier of America: Its Origins and History* (New York: Greenwood Press, [1880] 1969), 25–26.

22. Pacific Railway Act, 37th Cong., Sess. II, Ch. 120, 1862.

23. Waziyatawin Angela Wilson, *Remember This!: Dakota Decolonization and the Eli Taylor Narratives* (Lincoln: University of Nebraska Press, 2005), 6–7; Waziyatawin, *What Does Justice Look Like?,* 38–50; Estes, *Our History Is the Future.*

24. Maj. Gen. Grenville M. Dodge, *The Indian Campaign of the Winter of 1864–65,* read to the Colorado Commandery Loyal Legion of the United States at Denver, April 21, 1907, p. 17.

25. U.S. Senate, *Testimony Taken by the United States Pacific Railway Commission* (Washington, DC: Government Printing Office, 1887–88), 2589; Report of Jas. A. Evans, of Exploration from Camp Walback to Green River, January 3, 1865.

26. Charles H. Springer, *Soldiering in Sioux Country: 1865* (San Diego: Frontier Heritage Press, 1971), 37–53, 68.

27. Letter to Grenville Dodge, Fort Laramie, June 17, 1866; Wm. H. Yarthross to Grenville Dodge, Office Ordnance Depot, Fort Kearney, February 12, 1866; Ogden Edwards to D. H. Ainsworth, September 28, 1865, *Grenville Dodge Papers; Biography of Major General Grenville M. Dodge* (manuscript), report from Col. W. O. Collins, St. Louis, April 7, 1865, Council Bluffs Public Library.

28. *Union Pacific Railroad, Report of Chief Engineer, 1867,* pp. 3–4. *Union Pacific Railroad, Experiences of Thomas O'Donnell While a Workman in Building the Union Pacific Railroad.* Miscellaneous items from envelope marked "Union Pacific: History" in Nebraska State Historical Society, "North Platte in 1867," 1–5.

29. *Biography of Major General Grenville M. Dodge from 1831 to 1871, Written and Compiled by Himself at Different Times and Completed in 1914,* in five typewritten volumes, p. 388, *Grenville Dodge papers.*

30. *Letter from the Secretary of the Interior, communicating, In obedience to a resolution of the Senate of the 30th of January, information in relation to the late massacre of United States troops by Indians at or near Fort Phil. Kearney, in Dakota Territory,* pp. 2–4; *Samuel B. Reed Letters,* 1864–1869, August 2, Bitter Creek, Idaho, camp No. 40, August 17, 1864, May 14, 1867, Omaha, May 23, 1867, North Platte, May 27, 1867, North Platte; U.S. Senate, *Testimony Taken by the United States Pacific Railway Commission* (Washington, DC: Government Printing Office, 1887), 2588–89; Sherman to Dodge, St. Louis, January 5, 1867, *Grenville Dodge Papers; Biography of Dodge,* 610.

31. *Biography of Dodge,* 611–12; Statement of J. Hudnutt's Party, West of Laramie, February 1867 to July 1869.

32. Sherman to Dodge, February 20, 1867, *Grenville Dodge Papers;* "each imperialist power keeps an increasing army available for foreign service; rectification of frontiers, punitive expeditions, and other euphemisms for war have been an incessant progress." Hobson, *Imperialism,* 126.

33. Sherman letter to Dodge, St. Louis, May 7, 1867; Grenville Dodge to W. T. Sherman, Council Bluffs, May 21, 1867, P. Edw. Connor to Grenville Dodge, Stockton, Cal, June 30, 1867, *Grenville Dodge Papers*; *Biography of Dodge*, 623, 626, 628, 633, 637–38.

34. *Papers Relating to Talks and Councils Held with the Indians in Dakota and Montana Territories in the years 1866–1869* (Washington, DC: Government Printing Office, 1919), 52–53; Khalili, 59; Dunbar-Ortiz, *An Indigenous Peoples' History*, 8.

35. *Biography of Dodge*, 648.

36. Dunbar-Ortiz, *Great Sioux Nation*, 144.

37. *Papers Relating to Talks and Councils*, 88–89.

38. Ibid., 8–10.

39. 1868 Treaty talks, 11, 14–15. For a long history of these refusals, going back to the early 1850s, see Estes, *Our History Is the Future*.

40. Josephine Waggoner, *Witness: A Húnkpapha Historian's Strong-Heart Song of the Lakotas* (Lincoln: University of Nebraska Press, 2013), 45. Head Quarters, Fort Laramie, November 20, 1868, NARA Record Group 393; Records of U. S. Army Continental Commands, 1821–1920.

41. Dunbar-Ortiz, *Great Sioux Nation*, 43, 126, 138; Vine Deloria, Jr., "The United States Has No Jurisdiction in Sioux Land," in Dunbar-Ortiz, *Great Sioux Nation*, 143.

42. Rosa Luxemburg's analysis of militarism and accumulation provides a useful and relevant framework to consider the economic function of war against Lakota people and Lakota modes of relationship. Capitalism was reactive to the Lakota buffalo economy, and enmeshed with it, through militarism. "From the purely economic point of view, [war] is a pre-eminent means for the realization of surplus value": Rosa Luxemburg, *Accumulation of Capital*, 434; Delphine Red Shirt, *Turtle Lung Woman's Granddaughter*, 104.

43. *Papers Relating to Talks and Councils*, 15.

44. Ostler, *Plains Sioux and U. S. Colonialism*, 51–53; Estes, *Our History Is the Future*.

45. Circular to Commanding Officers, Headquarters Department of the Platte, Omaha, Nebraska, October 1, 1868. Deloria, *Indians in Unexpected Places*, 36–47.

46. Dunbar-Ortiz, *Great Sioux Nation*, 161.

CHAPTER FIVE

1. Peter Burnett, "Message to the California State Legislature," January 7, 1851, *California State Senate Journal* (1851), 15; Leland Stanford, *Inaugural Address of Leland Stanford, Governor of the State of California, January 10, 1862* (Sacramento: B. P. Avery, 1862); June Mei, "Socioeconomic Origins of Emigration: Guangdong to California, 1850–1882," in *Labor Immigration under Capitalism: Asian Immigrant Workers in the United States before World War II*, ed. Lucie Cheng and Edna

Bonacich (Berkeley: University of California Press, 1984); Iyko Day, *Alien Capital: Asian Racialization and the Logic of Settler Colonialism* (Durham, NC: Duke University Press, 2016), 48–53; Moreton-Robinson, *The White Possessive,* 144, 152.

2. U.S. 37th Cong., Sess. II, Chs. 25, 27, 1862, pp. 340–41; Robert Schwendinger, "Investigating Chinese Immigrant Ships and Sailors," in *The Chinese American Experience: Papers from the Second National Conference on Chinese American Studies,* ed. Genny Lim (San Francisco: Chinese Historical Society of America, 1980), 21; Robert Irick, *Ch'ing Policy toward the Coolie Trade, 1847–1878* (China: Chinese Materials Center, 1982), 153; Moon-Ho Jung, "Outlawing 'Coolies': Race, Nation, and Empire in the Age of Emancipation," *American Quarterly* 57, no. 3 (September 2005): 677–701; Moon-Ho Jung, *Coolies and Cane: Race, Labor, and Sugar in the Age of Emancipation* (Baltimore: Johns Hopkins University Press, 2006), 36–38; Lowe, *The Intimacies of Four Continents,* 25.

3. *An Act to Protect Free White Labor Against Competition with Chinese Coolie Labor, and to Discourage the Immigration of the Chinese Into the State of California,* April 26, 1862; Moon Ho-Jung, "What Is the 'Coolie Question'?" *Labour History* 113 (2017): 3; Albert Hurtado, "Controlling California's Indian Labor Force: Federal Administration of California Indian Affairs during the Mexican War," *Southern California Quarterly* 61, no. 3 (1979): 228. Taxes on Chinese miners provided at least 10 percent of total state revenue from the early 1850s through 1864. Chinese people in California faced additional, racially targeted taxes in California during these years. Mark Kanazawa, "Immigration, Exclusion, and Taxation: Anti-Chinese Legislation in Gold Rush California," *Journal of Economic History* 65, no. 3 (September 2005): 781, 785–87, 789.

4. Moreton-Robinson, *White Possessive,* 5; Kwong Ki-Chaou, interview by H. H. Bancroft.

5. Combined Asian American Resources Project: Oral History transcripts of tape-recorded interviews conducted 1974–76, p. 3; Albert Hurtado, *Indian Survival on the California Frontier* (New Haven, CT: Yale University Press, 1988), 93; Albert L. Hurtado, "California Indians and the Workaday West: Labor, Assimilation, and Survival," *California History* 69, no. 1 (Spring 1990): 5–6, 8; Tomás Almaguer, *Racial Fault Lines: The Historical Origins of White Supremacy in California* (Berkeley: University of California Press, 1994), 29–32; Yong Chen, "The Internal Origins of Chinese Emigration to California Reconsidered," *Western Historical Quarterly* 28, no. 4 (Winter 1997): 520–46 at 540; Richard Steven Street, *Beasts of the Field: A Narrative History of California Farmworkers, 1769–1913* (Stanford, CA: Stanford University Press, 2004), chaps. 6, 7; Michael Magliari, "Free Soil, Unfree Labor," *Pacific Historical Review* 73, no. 3 (August 2004): 349–50, 352–53; Michael Magliari, "Free State Slavery: Bound Indian Labor and Slave Trafficking in California's Sacramento Valley, 1850–1864," *Pacific Historical Review* 81, no. 2 (May 2012): 157; Brendan C. Lindsay, *Murder State: California's Native American Genocide, 1846–1873* (Lincoln: University of Nebraska Press, 2012), chap. 5; Kornel Chang, *Pacific Connections: The Making of the U.S.-Canadian Borderlands* (Berkeley: University of California Press, 2012), 12; Stacey L. Smith, *Freedom's Frontier: California and the Struggle*

over *Unfree Labor, Emancipation, and Reconstruction* (Chapel Hill: University of North Carolina Press, 2013), 23–24; Hurtado, "California's Indian Labor Force," 219, 220, 222; Kwee Hui Kian, "Chinese Economic Dominance in Southeast Asia: A Longue Duree Perspective," *Comparative Studies in Society and History* 55, no. 1 (2013): 21–22; Mei, "Socioeconomic Origins of Emigration," 488–89; David Chang, *The World and All the Things upon It: Native Hawaiian Geographies of Exploration* (Minneapolis: University of Minnesota Press, 2016), 163–84.

6. Rev. A. W. Loomis, "The Chinese Six Companies," *Overland Monthly* 1, no. 3 (September 1868): 221–27 at 222–23; William Hoy, *The Chinese Six Companies* (San Francisco: Chinese Consolidated Benevolent Association, 1942); Him Mark Lai, *Becoming Chinese American: A History of Communities and Institutions* (New York: Alta Mira Press, 2004), 46, 58–59; Mei, "Socioeconomic Origins of Emigration," 499–500; Kian, "Chinese Economic Dominance," 8, 16–19; Mae Ngai, "Chinese Gold Miners and the 'Chinese Question' in Nineteenth-Century California and Victoria," *Journal of American History* 101, no. 4 (2015): 1096.

7. Karl Marx, *Capital: A Critique of Political Economy, Vol. 1* (London: Penguin, 1976), 317. ". . . it is the wear and tear, the loss of value which they suffer as a result of continuous use over a period of time, which reappears as an element of value in the commodities which they produce": Hilferding, *Finance Capital*, 245; Sucheng Chan, *This Bittersweet Soil: The Chinese in California Agriculture, 1860–1910* (Berkeley: University of California Press, 1986), 347; Day, *Alien Capital*, 44; Vijay Prashad, *The Karma of Brown Folk* (Minneapolis: University of Minnesota Press, 2000), 90–91; Street, *Beasts of the Field*, chap. 12; Mae Ngai, *The Lucky Ones: One Family and the Extraordinary Invention of Chinese America* (Boston: Houghton Mifflin Harcourt, 2010), 30, 74; *Report of the Joint Special Committee to Investigate Chinese Immigration*, 44th Congress (New York: Arno Press, 1978), Charles Crocker testimony, p. 675.

8. Biographical Sketch of Edwin Bryant Crocker (manuscript). Judges played a central role in the California "apprenticeship" system, which amounted to a trade in indigenous children to wealthy landowners. Magliari, "Free Soil, Unfree Labor," 357.

9. Charles Crocker testimony, *Committee to Investigate Chinese Immigration*, 674, 723–28; Chang, *Pacific Connections*, 30; Jung, *Coolies and Cane*, 61.

10. *Proceedings of the California State Convention of Colored Citizens, 1865*, p. 92; Central Pacific Railroad Company, *Report of the President, 1866*, p. 33; Alexander Saxton, "The Army of Canton in the High Sierra," in *Chinese on the American Frontier*, ed. Arif Dirlik (Lanham, MD: Rowman & Littlefield, 2001), 29; William G. Thomas, *The Iron Way: Railroads, the Civil War, and the Making of Modern America* (New Haven, CT: Yale University Press, 2011), 181–82.

11. Hopkins to Huntington, May 31, 1865, *Huntington Papers*.

12. *Sacramento Daily Union*, June 18, 1866.

13. *Sacramento Daily Union*, December 18, 1866; *Sacramento Daily Union*, December 19, 1866. Archaeological research from a Chinese community in 1880s Truckee, California, found evidence that residents carried firearms for self-defense; R. Scott Baxter, "The Response of California's Chinese Populations in the Anti-

Chinese Movement," *Historical Archaeology* 42, no. 3 (2008): 33–34. Evidence from bodies of Chinese workers disinterred in Carlin, Nevada, suggest distinct patterns of cranial and facial trauma; Ryan P. Harrod, Jennifer L. Thompson, and Debra L. Martin, "Hard Labor and Hostile Encounters: What Human Remains Reveal about Institutional Violence and Chinese Immigrants Living in Carlin, Nevada (1885–1923)," *Historical Archaeology* 46, no. 4 (2012): 98, 100.

14. Mark Hopkins to Collis Huntington, January 2, 1867, *Huntington Papers*; *San Francisco Evening Bulletin,* January 2, 1867; Cynthia Wu, *Chang and Eng Reconnected: The Original Siamese Twins in American Culture* (Philadelphia: Temple University Press, 2012).

15. E. B. Crocker to Collis Huntington, January 10, 1867, *Huntington Papers.*

16. E. B. Crocker to Collis Huntington, January 14, 1867, *Huntington Papers*; Day, *Alien Capital,* 44, 47.

17. E. B. Crocker to Collis Huntington, January 31, 1867, *Huntington Papers.*

18. Charles Nordhoff, *California: For Health, Pleasure, and Residence—A Book for Travellers and Settlers* (Berkeley: Ten Speed Press, 1973; original 1873), 189–90; Ngai, "Chinese Gold Miners," 1089; Day, *Alien Capital,* chap. 1.

19. E. B. Crocker to Collis Huntington, February 12, 1867, *Huntington Papers.*

20. Chen, "Internal Origins of Chinese Emigration," 118–21; Chang, *Pacific Connections,* 31. On the queer domesticity of urban Chinese life in California during these decades, see Nayan Shah, *Contagious Divides: Epidemics and Race in San Francisco's Chinatown* (Berkeley: University of California Press), chap. 3; Hobson wrote of Chinese workers, who were "introduced into the Transvaal as mere economic machines, not as colonists to aid the industrial and social development of a new country. Their presence is regarded as a social danger": Hobson, *Imperialism,* 276.

21. E. B. Crocker to Collis Huntington, February 15, 1867, *Huntington Papers.*

22. E. B. Crocker to Collis Huntington, February 17, 1867, *Huntington Papers.*

23. Mark Hopkins to Collis Huntington, February 15, 1867, *Huntington Papers.*

24. E. B. Crocker to Collis Huntington, May 22, 1867; E. B. Crocker to Collis Huntington, May 27, 1867; E. B. Crocker to Collis Huntington, June 4, 1867, *Huntington Papers.*

25. Mark Hopkins to Collis Huntington, June 26, 1867, *Huntington Papers.*

26. *Sacramento Daily Union,* July 1, 1867.

27. E. B. Crocker to Collis Huntington, June 27, 1867, *Huntington Papers.*

28. Mark Hopkins to Collis Huntington, June 28, 1867, *Huntington Papers*; Du Bois, *Black Reconstruction,* 569.

29. E. B. Crocker to Collis Huntington, June 28, 1867, *Huntington Papers.*

30. Mark Hopkins to Collis Huntington, July 1, 1867, *Huntington Papers.*

31. E. B. Crocker to Collis Huntington, July 2, 1867, *Huntington Papers.*

32. *Sacramento Daily Union,* July 2, 1867. Whipping was standard practice in the management of Indigenous labor in California. Magliari, "Free Soil, Unfree Labor," 374.

33. E. B. Crocker to Collis Huntington, July 6, 1867, *Huntington Papers.*

34. E. B. Crocker to Collis Huntington, July 23, 1867, *Huntington Papers*.

35. E. B. Cocker to Collis Huntington, July 30, 1867, *Huntington Papers*.

36. *San Francisco Commercial Herald and Market Review*, July 10, 1867. A decade earlier, common arguments against Chinese exclusion revolved around the drain on public finances that would result from excluding a population that provided a significant source of state and local tax revenue; Kanazawa, "Immigration, Exclusion, and Taxation," 788.

37. E. B. Crocker to Collis Huntington, September 12, 1867; E. B. Crocker to Collis Huntington, January 8, 1868, *Huntington Papers*. Here, too, the Central Pacific Railroad was following patterns already set in southeast Asia. Kian, "Chinese Economic Dominance," 25.

38. E. B. Crocker to Collis Huntington, January 26, 1868; Collis Huntington to Charles Crocker, January 26, 1868; Letter to Huntington, February 13, 1868, *Huntington Papers*; Mei, "Socioeconomic Origins of Emancipation," 492.

39. E. B. Crocker to Collis Huntington, March 20, 1868, *Huntington Papers*.

40. C. Crocker to Collis Huntington, May 20, 1868; Mark Hopkins to Collis Huntington, May 26, 1868; Charles Crocker to Collis Huntington, June 15, 1868, *Huntington Papers*.

41. Collis Huntington to Leland Stanford, June 18, 1868; Collis Huntington to Mark Hopkins, June 19, 1868; Collis Huntington to E. B. Crocker, June 24, 1868; Charles Crocker to Collis Huntington, January 20, 1869, *Huntington Papers*.

42. *The Statutes of California Passed at the Eighteenth Session of the Legislature, 1869–1870* (Sacramento: D. W. Gelwicks, 1870), 332–33. There is a trans-Pacific reverberation of the compulsory registration of Chinese as part of the British liberal governance of its Hong Kong colony; Lowe, *Intimacies*, 123; Magliari, "Free State Slavery," 191.

43. *Memorial of the Six Chinese Companies: An Address to the Senate and House of Representatives of the United States. Testimony of California's Leading Citizens before the Joint Special Congressional Committee. Read and Judge Us* (San Francisco, 1877), 51–52.

44. State of California, Legislature, *Memorial to Congress on the Dangers of Chinese Immigration* (San Francisco: Benj. P. Avery, State Printer, 1862), 3, 7; E. H. Derby, *The Overland Route to the Pacific: A Report on the Condition, Capacity and Resources of the Union Pacific and Central Pacific Railways* (Boston: Lee & Shepard, 1869), 89; *Chinese Immigration; Its Social, Moral, and Political Effect, Report to the California State Senate of Its Special Committee on Chinese Immigration* (Sacramento: F. P. Thompson, supt. state printing, 1878); Audra Simpson, *Mohawk Interruptus: Political Life across the Borders of Settler States* (Durham, NC: Duke University Press, 2014), 129; Heidi Kiiwetinepinesiik Stark, "Criminal Empire: The Making of the Savage in a Lawless Land," *Theory & Event* 19, no. 4 (2016).

45. Frederick F. Low, *Political Affairs in California* (Berkeley: Bancroft Library, 1883), 72–73; Moreton-Robinson, *White Possessive*, 5; *Report of the Joint Special Committee*, 75; Hilferding, *Finance Capital*, 320–21. "The land thus cleared of natives passes into white possession, and white men must work it themselves, or introduce other lower industrial peoples to work it for them": Hobson, *Imperialism*, 258.

46. Chinese Exclusion Act, Sess. 1, Ch. 126; 22 Stat. 58, 47th Cong., May 6, 1882.

47. H. I. Cleveland, "The Massacre of Chinese at Rock Springs," *The Watchman* 81, no. 36 (1900): 13; George B. Pryde, "The Union Pacific Coal Company, 1868 to August 1952," *Annals of Wyoming* 25 (1953): 191–205; Yuji Ichioka, "Asian Immigrant Coal Miners and the United Mine Workers of America: Race and Class at Rock Springs, Wyoming, 1907," *Amerasia* 6, no. 2 (1979): 2–3, 5–6; Craig Storti, *Incident at Bitter Creek: The Story of the Rock Springs Chinese Massacre* (Ames: Iowa State University Press, 1991); David O. Wolff, *Industrializing the Rockies: Growth, Competition, and Turmoil in the Coalfields of Colorado and Wyoming, 1868–1914* (Boulder: University Press of Colorado, 2003), 239; Jean Pfaelzer, *Driven Out: The Forgotten War against Chinese Americans* (Berkeley: University of California Press, 2007), 209–15.

CHAPTER SIX

1. J. J. Aldrich, "Diary of a Twenty Days' Sport: Buffalo Hunting on the Plains with the Pawnees," *Omaha Weekly Herald*, August 19, 26, 1868; "Major North's Buffalo Hunt: Reply to 'Blue Cloud'," "Major Frank North and the Indians," *Omaha Weekly Herald*, September 2, 1868.

2. Robert Campbell, *A Narrative of Col. Robert Campbell's Experiences in the Rocky Mountains Fur Trade from 1825 to 1835*, The Huntington.

3. Treaty with the Pawnee Tribe, 1825, in Charles J. Kappler, ed., *Indian Affairs: Laws and Treaties*, vol. 2, *Treaties* (Washington, DC: Government Printing Office, 1904). Two bands had signed treaties of friendship with the United States in 1818. Khalili, 45–46.

4. *Ratified treaty no. 190, documents relating to the negotiation of the treaty of October 9, 1833, with the Pawnee Indians* (Washington, DC: National Archives, October 9, 1833); Treaty with the Pawnee, 1833, October 9, 1833, 7 Stat. 448, Proclamation, April 12, 1834, in Kappler, *Indian Affairs*, 416–18; James Riding In, "The United States v. Yellow Sun et al. (the Pawnee People): A Case Study of Institutional and Societal Racism and U. S. Justice in Nebraska from the 1850s to the 1870s," in *Native Historians Write Back: Decolonizing American Indian History*, ed. Susan A. Miller and James Riding In (Lubbock: Texas Tech University Press, 2011), 249n7.

5. Waldo Wedel, ed., *The Dunbar-Allis Letters on the Pawnee* (New York: Garland, 1985); Dunbar letter to Rev. D. Greene, Boston, July 10, 1843; Martha Royce Blaine, *Pawnee Passage: 1870–1875* (Norman: University of Oklahoma Press, 1990), 169; Adrea Lawrence, *Lessons from an Indian Day School: Negotiating Colonization in Northern New Mexico, 1902–1907* (Lawrence: University Press of Kansas, 2011), 151–52; Jennifer Denetdale, "The Uprising at Beautiful Mountain," in *Critically Sovereign: Indigenous Gender, Sexuality, and Feminist Studies,* ed. Joanne Barker (Durham, NC: Duke University Press, 2017), 73; Denetdale, "Chairmen, Presidents, and Princesses," 13; Sarah Hunt, "Representing Colonial Violence: Trafficking, Sex Work, and the Violence of Law," *Atlantis* 37, no. 1 (2015 / 16): 27.

6. Wedel, *Dunbar-Allis Letters,* 610–12; David Wishart, "The Roles and Status of Men and Women in Nineteenth-Century Omaha and Pawnee Societies: Postmodernist Uncertainties and Empirical Evidence," *American Indian Quarterly* 19, no. 4 (Autumn 1995): 510.

7. Charles Augustus Murray, *Travels in North America during the years 1834, 1835 & 1836, including A Summer Residence with the Pawnee Tribe of Indians, in the Remote Prairies of the Missouri, and a Visit to Cuba and the Azore Island,* vol. 1 (New York: Harper & Brothers, 1839), 234.

8. *Letters Received, Pawnee Agency 1859–1880,* Henry DePuy, July 22, 1861, Benjamin Lushbaugh, February 9, 1864; Wishart, "Roles and Status," 516.

9. Wedel, *Dunbar-Allis Letters,* Dunbar to Rev. D. Greene, Boston, September 9, 1844, Dunbar to Greene, October 9, 1844; *Letters Received, Pawnee Agency 1859–1880,* Henry DePuy, July 5, 1861 and May 23, 1863, Benjamin Lushbaugh, September 23, 1863; Goeman, *Mark My Words,* 48; Audra Simpson, *Mohawk Interruptus: Political Life across the Borders of Settler States* (Durham, NC: Duke University Press, 2014), 101.

10. Treaty with the Pawnee—Grand, Loups, Republicans, Etc., August 6, 1848, 9 Stat. 949, Ratified January 8, 1849; Kappler, *Indian Affairs,* 571; Blaine, *Pawnee Passage,* 37; Gottlieb F. Oehler and David Z. Smith, *Description of a Journey and Visit to the Pawnee Indians,* April 22–May 18, 1851, reprinted from the Moravian Church Miscellany of 1851–1852, New York, 1914, p. 29.

11. Oehler and Smith, *Description of a Journey,* 30–31; Wishart, "Roles and Status," 515–16; Daniel Pugh, "Scenes of Exclusion: Historical Transformation and Material Limitations to Pawnee Gender Representation," *Journal of Material Culture* 18, no. 1 (2013): 53–67; Nichols, "Disaggregating Primitive Accumulation."

12. Oehler and Smith, *Description of a Journey,* 7–8; Donald F. Danker, ed., *Man of the Plains: Recollections of Luther North* (Lincoln: University of Nebraska Press, 1961), 12, 49.

13. Treaty with the Pawnee, September 24, 1857, 11 Stats. 729, Ratified March 31, 1858, Proclaimed May 26, 1858; Kappler, *Indian Affairs,* 764–67.

14. *Letters Received, Pawnee Agency 1859–1880,* B. D. Holbrooke, U.S. Department of Surveys, November 18, 1859; Pawnee Loup Bill of Trade, Baltimore, April 26, 1859; Henry DePuy to Commissioner of Indian Affairs, February 10, 1862; Gene Weltfish, *Pawnee Field Notes,* Summer 1935, Book 10, p. 5.

15. *Letters Received by the Office of Indian Affairs, 1824–1880, Pawnee Agency 1859–1880,* J. L. Gillis to A. B. Greenwood, Commissioner of Indian Affairs, February 6, 1860. "... the government borrowed against a future in which the continent was already settled, in the absence of other means for financing conquest": K-Sue Park, "Insuring Conquest: U.S. Expansion and the Indian Depredation Claims System, 1796–1920," *History of the Present* 8, no. 1 (2018): 58–60.

16. Lawrie Tatum, *Our Red Brothers and the Peace Policy of President Ulysses S. Grant* (Lincoln: University of Nebraska Press, 1970), 88–92.

17. *Letters Received, Pawnee Agency 1859–1880,* Henry DePuy, July 10, 1861, Benjamin Lushbaugh, January 4, 1863; Goeman, *Mark My Words,* 49–50; L. Paul

Bremer III, *My Year in Iraq: The Struggle to Build a Future of Hope* (New York: Simon & Schuster, 2006); "Politically, the new Imperialism was an expansion of autocracy": Hobson, *Imperialism*, 27; Beth H. Piatote, "The Indian / Agent Aporia," *American Indian Quarterly* 37, no. 3 (2013): 46.

18. *Letters Received, Pawnee Agency 1859–1880*, J.L. Gillis to Commissioner of Indian Affairs, June 4, 1860; J.L. Gillis to Commissioner of Indian Affairs, June 22, 1860; J.L. Gillis to Commissioner of Indian Affairs, June 24, 1860; J.L. Gillis to John Black, June 24, 1860; J.L. Gillis, September 15, 1860; *Letters Received, Pawnee Agency 1859–1880*, Alfred Sully to Adjutant General, Department of the West, St. Louis, September 27, 1860, 1880.

19. *Letters Received, Pawnee Agency 1859–1880*, Henry DePuy, June 27, 1861, Henry DePuy, July 30, 1861; Simpson, *Mohawk Interruptus*, 7–8; Land, Coulthard writes, should be understood "*as a system of reciprocal relations and obligations*"; Glen Coulthard, *Red Skin, White Masks: Rejecting the Colonial Politics of Recognition* (Minneapolis: University of Minnesota Press, 2014), 13.

20. *Letters Received, Pawnee Agency 1859–1880*, Henry DePuy, December 29, 1861; Danker, *Man of the Plains*, 8; George Bird Grinnell, *Two Great Scouts and Their Pawnee Battalion: The Experiences of Frank J. North and Luther H. North, Pioneers in the Great West, 1856–1882, and Their Defence of the Building of the Union Pacific Railroad* (Lincoln: University of Nebraska Press, 1973), 63.

21. *Letters Received, Pawnee Agency 1859–1880*, Henry DePuy to Commissioner of Indian Affairs, January 2, 1862; Henry DePuy, telegraph to Commissioner of Indian Affairs, February 5, 1862.

22. E.G. Platt, February 2, 1892, reproduced in R.W. Hazen, "History of the Pawnee Indians," *Fremont Tribune*, 1893.

23. *Letters Received, Pawnee Agency 1859–1880*, Henry DePuy to B.F. Lushbaugh, June 30, 1862; Joseph McFadden to Commissioner of Indian Affairs, April 6, 1862. Enlistment procedures for Pawnee scouts in short-term contracts worked as a form of labor control, preventing the possibility of promotion beyond the ranks. Janne Lahti, "Colonized Labor: Apaches and Pawnees as Army Workers," *Western Historical Quarterly* 39, no. 3 (Autumn 2008): 283–302 at 295–96.

24. *Letters Received, Pawnee Agency 1859–1880*, B.F. Lushbaugh to Acting Commissioner of Indian Affairs, September 13, 1862; B.F. Lushbaugh to Commissioner of Indian Affairs, November 10, 1862; Frank J. North, sworn before B.F. Lushbaugh, December 10, 1862; B.F. Lushbaugh to Commissioner of Indian Affairs, January 19, 1863; B.F. Lushbaugh, June 24, 1863; B.F. Lushbaugh, May 12, 1863; "Earth hunger and the scramble for markets were responsible for the openly avowed repudiation of treaty obligations": Hobson, *Imperialism*, 13.

25. *Letters Received, Pawnee Agency 1859–1880*, C. Whaley to B. Lushbaugh, September 26, 1864; B.F. Lushbaugh, September 30, 1864; B.F. Lushbaugh, March 24, 1865; George F. Will and George E. Hyde, *Corn among the Indians of the Upper Missouri* (Lincoln: University of Nebraska Press, 1964), 83–84; Richard White, *The Roots of Dependency: Subsistence, Environment, and Social Change among the Choctaws, Pawnees, and Najavos* (Lincoln: University of Nebraska Press, 1983), 206.

26. *Letters Received, Pawnee Agency 1859–1880*, B.F. Lushbaugh to Commissioner of Indian Affairs, December 18, 1864; B.F. Lushbaugh, June 13, 1864; Robert Bruce, *The Fighting Norths and Pawnee Scouts: Narratives and Reminiscences of Military Service on the Old Frontier* (Lincoln: Nebraska State Historical Society, 1932), 24; Mark Van de Logt, *War Party in Blue: Pawnee Scouts in the U.S. Army* (Norman: University of Oklahoma Press, 2010), 53–55, 58, 81–82, 264.

27. *Letters Received, Pawnee Agency 1859–1880*, J.B. Whitfield, October 1, 1864. On the management of disease at the Sherman Institute, see Jean A. Keller, *Empty Beds: Indian Student Health at Sherman Institute, 1902–1922* (East Lansing: Michigan State University Press, 2002).

28. *Letters Received, Pawnee Agency 1859–1880*, J.B. Whitfield to D.H. Wheeler, Indian Agent, September 15, 1865. On unpaid labor by Choctaw schoolchildren in the 1820s, see Clara Sue Kidwell, *Choctaws and Missionaries in Mississippi, 1818–1918* (Norman: University of Oklahoma Press, 1995), 78–79.

29. *Letters Received, Pawnee Agency 1859–1880*, B.F. Lushbaugh, February 11, 1865; *Biography of Major General Grenville M. Dodge*, 339; Grinnell, *Two Great Scouts*, 80, 125; Van de Logt, *War Party in Blue*, 59–60.

30. Danker, *Man of the Plains*, 44–45; Van der Logt, *War Party in Blue*, 84.

31. *Letters Received, Pawnee Agency 1859–1880*, John Becker to Superintendent of Indian Affairs, January 26, 1867; C.C. Augur telegraph, Omaha, Nebraska, February 27, 1867; Ruth Spack, *America's Second Tongue: American Indian Education and the Ownership of English, 1860–1900* (Lincoln: University of Nebraska Press, 2002).

32. A. Mooney telegram to Grenville Dodge, UPRR Black Hills, July 11, 1867, *Grenville Dodge Papers*; *Biography of Dodge*, 637–38.

33. Murray, *Travels in North America*, 262; Grinnell, *Two Great Scouts*, 178–79, 208–9, 220; James R. Murie, *Pawnee Indian Societies*, Anthropological Papers of the American Museum of Natural History, vol. 11, pt. 7 (New York, 1914), 595–96.

34. Danker, *Man of the Plains*, 64–65.

35. James Riding In, "Six Pawnee Crania: Historical and Contemporary Issues Associated with the Massacre and Decapitation of Pawnee Indians in 1869," in Miller and Riding In, *Native Historians Write Back;* Van der Logt, *War Party in Blue*, 111–12, 115.

36. *Letters Received, Pawnee Agency 1859–1880*, Elvira Platt to Jacob Troth, September 3, 1869; Frances C. Carrington, *My Army Life: and the Fort Phil Kearney Massacre with an Account of the Celebration of "Wyoming Opened"* (Philadelphia: J.B. Lippincott, 1919), 55–56; James F. Brooks, *Captives and Cousins: Slavery, Kinship, and Community in the Southwest Borderlands* (Chapel Hill: University of North Carolina Press, 2002), 14–15; Ned Blackhawk, *Violence over the Land: Indians and Empires in the Early American West* (Cambridge, MA: Harvard University Press, 2006), 7.

37. August 1869 Clothing voucher for Company A, Pawnee Scouts, Nebraska State Historical Society.

38. *Guide to the Union Pacific Railroad Lands: 12,000,000 Acres Best Farming and Mineral Lands in America, For Sale by the Union Pacific Railroad Company, in Tracts to Suit Purchases and at Low Prices,* Omaha, Nebraska, 1870, pp. 6–7.

39. "At the same time imperialism involves a strengthening of the state power, an expansion of the armed forces and the bureaucracy in general, and thereby a reinforcement of the community of interests between financial capital and the large landowners": Hilferding, *Finance Capital,* 342; *Guide to the Union Pacific Railroad Lands,* 20; Wishart, "Roles and Status," 514; Philip Deloria, *Indians in Unexpected Places* (Lawrence: University Press of Kansas, 2004), chap. 3.

40. *Frank North Papers,* Box 1, letter to Lieut. General P. H. Sheridan, Sidney Barracks, Nebraska, April 13, 1877; Joanne Barker, *Native Acts: Law, Recognition, and Cultural Authenticity* (Durham, NC: Duke University Press, 2011), 6.

41. Lisa Knopp, *What the River Carries: Encounters with the Mississippi, Missouri, and Platte* (Columbia: University of Missouri Press, 2012), chap. 16; Clint Carroll, *Roots of Our Renewal: Ethnobotany and Cherokee Environmental Governance* (Minneapolis: University of Minnesota Press, 2015).

CHAPTER SEVEN

1. John Stands in Timber and Margot Liberty, *Cheyenne Memories* (New Haven, CT: Yale University Press, 1967), 173–75; John Stands in Timber and Margot Liberty, *A Cheyenne Voice; The Complete John Stands in Timber Interviews* (Norman: University of Oklahoma Press, 2013), 162–65.

2. This was a shift from collective relationships with corn, to collective relationships with buffalo. In the late nineteenth century, Cheyennes had living memories of life organized around farming corn, persisting through the 1830s. John H. Seger, *Tradition of the Cheyenne Indians,* Arapaho Beeprint, 1905; Karl H. Schlesier, *The Wolves of Heaven: Cheyenne Shamanism, Ceremonies, and Prehistoric Origins* (Norman: University of Oklahoma Press, 1987), 58. My understanding of deep historical changes and continuities in Cheyenne modes of relationship is informed by Roxanne Dunbar-Ortiz's argument that Indigenous civilizations in the Americas revolved around the cultivation of corn and the development of game management; "a kind of animal husbandry different from that developed in Africa and Asia": Dunbar-Ortiz, 15–17, 28; *George Bent Papers,* George Bent to George Hyde, March 4, 1912.

3. *Cheyenne and Sioux: The Reminiscences of Four Indians and a White Soldier,* compiled by Thomas B. Marquis (Stockton: Pacific Center for Western Historical Studies, 1973), 8; *George Bent Papers,* George Bent to George Hyde, March 6, 1905.

4. *Cheyenne and Sioux,* 35; David Lavender, *Bent's Fort* (Garden City, NY: Doubleday, 1954), 130–31, 312–13; William Wyckoff, *Creating Colorado: The Making of a Western American Landscape 1860–1940* (New Haven, CT: Yale University Press, 1999), 37–38.

5. *George Bent Papers,* George Bent to George Hyde, March 6, 1905; George Bent to George Hyde, March 19, 1906. William Bent's brother and business partner,

Charles, was appointed governor of New Mexico, and was killed in a rebellion against U.S. colonial power. His other business partner, Ceran St. Vrain, organized a counterinsurgent army, successfully drawing on the participation of elite New Mexicans. Roxanne Dunbar-Ortiz, *Roots of Resistance: A History of Land Tenure in New Mexico* (Norman: University of Oklahoma Press, 2007), chap. 4; Pekka Hämäläinen, *The Comanche Empire* (New Haven, CT: Yale University Press, 2008), 214–19; David A. Clary, *Eagles and Empire: The United States, Mexico, and the Struggle for a Continent* (New York: Bantam Books, 2009), 154, 173, 179; Lavender, *Bent's Fort*, 74, 132.

6. Joyce M. Szabo, *Imprisoned Art: Complex Patronage: Plains Drawings by Howling Wolf and Zotom at the Autry National Center* (Santa Fe: School for Advanced Research Press, 2011), 143; John Moore, *The Cheyenne Nation: A Social and Demographic History* (Lincoln: University of Nebraska Press, 1987), 185, 188; Stands in Timber and Liberty, *Cheyenne Memories*, 44; Leo Killsback, "The Legacy of Little Wolf: Rewriting and Rerighting Our Leaders Back into History," *Wicazo Sa Review* 26, no. 1 (Spring 2011): 88, 93.

7. *George Bent Papers*, George Bent to George Hyde, October 6, 1916.

8. *George Bent Papers*, George Bent to George Hyde, March 6, 1905; James Mooney, *In Sun's Likeness and Power: Cheyenne Accounts of Shield and Tipi Heraldry*, vol. 1 (Lincoln: University of Nebraska Press, 2013), 28.

9. Loretta Fowler, "Arapaho and Cheyenne Perspectives: From the 1851 Treaty to the Sand Creek Massacre," *American Indian Quarterly* 39, no. 4 (Fall 2015): 365–69; William S. Abruzzi, *Dam That River!: Ecology and Mormon Settlement in the Little Colorado River Basin* (Lanham, MD: University Press of America, 1993).

10. Donald Berthrong, *The Southern Cheyennes* (Norman: University of Oklahoma Press, 1963), 143; Elliot West, *The Contested Plains: Indians, Goldseekers, and the Rush to Colorado* (Lawrence: University of Kansas Press, 1998), 97–192; Wyckoff, *Creating Colorado*, 54; Sarah M. Nelson et al., *Denver: An Archaeological History* (Philadelphia: University of Pennsylvania Press, 2001), 170–71; *The Journal of Mollie Dorsey Sanford in Nebraska and Colorado Territories, 1857–1866* (Lincoln: University of Nebraska Press, 2003), 135.

11. Charles Kappler, ed., *Indian Affairs, Laws and Treaties,* vol. 2 (Washington, DC: Government Printing Office, 1904), 810; Hilferding, *Finance Capital,* 330, 431n20.

12. *Cheyenne and Sioux,* 7.

13. *George Bent Papers,* George Bent to George Hyde, March 6, 1905; George Bent to George Hyde, March 26, 1906; George Bent to George Hyde, November 22, 1908; Fowler, "Arapaho and Cheyenne Perspectives," 378–80; Hobson, *Imperialism,* 71; Denetdale, "The Uprising at Beautiful Mountain, 84.

14. *George Bent Papers,* George Bent to George Hyde, February 28, 1906.

15. George Hyde, *Life of George Bent: Written from His Letters* (Norman: University of Oklahoma Press, 1968), 139–42.

16. Biren Bonnerjea, *Reminiscences of a Cheyenne Indian,* from the *Journal de la Société des americanistes,* n.s., t. 27, Paris, 1935, 129–43 at 136.

17. *George Bent Papers,* George Bent to George Hyde, April 30, 1913; Bonnerjea, *Reminiscences of a Cheyenne Indian,* 136; Stands in Timber and Liberty, *Cheyenne Memories,* 168–70. In a meticulous archival reconstruction, Loretta Fowler argues that the camp at Sand Creek "was a product of a thirteen-year strategy of taking responsibility for maintaining peace with Americans, regardless the great sacrifice." This included the development of a mixed economy among Cheyennes and Arapahos, which incorporated hunting, domestic, and ranching work. Fowler, "Arapaho and Cheyenne Perspectives," 385. On women fighters among Indigenous nations on the Plains, see Beatrice Medicine Woman, *Learning to Be an Anthropologist and Remaining "Native"* (Urbana: University of Illinois Press, 2001), chap. 12.

18. *George Bent Papers,* George Bent to George Hyde, March 15, 1905; *George Bent Papers,* George Bent to George Hyde, May 3, 1906; George Bent to George Hyde, October 18, 1906; George Bent to George Hyde, April 24, 1905. Berthrong, *Southern Cheyennes,* 224, 226–27; Jean Afton, David Halaas, Andrew Masich, and Richard Ellis, *Cheyenne Dog Soldiers: A Ledgerbook History of Coups and Combat* (Denver: University Press of Colorado and Colorado Historical Society, 1997), 75; Denise Low, "Composite Indigenous Genre: Cheyenne Ledger Art as Literature," *Studies in American Indian Literatures* 18, no. 2 (Summer 2006): 84, 86.

19. *George Bent Papers,* George Bent to George Hyde, April 24, 1905; Hyde, *Life of George Bent,* 179, 186; George Bent to George Hyde, May 3, 1906; George Bent to George Hyde, October 12, 1905; George Bent to George Hyde, May 4, 1906.

20. *George Bent Papers,* George Bent to George Hyde, October 12, 1905; Berthrong, *Southern Cheyennes,* 236–37; Afton et al., *Cheyenne Dog Soldiers,* 263; Hyde, *Life of George Bent,* 180.

21. Afton et al., *Cheyenne Dog Soldiers,* 189.

22. Henry Mizner to H.G. Litchfield, November 13, 1866, NARA Record Group 393. "Investors who have put their money in foreign lands, upon terms which take full account of risks connected with the political conditions of the country, desire to use the resources of their Government to minimise these risks, and so to enhance the capital value and the interest of their private investments": Hobson, *Imperialism,* 56.

23. Afton et al., *Cheyenne Dog Soldiers,* 9, 139.

24. Ibid., 29.

25. Henry Mizner to Litchfield, May 9, 1867; Henry Mizner to C.C. Augur, May 10, 1867, NARA Record Group 393; Afton et al., *Cheyenne Dog Soldiers,* 33, 71.

26. Henry Mizner to C.C. Augur, May 12, 1867; Mizner to Lieut. William Harmon, May 14, 1867, NARA Record Group 393, Part V.

27. Henry Mizner to Litchfield, May 13, 1867; C.C. Augur to Colonel Mizner, May 17, 1867, NARA Record Group 393, Part V; Afton et al., *Cheyenne Dog Soldiers,* 27, 161, 227.

28. *Biography of Dodge,* 803.

29. Ibid., 792–95.

30. Henry C. Parry, "Letters from the Frontier," *General Magazine and Historical Chronicle,* University of Pennsylvania, April 1958, letters of June 9, 1867 and June 23, 1867.

31. Wm. Meyers to John Gibbon, July 22, 1867; Augur to John Gibbon, July 27, 1867, NARA Record Group 393.

32. Telegram to Lieut. Chas. Henry, 26th Infantry, NARA Record Group 393; Thomas Bates to John Gibbon, September 1, 1867, NARA Record Group 393, Part V.

33. See Loretta Fowler, *Tribal Sovereignty and the Historical Imagination: Cheyenne-Arapaho Politics* (Lincoln: University of Nebraska Press, 2002), chap. 1.

34. John Gibbon, December 31, 1867, NARA Record Group 393.

35. G. M. Dodge to C. C. Augur, January 14, 1868, NARA Record Group 393.

36. John Gibbon to Litchfield, February 15, 1868, NARA Record Group 393.

37. C. C. Augur to John Gibbon, February 27, 1868; G. M. Dodge to John Gibbon, April 17, 1868, NARA Record Group 393.

38. John Gibbon to Col. R. I. Dodge, 30th M. S. Infantry, April 22, 1868; C. C. Augur to Mizner, April 29, 1867; John Gibbon to R. I. Dodge, April 24, 1868; NARA Record Group 393.

39. John Gibbon to Ed Ball, April 26, 1868, NARA Record Group 393. "Counterinsurgency . . . is also dependent on the militarization of counterinsurgent civilians": Khalili, 207; Jean O'Brien, *Firsting and Lasting: Writing Indians Out of Existence in New England* (Minneapolis: University of Minnesota Press, 2010).

40. John Gibbon to Gen. A. B. Dyer, April 28, 1868, RG 393, NARA.

41. *Biography of Dodge,* 965.

42. Hyde, *Life of George Bent,* 332–35, 340; Killsback, "Legacy of Little Wolf," 103.

43. Stands in Timber and Liberty, *Cheyenne Memories,* 260.

44. Alex Ruuska, "Ghost Dancing and the Iron Horse: Surviving through Tradition and Technology," *Technology and Culture* 52, no. 3 (2011): 574–97.

CHAPTER EIGHT

1. Sarah Bradford, *Scenes in the Life of Harriet Tubman,* Auburn, NY: W. J. Moses, 1869; Sarah Bradford, *Harriet, the Moses of Her People* (New York: G. R. Lockwood & Son, 1886); Kate Clifford Larson, *Bound for the Promised Land: Harriet Tubman—Portrait of an American Hero* (New York: Ballantine, 2004), 244–45, 248.

2. Karl Marx, *Capital, Vol. 3* (New York: Penguin Books, 1993), 528; Du Bois, *Black Reconstruction,* 136; William G. Roy, *Socializing Capital: The Rise of the Large Industrial Corporation in America* Princeton, NJ: Princeton University Press, 1997), 10–11, 14.

3. This bears a relationship to the development of a concept of land as an equivalent of money, and money's association with debt. "The new liquidity of land made

it possible for real estate to become the basis of a new economy, as well as the growth of colonial states": Park, "Money, Mortgages," 1009, 1012; Paddy Ireland, Ian Grigg-Spall, and Dave Kelly, "The Conceptual Foundations of Modern Company Law," *Journal of Law and Society* 14, no. 1 (Spring 1987): 156; Harvey, *The Limits to Capital,* chap. 9.

4. Christopher Tomlins, "The Supreme Sovereignty of the State: A Genealogy of Police in American Constitutional Law, from the Founding Era to *Lochner,*" in *Police and the Liberal State,* ed. Markus D. Dubber and Mariana Valverde (Stanford, CA: Stanford University Press, 2008), 36; Khalili, 173; Roy, *Socializing Capital,* 47; Cedric Robinson, *Forgeries of Memory and Meaning: Blacks and the Regimes of Race in American Film before World War II* (Chapel Hill: University of North Carolina Press, 2007), 13–14; Frederick Engels, "On the Decline of Feudalism and the Emergence of National States," in Karl Marx and Frederick Engels, *On the National and Colonial Questions* (New Delhi: LeftWord Press, 2001).

5. John Dewey, "The Historic Background of Corporate Legal Personality," *Yale Law Journal* 70, no. 6 (April 1926): 669; Morris Cohen, "Property and Sovereignty," *Cornell Law Quarterly* 1, no. 1 (1927): 8–9; Eric Wilson, *The Savage Republic: De Indis of Hugo Grotius, Republicanism, and Dutch Hegemony within the Early Modern World-System (c. 1600–1619)* (Leiden: Martinus Nijhoff, 2008): 257; Lauren Benton, *A Search for Sovereignty: Law and Geography in European Empires, 1400–1900* (New York: Cambridge University Press, 2010), 131–37.

6. Joshua Barkan, *Corporate Sovereignty: Law and Government under Capitalism* (Minneapolis: University of Minnesota Press, 2013), 34–35, 51; Joanne Barker, "The Corporation and the Tribe," *American Indian Quarterly* 39, no. 3 (Summer 2015): 252.

7. On the roots of land as real estate, and land as security for credit, see Park, "Money, Mortgages," 1006–35; Ireland, Grigg-Spall, and Kelly, "Conceptual Foundations," 155; Stephanie Smallwood, *Saltwater Slavery: A Middle Passage from Africa to American Diaspora* (Cambridge, MA: Harvard University Press, 2007); Zenia Kish and Justin Leroy, "Bonded Life, " *Cultural Studies* 29, nos. 5–6 (2015): 630–51; Ian Baucom, *Specters of the Atlantic: Finance Capital, Slavery, and the Philosophy of History* (Durham, NC: Duke University Press, 2005); Christopher G. Tiedeman, *A Treatise on the Limitations of Police Power in the United States* (St. Louis: F. H. Thomas Law, 1886), 1–3; Mark Neocleous, *The Fabrication of Social Order: A Critical Theory of Police Power* (London: Pluto Press, 2000), 3–5, 11; Nikhil Singh, "The Whiteness of Police," *American Quarterly* 66, no. 4 (2014); Barkan, *Corporate Sovereignty,* 20, 26–27, 34, 42, 50–51, 53–54; Roy, *Socializing Capital,* 41, 50.

8. Fletcher v. Peck, 10 U.S. 87, 94–96 (1810); Cheryl Harris, "Finding Sojourner's Truth: Race, Gender and the Institution of Property," *Cardozo Law Review* 18, no. 2 (1996): 387–88; Charles Mills, *The Racial Contract* (Ithaca, NY: Cornell University Press, 1997), 49–51; Frank Shockey, " 'Invidious' American Indian Tribal Sovereignty: Morton v. Mancari Contra Adarand Constructors, Inc., v. Pena, Rice v. Cayetano, and Other Recent Cases," *American Indian Law Review* 25, no. 2 (2000 / 2001): 275–313; Charles F. Hobson, *The Great Yazoo Lands Sale: The Case of*

Fletcher v. Peck (Lawrence: University Press of Kansas, 2016); Barker, "Corporation and the Tribe," 255.

9. The Trustees of Dartmouth College v. Woodward, 17 U.S. 518, 633–34, 641 (1819); Paul A. Baran and Paul M. Sweezy, *Monopoly Capital: An Essay on the American Economic and Social Order* (New York: Monthly Review Press, 1966), 48; Barkan, *Corporate Sovereignty*, 3–4, 6, 52; Barker, "Corporation and the Tribe," 246; Ireland, Grigg-Spall, and Kelly, "Conceptual Foundations," 157; Harris, "Finding Sojourner's Truth," 345; Paddy Ireland, "Company Law and the Myth of Shareholder Ownership," *Modern Law Review* 62, no. 1 (1999): 46.

10. Samir Amin, "The Surplus of Monopoly Capital and the Imperialist Rent," *Monthly Review* 64, no. 3 (July / August 2012); Park, "Money, Mortgages," 1022; *Dartmouth v. Woodward*, 674, 659–62, 693; Marx, *Capital, Vol. 3*, 756.

11. Barker, "Corporation and the Tribe," 251, 253; Johnson and Graham's Lessee v. William M'Intosh, 21 U.S. 543, 572–74 (1923); Cheryl I. Harris, "Whiteness as Property," *Harvard Law Review* 106, no. 8 (1993): 1714. ". . . credit secured by land required land appropriation, and made more land appropriation possible": Park, "Money, Mortgages," 1014.

12. *Johnson v. M'Intosh*, 580, 586–87, 603.

13. The quote is from Margaret A. Burnham, "An Impossible Marriage: Slave Law and Family Law," *Law and Inequality* 5 (1987): 216. See also Burnham, "Impossible Marriage," 189, 216; "The sliding scale of political terminology along which no-man's land, or hinterland, passes into some kind of definite protectorate is often applied so as to conceal the process": Hobson, *Imperialism*, 15; A. Leon Higginbotham, Jr. and Barbara K. Kopytoff, "Property First, Humanity Second: The Recognition of the Slave's Human Nature in Virginia Civil Law," *Ohio State Law Journal* 50 (1989): 512; Andrew Fitzmaurice, "The Genealogy of Terra Nullius," *Australian Historical Studies* 38, no. 129 (2007): 1–15; Audra Simpson, "Captivating Eunice: Membership, Colonialism, and Gendered Citizenships of Grief," *Wicazo Sa Review* 24, no. 2 (2009): 119; Orlando Betancour, *The Matter of Empire: Metaphysics and Mining in Colonial Peru* (Pittsburgh: University of Pittsburgh Press, 2017), 46–57; Harris, "Finding Sojourner's Truth," 321, 328–30, 332, 338–39, 350–53; Dewey, "Corporate Legal Personality," 656.

14. Nicholas Mirzoeff, "The Sea and the Land: Biopower and Visuality from Slavery to Katrina," *Culture, Theory and Critique* 50, nos. 2–3 (2009): 292; Benjamin Straumann, "The *Corpus iuris* as a Source of Law between Sovereigns in Alberico Gentili's Thought," in *The Roman Foundations of the Law of Nations: Alberico Gentili and the Justice of Empire,* ed. Benedict Kingsbury and Benjamin Straumann (New York: Oxford University Press, 2010), 114; Colin Dayan, *The Law Is a White Dog: How Legal Rituals Make and Unmake Persons* (Princeton, NJ: Princeton University Press, 2011), 34–35, 140, 147–48, 150–51, 155; Harris, "Finding Sojourner's Truth," 316, 321–22; Higginbotham and Kopytoff, "Property First, Humanity Second," 514, 538.

15. Thanks to K-Sue Park for this insight.

16. Ireland, Grigg-Spall, and Kelly, "Conceptual Foundations," 152–54; Dayan, *Law Is a White Dog*, 148; Harris, "Finding Sojourner's Truth," 334, 336.

17. Samuel Worcester v. State of Georgia, 31 U.S. 515, 544–45 (1832); *Johnson v. M'Intosh*, 552; Shockey, "'Invidious' American Indian Tribal Sovereignty," 281; Ireland, Grigg-Spall, and Kelly, "Conceptual Foundations," 158. ". . . our increased military and naval expenditure during recent years may be regarded primarily as insurance premiums for protection of existing colonial markets and current outlay on new markets": Hobson, *Imperialism*, 64.

18. An Act to Provide a National Currency, secured by a pledge of United States stocks, and to provide for the circulation and redemption thereof: 37th Cong., Sess. III, Chs. 56, 58, 1863, pp. 665, 666, 679. Gerald Berk, *Alternative Tracks: The Constitution of American Industrial Order, 1865–1917* (Baltimore: Johns Hopkins University Press, 1994), 32; Paddy Ireland, "Capitalism without the Capitalist: The Joint Stock Company Share and the Emergence of the Modern Doctrine of Separate Corporate Personality," *Legal History* 17, no. 1 (April 1996): 63–67; John James and David Weiman, "The National Banking Acts and the Transformation of New York City Banking during the Civil War Era," *Journal of Economic History* 71, no. 2 (June 2011): 338–62; Samuel Decanio, *Democracy and the Origins of the American Regulatory State* (New Haven, CT: Yale University Press, 2015), 41, 44–47; Manu Karuka [as Manu Vimalassery], "Fugitive Decolonization," *Theory & Event* 19, no. 4 (2016); Ireland, Grigg-Spall, and Kelly, "Conceptual Foundations," 158–59; Roy, *Socializing Capital*, 116–17, 130–31. For the relationships between the development of banking and a bond market, and the ability to fight wars against Indigenous nations, see Adam Waterman, *The Corpse in the Kitchen: History, Necropolitics, and the Afterlives of the Black Hawk War* (Duke University Press, forthcoming), chap. 2.

19. Morton Horwitz, "*Santa Clara* Revisited: The Development of Corporate Theory," *West Virginia Law Review* 88 (1985–86): 210; James Ely, Jr., *Railroads and American Law* (Lawrence: University of Kansas Press, 2001), 58; Mary O' Sullivan, *Dividends of Development: Securities Markets in the History of US Capitalism, 1866–1922* (Oxford: Oxford University Press, 2016), 6–7, 26–34; Ireland, "Capitalism without the Capitalist," 42, 68; Baran and Sweezy, *Monopoly Capital*, 218–21; Berk, *Alternative Tracks*, 28–31.

20. Vine Deloria, *Behind the Trail of Broken Treaties: An Indian Declaration of Independence* (New York: Delacorte Press, 1974), 113; Charles S. Maier, *Once within Borders: Territories of Power, Wealth, and Belonging since 1500* (Cambridge, MA: Harvard University Press, 2016), 47, 76; "No matter how degraded the factory hand, he is not real estate": Du Bois, *Black Reconstruction*, 10–12; Zachary Sell, "Slavery beyond Slavery: The American South, British Imperialism, and the Circuits of Capital, 1833–1873," PhD dissertation, History, University of Illinois, Urbana Champaign, 2017, chap. 7; Thomas Morris, *Southern Slavery and the Law, 1619–1860* (Chapel Hill: University of North Carolina Press, 1996), chap. 3; Robinson, *Forgeries of Memory*, 58.

21. Tera Hunter, *To 'Joy My Freedom: Southern Black Women's Lives and Labors after the Civil War* (Cambridge, MA: Harvard University Press, 1997), 26–27; Saidiya Hartman, *Scenes of Subjection: Terror, Slavery, and Self-Making in Nineteenth-Century America* (New York: Oxford University Press, 1997), chap. 5; Nicholas Draper, *The Price of Emancipation: Slave-Ownership, Compensation and British*

Society at the End of Slavery (New York: Cambridge University Press, 2010); Sarah Haley, *No Mercy Here: Gender, Punishment, and the Making of Jim Crow Modernity* (Chapel Hill: University of North Carolina Press, 2016), 12–14, 67, 157; Clyde Woods, *Development Arrested: The Blues and Plantation Power in the Mississippi Delta* (New York: Verso, 2017), chaps. 4–6; Clyde Woods, *Development Drowned and Reborn: The Blues and Bourbon Restoration in Post-Katrina New Orleans*, ed. Jordan T. Camp and Laura Pulido (Athens: University of Georgia Press, 2017), 56–76; "Those who believed themselves the natural heirs to the racial privileges once claimed by slaveholders": Robinson, *Forgeries of Memory*, 153, 184–88; Dayan, *Law Is a White Dog*, 60; Ely, *Railroads and American Law*, 67–68; Tiedeman, *Limitations of Police Power*, 100–101.

22. W. E. B. Du Bois, *Darkwater: Voices from within the Veil* (New York: Harcourt, Brace and Howe, 1920), 44; Roy, *Socializing Capital*, 98. "The money capitalist as creditor has nothing to do with the use which is made of his capital in production, despite the fact that this utilization is a necessary condition of the loan relationship. His only function is to lend his capital and, after a period of time, to get it back with interest; a function which is accomplished in a legal transaction. So also the shareholder functions as a money capitalist. He advances money in order to get a return": Hilferding, *Finance Capital*, 107–10.

23. Dewey, "Corporate Legal Personality," 667–68; Lisa Lowe, *Intimacies of Four Continents* (Durham, NC: Duke University Press, 2015), 46.

24. Ireland, Grigg-Spall, and Kelly, "Conceptual Foundations," 157–61; Baran and Sweezy, *Monopoly Capital*, 29; Gail Bederman, *Manliness and Civilization: A Cultural History of Gender and Race in the United States, 1880–1917* (Chicago: University of Chicago Press, 1995).

25. Alexander Saxton, *The Rise and Fall of the White Republic: Class Politics and Mass Culture in Nineteenth-Century America* (New York: Verso, 1990), chap. 13; Horwitz, "*Santa Clara* Revisited," 206, 216, 219; Roy, *Socializing Capital*, 78–79, 123, 138, 270; Ireland, "Capitalism without the Capitalist," 69; Ireland, "Company Law," 34, 56. "The major operating unions did not remove their formal race bar until the 1960s, by which time black employment on the railroads had been largely eliminated": Ely, *Railroads and American Law*, 143–45.

26. Mark Neocleous, "Theoretical Foundations of the 'New Police Science,'" in *The New Police Science: The Police Power in Domestic and International Governance*, ed. Markus D. Dubber and Mariana Valverde (Stanford, CA: Stanford University Press, 2006), 24, 29; Lyman Johnson, "Law and Legal Theory in the History of Corporate Responsibility: Corporate Personhood," *Seattle University Law Review* 35, no. 4 (2012): 1145; David Squires, "Outlawry: Ida B. Wells and Lynch Law," *American Quarterly* 67, no. 1 (2015); Hartman, *Scenes of Subjection*, 131; Khalili, 67.

27. Tomlins, "Supreme Sovereignty," 40–43, 47–48, 53; Berk, *Alternative Tracks*, 49–50.

28. Lucy E. Salyer, *Laws Harsh as Tigers: Chinese Immigrants and the Shaping of Modern Immigration Law* (Chapel Hill: University of North Carolina Press, 1995); Erika Lee, *At America's Gates: Chinese Immigration during the Exclusion Era*,

1882–1943 (Chapel Hill: University of North Carolina Press, 2003); Gordon Chang, "China and the Pursuit of America's Destiny: Nineteenth-Century Imagining and Why Immigration Restriction Took So Long," *Journal of Asian American Studies* 15, no. 2 (June 2012): 145–69.

29. Tiedeman, *Limitations of Police Power*, 144–45; Cohen, "Property and Sovereignty," 12–13; Moreton-Robinson, *The White Possessive*, 147–48.

30. Roy, *Socializing Capital*, 89; Horwitz, "*Santa Clara* Revisited," 191, 201–2. On Standard Oil as a major importer of capital, see Baran and Sweezy, *Monopoly Capital*, 193–96.

31. Ida B. Wells, *Crusade for Justice: The Autobiography of Ida B. Wells* (Chicago: University of Chicago Press, 1970), 18–20. On the alliance between northern railroad corporations and the forces of racist reaction, see Robinson, *Forgeries of Memory*, 73–74; Chesapeake & Ohio & Southwestern Railroad Company v. Wells. 85 Tenn. 613 (1887).

32. Yick Wo v. Hopkins, 118 U.S. 356, 6 S. Ct. 1036, 30 L. Ed. 200, 365, 369–70, 373 (1886); Thomas Wuil Joo, "New 'Conspiracy Theory' of the Fourteenth Amendment: Nineteenth-Century Chinese Civil Rights Cases and the Development of Substantive Due Process Jurisprudence," *University of San Francisco Law Review* 29 (Winter 1995): 376, 377, 384, 385; Gabriel J. Chin, "Unexplainable on Grounds of Race: Doubts about *Yick Wo*," *University of Illinois Law Review* (2008): 1359 (online).

33. Santa Clara County v. Southern Pacific Railroad Company, 118 U.S. 394 (1886); Martin Sklar, *The Corporate Reconstruction of American Capitalism, 1890–1916: The Market, the Law, and Politics* (New York: Cambridge University Press, 1988), 49–51; Du Bois, *Black Reconstruction*, 691; Roy, *Socializing Capital*, 83; Barker, "Corporation and the Tribe," 262.

34. Stuart Hall, "Rethinking the Base and Superstructure," in Stuart Hall, *Cultural Studies 1983: A Theoretical History* (Durham, NC: Duke University Press, 2016); *Santa Clara v. Southern Pacific*, 123–25; Roy, *Socializing Capital*, 3–4. On the Trade and Intercourse Acts, see Barker, "Corporation and the Tribe," 248–49; Ireland, Grigg-Spall, and Kelly, "Conceptual Foundations," 150; Barkan, *Corporate Sovereignty*, 32, 68–70.

35. Richard D. Stone, *The Interstate Commerce Commission and the Railroad Industry: A History of Regulatory Policy* (New York: Praeger, 1991); Berk, *Alternative Tracks*, 7.

36. Bonita Lawrence, "Gender, Race, and the Regulation of Native Identity in Canada and the United States: An Overview," *Hypatia* 18, no. 2 (2003): 24; Rose Stremlau, *Sustaining the Cherokee Family: Kinship and the Allotment of an Indigenous Nation* (Chapel Hill: University of North Carolina Press, 2011), chaps. 4, 5; Barker, "Corporation and the Tribe," 243, 247, 251–52, 256, 258–60; Ely, *Railroads and American Law*, 149.

37. Christopher Grandy, *New Jersey and the Fiscal Origins of Modern American Corporation Law* (New York: Garland, 1993); Horwitz, "*Santa Clara* Revisited," 186–87, 195; Thomas W. Joo, "Yick Wo Revisited: Nonblack Nonwhites and Fourteenth Amendment History," *University of Illinois Law Review* (2008): 1428 (online).

38. While credit was productive for shareholders, K-Sue Park has tracked a long history of the destructive use of credit against Indigenous and other nonwhite communities, from the earliest period of colonization in North America; see Park, "Money, Mortgages." Credit and share-wages served to limit the liability of planters after emancipation. Gerald David Jaynes, *Branches without Roots: Genesis of the Black Working Class in the American South, 1862–1882* (New York: Oxford University Press, 1986), chap. 9; Paula J. Giddings, *Ida, A Sword among Lions: Ida B. Wells and the Campaign against Lynching* (New York: Amistad, 2008), 371; Plessy v. Ferguson, 163 U.S. 537, 549 (1896); Roy, *Socializing Capital*, 87, 158, 160, 163–64; Barker, "Corporation and the Tribe," 256; Dayan, *Law Is a White Dog*, 47.

39. *Plessy v. Ferguson*, 543–44, 549–50, 561–62. Louisiana segregation laws overturned two decades of nondiscrimination laws. A. Leon Higginbotham, Jr., *Shades of Freedom: Racial Politics and Presumptions of the American Legal Process* (New York: Oxford University Press, 1996), 109–11; Barbara Young Welke, *Recasting American Liberty: Gender, Race, Law and the Railroad Revolution, 1865–1920* (New York: Cambridge University Press, 2001), 314–16; Hoang Gia Phang, "'A Race So Different': Chinese Exclusion, The Slaughterhouse Cases, and Plessy v. Ferguson," *Labor History* 45, no. 2 (2004); Blair L.M. Kelley, *Right to Ride: Streetcar Boycotts and African American Citizenship in the Era of Plessy v. Ferguson* (Chapel Hill: University of North Carolina Press, 2010).

40. "To be a man meant to participate, separated from the actual experience, in a genocide": Michael Paul Rogin, "Liberal Society and the Indian Question," *Politics and Society* 1 (May 1971): 312. "An Act to Establish a Uniform System of Bankruptcy throughout the United States," U.S. 55th Cong., Sess. 2, Chs. 540, 541; Berk, *Alternative Tracks*, 58, 110; Horwitz, "*Santa Clara* Revisited," 181, 183; Baran and Sweezy, *Monopoly Capital*, 67. "To a larger extent every year Great Britain has been becoming a nation living upon tribute from abroad, and the classes who enjoy this tribute have had an ever-increasing incentive to employ the public policy, the public purse, and the public force to extend the field of their private investments, and to safeguard and improve their existing investments. . . . What was true of Great Britain was likewise true of France, Germany, the United States, and of all the countries in which modern capitalism had placed a large surplus savings in the hands of a plutocracy or of a thrifty middle class": Hobson, *Imperialism*, 53–54.

CHAPTER NINE

1. Blackhawk, 9; Wolfe, *Traces of History*, 38; Du Bois, *Black Reconstruction in America*, 211–12; Nikhil Pal Singh, *Race and America's Long War* (Oakland: University of California Press, 2017), 26; Dunbar-Ortiz, *An Indigenous Peoples' History*, 6; Jodi A. Byrd, "Follow the Typical Signs: Settler Sovereignty and Its Discontents," *Settler Colonial Studies* 4, no. 2 (2014): 153.

2. Frederick Jackson Turner, *The Frontier in American History* (Tucson: University of Arizona Press, 1997), 32; Goeman, *Mark My Words*, 14; Charles S. Maier, *Once*

within Borders: Territories of Power, Wealth, and Belonging since 1500 (Cambridge, MA: Harvard University Press, 2016), 229. Cedric Robinson wrote that colonialism in America required "the Savage" as a rationale, and that English colonialism drew upon a traveling notion of savagery that was rooted in the colonization of Ireland. While I was unable to incorporate it into this book, the historicization of the transcontinental railroad through the lens of imperialism should also entail a reckoning of Irish railroad workers through the long history of colonialism in Ireland, and not primarily through U. S. nationalism and amalgamated whiteness. Robinson, *Black Marxism*, 186–87. On the savage / civilized binary as a logic of counterinsurgency warfare, see Khalili, 43.

3. Turner, *Frontier in American History*, 31.

4. Ibid., 59. I have argued that continental imperialism, in North America, was actually achieved through, and preceded by, overseas imperialism. California, that is, was overseas, Pacific territory of the United States, before it was part of the continental territory of the U. S. In a related way, we might consider visions of the southward expansion of slavery, as a different conception of continental expansion, occurring across seas. See Johnson, *River of Dark Dreams;* Moon-Ho Jung, "Beyond Loyalties: Reflections on Regional and National Divides in the Study of Race," *Western Historical Quarterly* 34, no. 3 (2012): 291; J. Kēhaulani Kauanui, "Imperial Ocean: The Pacific as a Critical Site for American Studies," *American Quarterly* 67, no. 3 (2015): 625–36; Peter Hudson, *Banking and Empire: How Wall Street Colonized the Caribbean* (Chicago: University of Chicago Press, 2017). The concept of continental imperialism could be understood in productive interrelationship with concepts such as archipelagic imperialism. Lanny Thompson, *Imperial Archipelago: Representation and Rule in the Insular Territories under U. S. Dominion after 1898* (Honolulu: University of Hawai'i Press, 2010); Yolanda Martínez San-Miguel, *Coloniality of Diasporas: Rethinking Intra-Colonial Migrations in a Pan-Caribbean Context* (New York: Palgrave Macmillan, 2014); Setsu Shigematsu and Keith L. Camacho, eds., *Militarized Currents: Toward a Decolonized Future in Asia and the Pacific* (Minneapolis: University of Minnesota Press, 2010); Brian Russell Roberts and Michelle Ann Stephens, eds., *Archipelagic American Studies* (Durham, NC: Duke University Press, 2017); Alyosha Goldstein, "Promises Are Over: Puerto Rico and the Ends of Decolonization," *Theory and Event* 19, no. 4 (2016).

5. Luana Ross, *Inventing the Savage: The Social Construction of Native American Criminality* (Austin: University of Texas Press, 1998); Heidi Kiiwetinepinesiik Stark, "Criminal Empire: The Making of the Savage in a Lawless Land," *Theory & Event* 19, no. 4 (2016); Audra Simpson, "The Ruse of Consent and the Anatomy of 'Refusal': Cases from Indigenous North America and Australia," *Postcolonial Studies* 20, no. 1 (2017): 11; Turner, *Frontier in American History*, 60. On Turner's melancholy, see also Reddy, *Freedom with Violence*, 63; Jodi A. Byrd, "Beast of America: Sovereignty and the Wildness of Objects," *South Atlantic Quarterly* 117, no. 3 (July 2018): 608–9.

6. W. E. B. Du Bois, "The African Roots of War," *Atlantic Monthly,* May 1915, 30, 34; Manu Vimalassery, Juliana Hu Pegues, and Alyosha Goldstein, "Introduction:

On Colonial Unknowing," *Theory & Event* 10, no. 4 (2016); Manu Vimalassery, Juliana Hu Pegues, and Alyosha Goldstein, "Colonial Unknowing and Relations of Study," *Theory & Event* 20, no. 4 (2017).

7. Joanne Barker, "Self-Determination," *Critical Ethnic Studies* 1, no. 1 (2015): 23; Du Bois, "African Roots of War," 36. Reddy argues that Du Bois's analysis of race offers, "in the *figure* of 'land'," a trope that exceeds the regulative matrix of territory, culture, and identity underpinning Turner's thesis. Reddy, *Freedom with Violence*, 62–64, 67; Mishuana Goeman, "Ongoing Storms and Struggles: Gendered Violence and Resource Exploitation," in *Critically Sovereignty Matters*, ed. Barker, 102; Singh, *Race and America's Long War*, 137; Barker, *Native Acts*, 5–11; Turner, *Frontier in American History*, 53, 55.

8. Turner, *Frontier in American History*, 33; Samir Amin, *Ending the Crisis of Capitalism or Ending Capitalism?* (Cape Town: Pambazuka Press, 2011), 42, 55; Nick Estes, "Wounded Knee: Settler Colonial Property Regimes and Indigenous Liberation," *Capitalism, Nature, Socialism* 24, no. 3 (2013): 197–98. Contemporary politics of border controls against migrations from the South, in the wake of the social devastation of trade liberalization, climate crisis, and war, should be situated in this long historical arc.

9. Goeman, *Mark My Words*, 31; Maier, *Once within Borders*, 187; Turner, *Frontier in American History*, 41.

10. Du Bois, "African Roots of War," 31–33.

11. Turner, *Frontier in American History*, 47; Vladimir I. Lenin, *Imperialism: The Highest Stage of Capitalism* (New York: International, 1937), 25, 59, 124–25.

12. Lenin, *Imperialism*, 124; Goeman, "Ongoing Storms and Struggles," 116; Maier, *Once within Borders*, 188; Du Bois, "African Roots of War," 30–31, 35–36.

13. Turner, *Frontier in American History*, 42. Lenin, *Imperialism*, 25; Alyosha Goldstein, "Where the Nation Takes Place: Proprietary Regimes, Antistatism, and U.S. Settler-Colonialism," *South Atlantic Quarterly* 107, no. 4 (Fall 2008): 835.

14. Joy Harjo and Gloria Bird, *Reinventing the Enemy's Language: Contemporary Native Women's Writings of North America* (New York: W.W. Norton, 1997), 21; Russel Lawrence Barsh, "War and the Reconfiguring of American Indian Society," *Journal of American Studies* 35, no. 3 (2001): 371–411. John Grenier has argued that the roots of a distinctly U.S. military tradition lie in the purposeful destruction of noncombatants, villages, and food sources. John Grenier, *The First War of War: American War Making on the Frontier, 1607–1814* (New York: Cambridge University Press, 2005), 1, 10–13; Dunbar-Ortiz, *Indigenous Peoples' History*, 58–65; Winnemucca, *Life among the Piutes*, 78.

15. Du Bois, "African Roots of War," 28, 35.

16. Cedric Robinson argued "the development, organization, and expansion of capitalist society pursued essentially racial directions, so too did social ideology": Robinson, *Black Marxism*, 22. Du Bois, "African Roots of War," 29, 30, 35; Turner, *Frontier in American History*, 48. Turner's frontier thesis attempts to territorialize and separate "an emergent social or cultural formation," which Lisa Lowe has

charted, marked by the achievement of "imminent, potential alliances among sub-jugated people"; Lowe, *The Intimacies of Four Continents*, 34, 35, 37.

17. The land's apparent availability, Aileen Moreton-Robinson argued, is a "pro-prietary anchor within capitalist economies such as the United States": Moreton-Robinson, *The White Possessive*, xix. Lenin, *Imperialism*, 54; Turner, *Frontier in American History*, 33, 38, 48; Dunbar-Ortiz, *Indigenous Peoples' History*, 141.

18. "Consolidation of railway systems began with fighting, stealing, and cheat-ing": Du Bois, *Black Reconstruction*, 582. Lenin, *Imperialism*, 28, 37, 40–41, 45–46, 64, 81; Turner, *Frontier in American History*, 40; Elizabeth Cook-Lynn, *A Separate Country: Postcoloniality and American Indian Nations* (Lubbock: Texas Tech University Press, 2012), 30.

19. "Imperialism is not the latest stage of capitalism but its foundational war-rant": Wolfe, *Traces of History*, 23. Lenin, *Imperialism*, 21–23; Jeffrey Ostler, *The Plains Sioux and U.S. Colonialism from Lewis and Clark to Wounded Knee* (New York: Cambridge University Press, 2004), 52–53.

20. Lenin, *Imperialism*, 16–17, 57, 76; Goeman, "Ongoing Storms and Struggles."

21. Lenin, *Imperialism*, 25, 67, 68, 75; Moreton-Robinson, *White Possessive*, 67; Akwesasne Notes, *Basic Call to Consciousness* (Summertown, TN: Native Voices, 1978), 122. For Indigenous energy and food production as practices of tribal renewal, see Winona LaDuke, *Recovering the Sacred: The Power of Naming and Claiming* (Boston: South End Press, 2005). For pedagogies of Indigenous Hawaiian taro farm-ing and seafaring, see Noelani Goodyear-Kaʻōpua, *The Seeds We Planted: Portraits of a Native Hawaiian Charter School* (Durham, NC: Duke University Press, 2013), chaps. 3, 4.

22. Lenin, *Imperialism*, 26–27, 49, 99–101.

23. Ibid., 19–20, 34, 65, 83, 84, 88–99, 123–24; Du Bois, "African Roots of War," 32.

24. Lenin, *Imperialism*, 24–25, 61, 82, 126.

25. Ibid., 59, 67; Vine Deloria, Jr., *Behind the Trail of Broken Treaties: An Indian Declaration of Independence* (New York: Delacorte Press, 1974), 113.

26. Turner, *Frontier in American History*, 37; Saldaña-Portillo, *Indian Given*, 10; Lenin, *Imperialism*, 97–98.

27. Turner, *Frontier in American History*, 31, 34–36, 39.

28. Ibid., 37. Moreton-Robinson, *White Possessive*, 112–18; Goldstein, "Where the Nation Takes Place," 833–34; Goeman, "Ongoing Storms and Struggles," 105.

29. Turner, *Frontier in American History*, 38, 40; Tiffany Lethabo-King, "The Labor of (Re)Reading Plantation Landscapes Fungible(ly)," *Antipode* 48, no. 4 (2016): 1022–39.

30. Barker, "Introduction," *Critically Sovereign*; Moreton-Robinson, *White Possessive;* Elizabeth Povinelli, *Economies of Abandonment: Social Belonging and Endurance in Late Liberalism* (Durham, NC: Duke University Press, 2011).

31. Turner, *Frontier in American History*, 31–35, 41. ". . . the closing of Turner's frontier and the pacification of violent Indians met a kind of narrative harmony": Philip Deloria, *Indians in Unexpected Places* (Lawrence: University Press of Kansas, 2004), 62.

32. Turner, *Frontier in American History*, 55.

33. Robinson wrote, "capitalism was less a catastrophic revolution (negation) of feudalist social orders than the extension of these social relations into the larger tapestry of the modern world's political and economic relations": Robinson, *Black Marxism*, 10, 12. Roderick Ferguson, *The Reorder of Things: The University and Its Pedagogies of Minority Difference* (Minneapolis: University of Minnesota Press, 2012), 46; Goodyear-Ka'ōpua, *Seeds We Planted*, 24–26; Lenin, *Imperialism*, 81, 91; Du Bois, "African Roots of War," 36; Moreton-Robinson, *White Possessive*, 138–44.

34. Lenin, *Imperialism*, 35–36, 111.

35. Du Bois, "African Roots of War," 32, 36–39. Goeman focuses on a different dimension of this failure and refusal, what she terms "intentional neglect"; Goeman, "Ongoing Storms and Struggles," 109.

36. Dunbar-Ortiz, *Indigenous Peoples' History*, 1, 12; Leanne Simpson, "Looking after Gdoo-naaganinaa: Precolonial Nishnaabeg Diplomatic and Treaty Relationships," *Wicazo Sa Review* 23, no. 2 (Fall 2008): 29–42; Leanne Simpson, *Dancing on Our Turtle's Back: Stories of Nishnaabeg Re-Creation, Resurgence and a New Emergence* (Winnipeg: ARP Books, 2011), 143; Sarah Hunt, "Decolonizing Sex Work: Developing an Intersectional Indigenous Approach," in *Selling Sex: Experience, Advocacy, and Research on Sex Work in Canada,* ed. Emily van der Meulen, Elya M. Durisin, and Victoria Love (Vancouver: UBC Press, 2013); Sarah Hunt, "More than a Poster Campaign," in Kino-nda-niimi Collective, *The Winter We Danced: Voices from the Past, The Future, and the Idle No More Movement* (Winnipeg: ARP Books, 2014), 192; Hunt, "Ontologies of Indigeneity," 27, 30; Steven Salaita, *Inter/Nationalism: Decolonizing Native America and Palestine* (Minneapolis: University of Minnesota Press, 2016); Audra Simpson, "The State Is a Man: Theresa Spence, Loretta Saunders and the Gender of Settler Sovereignty," *Theory & Event* 19, no. 4 (2016); Goeman, "Ongoing Storms and Struggles," 123; Coulthard, *Red Skin, White Masks*, 60; Barker, "Introduction," *Critically Sovereign*, 22.

EPILOGUE

1. Roxanne Dunbar-Ortiz, *Roots of Resistance: A History of Land Tenure in New Mexico* (Norman: University of Oklahoma Press, 2007), 71; Byrd, *The Transit of Empire*, 4, 223; Left Quarter Collective, "White Supremacist Constitution of the U.S. Empire-State: A Short Conceptual Look at the Long First Century," *Political Power and Social Theory* 20 (2009): 167–200.

2. Project for the New American Century (PNAC), *Rebuilding America's Defenses: Strategy, Forces and Resources for a New Century,* [September] 2000, i–ii, iv, 2–5.

3. PNAC, iii, 1, 22, 23, 26, 29, 70–71, 75; Jordan T. Camp, "The Bombs Explode at Home: Policing, Prisons, and Permanent War," *Social Justice* 44, nos. 2–3 (2017):

11–30; Roxanne Dunbar-Ortiz, *Loaded: A Disarming History of the Second Amendment* (San Francisco: City Lights Books, 2018), 57.

4. PNAC, 6, 10, 13–15, 19, 25, 27, 30, 37, 38, 74; Cynthia Enloe, *Bananas, Beaches, and Bases: Making Feminist Sense of International Politics* (Oakland: University of California Press, 2014); David Vine, *Base Nation: How U.S. Military Bases Abroad Harm America and the World* (New York: Metropolitan Books, 2015).

5. PNAC, 11, 16–18, 20, 51–52.

6. PNAC, iv, 4–8, 22, 30, 51, 54–56, 59, 60–62.

7. *Report of the National Energy Policy Development Group,* May 2001, ix, 1.1; *National Energy Policy,* xii, xv, 1.6, 2.6, 2.11, 3.9, 5.6–5.7, 7.1, 8.3, 8.10–8.11; Coulthard, *Red Skin, White Masks,* 56–57. A move by financial capital and the major agricultural and chemical companies toward the production of agro-fuels, attendant on large-scale monocrop cultivation of sugar, maize, soybean, peanut, rapeseed, and palm oil, has greatly exacerbated the impact of the food and agricultural crisis and its aftermath. João Pedro Stedile, "Latin America: Reflections on the Tendencies of Capital in Agriculture and Challenges for Peasant Movements in Latin America," in *The Struggle for Food Sovereignty: Alternative Development and the Renewal of Peasant Societies Today,* ed. Remy Herrera and Kin Chi Lau (London: Pluto Press, 2015), 37; Fred Magdoff and Brian Tokar, eds., *Agriculture and Food in Crisis: Conflict, Resistance, and Renewal* (New York: Monthly Review Press, 2010); Sam Moyo, "Agrarian Transformation in Africa and its Decolonisation," in *Agricultural Development and Food Security in Africa: The Impact of Chinese, Indian and Brazilian Investments,* ed. Fantu Cheru and Renu Modi (London: Zed Books, 2013), 48.

8. Vijay Prashad, *Fat Cats and Running Dogs: The Enron Stage of Capitalism* (Monroe, ME: Common Courage Press, 2003), 11–26; Mike Davis, *Prisoners of the American Dream: Politics and Economy in the History of the U.S. Working Class* (New York: Verso, 2018), 134; Woods, *Development Drowned and Reborn,* 222–31.

9. Energy Transfer Equity, L.P. (ETE), *Annual Report,* 2010, 35, 42, 44, 50, 51, 53; Energy Transfer Partners (ETP), *Annual Report,* 2010, 34, 44–45; ETE, *Annual Report,* 2011, 44, 45; ETP, *Annual Report,* 2011, 36–37; ETP, *Annual Report,* 2012, 58–59; ETE, *Annual Report,* 2012, 56; ETP, *Annual Report,* 2013, 48–49, 55–56; ETP, *Annual Report,* 2014, 58–59; ETE, *Annual Report,* 2016, 60.

10. ETE, *Annual Report,* 2015, 3, 4, 9, 49; ETP, *Annual Report,* 2015, 3–4; Sunoco Logistics Partners L.P. *Annual Report,* 2015, 3; ETE, *Annual Report,* 2016, 43–44, 52, 58; ETP, *Annual Report,* 2016, 53–54.

11. Enbridge, *Annual Review,* 2012, 3, 11, 24; Enbridge, *Annual Review,* 2016, 40–41, 62, 102; Enbridge, *Annual Report,* 2017, 6, 10, 34, 41, 46.

12. https://theintercept.com/document/2017/06/03/internal-tigerswan-situation-report-2016–10–03/; https://theintercept.com/2017/05/27/leaked-documents-reveal-security-firms-counterterrorism-tactics-at-standing-rock-to-defeat-pipeline-insurgencies/; https://theintercept.com/2017/06/03/standing-rock-documents-expose-inner-workings-of-surveillance-industrial-complex/; https://theintercept.com/2017/06/21/as-standing-rock-camps-cleared-out-tigerswan-expanded-surveillance-to-array-of-progressive-causes/ "Internal TigerSwan Situation Report 2016–09–

07"; https://theintercept.com/document/2017/05/27/internal-tigerswan-situation-report-2016–09–07/; Pasternak, *Grounded Authority*, 234–40.

13. Samir Amin, *Empire of Chaos* (New York: Monthly Review Press, 1992), 12; Samir Amin, *Obsolescent Capitalism: Contemporary Politics and Global Disorder* (London: Zed Books, 2003), 80; Samir Amin, *From Capitalism to Civilization: Reconstructing the Socialist Perspective* (New Delhi: Tulika Books, 2010), 22; Ho-Fung Hung, "China and the Lingering Pax Americana," in *BRICS: An Anti-Capitalist Critique,* ed. Patrick Bond and Ana Garcia (Chicago: Haymarket Books, 2015), 255; Achin Vanaik, "The Future Trajectory of BRICS," in Bond and Garcia, *BRICS*, 262. Utsa and Prabhat Patnaik argue that imperialism is a structural feature of capitalism. Third World traditional petty producers have historically played a central role in stabilizing the value of imperial currencies. Extended growing seasons and multiple harvests in the tropical and subtropical landmass enable the stabilization of reproduction costs in the global North. The Patnaiks argue that periods of unbridled capitalist expansion are periods of rapid immiseration of the majority of petty producers in the Third World. Utsa Patnaik and Prabhat Patnaik, *A Theory of Imperialism* (New York: Columbia University Press, 2016). On the comparative consumption of food grains in India and the United States (where it is more than five times higher, most going to animal feed), see Utsa Patnaik and Sam Moyo, *The Agrarian Question in the Neoliberal Era: Primitive Accumulation and the Peasantry* (Cape Town: Pambazuka Press, 2011), 44. On parallels between the end of railroad colonialism and the 1970s global crisis of accumulation, see Davis, *Prisoners of the American Dream*, 204.

14. Patrick Bond, *Looting Africa: The Economics of Exploitation* (London: Zed Books, 2006), 38–39; William K. Tabb, "The Global Food Crisis and What Has Capitalism to Do with It?," paper presented at "The Global Food Crisis" conference, Brecht Forum, New York, July 12, 2008; Jomo Kwame Sundaram, *Economic Liberalisation and Development in Africa* (Dakar: Council for the Development of Social Science Research in Africa, 2008), 1–9; Neferti X. M. Tadiar, "Life-Times in Fate Playing," *South Atlantic Quarterly* 111, no. 4 (Fall 2012): 784; Yilmaz Akyüz, *The Financial Crisis and the Global South: A Development Perspective* (London: Pluto Press, 2013), 3, 17; Walden Bello, *Capitalism's Last Stand?: Deglobalization in the Age of Austerity* (London: Zed Books, 2013), 3–16, 151–52; Issa Shivji, preface in Patnaik and Moyo, *Agrarian Question*, 3; Herrera and Lau, *Struggle for Food Sovereignty*, 1–2; Thandika Mkandawire and Charles C. Soludo, *Our Continent, Our Future: African Perspectives on Structural Adjustment* (Dakar: Council for the Development of Social Science Research in Africa, 1999), 71–73, 75–77, 88; Samir Amin, "Food Sovereignty and the Agrarian Question: Constructing Convergence of Struggles with Diversity," in Herrera and Lau, *Struggle for Food Sovereignty*, 17; Moyo, "Agrarian Transformation in Africa," in Herrera and Lau, *Struggle for Food Sovereignty*, 45.

15. "One of the most startling and disturbing features of the decade of the 1990s was the coexistence of two contradictory processes: the reduction of access to cheap food for a significant proportion of the population, and the emergence of huge and

growing excess foodgrain stocks held by the public sector": C. P. Chandrasekhar and Jayati Ghosh, *The Market That Failed: A Decade of Neoliberal Economic Reforms in India* (New Delhi: LeftWord Books, 2002), 159; Atilio Boron and Gladys Lechini, eds., *Politics and Social Movements in an Hegemonic World: Lessons from Africa, Asia and Latin America* (Buenos Aires: CLACSO, 2005); Emir Sader, "Latin America in the XXI Century," in Boron and Lechini, *Politics and Social Movements*, 55–57, 71–74; Utsa Patnaik, "Poverty and Neo-Liberalism," *Pune: Gokhale Institute of Politics and Economics*, 2005, 5, 12–14; Utsa Patnaik, *The Republic of Hunger and Other Essays* (Gurgaon: Three Essays Collective, 2007), 212–30; Jayati Ghosh, *Never Done and Poorly Paid: Women's Work in Globalising India* (New Delhi: Women Unlimited, 2009), 60–61; Sam Moyo, "Africa: Rebuilding African Peasantries: Inalienability of Land Rights and Collective Food Sovereignty in Southern Africa," in Herrera and Lau, *Struggle for Food Sovereignty*, 58–65, 76. Critics of large-scale leases argue that what is being presented as "unutilized land" is in fact a primary land base for pastoral communities, and also essential for wildlife migrations. Sam Moyo, "Agrarian Transformation," in Cheru and Modi, *Agricultural Development and Food Security*, 38, 51; Patnaik and Moyo, *Agrarian Question*, 1, 73–78; P. Sainath, *Everybody Loves a Good Drought: Stories from India's Poorest Districts* (New Delhi: Penguin Books, 1996).

16. Public Law 107–40, 115 Stat. 224, September 18, 2001; Aijaz Ahmad, *Iraq, Afghanistan, and the Imperialism of Our Time* (New Delhi: LeftWord Books, 2004), 8–9, 13, 57, 64, 66.

17. Bremer quote is from Andrew Murray, "Hostages of the Empire," *The Guardian*, June 30, 2003.

18. "Militant-Turned-Populist Cleric Sadr Wins Iraqi Election," *Washington Post*, May 18, 2018; Walden Bello, *Dilemmas of Domination: The Unmaking of the American Empire* (London: Zed Books, 2005), 5; Patrick Cockburn, *The Occupation: War and Resistance in Iraq* (New York: Verso, 2007); Samir Amin, *The World We Wish to See: Revolutionary Objectives in the Twenty-First Century* (New York: Monthly Review Press, 2008), 30; Patrick Cockburn, *Muqtada: Muqtada al-Sadr, the Shia Revival, and the Struggle for Iraq* (New York: Scribner, 2008); Eqbal Ahmad and David Barsamian, *Confronting Empire* (Chicago: Haymarket Books, 2017), 37–39; " . . . in guerilla warfare, a stalemate is a triumph for the guerillas": Ahmad, *Imperialism of Our Time*, 24–25, 52, 199, 211–26; Samir Amin, *Obsolescent Capitalism*, 1; Samir Amin, *Spectres of Capitalism: A Critique of Current Intellectual Fashions* (New York: Monthly Review Press, 1998), 8–9; Prabhat Patnaik, "Introduction," *No to Terrorism, No to War* (New Delhi: CPI(M), 2001), iii–v; Neferti X. M. Tadiar, "Metropolitan Life and Uncivil Death," *PMLA* 122, no. 1 (2007): 317; Naomi Klein, *The Shock Doctrine: The Rise of Disaster Capitalism* (New York: Picador, 2008), chap. 20; Neferti X. M. Tadiar, "City Everywhere," *Theory, Culture & Society* 33, nos. 7–8 (2016): 60–61; Amin, *From Capitalism to Civilization*, 21. Ahmad wrote: "Baghdad is increasingly coming to resemble the Saigon of the early 1960s and early 1970s": Ahmad, *Imperialism of Our Time*, 27.

19. José Seoane, Emilio Taddei, and Clara Algranati, "The New Configurations of Popular Movements in Latin America," in Boron and Lechini, *Politics and Social*

Movements, 239–40; Amin, *Obsolescent Capitalism,* 98, 126–27; Bello, *Dilemmas of Domination,* 64; Matthew Gutmann and Catherine Lutz, *Breaking Ranks: Iraq Veterans Speak Out against the War* (Berkeley: University of California Press, 2010); Iraq Veterans Against the War, *Winter Soldier: Iraq and Afghanistan* (Chicago: Haymarket Books, 2008).

20. Julius Nyerere, "Foreword," in Chakravarti Raghavan, *Recolonization: GATT, the Uruguay Round and the Third World* (Penang: Third World Network, 1990); Walden Bello, *Deglobalization: Ideas for a New World Economy* (Quezon City: Ateneo de Manila University Press, 2006) xiv–xxv, 2–3, 108–18. See also Issa G. Shivji, "Revisiting the Debate on National Autonomous Development," in *The African Union and New Strategies for Development in Africa,* ed. Said Adejumobi and Adebayo Olukoshi (Amherst: Cambria Press, 2008), 199. Thandika Mkandawire argued for re-enlivening pan-Africanism as a means to establish political and economic unification of the continent; Thandika Mkandawire, "Rethinking Pan-Africanism, Nationalism and the New Regionalism," in *Reclaiming the Nation,* eds. Moyo and Yeros (London: Pluto Press, 2011). See Bello, *Capitalism's Last Stand?,* 273–75; Akyüz, *Financial Crisis and the Global South,* xvi–xvii, 131, 171; JP Morgan Chase & Co., *Annual Report,* 2016, p. 11; Jodi Kim, "Settler Modernity, Debt Imperialism, and the Necropolitics of the Promise," *Social Text* 36, no. 2 (June 2018): 41–61; Issa Shivji, *Accumulation in an African Periphery: A Theoretical Framework* (Dar es Salaam: Mkuki na Nyota, 2009), 63–66, 86–87.

21. Dzodzi Tsikata and Joanna Kerr, *Demanding Dignity: Women Confronting Economic Reforms in Africa* (Accra: Third World Network–Africa, 2000), 20–25; Mahmood Mamdani, *General Assembly Distinguished Lectures* (Kampala: CODESRIA, 2002); "An African Perspective on Nine Eleven," 30; Samir Amin, *Financial Crisis? Systemic Crisis?* (Dakar: CODESRIA, 2010), 13; Samir Amin, *The Implosion of Contemporary Capitalism* (New York: Monthly Review Press, 2013), 16–17; Samir Amin, *Three Essays on Marx's Theory of Value* (New York: Monthly Review Press, 2013), 74–76; Jodi A. Byrd, "Still Waiting for the 'Post' to Arrive: Elizabeth Cook-Lynn and the Imponderables of American Indian Postcoloniality," *Wicazo Sa Review* 31, no. 1 (Spring 2016): 83; Amin, *From Capitalism to Civilization,* 37–38; Baran and Sweezy, *Monopoly Capital,* 6–11; Alyosha Goldstein, "The Ground Not Given: Colonial Dispositions of Land, Race, and Hunger," *Social Text* 36, no. 2 (June 2018): 83–106; João Pedro Stedile, "The Neoliberal Agrarian Model in Brazil," *Monthly Review* 58, no. 9 (February 2007): 51; Wen Tiejun, "Centenary Reflections on the 'Three Dimensional Problem' of Rural China," *Inter-Asia Cultural Studies* 2, no. 2 (2001): 287–95; Mike Davis, *Planet of Slums* (New York: Verso, 2006); Mishuana R. Goeman, "Notes toward a Native Feminism's Spatial Practice," *Wicazo Sa Review* 24, no. 2 (2009): 171–72, 175; Utsa Patnaik, *The Agrarian Question in Marx and His Successors,* vol. 2 (New Delhi: LeftWord Books, 2011), 29; Abidin Kusno, "Peasants in Indonesia and the Politics of (Peri)Urbanization," in *Global Capitalism and the Future of Agrarian Society,* ed. Arif Dirlik, Roxann Prazniak, and Alexander Woodside (Boulder, CO: Paradigm, 2012); Mishuana R. Goeman, "Disrupting a Settler-Colonial Grammar of Place: The Visual Memoir of Hulleah Tsinhnahjin-

nie," in *Theorizing Native Studies,* ed. Audra Simpson and Andrea Smith (Durham, NC: Duke University Press, 2014), 245; Eric Tang, *Unsettled: Cambodian Refugees in the NYC Hyperghetto* (Philadelphia: Temple University Press, 2015); Jennifer Nez Denetdale, " 'No Explanation, No Resolution, and No Answers': Border-Town Violence and Navajo Resistance to Settler Colonialism," *Wicazo Sa Review* 31, no. 1 (2016): 111–31; Christina Heatherton, "Policing the Crisis of Indigenous Lives: An Interview with the Red Nation," in *Policing the Planet: Why the Policing Crisis Led to Black Lives Matter,* ed. Christina Heatherton and Jordan T. Camp (New York: Verso, 2016); Jaskiran Dhillon, *Prairie Rising: Indigenous Youth, Decolonization, and the Politics of Intervention* (Toronto: University of Toronto Press, 2017), 158–84; Rebecca Schreiber, *The Undocumented Everyday: Migrant Lives and the Politics of Visibility* (Minneapolis: University of Minnesota Press, 2018), 268; Bello, *Capitalism's Last Stand?,* 28–29; Seoane, Taddei, and Algranati, "New Configurations," in Boron and Lechini, *Politics and Social Movements;* Amin, *Implosion,* 32–33; Lisa Lowe, *The Intimacies of Four Continents* (Durham, NC: Duke University Press, 2015), 150; Wolfe, *Traces of History,* 31; Goeman, 139; Coulthard, *Red Skin, White Masks,* 173–76; Vijay Prashad, *The Poorer Nations: A Possible History of the Global South* (New York: Verso, 2012), 271–78; Ananya Roy, "Slumdog Cities: Rethinking Subaltern Urbanism," *International Journal of Urban and Regional Research* 35, no. 2 (March 2011): 223–38.

22. Steffanie Scott, Danièle Bélanger, Nguyen Thi Van Anh, and Khuat Thu Hong, "Gender, Kinship and Agrarian Transitions in Vietnam," in *Land Tenure, Gender and Globalisation: Research and Analysis from Africa, Asia and Latin America,* ed. Dzodzi Tsikata and Pamela Golah (New Delhi: Zubaan, 2010), 265; Tsikata and Kerr, *Demanding Dignity,* 8–10; Singh, *Race and America's Long War,* 109; Ahmad, *Imperialism of Our Times,* 190–91; Jodi Melamed, *Represent and Destroy: Rationalizing Violence in the New Racial Capitalism* (Minneapolis: University of Minnesota Press, 2011); Prashad, *Poorer Nations,* 251–52; Davis, *Prisoners of the American Dream,* 235, 254–55; Briggs, 11–12; Shivji, *Accumulation in an African Periphery,* 14.

23. Samir Amin, *The Liberal Virus: Permanent War and the Americanization of the World* (New York: Monthly Review Press, 2004), 20–21, 27; Melamed, *Represent and Destroy;* Ruth Wilson Gilmore, "In the Shadow of the Shadow State," in *The Revolution Will Not Be Funded,* ed. INCITE! Women of Color Against Violence (Boston: South End Press, 2009); Ruth Wilson Gilmore, "Abolition Geography and the Problem of Innocence," in *Futures of Black Radicalism,* ed. Gaye Theresa Johnson and Alex Lubin (New York: Verso, 2017), 235; Amin, *Spectres of Capitalism,* 35, 38; Amin, *Obsolescent Capitalism,* 114; Amin, *From Capitalism to Civilization,* 20; Ahmad, *Imperialism of Our Times,* 28–29; Utsa Patnaik, "Poverty and Neo-Liberalism," 9–10; Moyo, "Agrarian Transformation in Africa," 43.

24. Victor Manuel Figueroa Albelo, "Cuba: An Experience of Rural Development," in *Agrarian Studies: Essays on Agrarian Relations in Less-Developed Countries,* ed. V. K. Ramachandran and Madhura Swaminathan (London: Zed Books, 2003); Sinan Koont, *Sustainable Urban Agriculture in Cuba* (Gainesville:

University of Florida Press, 2011); K. T. Chandramohanan and K. V. Mohanan, "Kaipad Rice Farming in North Kerala: An Indigenous Saline-Resistant Organic Farming System," *Indian Journal of Traditional Knowledge* 11, no. 1 (2012): 185–89; Carey Clouse, *Farming Cuba: Urban Agriculture from the Ground Up* (New York: Princeton Architectural Press, 2014); Chellappan Mohanakumaran Nair, Krishna Rugmini Salin, Juliet Joseph, Bahuleyan Aneesh, Vaidhyanathan Geethalakshmi, and Michael Bernard New, "Organic Rice-Prawn Farming Yields 20% Higher Revenues," *Agronomy for Sustainable Development* 34 (2014): 569–81; Dean Saranillio, "Alternative Economies for Alternative Futures," in *The Value of Hawai'i 2: Ancestral Routes, Oceanic Visions,* ed. Aiko Yamashiro and Noelani Goodyear-Kaʻōpua (Honolulu: University of Hawai'i Press, 2014); Dean Saranillio, "The Insurrection of Subjugated Futures," *American Quarterly* 67, no. 3 (2015): 637–44; José E. Martínez-Reyes, *Moral Ecology of a Forest: The Nature Industry and Maya Post-Conservation* (Tucson: University of Arizona Press, 2016); Patnaik and Moyo, *Agrarian Question,* 50, 52; Bond, *Looting Africa,* 56, 58, 60–61; Moyo, "Agrarian Transformation in Africa," 42; Waziyatawin, *What Does Justice Look Like?,* 12–13; John Mohawk, *Thinking in Indian: A John Mohawk Reader* (Golden, CO: Fulcrum, 2010), 102–3.

25. Quote is from Davis, *Prisoners of the American Dream,* 262. Vijay Prashad, "Does the South Have a Possible History?" in Bond and Garcia, *BRICS,* 268; Vijay Prashad, *Arab Spring, Libyan Winter* (New Delhi: LeftWord Books, 2012), 240–41; Prashad, *Poorer Nations,* 225–30; Amin, *Empire of Chaos,* 74; Bello, *Deglobalization,* 117; Ahmad, *Imperialism of Our Time,* 130, 135, 140–41.

26. On accumulation by encroachment, see Prabhat Patnaik, *Re-Envisioning Socialism* (New Delhi: Tulika Books, 2011), 26–27; Pasternak, *Grounded Authority,* 32, 240–44. On blockades among jobless workers in Argentina, and among Indigenous coca-growers in the Andes, see Seoane, Taddei, and Algranati, "New Configurations," in Boron and Lechini, *Politics and Social Movements,* 233; Coulthard, *Red Skin, White Masks,* 166–70; Noelani Goodyear Kaʻōpua, "Protectors of the Future, Not Protestors of the Past: Indigenous Pacific Activism and Mauna a Wākea" *South Atlantic Quarterly* 116, no. 1 (2017): 184–86, 188–90; Manissa M. Maharawal, "Black Lives Matter, Gentrification and the Security State in the San Francisco Bay Area," *Anthropological Theory* 17, no. 3 (2017): 338–64; Darius Carr, "Black Lives Matter: An Autoethnographic Account of Ferguson, Missouri, Civil Unrest of 2014," *Journal for the Study of Peace and Conflict* (2016): 12–15; Richard Pithouse, "Forging New Political Identities in the Shanty Towns of Durban, South Africa," *Historical Materialism* 26, no. 2 (2018): 178–97; José Antonio Lucero, *Struggles of Voice: The Politics of Indigenous Representation in the Andes* (Pittsburgh: University of Pittsburgh Press, 2008), 84–86, 138–41; Sergio Miguel Huarcaya, "Performativity, Performance, and Indigenous Activism in Ecuador and the Andes," *Comparative Studies in Society and History* 57, no. 3 (July 2015): 822–24.

27. João Pedro Stedile, "Landless Battalions: The Sem Terra Movement of Brazil," *New Left Review* 15 (2002): 76–104; Raghavan, *Recolonization,* 294–95, 308–9; Noenoe K. Silva, *The Power of the Steel-Tipped Pen: Reconstructing Native Hawaiian*

Intellectual History (Durham, NC: Duke University Press, 2017), 2–3; Patnaik and Moyo, *Agrarian Question*, 8, 62–63; Prabhat Patnaik, *Re-Envisioning Socialism*, 30–35; Tsikata and Kerr, *Demanding Dignity*, 26; Richard Pithouse, "The Shack Settlement as a Site of Politics: Reflections from South Africa," *Agrarian South: Journal of Political Economy* 3, no. 2 (2014): 191–95; Issa Shivji, *Class Struggles in Tanzania* (New York: Monthly Review Press, 1976), 111–20.

28. Karl Kautsky, "Ultra-Imperialism," *Der Neue Zeit*, September 11, 1914; V.I. Lenin, with G.Y. Zinoviev, *Socialism and War: The Attitude of the Russian Social-Democratic Labour Party Towards the War*, www.marxists.org/archive/lenin /works/1915/s+w/index.htm (accessed August 28, 2018); Amin, *From Capitalism to Civilization*, 92; Ahmad and Barsamian, *Confronting Imperialism*, 50.

29. Chris Busby, Malak Hamdan, and Enteser Ariabi, "Cancer, Infant Mortality, and Birth-Sex Ratio in Fallujah, Iraq, 2005–2009," *International Journal of Environmental Research and Public Health* 7, no. 7 (2010): 2828–37; Avery Anopol, "Lindsey Graham: War with North Korea Would Be 'Worth It' in the Long Run," *The Hill*, March 2, 2018; Ahmad and Barsamian, *Confronting Imperialism*, 43–45; Grace Kyungwon Hong, "Ghosts of Camptown," *MELUS* 39, no. 3 (2014): 53–55; Bello, *Deglobalization*, 30; Peter Hudis and Kevin B. Anderson, eds., *The Rosa Luxemburg Reader* (New York: Monthly Review Press, 2004); Amin, *Spectres of Capitalism*, 62–63, 67–68, 85; Hugo Chavez Frias, "Speech to the 6th World Social Forum," January 27, 2006, Caracas, Venezuela, https://venezuelanalysis.com /analysis/1728 (accessed August 19, 2018).

30. "The only way to end this 'terrorism' is to rebuild that revolutionary movement of the left whose place it occupies and with whose mantle it masquerades": Ahmad, *Imperialism of Our Time*, 54, 107, 109–10, 118, 121–22; Lisa Lowe, "Other Humanities and the Limits of the Human: Response to Lisa Rofel and Stephanie Smallwood," *Cultural Dynamics* 29, nos. 1–2 (2017): 98; Noelani Goodyear Kaʻōpua and Bryan Kamaoli Kuwada, "Making 'Aha: Independent Hawaiian Pasts, Presents and Futures," *Daedalus* 147, no. 1 (2018): 49–59; Amin, *From Capitalism to Civilization*, 2; Goldstein, "Where the Nation Takes Place," 836, 842; Estes, " 'No Two Sides to This Story,' " 39; Coulthard, *Red Skin, White Masks*, 64–75; Bello, *Dilemmas of Domination*, 216–17; Amin, *Liberal Virus*, 81.

BIBLIOGRAPHY

NEWSPAPERS

Fremont Tribune
The Guardian
The Hill
The Intercept
New York Tribune
Omaha Weekly Herald
Overland Monthly
Sacramento Daily Union
San Francisco Chronicle
San Francisco Commercial Herald and Market Review
San Francisco Evening Bulletin
Washington Post

COLLECTIONS

George Bent Papers
Grenville Dodge Papers
Mark Hopkins Papers
Collis Huntington Papers
Frank North Papers
Samuel B. Reed Letters

NATIONAL ARCHIVES

Records of the Office of the Secretary of the Interior, Record Group 48
Records of the Bureau of Indian Affairs, Record Group 75
Records of U. S. Army Continental Commands, 1821–1920, Record Group 393

CONGRESSIONAL AND STATE DOCUMENTS

Peter Burnett, "Message to the California State Legislature," January 7, 1851
Documents relating to the negotiation of the treaty of October 9, 1833, with the Pawnee Indians
Papers Relating to Talks and Councils Held with the Indians in Dakota and Montana Territories in the Years 1866–1869, Washington, DC: Government Printing Office, 1919
Report to the California State Senate of Its Special Committee on Chinese Immigration, 1878
Report of the Joint Special Committee to Investigate Chinese Immigration, Forty-Fourth Congress, New York: Arno Press, 1978
Report of the National Energy Policy Development Group, 2001
U. S. Senate, *Letter from the Secretary of the Interior in relation to the massacre of United States troops by Indians at or near Fort Phil. Kearney*, 1867
U. S. Senate, *Testimony Taken by the United States Pacific Railway Commission*, Washington, DC: Government Printing Office, 1887–1888
"Slave Trade in Africa," September 22, 1890
Leland Stanford, "Inaugural Address of Leland Stanford," January 10, 1862
State of California, Legislature, *Memorial to Congress on the Dangers of Chinese Immigration*, 1862

LAWS AND TREATIES

1825 Treaty with the Pawnee Tribe
1833 Treaty with the Pawnee
1848 Treaty with the Pawnee
1851 Treaty of Fort Laramie with the Sioux
1857 Treaty with the Pawnee
1862 Act to Prohibit the "Coolie Trade"
1862 Act to Protect Free White Labor Against Competition with Chinese Coolie Labor, and to Discourage the Immigration of the Chinese into the State of California
1862 Pacific Railway Act
1863 National Currency Act

1882 Chinese Exclusion Act
1898 Bankruptcy Act
2001 Authorization for Use of Military Force Against Terrorists

SUPREME COURT DECISIONS

Fletcher v. Peck, 1810
The Trustees of Dartmouth College v. Woodward, 1819
Johnson and Graham's Lessee v. William M'Intosh, 1823
Samuel Worcester v. State of Georgia, 1832
Chesapeake & Ohio & Southwestern Railroad Company v. Ida B. Wells [Tennessee
     Supreme Court], 1885
Yick Wo v. Hopkins, 1886
Santa Clara County v. Southern Pacific Railroad Company, 1886
Plessy v. Ferguson, 1896

CORPORATE DOCUMENTS

Central Pacific Railroad Company, *Report of the President*
Enbridge, *Annual Review*
Energy Transfer Equity, *Annual Reports*
Energy Transfer Partners, *Annual Reports*
Guide to the Union Pacific Railroad Lands
JP Morgan Chase & Co., *Annual Report*
Sunoco Logistics Partners, *Annual Reports*
Union Pacific Railroad, *Report of Chief Engineer*

UNPUBLISHED MANUSCRIPTS

Asian American Resources Project: Oral History Transcripts, 1974–1976
Robert Campbell, *A Narrative of Col. Robert Campbell's Experiences in the Rocky
     Mountains Fur Trade from 1825 to 1835*
Edwin Bryant Crocker, Biographical Sketch
Maj. Gen. Grenville M. Dodge, *The Indian Campaign of the Winter of 1864–65*
Biography of Major General Grenville M. Dodge
Kwong Ki-Chaou, interview by H. H. Bancroft
Frederick F. Low, *Political Affairs in California,* Bancroft Library, 1883
Experiences of Thomas O'Donnell While a Workman in Building the Union Pacific
     Railroad
Proceedings of the California State Convention of Colored Citizens, 1865
Gene Weltfish, *Pawnee Field Notes*

DISSERTATIONS

Chun-lin Tan. "The Boxer Catastrophe." PhD dissertation, Political Science, Columbia University, 1952.

Sell, Zachary. "Slavery beyond Slavery: The American South, British Imperialism, and the Circuits of Capital, 1833–1873." PhD dissertation, History, University of Illinois, Urbana-Champaign, 2017.

Tsey, Christian. "Gold Coast Railways: The Making of a Colonial Economy." PhD dissertation, University of Glasgow, Faculty of Social Sciences, 1986.

WORKS CITED

Abruzzi, William S. *Dam That River!: Ecology and Mormon Settlement in the Little Colorado River Basin.* Lanham, MD: University Press of America, 1993.

Adejumobi, Said, and Adebayo Olukoshi. *The African Union and New Strategies for Development in Africa.* Amherst, NY: Cambria Press, 2008.

Afton, Jean, David Halaas, Andrew Masich, and Richard Ellis. *Cheyenne Dog Soldiers: A Ledgerbook History of Coups and Combat.* Denver: University Press of Colorado and Colorado Historical Society, 1997.

Aguiar, Marian. *Tracking Modernity: India's Railway and the Culture of Mobility.* Minneapolis: University of Minnesota Press, 2011.

Ahmad, Aijaz. *Iraq, Afghanistan, and the Imperialism of Our Time.* New Delhi: LeftWord Books, 2004.

Ahmad, Eqbal, and David Barsamian. *Confronting Empire.* Chicago: Haymarket Books, 2017.

Akwesasne Notes. *Basic Call to Consciousness.* Summertown, TN: Native Voices, 1978.

Akyüz, Yilmaz. *The Financial Crisis and the Global South: A Development Perspective.* London: Pluto Press, 2013.

Albers, Patricia, and Beatrice Medicine Woman, eds. *The Hidden Half: Studies of Plains Indian Women.* Washington, DC: University Press of America, 1983.

Allen, Paula Gunn. *The Sacred Hoop: Recovering the Feminine in American Indian Traditions.* Boston: Beacon Press, 1986.

Almaguer, Tomás. *Racial Fault Lines: The Historical Origins of White Supremacy in California.* Berkeley: University of California Press, 1994.

Amin, Samir. *Empire of Chaos.* New York: Monthly Review Press, 1992.

———. *Spectres of Capitalism: A Critique of Current Intellectual Fashions,* New York: Monthly Review Press, 1998.

———. *Obsolescent Capitalism: Contemporary Politics and Global Disorder.* London: Zed Books, 2003.

———. *The Liberal Virus: Permanent War and the Americanization of the World.* New York: Monthly Review Press, 2004.

———. *The World We Wish to See: Revolutionary Objectives in the Twenty-First Century.* New York: Monthly Review Press, 2008.

————. *Financial Crisis? Systemic Crisis?* Dakar: CODESRIA, 2010.

————. *From Capitalism to Civilization: Reconstructing the Socialist Perspective.* New Delhi: Tulika Books, 2010.

————. *Ending the Crisis of Capitalism or Ending Capitalism?* Cape Town: Pambazuka Press, 2011.

————. "The Surplus of Monopoly Capital and the Imperialist Rent." *Monthly Review* 64, no. 3 (July / August 2012): 78–85.

————. *The Implosion of Contemporary Capitalism.* New York: Monthly Review Press, 2013.

————. *Three Essays on Marx's Theory of Value.* New York: Monthly Review Press, 2013.

Angevine, Robert G. *The Railroad and the State: War, Politics, and Technology in Nineteenth-Century America.* Stanford, CA: Stanford University Press, 2004.

Arkush, Brooke S. *The Archaeology of CA-Mno-2122: A Study of Pre-Contact and Post-Contact Lifeways among the Mono Basin Paiute.* Berkeley: University of California Press, 1995.

Arnesen, Eric. *Brotherhoods of Color: Black Railroad Workers and the Struggle for Equality.* Cambridge, MA: Harvard University Press, 2001.

Ashabranner, Brent. *Morning Star, Black Sun: The Northern Cheyenne Indians and America's Energy Crisis.* New York: Dodd, Mead, 1982.

Atleo, E. Richard. *Principles of Tsawalk: An Indigenous Approach to Global Crisis.* Vancouver: UBC Press, 2011.

Awasthi, Aruna. *History and Development of Railways in India.* New Delhi: Deep & Deep, 1994.

Balce, Nerissa. *Body Parts of Empire: Visual Abjection, Filipino Imagines, and the American Archive.* Ann Arbor: University of Michigan Press, 2016.

Bamforth, Douglas B. *Ecology and Human Organization on the Great Plains.* New York: Plenum Press, 1988.

Barak, On. *On Time: Technology and Temporality in Modern Egypt.* Berkeley: University of California Press, 2013.

Baran, Paul A., and Paul M. Sweezy. *Monopoly Capital: An Essay on the American Economic and Social Order.* New York: Monthly Review Press, 1966.

Barkan, Joshua. *Corporate Sovereignty: Law and Government under Capitalism.* Minneapolis: University of Minnesota Press, 2013.

Barker, Joanne, ed. *Sovereignty Matters: Locations of Contestation and Possibility in Indigenous Struggles for Self-Determination.* Lincoln: University of Nebraska Press, 2005.

————. *Native Acts: Law, Recognition, and Cultural Authenticity.* Durham, NC: Duke University Press, 2011.

————. "The Corporation and the Tribe." *American Indian Quarterly* 39, no. 3 (Summer 2015): 243–70.

————. "Self-Determination." *Critical Ethnic Studies* 1, no. 1 (2015): 11–26.

————, ed. *Critically Sovereign: Indigenous Gender, Sexuality, and Feminist Studies.* Durham, NC: Duke University Press, 2017.

———. "Territory as Analytic: The Dispossession of Lenapehoking and the Subprime Crisis." *Social Text* 36, no. 2 (2018): 19–39.

Barsh, Russel Lawrence. "War and the Reconfiguring of American Indian Society." *Journal of American Studies* 35, no. 3 (2001): 371–411.

Baucom, Ian. *Specters of the Atlantic: Finance Capital, Slavery, and the Philosophy of History*. Durham, NC: Duke University Press, 2005.

Bauer Jr., William J. *We Were All Like Migrant Workers Here: Work, Community, and Memory on California's Round Valley Reservation, 1850–1941*. Chapel Hill: University of North Carolina Press, 2009.

Baxter, R. Scott. "The Response of California's Chinese Populations in the Anti-Chinese Movement." *Historical Archaeology* 42, no. 3 (2008): 29–36.

Bear, Laura. *Lines of the Nation: Indian Railway Workers, Bureaucracy, and the Intimate Historical Self*. New York: Columbia University Press, 2007.

Bederman, Gail. *Manliness and Civilization: A Cultural History of Gender and Race in the United States, 1880–1917*. Chicago: University of Chicago Press, 1995.

Bell, Colleen. *The Freedom of Security: Governing Canada in the Age of Counter-Terrorism*. Vancouver: UBC Press, 2011.

Bello, Walden. *Dilemmas of Domination: The Unmaking of the American Empire*. London: Zed Books, 2005.

———. *Deglobalization: Ideas for a New World Economy*. Quezon City: Ateneo de Manila University Press, 2006.

———. *Capitalism's Last Stand?: Deglobalization in the Age of Austerity*. London: Zed Books, 2013.

Benton, Lauren. *A Search for Sovereignty: Law and Geography in European Empires, 1400–1900*. New York: Cambridge University Press, 2010.

Berk, Gerald. *Alternative Tracks: The Constitution of American Industrial Order, 1865–1917*. Baltimore: Johns Hopkins University Press, 1994.

Berthrong, Donald J. *The Southern Cheyennes*. Norman: University of Oklahoma Press, 1963.

Betancourt, Orlando. *The Matter of Empire: Metaphysics and Mining in Colonial Peru*. Pittsburgh: University of Pittsburgh Press, 2017.

Biermann, Werner. *Tanganyika Railways—Carrier of Colonialism: An Account of Economic Indicators and Social Fragments*. Münster: Lit Verlag, 1995.

Billeb, Emil. *Mining Camp Days*. Berkeley: Howell-North Books, 1968.

Black III, Robert C. *The Railroads of the Confederacy*. Chapel Hill: University of North Carolina Press, 1952.

Blackhawk, Ned. *Violence over the Land: Indians and Empires in the Early American West*. Cambridge, MA: Harvard University Press, 2006.

Blaine, Martha Royce. *Pawnee Passage: 1870–1875*. Norman: University of Oklahoma Press, 1990.

Boag, Peter. *Same-Sex Affairs: Constructing and Controlling Homosexuality in the Pacific Northwest*. Berkeley: University of California Press, 2003.

Bond, Patrick. *Looting Africa: The Economics of Exploitation*. London: Zed Books, 2006.

———— and Ana Garcia, eds. *BRICS: An Anti-Capitalist Critique.* Chicago: Haymarket Books, 2015.

Bonnerjea, Biren. *Reminiscences of a Cheyenne Indian.* From the *Journal de la Société des americaniste*, n.s., t. 27, Paris, 1935.

Bordeaux Bettelyoun, Susan, and Josephine Waggoner. *With My Own Eyes: A Lakota Woman Tells Her People's History.* Lincoln: University of Nebraska Press, 1998.

Boron, Atilio, and Gladys Lechini, eds. *Politics and Social Movements in an Hegemonic World: Lessons from Africa, Asia and Latin America.* Buenos Aires: CLACSO, 2005.

Boughter, Judith A. *Betraying the Omaha Nation, 1790–1916.* Norman: University of Oklahoma Press, 1998.

Bradford, Sarah. *Scenes in the Life of Harriet Tubman.* Auburn, NY: W.J. Moses, 1869.

————. *Harriet, the Moses of Her People.* New York: G.R. Lockwood & Son, 1886.

Braun, Bruce, and Sarah Whatmore, eds. *Political Matter: Technoscience, Democracy, and Public Life.* Minneapolis: University of Minnesota Press, 2010.

Bremer III, L. Paul. *My Year in Iraq: The Struggle to Build a Future of Hope.* New York: Simon & Schuster, 2006.

Briggs, Laura. *How All Politics Became Reproductive Politics: From Welfare Reform to Foreclosure to Trump.* Oakland: University of California Press, 2017.

Brooks, James F. *Captives and Cousins: Slavery, Kinship, and Community in the Southwest Borderlands.* Chapel Hill: University of North Carolina Press, 2002.

Brown, Vincent. *The Reaper's Garden: Death and Power in the World of Atlantic Slavery.* Cambridge, MA: Harvard University Press, 2008.

Bruce, Robert. *The Fighting Norths and Pawnee Scouts: Narratives and Reminiscences of Military Service on the Old Frontier.* Lincoln: Nebraska State Historical Society, 1932.

Burnham, Margaret A. "An Impossible Marriage: Slave Law and Family Law." *Law and Inequality* 5 (1987): 187–225.

Busby, Chris, Malak Hamdan, and Enteser Ariabi. "Cancer, Infant Mortality, and Birth-Sex Ratio in Fallujah, Iraq, 2005–2009." *International Journal of Environmental Research and Public Health* 7, no. 7 (2010): 2828–37.

Byrd, Jodi A. "In the City of Blinding Lights." *Cultural Studies Review* 15, no. 2 (2009): 13–28.

————. *The Transit of Empire: Indigenous Critiques of Colonialism.* Minneapolis: University of Minnesota Press, 2011.

————. "Follow the Typical Signs: Settler Sovereignty and Its Discontents." *Settler Colonial Studies* 4, no. 2 (2014): 151–54.

————. "'Do They Not Have Rational Souls?': Consolidation and Sovereignty in Digital New Worlds." *Settler Colonial Studies* 6, no. 4 (2016): 423–37.

————. "Still Waiting for the 'Post' to Arrive: Elizabeth Cook-Lynn and the Imponderables of American Indian Postcoloniality." *Wicazo Sa Review* (Spring 2016): 75–89.

————. "Beast of America: Sovereignty and the Wildness of Objects." *South Atlantic Quarterly* 117, no. 3 (July 2018): 597–613.

Camp, Jordan T. *Incarcerating the Crisis: Freedom Struggles and the Rise of the Neoliberal State.* Oakland: University of California Press, 2016.

————. "The Bombs Explode at Home: Policing, Prisons, and Permanent War." *Social Justice* 44, nos. 2–3 (2017): 11–30.

Campbell, Gregory R. "Northern Cheyenne Ethnicity, Religion, and Coal Development." *Plains Anthropologist* 32, no. 118 (1987): 378–88.

Carr, Darius. "Black Lives Matter: An Autoethnographic Account of Ferguson, Missouri, Civil Unrest of 2014." *Journal for the Study of Peace and Conflict* (2016): 6–20.

Carrington, Frances C. *My Army Life, and the Fort Phil Kearney Massacre with an Account of the Celebration of "Wyoming Opened."* Philadelphia: J. B. Lippincott, 1919.

Carroll, Clint. *Roots of Our Renewal: Ethnobotany and Cherokee Environmental Governance.* Minneapolis: University of Minnesota Press, 2015.

Carroll, Patrick. *Science, Culture, and Modern State Formation.* Berkeley: University of California Press, 2006.

Chan, Sucheng. *This Bittersweet Soil: The Chinese in California Agriculture, 1860–1910.* Berkeley: University of California Press, 1986.

Chandramohanan, K. T., and K. V. Mohanan. "Kaipad Rice Farming in North Kerala: An Indigenous Saline-Resistant Organic Farming System." *Indian Journal of Traditional Knowledge* 11, no. 1 (2012): 185–89.

Chandrasekhar, C. P., and Jayati Ghosh. *The Market That Failed: A Decade of Neoliberal Economic Reforms in India.* New Delhi: LeftWord Books, 2002.

Chang, David. *The Color of the Land: Race, Nation, and the Politics of Landownership in Oklahoma, 1832–1929.* Chapel Hill: University of North Carolina Press, 2010.

————. *The World and All the Things upon It: Native Hawaiian Geographies of Exploration.* Minneapolis: University of Minnesota Press, 2016.

Chang, Gordon. "China and the Pursuit of America's Destiny: Nineteenth-Century Imagining and Why Immigration Restriction Took So Long." *Journal of Asian American Studies* 15, no. 2 (June 2012): 145–69.

Chang, Kornel. *Pacific Connections: The Making of the U. S.–Canadian Borderlands.* Berkeley: University of California Press, 2012.

Chavez Frías, Hugo. "Speech to the 6th World Social Forum." January 27, 2006, Caracas, Venezuela. Accessed August 19, 2018. https://venezuelanalysis.com /analysis/1728.

Chen, Yong. "The Internal Origins of Chinese Emigration to California Reconsidered." *Western Historical Quarterly* 28, no. 4 (Winter 1997): 520–46.

Cheng, Lucie, and Edna Bonacich, eds. *Labor Immigration under Capitalism: Asian Immigrant Workers in the United States before World War II.* Berkeley: University of California Press, 1984.

Cheru, Fantu, and Renu Modi, eds. *Agricultural Development and Food Security in Africa: The Impact of Chinese, Indian and Brazilian Investments.* London: Zed Books, 2013.

Chew, William F. *Nameless Builders of the Transcontinental Railroad: The Chinese Workers of the Central Pacific Railroad.* Victoria: Trafford, 2004.

Cheyenne and Sioux: The Reminiscences of Four Indians and a White Soldier. Compiled by Thomas B. Marquis. Stockton: Pacific Center for Western Historical Studies, 1973.

Chin, Gabriel J. "Unexplainable on Grounds of Race: Doubts about *Yick Wo.*" *University of Illinois Law Review* (2008): online.

Chittenden, Hiram, and Alfred Talbot Richardson, eds. *Life, Letters, and Travels of Father De Smet,* vol. 2. New York: Arno Press, 1969.

Clark, Jr., John E. *Railroads in the Civil War: The Impact of Management on Victory and Defeat.* Baton Rouge: Louisiana State University Press, 2001.

Clary, David A. *Eagles and Empire: The United States, Mexico, and the Struggle for a Continent.* New York: Bantam Books, 2009.

Cleveland, H. I. "The Massacre of Chinese at Rock Springs." *The Watchman* 81, no. 36 (1900): 13.

Clouse, Carey. *Farming Cuba: Urban Agriculture from the Ground Up.* New York: Princeton Architectural Press, 2014.

Coatsworth, John. *Growth against Development: The Economic Impact of Railroads in Porfirian Mexico.* DeKalb: Northern Illinois University Press, 1981.

Cockburn, Patrick. *The Occupation: War and Resistance in Iraq.* New York: Verso, 2007.

———. *Muqtada: Muqtada al-Sadr, the Shia Revival, and the Struggle for Iraq.* New York: Scribner, 2008.

Cohen, Morris. "Property and Sovereignty." *Cornell Law Quarterly* 1, no. 1 (1927): 8–30.

Cohen, Paul A. *History in Three Keys: The Boxers as Event, Experience, and Myth.* New York: Columbia University Press, 1997.

Connolly, William. "Tocqueville, Territory, and Violence." *Theory, Culture, and Society* 11, no. 1 (1994): 19–40.

Cook-Lynn, Elizabeth. *A Separate Country: Postcoloniality and American Indian Nations.* Lubbock: Texas Tech University Press, 2012.

Cotera, María Eugenia. *Native Speakers: Ella Deloria, Zora Neale Hurston, Jovita González, and the Poetics of Culture.* Austin: University of Texas Press, 2008.

Coulthard, Glen. *Red Skin, White Masks: Rejecting the Colonial Politics of Recognition.* Minneapolis: University of Minnesota Press, 2014.

Coward, John M. *The Newspaper Indian: Native American Identity in the Press, 1820–90.* Urbana: University of Illinois Press, 1999.

Crawford, J. B. *The Credit Mobilier of America: Its Origins and History.* New York: Greenwood Press, [1880] 1969.

Culin, Stewart. "The Chinese Drug Stores in America." *American Journal of Pharmacy* 59 (1887): 593–98.

Danker, Donald F., ed. *Man of the Plains: Recollections of Luther North.* Lincoln: University of Nebraska Press, 1961.

Davis, Clarence B., and Kenneth E. Wilburn, Jr., eds. *Railway Imperialism.* New York: Greenwood Press, 1991.

Davis, Mike. *Late Victorian Holocausts: El Niño Famines and the Making of the Third World*. New York: Verso, 2002.

———. *Planet of Slums*. New York: Verso, 2006.

———. *Prisoners of the American Dream: Politics and Economy in the History of the U. S. Working Class*. New York: Verso, 2018.

Day, Iyko. *Alien Capital: Asian Racialization and the Logic of Settler Colonialism*. Durham, NC: Duke University Press, 2016.

Dayan, Colin. *The Law Is a White Dog: How Legal Rituals Make and Unmake Persons*. Princeton, NJ: Princeton University Press, 2011.

Decanio, Samuel. *Democracy and the Origins of the American Regulatory State*. New Haven, CT: Yale University Press, 2015.

Decker, Leslie E. *Railroads, Lands, and Politics: The Taxation of the Railroad Land Grants, 1864–1897*. Providence: Brown University Press, 1964.

Deer, Sarah. *The Beginning and End of Race: Confronting Sexual Violence in Native America*. Minneapolis: University of Minnesota Press, 2015.

Deloria, Ella. *Iron Hawk*. Albuquerque: University of New Mexico Press, 1993.

———. *Buffalo People*. Albuquerque: University of New Mexico Press, 1994.

———. *Waterlily*. Omaha: University of Nebraska Press, 2009.

Deloria, Jr., Vine. *Behind the Trail of Broken Treaties: An Indian Declaration of Independence*. New York: Delacorte Press, 1974.

——— and Raymond J. DeMallie. *Documents of American Indian Diplomacy: Treaties, Agreements, and Conventions, 1775–1979*, vol. 1. Norman: University of Oklahoma Press, 1999.

Deloria, Philip. *Indians in Unexpected Places*. Lawrence: University Press of Kansas, 2004.

Denetdale, Jennifer Nez. "Planting Seeds of Ideas and Raising Doubts about What We Believe: An Interview with Vine Deloria, Jr." *Journal of Social Archaeology* 42, no. 2 (2004): 131–46.

———. "Chairmen, Presidents, and Princesses: The Navajo Nation, Gender, and the Politics of Tradition." *Wicazo Sa Review* 21, no. 1 (2006): 9–28.

———. "'No Explanation, No Resolution, and No Answers': Border Town Violence and Navajo Resistance to Settler Colonialism." *Wicazo Sa Review* 31, no. 1 (2016): 111–31.

Dennison, Jean. *Colonial Entanglement: Constituting a Twenty-First-Century Osage Nation*. Chapel Hill: University of North Carolina Press, 2012.

De Quille, Dan. *The Big Bonanza: An Authentic Account of the Discovery, History, and Working of the World-Renowned Comstock Lode of Nevada*. New York: Thomas Crowell, 1947.

Derby, E. H. *The Overland Route to the Pacific: A Report on the Condition, Capacity and Resources of the Union Pacific and Central Pacific Railways*. Boston: Lee & Shepard, 1869.

Deustua, José R. *The Bewitchment of Silver: The Social Economy of Mining in Nineteenth-Century Peru*. Athens: Ohio University Press, 2000.

Dewey, John. "The Historic Background of Corporate Legal Personality." *Yale Law Journal* 70, no. 6 (April 1926): 655–73.

Dhillon, Jaskiran. *Prairie Rising: Indigenous Youth, Decolonization, and the Politics of Intervention.* Toronto: University of Toronto Press, 2017

Dirlik, Arif., ed. *Chinese on the American Frontier.* Lanham, MD: Rowman & Littlefield, 2001.

———, Roxann Prazniak, and Alexander Woodside, eds. *Global Capitalism and the Future of Agrarian Society.* Boulder, CO: Paradigm, 2012.

Dobbin, Frank. *Forging Industrial Policy: The United States, Britain, and France in the Railway Age.* New York: Cambridge University Press, 1994.

Downs, James. *Two Worlds of the Washo.* New York: Holt, Rinehart, and Winston, 1966.

Draper, Nicholas. *The Price of Emancipation: Slave-Ownership, Compensation and British Society at the End of Slavery.* New York: Cambridge University Press, 2010.

Dubber, Markus D., and Mariana Valverde, eds. *The New Police Science: The Police Power in Domestic and International Governance.* Stanford, CA: Stanford University Press, 2006.

———. *Police and the Liberal State.* Stanford, CA: Stanford University Press, 2008.

DuBois, Laurent. *A Colony of Citizens: Revolution and Slave Emancipation in the French Caribbean, 1787–1804.* Chapel Hill: University of North Carolina Press, 2004.

Du Bois, W. E. B. "The African Roots of War." *Atlantic Monthly,* May 1915, 707–14.

———. *Darkwater: Voices from within the Veil.* New York: Harcourt, Brace and Howe, 1920.

———. *Black Reconstruction in America.* New York: Free Press, 1998.

———. *Dusk of Dawn: An Essay toward and Autobiography of a Race Concept.* New York: Oxford University Press, 2007.

Dunbar-Ortiz, Roxanne. *Roots of Resistance: A History of Land Tenure in New Mexico.* Norman: University of Oklahoma Press, 2007.

———. *The Great Sioux Nation: Sitting in Judgement of America.* Lincoln: University of Nebraska Press, 2013.

———. *An Indigenous Peoples' History of the United States.* Boston: Beacon Press, 2014.

———. *Loaded: A Disarming History of the Second Amendment.* San Francisco: City Lights Books, 2018.

Eastman, Charles A. *Indian Heroes and Great Chieftains,* Lincoln: University of Nebraska Press, 1991.

Elden, Stuart. *Terror and Territory: The Spatial Extent of Sovereignty.* Minneapolis: University of Minnesota Press, 2009.

Ely, Jr., James. *Railroads and American Law.* Lawrence: University of Kansas Press, 2001.

Endres, Danielle. "Animist Intersubjectivity as Argumentation: Western Shoshone and Southern Paiute Arguments against a Nuclear Waste Site at Yucca Mountain." *Argumentation* 27, no. 2 (2013): 183–200.

Enloe, Cynthia. *Bananas, Beaches, and Bases: Making Feminist Sense of International Politics.* Oakland: University of California Press, 2014.

Ennis, Thomas E. *French Policy and Developments in Indochina.* New York: Russell & Russell, 1936.

Eschen, Penny von. *Race against Empire: Black Americans and Anticolonialism, 1937–1957.* Ithaca, NY: Cornell University Press, 1997.

Estes, Nick. "Wounded Knee: Settler Colonial Property Regimes and Indigenous Liberation." *Capitalism, Nature, Socialism* 24, no. 3 (2013): 190–202.

———. " 'There Are No Two Sides to This Story': An Interview with Elizabeth Cook-Lynn." *Wicazo Sa Review* 31, no. 1 (2016): 27–45.

———. *Our History Is the Future: #NoDAPL, Standing Rock, and the Long Tradition of Indigenous Resistance.* New York: Verso, forthcoming.

Ewers, John C. *Indian Life on the Upper Missouri.* Norman: University of Oklahoma Press, 1968.

Farge, Arlette, and Jacques Revel. *The Vanishing Children of Paris: Rumor and Politics before the French Revolution.* Cambridge, MA: Harvard University Press, 1991.

Ferguson, Roderick. *The Reorder of Things: The University and Its Pedagogies of Minority Difference.* Minneapolis: University of Minnesota Press, 2012.

Ferraro, Pat, and Bob Ferraro. *The Past in Glass.* Sparks, NV: Western Printing, 1964.

Fine, Gary, and Patricia Turner. *Whispers on the Color Line: Rumor and Race in America.* Berkeley: University of California Press, 2001.

Fitzmaurice, Andrew. "The Genealogy of Terra Nullius." *Australian Historical Studies* 38, no. 129 (2007): 1–15.

Flanagan, Thomas. *Riel and the Rebellion: 1885 Reconsidered.* Toronto: University of Toronto Press, 2000.

Foner, Philip S. *The Great Labor Uprising of 1877.* New York: Monad Press, 1977.

Forbes, Jack D. "Indigenous Americans: Spirituality and Ecos." *Daedalus* 130, no. 4 (2001), 283–300.

Fowler, Loretta. *Tribal Sovereignty and the Historical Imagination: Cheyenne-Arapaho Politics.* Lincoln: University of Nebraska Press, 2002.

———. "Arapaho and Cheyenne Perspectives: From the 1851 Treaty to the Sand Creek Massacre." *American Indian Quarterly* 39, no. 4 (Fall 2015): 364–90.

Fraser, Donald. *"Katy": Pioneer Railroad of the Southwest!: 1865.* New York: Newcomen Society, 1953.

Gallo, Kevin, and Eric Wood. "Historical Drought Events of the Great Plains Recorded by Native Americans." *Great Plains Research* 25, no. 2 (2015).

Gann, L. H., and Peter Duignan. *The Rulers of British Africa: 1870–1914.* Stanford, CA: Stanford University Press, 1978.

Gao, James. *Meeting Technology's Advance: Social Change in China and Zimbabwe in the Railroad Age.* Westport, CT: Greenwood Press, 1997.

Gewald, Jan-Bart. *Herero Heroes: A Socio-Political History of the Herero of Nimibia, 1890–1923*. Athens: Ohio University Press.

Ghosh, Jayati. *Never Done and Poorly Paid: Women's Work in Globalising India*. New Delhi: Women Unlimited, 2009.

Giddings, Paula J. *Ida, A Sword among Lions: Ida B. Wells and the Campaign against Lynching*. New York: Amistad, 2008.

Givens, Michael. *The Archaeology of the Colonized*. London: Routledge, 2004.

Go, Julian. "Chains of Empire, Projects of State: Political Education and U. S. Colonial Rule in Puerto Rico and the Philippines." *Comparative Studies in Society and History* 42 (2000): 333–62.

Godfrey, Joyzelle Gingway, and Susan Gardner. "Speaking of Ella Deloria: Conversations with Joyzelle Gingway Godfrey, 1998–2000, Lower Brule Community College, South Dakota." *American Indian Quarterly* 24, no. 3 (Summer 2000): 456–81.

Goeman, Mishuana. "From Place to Territories and Back Again: Centering Storied Land in the Discussion of Indigenous Nation-Building." *International Journal of Critical Indigenous Studies* 1, no. 1 (2008): 23–34.

———. "Notes toward a Native Feminism's Spatial Practice." *Wicazo Sa Review* 24, no. 2 (2009): 169–87.

———. *Mark My Words: Native Women Mapping Our Nations*. Minneapolis: University of Minnesota Press, 2013.

Goldberg-Hiller, Jonathan, and Noenoe K. Silva. "Sharks and Pigs: Animating Hawaiian Sovereignty against the Anthropological Machine." *South Atlantic Quarterly* 110, no. 2 (2011): 429–46.

Golden, James Reed. *Investment Behavior by United States Railroads, 1870–1914*. New York: Arno Press, 1975.

Goldstein, Alyosha. "Where the Nation Takes Place: Proprietary Regimes, Antistatism, and U. S. Settler-Colonialism." *South Atlantic Quarterly* 107, no. 4 (Fall 2008): 833–61.

———. *Formations of United States Colonialism*. Durham, NC: Duke University Press, 2014.

———. "Promises Are Over: Puerto Rico and the Ends of Decolonization." *Theory and Event* 19, no. 4 (2016).

———. "The Ground Not Given: Colonial Dispositions of Land, Race, and Hunger." *Social Text* 36, no. 2 (June 2018): 83–106.

Gómez-Barris, Macarena. *The Extractive Zone: Social Ecologies and Decolonial Perspectives*. Durham, NC: Duke University Press, 2017.

Goodyear-Kaʻōpua, Noelani. *The Seeds We Planted: Portraits of a Native Hawaiian Charter School*. Durham, NC: Duke University Press, 2013.

——— and Bryan Kamaoli Kuwada. "Making ʻAha: Independent Hawaiian Pasts, Presents and Futures." *Daedalus* 147, no. 1 (2018): 49–59.

Goswami, Manu. *Producing India: From Colonial Economy to National Space*. Chicago: University of Chicago Press, 2004.

Graham, Stephen, ed. *Disrupted Cities: When Infrastructure Fails*. New York: Routledge Press, 2010.

Grandy, Christopher. *New Jersey and the Fiscal Origins of Modern American Corporation Law*. New York: Garland, 1993.

Grenier, John. *The First War of War: American War Making on the Frontier, 1607–1814*. New York: Cambridge University Press, 2005.

Griffiths, Tom, and Libby Ronin, eds. *Ecology and Empire: Environmental History of Settler Societies*. Seattle: University of Washington Press, 1997.

Grinnell, George Bird. *Two Great Scouts and Their Pawnee Battalion: The Experiences of Frank J. North and Luther H. North, Pioneers in the Great West, 1856–1882, and Their Defence of the Building of the Union Pacific Railroad*. Lincoln: University of Nebraska Press, 1973.

Guha, Ranajit. *History at the Limits of World-History*. New York: Columbia University Press, 2002.

———— and Gayatri Chakravorty Spivak, eds. *Selected Subaltern Studies*. New York: Oxford University Press, 1988.

Gutmann, Matthew, and Catherine Lutz. *Breaking Ranks: Iraq Veterans Speak Out against the War*. Berkeley: University of California Press, 2010.

Haley, Sarah. *No Mercy Here: Gender, Punishment, and the Making of Jim Crow Modernity*. Chapel Hill: University of North Carolina Press, 2016.

Hall, Stuart. "A 'Reading' of Marx's 1857 Introduction to *The Grundrisse*." Centre for Cultural Studies, University of Birmingham, November–December 1973.

————. *Cultural Studies 1983: A Theoretical History*. Durham, NC: Duke University Press, 2016.

Hämäläinen, Pekka. *The Comanche Empire*. New Haven, CT: Yale University Press, 2008.

————. "Reconstructing the Great Plains: The Long Struggle for Sovereignty and Dominance in the Heart of the Continent." *Journal of the Civil War Era* 6, no. 4 (2016): 481–509.

Harjo, Joy, and Gloria Bird. *Reinventing the Enemy's Language: Contemporary Native Women's Writings of North America*. New York: W. W. Norton, 1997.

Harjo, Suzan Shown, ed. *Nation to Nation: Treaties between the United States and American Indian Nations*. Washington, DC: Smithsonian, 2014.

Harris, Cheryl I. "Whiteness as Property." *Harvard Law Review* 106, no. 8 (1993): 1707–91.

————. "Finding Sojourner's Truth: Race, Gender and the Institution of Property." *Cardozo Law Review* 18, no. 2 (1996): 309–410.

Harrod, Ryan P., Jennifer L. Thompson, and Debra L. Martin. "Hard Labor and Hostile Encounters: What Human Remains Reveal about Institutional Violence and Chinese Immigrants Living in Carlin, Nevada (1885–1923)." *Historical Archaeology* 46, no. 4 (2012): 85–111.

Hartman, Saidiya. *Scenes of Subjection: Terror, Slavery, and Self-Making in Nineteenth-Century America*. New York: Oxford University Press, 1997.

————. "Venus in Two Acts." *small axe* 26 (June 2008): 1–14.

Harvey, David. *The Limits to Capital*. New York: Verso, 1999.

Headrick, Daniel. *The Tools of Empire: Technology and European Imperialism in the Nineteenth Century.* New York: Oxford University Press, 1981.

———. *The Tentacles of Progress: Technology Transfer in the Age of Imperialism, 1850–1940.* New York: Oxford University Press, 1988.

Heatherton, Christina, and Jordan T. Camp, eds. *Policing the Planet: Why the Policing Crisis Led to Black Lives Matter.* New York: Verso, 2016.

Herrera, Remy, and Kin Chi Lau. *The Struggle for Food Sovereignty: Alternative Development and the Renewal of Peasant Societies Today.* London: Pluto Press, 2015.

Higginbotham, Jr., A. Leon. *Shades of Freedom: Racial Politics and Presumptions of the American Legal Process.* New York: Oxford University Press, 1996.

——— and Barbara K. Kopytoff. "Property First, Humanity Second: The Recognition of the Slave's Human Nature in Virginia Civil Law." *Ohio State Law Journal* 50 (1989): 511–40.

Higham, John. *Strangers in the Land: Patterns of American Nativism, 1860–1925.* New York: Atheneum, 1963.

Hilferding, Rudolph. *Finance Capital: A Study in the Latest Phase of Capitalist Development.* London: Routledge, 2006.

Hill, M. F. *Permanent Way: The Story of the Kenya and Uganda Railway.* Nairobi: East African Railways and Harbours, 1961.

Hobsbawm, Eric. *The Age of Empire: 1875–1914.* New York: Vintage, 1989.

Hobson, Charles F. *The Great Yazoo Lands Sale: The Case of Fletcher v. Peck.* Lawrence: University Press of Kansas, 2016.

Hobson, J. A. *Imperialism: A Study.* Ann Arbor: University of Michigan Press, 1965.

Holland, Sharon. *Raising the Dead: Readings of Death and (Black) Subjectivity.* Durham, NC: Duke University Press, 2000.

Hong, Grace Kyungwon. "Ghosts of Camptown." *MELUS* 39, no. 3 (2014): 49–67.

Hoover, Elizabeth. *The River Is in Us: Fighting Toxics in a Mohawk Community.* Minneapolis: University of Minnesota Press, 2017.

Horne, Gerald. *The Counter-Revolution of 1776: Slave Resistance and the Origins of the United States of America.* New York: NYU Press, 2014.

Horwitz, Morton. "*Santa Clara* Revisited: The Development of Corporate Theory." *West Virginia Law Review* 88, no. 2 (Fall 1985): 173–224.

Hoy, William. *The Chinese Six Companies.* San Francisco: Chinese Consolidated Benevolent Association, 1942.

Huarcaya, Sergio Miguel. "Performativity, Performance, and Indigenous Activism in Ecuador and the Andes." *Comparative Studies in Society and History* 57, no. 3 (July 2015): 806–37.

Hudis, Peter, and Kevin B. Anderson, eds. *The Rosa Luxemburg Reader.* New York: Monthly Review Press, 2004.

Hudson, Peter. *Banking and Empire: How Wall Street Colonized the Caribbean.* Chicago: University of Chicago Press, 2017.

Huenemann, Ralph William. *The Dragon and the Iron Horse: The Economics of Railroads in China, 1876–1937.* Cambridge, MA: Harvard University Press, 1984.

Hunt, Sarah. "Ontologies of Indigeneity: The Politics of Embodying a Concept." *Cultural Geographies* 21 (2014): 27–32.

———. "Representing Colonial Violence: Trafficking, Sex Work, and the Violence of Law." *Atlantis* 37, no. 1 (2015–16): 25–39.

——— and Cindy Holmes. "Everyday Decolonization: Living a Decolonizing Queer Politics." *Journal of Lesbian Studies* 19, no. 2 (2015): 154–72.

Hunter, Tera. *To 'Joy My Freedom: Southern Black Women's Lives and Labors after the Civil War.* Cambridge, MA: Harvard University Press, 1997.

Hurtado, Albert. "Controlling California's Indian Labor Force: Federal Administration of California Indian Affairs during the Mexican War." *Southern California Quarterly* 61, no. 3 (1979): 217–38.

———. *Indian Survival on the California Frontier.* New Haven, CT: Yale University Press, 1988.

———. "California Indians and the Workaday West: Labor, Assimilation, and Survival." *California History* 69, no. 1 (Spring 1990): 2–11.

Hyde, George. *Life of George Bent, Written from His Letters.* Norman: University of Oklahoma Press, 1968.

Hyman, Colette. *Dakota Women's Work: Creativity, Culture, and Exile.* St. Paul: Minnesota Historical Society Press, 2012.

Ichioka, Yuji. "Asian Immigrant Coal Miners and the United Mine Workers of America: Race and Class at Rock Springs, Wyoming, 1907." *Amerasia* 6, no. 2 (1979): 1–23.

Ilaiah, Kancha. *Buffalo Nationalism: A Critique of Spiritual Fascism.* Kolkata: Samya, 2004.

INCITE! Women of Color Against Violence, ed. *The Revolution Will Not Be Funded.* Boston: South End Press, 2009.

Iraq Veterans Against the War. *Winter Soldier: Iraq and Afghanistan.* Chicago: Haymarket Books, 2008.

Ireland, Paddy. "Capitalism without the Capitalist: The Joint Stock Company Share and the Emergence of the Modern Doctrine of Separate Corporate Personality." *Legal History* 17, no. 1 (April 1996): 41–73.

———. "Company Law and the Myth of Shareholder Ownership." *Modern Law Review* 62, no. 1 (1999): 32–57.

———, Ian Grigg-Spall, and Dave Kelly. "The Conceptual Foundations of Modern Company Law." *Journal of Law and Society* 14, no. 1 (Spring 1987): 149–65.

Irick, Robert. *Ch'ing Policy toward the Coolie Trade, 1847–1878.* China: Chinese Materials Center, 1982.

Jacobson, Matthew Frye. *Barbarian Virtues: The United States Encounters Foreign Peoples at Home and Abroad, 1876–1917.* New York: Hill and Wang, 2000.

James, C. L. R. *Modern Politics.* Oakland: PM Press, 2013.

James, John, and David Weiman. "The National Banking Acts and the Transformation of New York City Banking during the Civil War Era." *Journal of Economic History* 71, no. 2 (June 2011): 338–62.

Jaynes, Gerald David. *Branches without Roots: Genesis of the Black Working Class in the American South, 1862–1882*. New York: Oxford University Press, 1986.

Jeffries, Richard. *Class, Power and Ideology in Ghana: The Railwaymen of Sekondi.* London: Cambridge University Press, 1978.

Johnson, Edward C. *Walker River Paiutes: A Tribal History.* Schurz, NV: Walker River Paiute Tribe, 1975.

Johnson, Gaye Theresa, and Alex Lubin, eds. *Futures of Black Radicalism.* New York: Verso, 2017.

Johnson, Lyman. "Law and Legal Theory in the History of Corporate Responsibility: Corporate Personhood." *Seattle University Law Review* 35, no. 4 (2012): 1135–64.

Johnson, Walter. *River of Dark Dreams: Slavery and Empire in the Cotton Kingdom.* Cambridge, MA: Harvard University Press, 2013.

Joo, Thomas Wuil. "New 'Conspiracy Theory' of the Fourteenth Amendment: Nineteenth-Century Chinese Civil Rights Cases and the Development of Substantive Due Process Jurisprudence." *University of San Francisco Law Review* 29 (Winter 1995): 353–88.

———. "Yick Wo Revisited: Nonblack Nonwhites and Fourteenth Amendment History." *University of Illinois Law Review* (2008): online.

Jung, Moon-Ho. "Outlawing 'Coolies': Race, Nation, and Empire in the Age of Emancipation." *American Quarterly* 57, no. 3 (September 2005): 677–701.

———. *Coolies and Cane: Race, Labor, and Sugar in the Age of Emancipation.* Baltimore: Johns Hopkins University Press, 2006.

———. "Beyond Loyalties: Reflections on Regional and National Divides in the Study of Race." *Western Historical Quarterly* 34, no. 3 (2012): 289–91.

———. "What Is the 'Coolie Question'?" *Labour History* 113 (2017): 1–8.

Kanazawa, Mark. "Immigration, Exclusion, and Taxation: Anti-Chinese Legislation in Gold Rush California." *Journal of Economic History* 65, no. 3 (September 2005): 779–805.

Kapila, Neera. *Race, Rail and Society: Roots of Modern Kenya.* Nairobi: Kenway, 2009.

Kaplan, Amy. *The Anarchy of Empire in the Making of U.S. Culture.* Cambridge, MA: Harvard University Press, 2002.

——— and Donald Pease, eds. *Cultures of United States Imperialism.* Durham, NC: Duke University Press, 1993.

Kappler, Charles J., ed. *Indian Affairs: Laws and Treaties,* vol. 2, *Treaties.* Washington, DC: Government Printing Office, 1904.

Karuka, Manu [as Manu Vimalassery]. "Counter-Sovereignty." *J19: The Journal of Nineteenth-Century Americanists* 2, no. 1 (2014): 142–48.

———. "Fugitive Decolonization." *Theory & Event* 19, no. 4 (2016).

———, with Juliana Hu Pegues and Alyosha Goldstein. "Introduction: On Colonial Unknowing." *Theory & Event* 19, no. 4 (2016).

———, with Juliana Hu Pegues and Alyosha Goldstein. "Colonial Unknowing and Relations of Study." *Theory & Event* 20, no. 4 (2017).

Kauanui, J. Kēhaulani. "Imperial Ocean: The Pacific as a Critical Site for American Studies." *American Quarterly* 67, no. 3 (2015): 625–36.

Kaur, Amarjit. *Bridge and Barrier: Transport and Communications in Colonial Malaya, 1870–1957.* New York: Oxford University Press, 1975.

Kautsky, Karl. "Ultra-Imperialism." *Der Neue Zeit*, September 11, 1914.

Keller, Jean A. *Empty Beds: Indian Student Health at Sherman Institute, 1902–1922.* East Lansing: Michigan State University Press, 2002.

Kelley, Blair L. M. *Right to Ride: Streetcar Boycotts and African American Citizenship in the Era of Plessy v. Ferguson.* Chapel Hill: University of North Carolina Press, 2010.

Kelly, Isabel T. *Southern Paiute Ethnography.* Anthropological Papers, Department of Anthropology, University of Utah, Number 69 (Glen Canyon Series Number 21), May 1964.

Kerr, Ian J., ed. *27 Down: New Departures in Indian Railway Studies.* New Delhi: Orient Longman, 2007.

Kerwin, Dale. *Aboriginal Dreaming Paths and Trading Routes: The Colonisation of the Australian Landscape.* Brighton: Sussex Academic Press, 2010.

Khalili, Laleh. *Time in the Shadows: Confinement in Counterinsurgencies.* Stanford, CA: Stanford University Press, 2013.

Khuri-Makdisi, Ilham. *The Eastern Mediterranean and the Making of Global Radicalism, 1860–1914.* Berkeley: University of California Press, 2010.

Kidwell, Clara Sue. *Choctaws and Missionaries in Mississippi, 1818–1918.* Norman: University of Oklahoma Press, 1995.

Killsback, Leo. "The Legacy of Little Wolf: Rewriting and Rerighting Our Leaders Back into History." *Wicazo Sa Review* 26, no. 1 (Spring 2011): 85–111.

Kim, Jodi, "Settler Modernity, Debt Imperialism, and the Necropolitics of the Promise." *Social Text* 36, no. 2 (June 2018): 41–61.

Kim, Nadia. *Imperial Citizens: Koreans and Race from Seoul to LA.* Stanford, CA: Stanford University Press, 2008.

Kingsbury, Benedict, and Benjamin Straumann, eds. *The Roman Foundations of the Law of Nations: Alberico Gentili and the Justice of Empire.* New York: Oxford University Press, 2010.

Kino-nda-niimi Collective. *The Winter We Danced: Voices from the Past, the Future, and the Idle No More Movement.* Winnipeg: ARP Books, 2014.

Kish, Zenia, and Justin Leroy. "Bonded Life." *Cultural Studies* 29, nos. 5–6 (2015): 630–51.

Klein, Naomi. *The Shock Doctrine: The Rise of Disaster Capitalism.* New York: Picador, 2008.

Klopotek, Brian. *Recognition Odysseys: Indigeneity, Race, and Federal Tribal Recognition Policy in Three Louisiana Communities.* Durham, NC: Duke University Press, 2011.

Knack, Martha C., and Omer C. Stewart. *As Long as the River Shall Run.* Berkeley: University of California Press, 1984.

Knopf, Terry Ann. *Rumors, Race and Riots*. New Brunswick, NJ: Transaction Books, 1975.

Knopp, Lisa. *What the River Carries: Encounters with the Mississippi, Missouri, and Platte*. Columbia: University of Missouri Press, 2012.

Koont, Sinan. *Sustainable Urban Agriculture in Cuba*. Gainesville: University of Florida Press, 2011.

Kuokkanen, Rauna. "Indigenous Economies, Theories of Subsistence, and Women: Exploring the Social Economy Model for Indigenous Governance." *American Indian Quarterly* 35, no. 2 (2011): 215–40.

Kwee Hui Kian. "Chinese Economic Dominance in Southeast Asia: A Longue Duree Perspective." *Comparative Studies in Society and History* 55, no. 1 (2013): 5–34.

LaDuke, Winona. *Recovering the Sacred: The Power of Naming and Claiming*. Boston: South End Press, 2005.

———. *The Militarization of Indian Country*. East Lansing: Michigan State University Press, 2013.

———. *All Our Relations: Native Struggles for Land and Life*. Chicago: Haymarket Books, 2015.

Lahti, Janne. "Colonized Labor: Apaches and Pawnees as Army Workers." *Western Historical Quarterly* 39, no. 3 (Autumn 2008): 283–302.

Lai, Him Mark. *Becoming Chinese American: A History of Communities and Institutions*. New York: Alta Mira Press, 2004.

Larkin, Brian. *Signal and Noise: Media, Infrastructure, and Urban Culture in Nigeria*. Durham, NC: Duke University Press, 2008.

Larsen, Soren C., and Jay T. Johnson. *Being Together in Place: Indigenous Coexistence in a More Than Human World*. Minneapolis: University of Minnesota Press, 2017.

Larson, Kate Clifford. *Bound for the Promised Land: Harriet Tubman—Portrait of an American Hero*. New York: Ballantine, 2004

Lavender, David. *Bent's Fort*. Garden City, NY: Doubleday, 1954.

Lawrence, Adrea. *Lessons from an Indian Day School: Negotiating Colonization in Northern New Mexico, 1902–1907*. Lawrence: University Press of Kansas, 2011.

Lawrence, Bonita. "Gender, Race, and the Regulation of Native Identity in Canada and the United States: An Overview." *Hypatia* 18, no. 2 (2003): 3–31.

Lee, Erika. *At America's Gates: Chinese Immigration during the Exclusion Era, 1882–1943*. Chapel Hill: University of North Carolina Press, 2003.

Lee, Robert. *The Greatest Public Work: The New South Wales Railways, 1848–1889*. Sydney: Hale & Iremonger, 1988.

———. *France and the Exploitation of China, 1885–1901*. Oxford: Oxford University Press, 1989.

———. *Colonial Engineer: John Whitton: 1818–1899 and the Building of Australia's Railways*. Sydney: University of New South Wales Press, 2000.

Lefebvre, Henri. *The Production of Space*. Malden, MA: Blackwell, 1991.

Left Quarter Collective. "White Supremacist Constitution of the U.S. Empire-State: A Short Conceptual Look at the Long First Century." *Political Power and Social Theory* 20 (2009): 167–200.

Lenin, Vladimir I. *Imperialism: The Highest Stage of Capitalism*. New York: International, 1937.

———, with G. Y. Zinoviev. *Socialism and War: The Attitude of the Russian Social-Democratic Labour Party towards the War* (1915). Accessed August 28, 2018. www.marxists.org/archive/lenin/works/1915/s+w/index.htm.

Leonard, Frank. *A Thousand Blunders: The Grand Trunk Pacific Railway and Northern British Columbia*. Vancouver: UBC Press, 1996.

Lethabo-King, Tiffany. "The Labor of (Re)Reading Plantation Landscapes Fungible(ly)." *Antipode* 48, no. 4 (2016): 1022–39.

Liang, Ernest P. *China: Railways and Agricultural Development, 1875–1935*. Chicago: Department of Geography, 1982.

Lim, Genny, ed. *The Chinese American Experience: Papers from the Second National Conference on Chinese American Studies*. San Francisco: Chinese Historical Society of America, 1980.

Linder, Marc. *Projecting Capitalism: A History of the Internationalization of the Construction Industry*. Westport, CT: Greenwood Press, 1994.

Lindsay, Brendan C. *Murder State: California's Native American Genocide, 1846–1873*. Lincoln: University of Nebraska Press, 2012.

Longo, Peter J., and David W. Yoskowitz, eds. *Water on the Great Plains: Issues and Resources*. Lubbock: Texas Tech University Press, 2002.

Loomis, Rev. A. W. "The Chinese Six Companies." *Overland Monthly* 1, no. 3 (September 1868): 221–27.

Loring, Stephen, Moira T. McCaffrey, Peter Armitage, and Daniel Ashini, "The Archaeology and Ethnohistory of a Drowned Land: Innu Nation Research along the Former Michikamits Lake Shore in Nitassinan (Interior Labrador)." *Archaeology of Eastern North America* 31 (2003): 45–72.

Low, Denise. "Composite Indigenous Genre: Cheyenne Ledger Art as Literature." *Studies in American Indian Literatures* 18, no. 2 (Summer 2006): 83–104.

Lowe, Lisa. *Immigrant Acts: On Asian American Cultural Politics*. Durham, NC: Duke University Press, 1996.

———. *The Intimacies of Four Continents*. Durham, NC: Duke University Press, 2015.

———. "History Hesitant." *Social Text* 13, no. 4 (2015): 85–107.

———. "Other Humanities and the Limits of the Human: Response to Lisa Rofel and Stephanie Smallwood." *Cultural Dynamics* 29, nos. 1–2 (2017): 94–99.

Lucero, José Antonio. *Struggles of Voice: The Politics of Indigenous Representation in the Andes*. Pittsburgh: University of Pittsburgh Press, 2008.

Lukens, Margo. "Her 'Wrongs and Claims': Sarah Winnemucca's Strategic Narratives of Abuse." *Wicazo Sa Review* 13, no. 1 (Spring 1998): 93–108.

Lutterman, Annette. "Draining Energy from the Innu of Nitassinan." *Cultural Survival Quarterly* 24, no. 2 (2000).

Luxemburg, Rosa. *The Accumulation of Capital*. New York: Routledge, 2003.

MacLachlan, Ian. *Kill and Chill: Restructuring Canada's Beef Commodity Chain*. Toronto: University of Toronto Press, 2001.

Magdoff, Fred, and Brian Tokar, eds. *Agriculture and Food in Crisis: Conflict, Resistance, and Renewal*. New York: Monthly Review Press, 2010.

Magliari, Michael. "Free Soil, Unfree Labor." *Pacific Historical Review* 73, no. 3 (August 2004): 349–90.

———. "Free State Slavery: Bound Indian Labor and Slave Trafficking in California's Sacramento Valley, 1850–1864." *Pacific Historical Review* 81, no. 2 (May 2012): 155–92.

Maharawal, Manissa M. "Black Lives Matter, Gentrification, and the Security State in the San Francisco Bay Area." *Anthropological Theory* 17, no. 3 (2017): 338–64.

Maier, Charles S. *Once within Borders: Territories of Power, Wealth, and Belonging since 1500*. Cambridge, MA: Harvard University Press, 2016.

Mamdani, Mahmood. *General Assembly Distinguished Lectures*. Kampala: CODESRIA, 2002.

———. *Define and Rule: Native as Political Identity*. Cambridge, MA: Harvard University Press, 2012.

Marquis, Thomas B. *Cheyenne and Sioux: The Reminiscences of Four Indians and a White Soldier*. Stockton, CA: Pacific Center for Western Historical Studies, 1973.

Marrs, Aaron W. *Railroads in the Old South: Pursuing Progress in a Slave Society*. Baltimore: Johns Hopkins University Press, 2009.

Marshall III, Joseph M. *The Journey of Crazy Horse: A Lakota History*. New York: Viking, 2004.

Martínez-Reyes, José E. *Moral Ecology of a Forest: The Nature Industry and Maya Post-Conservation*. Tucson: University of Arizona Press, 2016.

Martínez San-Miguel, Yolanda. *Coloniality of Diasporas: Rethinking Intra-Colonial Migrations in a Pan-Caribbean Context*. New York: Palgrave Macmillan, 2014.

Marx, Karl. *The Poverty of Philosophy*. New York: International, 1963.

———. *A Contribution to the Critique of Political Economy*. New York: International, 1970.

———. *Grundrisse: Foundations of the Critique of Political Economy*. New York: Penguin, 1973.

———. *Capital, Vol. 1*. New York: Penguin, 1992.

———. *Capital, Vol. 2*. New York: Penguin, 1992.

———. *Capital, Vol. 3*. New York: Penguin, 1993.

——— and Frederick Engels. *On the National and Colonial Questions*. New Delhi: LeftWord Press, 2001.

Mathews, Mary McNair. *Ten Years in Nevada or Life on the Pacific Coast*. Lincoln: University of Nebraska Press, [1880] 1985.

Matthews, Michael. *The Civilizing Machine: A Cultural History of Mexican Railroads, 1876–1910*. Lincoln: University of Nebraska Press, 2013.

McChristian, Douglas. *Fort Laramie: Military Bastion of the High Plains*. Norman, OK: Arthur H. Clark, 2008.

McCrady, David G. *Living with Strangers: The Nineteenth-Century Sioux and the Canadian-American Borderlands.* Lincoln: University of Nebraska Press, 2006.

McMurray, Jonathan S. *Distant Ties: Germany, the Ottoman Empire, and the Construction of the Baghdad Railway.* Westport, CT: Praeger, 2001.

Medicine Woman, Beatrice. *Learning to Be an Anthropologist and Remaining "Native."* Urbana: University of Illinois Press, 2001.

Meinig, D. W. *The Shaping of America: A Geographical Perspective on 500 Years of History,* vol. 2, *Continental America, 1800–1876.* New Haven, CT: Yale University Press, 1993.

Melamed, Jodi. *Represent and Destroy: Rationalizing Violence in the New Racial Capitalism.* Minneapolis: University of Minnesota Press, 2011.

Meyer, Melissa L. *The White Earth Tragedy: Ethnicity and Dispossession at a Minnesota Anishinaabe Reservation, 1889–1920.* Lincoln: University of Nebraska Press, 1994.

Miller, Christine, and Patricia Chuchryk. *Women of the First Nations: Power, Wisdom, and Strength.* Winnipeg: University of Manitoba Press, 1996.

Miller, Susan A., and James Riding In, eds. *Native Historians Write Back: Decolonizing American Indian History.* Lubbock: Texas Tech University Press, 2011.

Million, Dian. "Felt Theory: An Indigenous Feminist Approach to Affect and History." *Wicazo Sa Review* 24, no. 2 (2009).

Mills, Charles. *The Racial Contract.* Ithaca, NY: Cornell University Press, 1997.

Miner, H. Craig. *The Corporation and the Indian: Tribal Sovereignty and Industrial Civilization in Indian Territory, 1865–1907.* Norman: University of Oklahoma Press, 1976.

Mirzoeff, Nicholas. "The Sea and the Land: Biopower and Visuality from Slavery to Katrina." *Culture, Theory and Critique* 50, no. 2 (2009): 289–305.

Mkandawire, Thandika, and Charles C. Soludo. *Our Continent, Our Future: African Perspectives on Structural Adjustment.* Dakar: Council for the Development of Social Science Research in Africa, 1999.

Mohanakumaran Nair, Chellappan, Krishna Rugmini Salin, Juliet Joseph, Bahuleyan Aneesh, Vaidhyanathan Geethalakshmi, and Michael Bernard New. "Organic Rice-Prawn Farming Yields 20% Higher Revenues." *Agronomy for Sustainable Development* 34 (2014): 569–81.

Mohawk, John. *Thinking in Indian: A John Mohawk Reader.* Golden, CO: Fulcrum, 2010.

Montoya, María. *Translating Property: The Maxwell Land Grant and the Conflict over Land in the American West.* Lawrence: University of Kansas Press, 2002.

Monture, Patricia. "Women's Words: Power, Identity, and Indigenous Sovereignty." *Canadian Women's Studies* 26, nos. 3–4 (2008): 154–59.

Mooney, James. *In Sun's Likeness and Power: Cheyenne Accounts of Shield and Tipi Heraldry,* vol. 1. Lincoln: University of Nebraska Press, 2013.

Moore, John. *The Cheyenne Nation: A Social and Demographic History.* Lincoln: University of Nebraska Press, 1987.

Moreton-Robinson, Aileen. *The White Possessive: Property, Power, and Indigenous Sovereignty.* Minneapolis: University of Minnesota Press, 2015.

Morris, Amanda. "Twenty-First-Century Debt Collectors: Idle No More Combats a Five-Hundred-Year-Old Debt." *Women's Studies Quarterly* 42, nos. 1–2 (2014), 244–260.

Morris, Thomas. *Southern Slavery and the Law, 1619–1860.* Chapel Hill: University of North Carolina Press, 1996.

Moyo, Sam, and Paris Yeros, eds. *Reclaiming the Nation: The Return of the National Question in Africa, Asia, and Latin America.* London: Pluto Press, 2011.

Murie, James R. *Pawnee Indian Societies.* Anthropological Papers of the American Museum of Natural History, vol. 11, part 7. New York, 1914.

Murphy, Michelle. *The Economization of Life.* Durham, NC: Duke University Press, 2017.

Murray, Charles Augustus. *Travels in North America during the years 1834, 1835 & 1836, including A Summer Residence with the Pawnee Tribe of Indians, in the Remote Prairies of the Missouri, and a Visit to Cuba and the Azore Island,* vol. 1. New York: Harper & Brothers, 1839.

Needham, Andrew. *Power Lines: Phoenix and the Making of the Modern Southwest.* Princeton, NJ: Princeton University Press, 2014.

Nelson, Melissa K., ed. *Original Instructions: Indigenous Teachings for a Sustainable Future.* Rochester: Bear & Company, 2008.

Nelson, Sarah M., et al. *Denver: An Archaeological History.* Philadelphia: University of Pennsylvania Press, 2001.

Neocleous, Mark. *The Fabrication of Social Order: A Critical Theory of Police Power.* London: Pluto Press, 2000.

———. "Off the Map: On Violence and Cartography." *European Journal of Social Theory* 6, no. 4 (2003): 409–25.

Ngai, Mae. *The Lucky Ones: One Family and the Extraordinary Invention of Chinese America.* Boston: Houghton Mifflin Harcourt, 2010.

———. "Chinese Gold Miners and the 'Chinese Question' in Nineteenth-Century California and Victoria." *Journal of American History* 101, no. 4 (2015): 1082–105.

Nicholas, Andrea Bear. "Colonialism and the Struggle for Liberation: The Experience of Maliseet Women." *University of New Brunswick Law Journal* 43 (1994): 223–39.

Nichols, Robert. "Disaggregating Primitive Accumulation." *Radical Philosophy* 194 (November / December 2015): 18–28.

———. "Theft Is Property! The Recursive Logic of Dispossession." *Political Theory* 46, no. 1 (2018): 3–28.

Nordhoff, Charles. *California: For Health, Pleasure, and Residence—A Book for Travellers and Settlers.* Berkeley: Ten Speed Press, 1973 (original 1873).

Numa: A Northern Paiute History, Reno: Inter-Tribal Council of Nevada, 1976.

Oberholtzer, Ellis. *Jay Cooke: Financier of the Civil War, Vol. 2.* Philadelphia: George W. Jacobs, 1907.

O'Brien, Jean. *Firsting and Lasting: Writing Indians Out of Existence in New England*. Minneapolis: University of Minnesota Press, 2010.

Oehler, Gottlieb F., and David Z. Smith. *Description of a Journey and Visit to the Pawnee Indians, April 22—May 18, 1851*, reprinted from the Moravian Church Miscellany of 1851–1852, New York, 1914.

Okihiro, Gary. *Cane Fires: The Anti-Japanese Movement in Hawaii, 1865–1945*. Philadelphia: Temple University Press, 1991.

Olusoga, David. *The Kaiser's Holocaust: Germany's Forgotten Genocide and the Colonial Roots of Nazism*. London: Faber and Faber, 2010.

Onuf, Peter. *Jefferson's Empire: The Language of American Nationhood*. Charlottesville: University of Virginia Press, 2000.

Opie, John. *Ogallala: Water for a Dry Land*. Lincoln: University of Nebraska Press, 2000.

Ortiz, Simon, ed., *Speaking for the Generations: Native Writers on Writing*. Tucson: University of Arizona Press, 1998.

Ostler, Jeffrey. *The Plains Sioux and U.S. Colonialism from Lewis and Clark to Wounded Knee*. New York: Cambridge University Press, 2004.

O'Sullivan, Mary. *Dividends of Development: Securities Markets in the History of US Capitalism, 1866–1922*. Oxford: Oxford University Press, 2016.

Otter, A. A. den. *The Philosophy of Railways: The Transcontinental Railway Idea in British North America*. Toronto: University of Toronto Press, 1997.

Palumbo-Liu, David. *Asian/American: Historical Crossings of a Racial Frontier*. Stanford, CA: Stanford University Press, 1999.

Park, K-Sue. "Money, Mortgages, and the Conquest of America." *Law & Social Inquiry* 41, no. 4 (Fall 2016): 1006–35.

———. "Insuring Conquest: U.S. Expansion and the Indian Depredation Claims System, 1796–1920." *History of the Present* 8, no. 1 (2018): 57–87.

Parry, Henry C. "Letters from the Frontier." *General Magazine and Historical Chronicle*, University of Pennsylvania, April 1958.

Pasternak, Shiri. *Grounded Authority: The Algonquins of Barriere Lake against the State*. Minneapolis: University of Minnesota Press, 2017.

Patnaik, Prabhat, ed. *Lenin and Imperialism: An Appraisal of Theories and Contemporary Reality*. New Delhi: Orient Longman, 1986.

———. "Introduction," *No to Terrorism, No to War*. New Delhi: CPI(M), 2001.

———. *Re-Envisioning Socialism*. New Delhi: Tulika Books, 2011.

Patnaik, Utsa. "Poverty and Neo-Liberalism." Pune: Gokhale Institute of Politics and Economics, 2005.

———. *The Republic of Hunger and Other Essays*. Gurgaon: Three Essays Collective, 2007.

———. *The Agrarian Question in Marx and His Successors, Vol. 2*. New Delhi: LeftWord Books, 2011.

——— and Sam Moyo. *The Agrarian Question in the Neoliberal Era: Primitive Accumulation and the Peasantry*. Cape Town: Pambazuka Press, 2011.

———— and Prabhat Patnaik. *A Theory of Imperialism.* New York: Columbia University Press, 2016.

Paul, R. Eli. *Blue Water Creek and the First Sioux War, 1854–1856.* Norman: University of Oklahoma Press, 2004.

Penman, Sarah, ed. *Honor the Grandmothers: Dakota and Lakota Women Tell Their Stories.* St. Paul: Minnesota Historical Society Press, 2000.

Perdue, Theda. *Cherokee Women: Gender and Culture Change, 1700–1835.* Lincoln: University of Nebraska Press, 1998.

Pfaelzer, Jean. *Driven Out: The Forgotten War against Chinese Americans.* Berkeley: University of California Press, 2007.

Phang, Hoang Gia. "'A Race So Different': Chinese Exclusion, The Slaughterhouse Cases, and Plessy v. Ferguson." *Labor History* 45, no. 2 (2004): 133–63.

Piatote, Beth H. "The Indian / Agent Aporia." *American Indian Quarterly* 37, no. 3 (2013): 45–62.

Pithouse, Richard. "The Shack Settlement as a Site of Politics: Reflections from South Africa." *Agrarian South: Journal of Political Economy* 3, no. 2 (2014): 179–201.

————. "Forging New Political Identities in the Shanty Towns of Durban, South Africa." *Historical Materialism* 26, no. 2 (2018): 178–97.

Pomeranz, Kenneth. *The Great Divergence: China, Europe, and the Making of the Modern World Economy.* Princeton, NJ: Princeton University Press, 2000.

Povinelli, Elizabeth. *Economies of Abandonment: Social Belonging and Endurance in Late Liberalism.* Durham, NC: Duke University Press, 2011.

Prashad, Vijay. *The Karma of Brown Folk.* Minneapolis: University of Minnesota Press, 2000.

————. *Fat Cats and Running Dogs: The Enron Stage of Capitalism.* Monroe, ME: Common Courage Press, 2003.

————. *The Darker Nations: A People's History of the Third World.* New York: New Press, 2007.

————. *Arab Spring, Libyan Winter.* New Delhi: LeftWord Books, 2012.

————. *The Poorer Nations: A Possible History of the Global South.* New York: Verso, 2012.

Price, Catherine. *The Oglala People, 1841–1879: A Political History.* Lincoln: University of Nebraska Press, 1996.

Prior, Christopher. *Exporting Empire: Africa, Colonial Officials and the Construction of the British Imperial State, c. 1900–1939.* Manchester: Manchester University Press, 2013.

Project for the New American Century. *Rebuilding America's Defenses: Strategy, Forces and Resources for a New Century,* [September] 2000.

Pryde, George B. "The Union Pacific Coal Company, 1868 to August 1952." *Annals of Wyoming* 25 (1953): 191–205.

Pugh, Daniel. "Scenes of Exclusion: Historical Transformation and Material Limitations to Pawnee Gender Representation." *Journal of Material Culture* 18, no. 1 (2013): 53–67.

Raghavan, Chakravarti. *Recolonization: GATT, the Uruguay Round and the Third World*. Penang: Third World Network, 1990.

Ramachandran, V. K., and Madhura Swaminathan, eds. *Agrarian Studies: Essays on Agrarian Relations in Less-Developed Countries*. London: Zed Books, 2003.

Ranger, T. O. *Revolt in Southern Rhodesia, 1896–7*. London: Heinemann, 1967.

———. *Bulawayo Burning: The Social History of a Southern African City, 1893–1960*. Rochester: Boydell & Brewer, 2010.

Rao, M. A. *Indian Railways*. New Delhi: National Book Trust, 1975.

Razack, Sherene, ed. *Race, Space, and the Law: Unmapping a White Settler Society*. Toronto: Between the Lines, 2002.

Red Shirt, Delphine. *Turtle Lung Woman's Granddaughter*. Lincoln: University of Nebraska Press, 2002.

Reddy, Chandan. *Freedom with Violence: Race, Sexuality, and the U. S. State*. Durham, NC: Duke University Press, 2011.

Richter, Amy C. *Home on the Rails: Women, the Railroad, and the Rise of Public Domesticity*. Chapel Hill: University of North Carolina Press, 2005.

Rifkin, Mark. *When Did Indians Become Straight?: Kinship, the History of Sexuality, and Native Sovereignty*. New York: Oxford University Press, 2011.

Robbins, William. *Colony and Empire: The Capitalist Transformation of the American West*. Lawrence: University of Kansas Press, 1994.

Roberts, Brian Russell, and Michelle Ann Stephens, eds. *Archipelagic American Studies*. Durham, NC: Duke University Press, 2017.

Robinson, Cedric. *Black Marxism: The Making of the Black Radical Tradition*. Chapel Hill: University of North Carolina Press, 2000.

———. *Forgeries of Memory and Meaning: Blacks and the Regimes of Race in American Film before World War I*. Chapel Hill: North Carolina Press, 2007.

Rodney, Walter. *How Europe Underdeveloped Africa*. Baltimore: Black Classic Press, 1972.

Roediger, David, and Elizabeth Esch. *The Production of Difference: Race and the Management of Labor in U. S. History*. New York: Oxford University Press, 2012.

Rogin, Michael Paul. "Liberal Society and the Indian Question." *Politics and Society* 1 (May 1971): 269–312.

Rosnow, Ralph, and Gary Fine. *Rumor and Gossip: The Social Psychology of Hearsay*. New York: Elsevier, 1976.

Ross, Luana. *Inventing the Savage: The Social Construction of Native American Criminality*. Austin: University of Texas Press, 1998.

Roy, Ananya. "Slumdog Cities: Rethinking Subaltern Urbanism." *International Journal of Urban and Regional Research* 35, no. 2 (March 2011): 223–38.

Roy, William G. *Socializing Capital: The Rise of the Large Industrial Corporation in America*. Princeton, NJ: Princeton University Press, 1997.

Ruuska, Alex. "Ghost Dancing and the Iron Horse: Surviving through Tradition and Technology." *Technology and Culture* 52, no. 3 (2011): 574–97.

Sainath, P. *Everybody Loves a Good Drought: Stories from India's Poorest Districts*. New Delhi: Penguin Books, 1996.

St. Pierre, Mark, and Tilda Long Soldier. *Walking in the Sacred Manner: Healers, Dreamers, and Pipe Carriers—Medicine Women of the Plains Indians*. New York: Touchstone, 1995.

Salaita, Steven. *Inter/Nationalism: Decolonizing Native America and Palestine*. Minneapolis: University of Minnesota Press, 2016.

Saldaña-Portillo, María Josefina. *Indian Given: Racial Geographies across Mexico and the United States*. Durham, NC: Duke University Press, 2016.

Salyer, Lucy E. *Laws Harsh as Tigers: Chinese Immigrants and the Shaping of Modern Immigration Law*. Chapel Hill: University of North Carolina Press, 1995.

Sanderson, Nathan B. "We Were All Trespassers: George Edward Lemmon, Anglo-American Cattle Ranching, and the Great Sioux Reservation." *Agricultural History* 85, no. 1 (2011): 50–71.

Sanford, Mollie. *The Journal of Mollie Dorsey Sanford in Nebraska and Colorado Territories, 1857–1866*. Lincoln: University of Nebraska Press, 2003.

Saranillio, Dean. "The Insurrection of Subjugated Futures." *American Quarterly* 67, no. 3 (2015): 637–44.

Sassen, Saskia. "Territory and Territoriality in the Global Economy." *International Sociology* 15, no. 2 (2000): 372–93.

———. "When Territory Deborders Territoriality." *Territory, Politics, Governance* 1, no. 1 (2013): 21–45.

Saxton, Alexander. "The Army of Canton in the High Sierra." *Pacific Historical Review* 35, no. 2 (1966): 141–52.

———. *The Rise and Fall of the White Republic: Class Politics and Mass Culture in Nineteenth-Century America*. New York: Verso, 1990.

Schlesier, Karl H. *The Wolves of Heaven: Cheyenne Shamanism, Ceremonies, and Prehistoric Origins*. Norman: University of Oklahoma Press, 1987.

Schreiber, Rebecca. *The Undocumented Everyday: Migrant Lives and the Politics of Visibility*. Minneapolis: University of Minnesota Press, 2018.

Scott, Lalla. *Karnee: A Paiute Narrative*. Reno: University of Nevada Press, 1966.

See, Sarita. *The Filipino Primitive: Accumulation and Resistance in the American Museum*. New York: NYU Press, 2017.

Seger, John H. *Tradition of the Cheyenne Indians*. Arapaho Beeprint, 1905.

Sell, Zach. "Worst Conceivable Form: Race, Global Capital, and the Making of the English Working Class." *Historical Reflections* 41, no. 1 (2015): 54–69.

Shah, Nayan. *Contagious Divides: Epidemics and Race in San Francisco's Chinatown*. Berkeley: University of California Press, 2001.

———. *Stranger Intimacy: Contesting Race, Sexuality, and the Law in the North American West*. Berkeley: University of California Press, 2011.

Shesadri-Crooks, Kalpana. *Desiring Whiteness: A Lacanian Analysis of Race*. London: Routledge, 2000.

Shibutani, Tamotsu. *Improvised News: A Sociological Study of Rumor*. Indianapolis: Bobbs-Merrill, 1966.

Shigematsu, Setsu, and Keith L. Camacho, eds. *Militarized Currents: Toward a Decolonized Future in Asia and the Pacific*. Minneapolis: University of Minnesota Press, 2010.

Shivji, Issa. *Class Struggles in Tanzania*. New York: Monthly Review Press, 1976.

———. *Accumulation in an African Periphery: A Theoretical Framework*. Dar es Salaam: Mkuki na Nyota Publishers, 2009.

Shockey, Frank. "'Invidious' American Indian Tribal Sovereignty: Morton v. Mancari Contra Adarand Constructors, Inc., v. Pena, Rice v. Cayetano, and Other Recent Cases." *American Indian Law Review* 25, no. 2 (2000 / 2001): 275–313.

Sikainga, Ahmad Alawad. *"City of Steel and Fire": A Social History of Atbara, Sudan's Railway Town, 1906–1984*. Portsmouth: Heinemann, 2002.

Silva, Noenoe K. *The Power of the Steel-Tipped Pen: Reconstructing Native Hawaiian Intellectual History*. Durham, NC: Duke University Press, 2017.

Simpson, Audra. "Captivating Eunice: Membership, Colonialism, and Gendered Citizenships of Grief." *Wicazo Sa Review* 24, no. 2 (2009): 105–29.

———. *Mohawk Interruptus: Political Life across the Borders of Settler States*. Durham, NC: Duke University Press, 2014.

———. "Consent's Revenge." *Cultural Anthropology* 31, no. 3 (2016): 326–33.

———. "The State Is a Man: Theresa Spence, Loretta Saunders and the Gender of Settler Sovereignty." *Theory & Event* 19, no. 4 (2016).

———. "The Ruse of Consent and the Anatomy of 'Refusal': Cases from Indigenous North America and Australia." *Postcolonial Studies* 20, no. 1 (2017): 18–33.

———. "'Tell Me Why, Why, Why': A Critical Commentary on the Visuality of Settler Expectation." *Visual Anthropology Review* 34, no. 1 (2018): 60–66.

——— and Andrea Smith. *Theorizing Native Studies*. Durham, NC: Duke University Press, 2014.

Simpson, Leanne. "Looking after Gdoo-naaganinaa: Precolonial Nishnaabeg Diplomatic and Treaty Relationships." *Wicazo Sa Review* 23, no. 2 (Fall 2008): 29–42.

———. *Dancing on Our Turtle's Back: Stories of Nishnaabeg Re-Creation, Resurgence and a New Emergence*. Winnipeg: ARP Books, 2011.

———. *As We Have Always Done: Indigenous Freedom through Radical Resurgence*. Minneapolis: University of Minnesota Press, 2017.

Singh, Nikhil Pal. "The Whiteness of Police." *American Quarterly* 66, no. 4 (2014): 1091–99.

———. *Race and America's Long War*. Oakland: University of California Press, 2017.

Six Companies. *Memorial of the Six Chinese Companies: An Address to the Senate and House of Representatives of the United States. Testimony of California's Leading Citizens before the Joint Special Congressional Committee. Read and Judge Us*. San Francisco, 1877.

Sklar, Martin. *The Corporate Reconstruction of American Capitalism, 1890–1916: The Market, the Law, and Politics*. New York: Cambridge University Press, 1988.

Smallwood, Stephanie. *Saltwater Slavery: A Middle Passage from Africa to American Diaspora*. Cambridge, MA: Harvard University Press, 2007.

Smith, Claire, and H. Martin Wobst, eds. *Indigenous Archaeologies: Decolonizing Theory and Practice.* New York: Routledge, 2005.

Smith, Matthew Hale. *Bulls and Bears of New York.* Hartford: J. B. Burr, 1875.

Smith, Merrit Roe, ed. *Military Enterprise and Technological Change: Perspectives on the American Experience.* London: MIT Press, 1985.

Smith, Stacey L. *Freedom's Frontier: California and the Struggle over Unfree Labor, Emancipation, and Reconstruction.* Chapel Hill: University of North Carolina Press, 2013.

Smits, David D. "The Frontier Army and the Destruction of the Buffalo, 1865–1883." *Western Historical Quarterly* 25, no. 3 (1994): 312–38.

Sneve, Virginia Driving Hawk. *Completing the Circle.* Lincoln: University of Nebraska Press, 1995.

Spack, Ruth. *America's Second Tongue: American Indian Education and the Ownership of English, 1860–1900.* Lincoln: University of Nebraska Press, 2002.

Spillers, Hortense. "Mama's Baby, Papa's Maybe: An American Grammar Book." *Diacritics* (Summer 1987): 64–81.

Springer, Charles H. *Soldiering in Sioux Country: 1865.* San Diego: Frontier Heritage Press, 1971.

Spude, Robert. *Promontory Summit,* May 10, 1869. National Park Service, 2005.

Squires, David. "Outlawry: Ida B. Wells and Lynch Law." *American Quarterly* 67, no. 1 (2015): 141–63.

Standing Bear, Luther. *Stories of the Sioux.* Lincoln: University of Nebraska Press, 1988.

Stands in Timber, John, and Margot Liberty. *Cheyenne Memories.* New Haven, CT: Yale University Press, 1967.

———. *A Cheyenne Voice: The Complete John Stands in Timber Interviews.* Norman: University of Oklahoma Press, 2013.

Stark, Heidi Kiiwetinepinesiik. "Criminal Empire: The Making of the Savage in a Lawless Land." *Theory & Event* 19, no. 4 (2016).

Stedile, João Pedro. "Landless Battalions: The Sem Terra Movement of Brazil." *New Left Review* 15 (2002): 76–104.

———. "The Neoliberal Agrarian Model in Brazil." *Monthly Review* 58, no. 9 (February 2007): 50–54.

Stewart, Watt. *Henry Meiggs: Yankee Pizarro.* Durham, NC: Duke University Press, 1946.

———. *Chinese Bondage in Peru: A History of the Chinese Coolie in Peru, 1849–1874.* Durham, NC: Duke University Press, 1951.

Stone, Richard D. *The Interstate Commerce Commission and the Railroad Industry: A History of Regulatory Policy.* New York: Praeger, 1991.

Storti, Craig. *Incident at Bitter Creek: The Story of the Rock Springs Chinese Massacre.* Ames: Iowa State University Press, 1991.

Stover, John. *American Railroads.* Chicago: University of Chicago Press, 1961.

Stowell, David O. *Streets, Railroads, and the Great Strike of 1877.* Chicago: University of Chicago Press, 1999.

Strahorn, Robert E. *The Handbook of Wyoming and Guide to the Black Hills and Big Horn Regions, for Citizen, Emigrant, and Tourist, Cheyenne, Wyoming.* Robert E. Strahorn, 1877.

Strange, Susan. *Sterling and British Policy: A Political Study of an International Currency in Decline.* London: Oxford University Press, 1971.

Street, Richard Steven. *Beasts of the Field: A Narrative History of California Farmworkers, 1769–1913.* Stanford, CA: Stanford University Press, 2004.

Stremlau, Rose. *Sustaining the Cherokee Family: Kinship and the Allotment of an Indigenous Nation.* Chapel Hill: University of North Carolina Press, 2011.

Sturm, Circe. "Reflections on the Anthropology of Sovereignty and Settler Colonialism: Lessons from Native North America." *Cultural Anthropology* 32, no. 3 (2017): 340–48.

Summer, Mark W. *Railroads, Reconstruction, and the Gospel of Prosperity.* Princeton, NJ: Princeton University Press, 1984.

Summerhill, William R. *Order against Progress: Government, Foreign Investment, and Railroads in Brazil, 1854–1913.* Stanford, CA: Stanford University Press, 2003.

Sun, E-tu Zen. *Chinese Railways and British Interests, 1898–1911.* New York: King's Crown Press, 1954.

Sundaram, Jomo Kwame. *Economic Liberalisation and Development in Africa.* Dakar: Council for the Development of Social Science Research in Africa, 2008.

Sweeney, Stuart. *Financing India's Imperial Railways, 1875–1914.* London: Pickering & Chatto, 2011.

Szabo, Joyce M. *Imprisoned Art, Complex Patronage: Plains Drawings by Howling Wolf and Zotom at the Autry National Center.* Santa Fe: School for Advanced Research Press, 2011.

Tabb, William K. "The Global Food Crisis and What Has Capitalism to Do with It?" Paper presented at "The Global Food Crisis" conference, Brecht Forum, New York, July 12, 2008.

Tadiar, Neferti X. M. "Metropolitan Life and Uncivil Death." *PMLA* 122, no. 1 (2007): 316–20.

———. *Things Fall Away: Philippine Historical Experience and the Makings of Globalization.* Durham, NC: Duke University Press, 2009.

———. "Life-Times in Fate Playing." *South Atlantic Quarterly* 111, no. 4 (Fall 2012): 783–802.

———. "Decolonization, 'Race,' and Remaindered Life under Empire." *Qui Parle* 23, no. 2 (2015): 135–60.

———. "City Everywhere." *Theory, Culture & Society* 33, nos. 7–8 (2016): 57–83.

Takaki, Ronald. *Iron Cages: Race and Culture in Nineteenth-Century America.* New York: Knopf, 1979.

Tang, Eric. *Unsettled: Cambodian Refugees in the NYC Hyperghetto.* Philadelphia: Temple University Press, 2015.

Tatum, Lawrie. *Our Red Brothers and the Peace Policy of President Ulysses S. Grant.* Lincoln: University of Nebraska Press, 1970.

Ter Haar, Barend J. *Telling Stories: Witchcraft and Scapegoating in Chinese History*. Leiden: Brill, 2006.

Thomas, William G. *The Iron Way: Railroads, the Civil War, and the Making of Modern America*. New Haven, CT: Yale University Press, 2011.

Thompson, Lanny. *Imperial Archipelago: Representation and Rule in the Insular Territories under U.S. Dominion after 1898*. Honolulu: University of Hawai'i Press, 2010.

Tiedeman, Christopher G. *A Treatise on the Limitations of Police Power in the United States*. St. Louis: F. H. Thomas Law, 1886.

Torbit, Stephen C., and Louis LaRose. "A Commentary on Bison and Cultural Restoration: Partnership between the National Wildlife Federation and the Intertribal Bison Cooperative." *Great Plains Research* 11, no. 1 (2001): 175–82.

Truett, Samuel. *Fugitive Landscapes: The Forgotten History of the U.S.-Mexico Borderlands*. New Haven, CT: Yale University Press, 2006.

Tsey, Komla. *From Head-Loading to the Iron Horse: Railway Building in Colonial Ghana and the Origins of Tropical Development*. Bamenda, Cameroon: Langaa Research, 2013.

Tsikata, Dzodzi, and Joanna Kerr. *Demanding Dignity: Women Confronting Economic Reforms in Africa*. Accra: Third World Network–Africa, 2000.

Tsikata, Dzodzi, and Pamela Golah. *Land Tenure, Gender and Globalisation: Research and Analysis from Africa, Asia and Latin America*. New Delhi: Zubaan, 2010.

Tsing, Anna. *Friction: An Ethnography of Global Connection*. Princeton, NJ: Princeton University Press, 2005.

Turner, Frederick Jackson. *Rereading Frederick Jackson Turner: "The Significance of the Frontier in American History" and Other Essays*. New Haven, CT: Yale University Press, 1994.

Van de Logt, Mark. *War Party in Blue: Pawnee Scouts in the U.S. Army*. Norman: University of Oklahoma Press, 2010.

Van der Meulen, Emily, Elya M. Durisin, and Victoria Love, eds. *Selling Sex: Experience, Advocacy, and Research on Sex Work in Canada*. Vancouver: UBC Press, 2013.

Veenendaal, Jr., Augustus J. *Slow Train to Paradise: How Dutch Investment Helped Build American Railroads*. Stanford, CA: Stanford University Press, 1996.

Vine, David. *Base Nation: How U.S. Military Bases Abroad Harm America and the World*. New York: Metropolitan Books, 2015.

Voiles, Traci Brynne. *Wastelanding: Legacies of Uranium Mining in Navajo Country*. Minneapolis: University of Minnesota Press, 2015.

Waggoner, Josephine. *Witness: A Húnkpapha Historian's Strong-Heart Song of the Lakotas*. Lincoln: University of Nebraska Press, 2013.

Waldorf, John Taylor. *A Kid on the Comstock*. Berkeley: Friends of the Bancroft Library, 1968.

Ward, James A. *Railroads and the Character of America, 1820–1887*. Knoxville: University of Tennessee Press, 1986.

Warrior, Robert Allen. "Canaanites, Cowboys, and Indians: Deliverance, Conquest, and Liberation Theology Today." *Christianity and Crisis* 49, no. 12 (1989): 261–65.

Water Technology News. "Ogallala Aquifer Depleted by Drought." March 1, 2003.

Waterman, Adam, *The Corpse in the Kitchen: History, Necropolitics, and the Afterlives of the Black Hawk War.* Duke University Press, forthcoming.

Waziyatawin. *Remember This!: Dakota Decolonization and the Eli Taylor Narratives.* Lincoln: University of Nebraska Press, 2005.

———. *What Does Justice Look Like?: The Struggle for Liberation in Dakota Homeland,* St. Paul: Living Justice Press, 2008.

Weber, Thomas. *The Northern Railroads in the Civil War, 1861–1865.* Westport, CT: Greenwood Press, 1972.

Wedel, Waldo, ed. *The Dunbar-Allis Letters on the Pawnee.* New York: Garland, 1985.

Welke, Barbara Young. *Recasting American Liberty: Gender, Race, Law and the Railroad Revolution, 1865–1920.* New York: Cambridge University Press, 2001.

Wells, Ida B. *Crusade for Justice: The Autobiography of Ida B. Wells.* Chicago: University of Chicago Press, 1970.

Wen Tiejun. "Centenary Reflections on the 'Three Dimensional Problem' of Rural China." *Inter-Asia Cultural Studies* 2, no. 2 (2001): 287–95.

West, Elliot. *The Contested Plains: Indians, Goldseekers, and the Rush to Colorado.* Lawrence: University of Kansas Press, 1998.

White, Luise. *Speaking with Vampires: Rumor and History in Colonial Africa.* Berkeley: University of California Press, 2000.

White, Richard. "The Winning of the West: The Expansion of the Western Sioux in the Eighteenth and Nineteenth Centuries." *Journal of American History* 65, no. 2 (September 1978): 319–43.

———. *The Roots of Dependency: Subsistence, Environment, and Social Change among the Choctaws, Pawnees, and Najavos.* Lincoln: University of Nebraska Press, 1983.

———. *Railroaded: The Transcontinentals and the Making of Modern America.* New York: W. W. Norton, 2011.

Whiting, Beatrice Blyth. *Paiute Sorcery.* New York: Viking Fund Publications in Anthropology, no. 15, 1950.

Wicker, Elmus. *Banking Panics of the Gilded Age.* New York: Cambridge University Press, 2000.

Wilks, Ivor. *Asante in the Nineteenth Century: The Structure and Evolution of a Political Order.* New York: Cambridge University Press.

Will, George F., and George E. Hyde. *Corn among the Indians of the Upper Missouri.* Lincoln: University of Nebraska Press, 1964.

Williams, Carol, ed. *Indigenous Women and Work: From Labor to Activism.* Urbana: University of Illinois Press, 2012.

Williams, Robert A. *The American Indian in Western Legal Thought: The Discourses of Conquest.* New York: Oxford University Press, 1990.

Wilson, Eric. *The Savage Republic: De Indis of Hugo Grotius, Republicanism, and Dutch Hegemony within the Early Modern World-System (c. 1600–1619)*. Leiden: Martinus Nijhoff, 2008.

Winnemucca, Sarah. *Life among the Piutes: Their Wrongs and Claims*. New York: Putnam, 1883.

Wishart, David. *The Fur Trade of the American West, 1807–1840: A Geographical Synthesis*. Lincoln: University of Nebraska Press, 1992.

———. "The Roles and Status of Men and Women in Nineteenth-Century Omaha and Pawnee Societies: Postmodernist Uncertainties and Empirical Evidence." *American Indian Quarterly* 19, no. 4 (Autumn 1995): 509–18.

Wolfe, Patrick. *Traces of History: Elementary Structures of Race*. New York: Verso, 2016.

Wolff, David O. *Industrializing the Rockies: Growth, Competition, and Turmoil in the Coalfields of Colorado and Wyoming, 1868–1914*. Boulder: University Press of Colorado, 2003.

Woods, Clyde. *Development Arrested: The Blues and Plantation Power in the Mississippi Delta*. New York: Verso, 2017.

———. *Development Drowned and Reborn: The Blues and Bourbon Restoration in Post-Katrina New Orleans*, edited by Jordan T. Camp and Laura Pulido. Athens: University of Georgia Press, 2017.

Wu, Cynthia. *Chang and Eng Reconnected: The Original Siamese Twins in American Culture*. Philadelphia: Temple University Press, 2012.

Wyckoff, William. *Creating Colorado: The Making of a Western American Landscape, 1860–1940*. New Haven, CT: Yale University Press, 1999.

Yamashiro, Aiko, and Noelani Goodyear-Ka'ōpua, eds. *The Value of Hawai'i 2: Ancestral Routes, Oceanic Visions*. Honolulu: University of Hawai'i Press, 2014.

Young, Crawford. *The African Colonial State in Comparative Perspective*. New Haven, CT: Yale University Press, 1994.

Ziolkowska, Jadwiga R. "Shadow Price of Water for Irrigation: A Case of the High Plains." *Agricultural Water Management* 153, no. 1 (2015): 20–31.

Zontek, Ken. *Buffalo Nation: American Indian Efforts to Restore the Bison*. Lincoln: University of Nebraska Press, 2007.

INDEX

abolitionism, 18

Afghanistan: Afghan campaign of 1878 (Second Anglo-Afghan War), 47; counterinsurgency operations in, 191; U.S. War in Afghanistan, 191, 194–195

African Trade Unions, 57

agency farmers, 108–109, 114, 117

Ahmad, Aijaz, 193–194, 196

Ahmad, Eqbal, 199

allotment policy, 54, 165

American Horse, 77

Ames, Oliver, 146

Amin, Samir, 192, 196, 200

Anatolian Railway Company, 51

annuity goods distribution system, 112–117, 119, 121

anticolonial internationalism, xiv, 23, 34, 36, 154, 186, 199–200

anti-imperialism, 32, 34, 36–37, 183–184, 185–200

anxiety: about whiteness, 4, 14, 18, 25; of countersovereignty, 1, 4, 10–11, 12, 14, 82, 94, 97, 176, 183; racial and class anxieties, 82, 97; in Turner's frontier thesis, 169

Arapaho people, 64, *127*, 130, 132, 143, 235n17

Arikara people, 64, 132

Assiniboine people, 64, 132

Augur, Christopher, 73, 74, 120, 139–140, 142, 145

Authorization to Use Military Force, U.S. (post-9/11), 186, 193–194

Baghdad Railway Company, 55

Balaklava Railway, 44

banks and banking, 47, 150, 156–157, 175–176, 178, 196

Bayhylle, Baptiste, 116

Bent, George, 134, 136

Bent's fort, *127*, 130–131

Berlin Compromise, 55

Black Hawk, 65

Black Hills, 22, 67, 70, 74–75, 120, 130, 138, 141

Black Lives Matter movement, 198

Big Crow, 139–140

body/bodies, 87, 110; control of in space, xiii, 161–166, 170, 183; and countersovereignty, 65; dead bodies, 155; and fictitious capital, 150; isolation of, 182; rail construction and relations between bodies, 53–54

Boxer Rebellion, 52–53

breech loading rifles, 72

Bremer, L. Paul, 194

British South Africa Company, 49–50

buffalo: buffalo commons and decolonization, 36; Cheyenne buffalo economy, 130–132, 147; circular trails of, 181; and collective mode of relationship, 30–31; depletion and displacement of, 32, 34, 45, 78, 119–120, 147; domestication of as colonial violence, 30–32; Lakota buffalo economy, 21, 60, 61–63, 69, 75, 78, 224n42; movement and migration of, 20, 60–62, 65, 69; Pawnee buffalo

buffalo *(continued)*
    economy, 104, 108, 109, 119–120; Sherman's threat to replace buffalo, 75; slaughter of 1996–97, 32
Bull Bear, Edith, 77–78

California: Act for the Government and Protection of Indians, 84; Act to Prevent the Importation of Chinese Criminals and to Prevent the Establishment of Coolie Slavery, 98–99; Anti-Coolie Act, 83; Central Pacific's charter from, 9; and Chinese labor, 46, *81–82*, 86–101; Chinese migrants to, 84–85; colonization of, 82–83; Gold Rush, 84, 131; violence against indigenous populations in, 84. *See also* Stanford, Leland
cannibalism, 10, 26–27, 30; figurative use of the term (economy), 122, 182, 192
capitalism, xii-xv; accumulation of, 192, 197, 198; assimilation of capital to indigenous modes of relationship, 64; cannibalism and, 27; as closed structure, 169; expansion of, 18, 60, 65; financialization, 69, 70, 113, 139, 143, 178, 197; finance capital, 46, 87, 123, 150, 176–180; finance capitalism, 172, 178, 183; as imperialism, 191–192; Lakota buffalo economy as distinct from, 63; as mode of relationship, xii-xiii, 63–64; and shareholder whiteness, 160. *See also* monopoly; profit; war-finance nexus
census records, 7, 182
Central Pacific Railroad, 40, 72, *81*, 144; and Chinese labor, 1–3, 8–10, 82, 85–100; Chinese workers' strike (July 1867), 9–10, 91–95; and finance capitalism, 178; gendered expropriation by, 28–29; land grants to, 2, 9, 15; and lumber; 15; militarized labor structure of, 89–90; Santa Clara v. Southern Pacific, 163; and Sierra Nevada summit tunnel, 9–11, 89
centralization: of banks, 175; of capital, 157, 162, 165; Lenin on, 175; and monopolies, 175; of North American energy infrastructure, 189–190; of trade, 130; and ultra-imperialism thesis, 199

Cherokee nation and people, 152, 156
Chesapeake & Ohio & Southwestern Railroad Company v. Ida B. Wells, 162, 165–166
Cheyenne Nation and people: buffalo economy of, 130–132, 147; and cholera epidemic, 131–132; colonial violence against, 134; derailing of Union Pacific train by (1867), 128–129, 143; Dog Soldiers, 132, 134–142, 144–145, 147; and Fort Laramie Treaty, 64; gentling approach to wild horses, 129; horses as mode of relationship, 128–129; manhastoz, 131–134, 138, 143; maps, *126–127;* modes of relationship of, 129, 131, 135, 139–143; and North Pacific Railway, 33; raiding as expropriation, 135–138; Stone Calf, xi-xii; and war-finance nexus, 128, 140–141, 146
childbirth, 21–23, 155. *See also* rebirth, frontier as
Chinese Eastern Railway, 52, 55–56
Chinese Exclusion Act (1882), 100–101, 161–163
Chinese migrants and labor, *80–81;* Act to prohibit the "Coolie Trade" by American Citizens in American Vessels, An, 83, 100–101; anti-Chinese movements and rallies, 14, 18, 46; Anti-Coolie Act (California), 83; Chinese Exclusion Act (1882), 100–101, 161–163; Chinese Six Companies (San Francisco district associations), 85, 99; Chinese workers' strike (July 1867), 9–10, 91–95; and continental imperialism, 82, 88, 93, 95, 99–100; and district associations (huiguan), 84–85, 99; free labor question, 86, 94–97; isolation of, 89; and racialized labor, 82–83, 86–87, 89–101; and racialized violence, 82, 84, 86, 88, 94, 96, 99–101; Rock Springs coal mine massacre, 70, 101; and war-finance nexus, 82, 90, 93
Chivington, John, 135
coal mining, 33, 101, 145, 175, 180, 188, 198; Rock Springs mine massacre, 70, 101
Cold War, 187, 194
Conquering Bear, 66
constabulary missions, 187–188

constant capital, 85, 100

continental imperialism: British, 49–50; California as site of, 82, 88; and capitalism, 174–180; and Chinese labor, 82, 88, 93, 95, 99–100; colonized versus "national" U.S. territory, xii; and control over extraction and infrastructure, 33–35, 198; and countersovereignty, 180–184; definition of, xii; destructive approach to energy production, 33–34; and DuBois's imperialism in Africa argument, 169–174; exclusion and restriction of movement as features of, 75, 82, 99–100, 162; gendered borders of, 168, 170; and gendered expropriation, 107–110, 123–124; and Lenin's theory of imperialism, 168, 170, 172–173, 175–180, 183, 199; mode of relationship of, 64, 131, 172; and nation, 169–174; partition and isolation as goals of, 130; and Pawnee scouts as countersovereignty, 122–123; racial borders of, 168, 170, 178; reconstruction as, 72; relationship between North American and African, 197; rumor community of, 3–6, 14, 18; and shareholder whiteness, 150, 152, 157, 162, 164, 167; and slavery, 107, 174; transcontinental railroad as core infrastructure of, 33, 54, 75, 82, 173; U.S. Indian policy moved to Department of the Interior, 168, 173; and war-finance nexus, 34–36, 69, 93–95, 105, 131–144, 157, 168, 182–183, 185–187. See also Du Bois, W. E. B.; frontier; Lenin, Vladimir

Cook-Lynn, Elizabeth, 203n4

coolie, 170; Act to Prevent the Importation of Chinese Criminals and to Prevent the Establishment of Coolie Slavery (1870, California), 98–99; Act to prohibit the "Coolie Trade" by American Citizens in American Vessels (1862, U.S.), 83, 100–101; Anti-Coolie Act (1962, California), 83; and Chinese Exclusion Act (1882, U.S.), 100; "coolie class" introduced by Indian railways, 44; as debt and labor structure (U.S. law), 83; as racial slur (California law), 83

corn: and Cheyenne people, xi, 233n2; and colonial concepts of property and ownership, 108–109; and credit, 115; and Dakota people, 21; eagle corn, 124; and Pawnee people, 104, 105, 108–209, 115, 124–125; Pawnee crop failure as colonial control, 117; Pawnee traditional corn as decolonization, 124–125; and treaties, 106, 108

corporations: and charters and treaties, 152–154; and emancipation, 150; and emancipation of capital, 157–161; emptiness and gaps of, 154–157; and exclusion and possession, 161–164; interrelationship between state and, 150–152; limited liability of whiteness, 164–167; personhood of, 158–159, 164–165; and war-finance nexus, 153, 156–165

cotton industry, 40, 43, 47, 48, 53, 54, 56, 59, 95, 157

cottonwood trees, 62, 131

counterinsurgency, 46, 48, 56; and countersovereignty, xii, 61; industrialization as, 71; U.S. sovereignty as project of, 69, 79; warfare, 106, 191

counterrevolution, 55–56, 149, 163, 165, 196, 199–200

countersovereignty: and anxiety about unfinished colonial project, 1, 11; and capital accumulation, 68; and continental imperialism, 180–184; and corporate power, 89, 150–151; and counter-messaging, 191; and counterinsurgency, xii, 61; and counterintelligence, xii; and counterrevolution, xii; definition of, xii, 65; and desolation, 75; and exclusion, 100; and extraction, 70; filius nullius (bastard child) as element of, 154–155; and financialization, 69, 70; imagination of, 74; and indigenous modes of relationship, 2, 8, 65, 106, 120, 122, 124; as inoculation against violence, 122; and labor exploitation, 138–141; prose of, 8–19; as reactive, 2, 33, 89, 154, 182–183, 185, 193; and rumor, 3–13, 17–19; terra nullius (empty place) as element of, 11, 154, 174–175; U.S. sovereignty as, 154; and treaties and charters, 117, 152–154; war and violence as elements of, 6, 67, 74–75, 79, 147 credit: and anti-imperialism, 195–196, 198; and emancipation, 69, 158–160; and financial crisis of 2008–09, 192; and Lakota people, 63, 65, 67; and Panic of 1873, 47; and Pawnee people, 114–115, 119, 123; and shareholder whiteness, 158–160, 166; and war-finance nexus, 63, 65, 67, 73. *See also* debt

Crédit Mobilier scandal, 47, 167, 178

Creek Nation, 54

Crimean War, 44

Crocker, Charles, 1–3, 8–11, 85–86, 88–89, 97–98

Crocker, Clark, 86

Crocker, Edwin Bryant, 85–86, 88–94, 96–97

Crow Dog, Leonard, 64

Crow people, 33, 64, 132, 188

Dakota Access pipeline, 190

Dakota mode of relationship, 23–27

Dakota people: and gendered labor, 63; tiospaye (larger family of related households), 22–23; *Waterlily* (Deloria), 21–27

Dakota Uprising, 46, 68–69

Dawes Act (1887), 164–165

debt: Act for the Government and Protection of Indians (1850), 84; American Civil War, 157; corporate debt, 161; Crédit Mobilier scandal, 47, 167, 178; emancipation and black indebtedness, 69, 73, 158; in India, 43; Lenin on, 178–179; limited liability, 165–166; and Pawnee people, 112; public debt, 43; railway debt, 43, 47; of Tubman, Harriet, 149. *See also* credit

decolonization, 29–30, 32–33, 36–37, 52, 57, 64, 173, 184; significance of for North America, 185–200

Deloria, Ella, xiv, 21–27, 200; critique of political economy by, 23; on "universal kinship of humans," 23. 36; *Waterlily*, 21–27

Deloria, Vine, Jr., 76, 77–78, 179

Department of the Interior, 168, 173

depersonalization, 158, 160

disease, 9, 12, 96; cholera, 131–132, 143; diphtheria, 117; measles, 117, 122; smallpox, 9, 12, 21, 98

displacement, 2, 6–7, 10, 12–13, 105, 178, 196, 203n4, 203–204n5

Dodge, Grenville, 45, 69–75, 119, 120, 138–142, 144–146

Donner Party, 10, 26

Du Bois, W. E. B., xv, 183; "African Roots of War, The," 169–170; *Black Reconstruction*, 198–199; on the Color Line, 172, 184; on "counter-revolution of property," 149; on "dividends of whiteness," 159; on imperialism in Africa, 169–174; on nation and colonial conquest, 178; on racism as refusal of relationship, 183

East India Company, 43, 151

emancipation, 149–150; of capital, 157–161; Fourteenth Amendment, 149, 163; and war-finance nexus, 149, 153, 156–165. *See also* corporations; shareholder whiteness

Emancipation Proclamation, 69

Enbridge, 190–191

energy security, 189

Energy Transfer Equity, 189–190

Energy Transfer Partners, 198, 191

exceptionalism, myth of U.S., 40, 172, 177

extinction, 31, 200

extraction, resource, 33, 56, 70, 145, 165. 180, 194, 196, 198

extractive economies, 70, 165, 180, 194, 196

extractive social order, 6–7, 145

femininity, 17, 23–25, 36, 109

financialization, 69, 70, 113, 139, 143, 178, 197

finance capital, 46, 87, 123, 150, 176–180

finance capitalism, 172, 178, 183

Fletcher v. Peck, 152

food, destruction of, 26

food sovereignty, 195–196

Fort Kearny, 71, 114, 119

Fort Laramie Treaty, 47, 64–66, 75, 132

Fourteenth Amendment, 149, 163

Fowler, Loretta, 235n17

Freedmen's Bureau, 92–93
frontier: circular versus linear frontier process, 175, 180–181; frontier dynamic, 168; as imperialistic creation story, 170; and "Indian question," 180–182; mercantilistic frontier, 174–175; and racism, 170–172, 174, 177, 183; nation and frontier, 170–173; terra nullius of frontier, 174–175; and transcontinental railroad, 179–180; Turner's frontier thesis, 168–182; and white supremacy, 170, 181. *See also* Turner, Frederick Jackson
Fugitive Slave Law, 156, 161

Gap, George, 79
gender: and control of bodies, 87, 162; gendered division of labor, 17–18, 29, 109–118; gendered expropriation, 28, 107–110, 123–124, 138; gendered ownership, 133, 165; gendered relationships, 23, 25, 129; gendered violence, 63, 84, 168; gendered vulnerability, 22; and territorialization, 170
genocide, 9, 31, 69, 71, 74, 75, 141, 146
Ghost Dance, 147–148
globalization, 192, 195, 197, 200
gold mining, 83–84, 89, 91
gold rushes, 6–7, 44, 132–133; California Gold Rush, 84, 131
golden spike ceremony, xi-xiv; and continental imperialism, xiv; "Done" telegraph, xii, xiii. *See also* Promontory Point
Goldman Sachs, 157
grandmothers and great-grandmothers, 34, 78, 105, 107, 111
Grotius, Hugo, 151
Grundrisse: Foundations of the Critique of Political Economy (Marx), xii
Guha, Ranajit, 11
gunpowder, 17, 89

Harney, William, 66, 76
Herero uprising and genocide, 53
Hidatsa people, 62, 64, 132
Higham, John, 18

Hilferding, Rudolph, 178, 215n1, 221n10, 233n39, 240n22
Hobson, J. A., 43, 113, 134, 223n32, 227n20, 228n45, 231n17, 232n24, 235n22, 238–238n13, 239n17, 242n40
Holland, Sharon, 19
"homeland security," 186–187
Hopkins, Mark, 86–87, 91–94, 97–98
Howling Wolf, 131
Huntington, Collis, 86–98, 162

imperial sovereignty, 32, 68, 151, 186, 193–196
imperialism: capitalism as, 191–192; ultra-imperialism, 199; Lenin's theory of, 168, 170, 172–173, 175–180, 183, 199. *See also* anti-imperialism; continental imperialism
Indian Appropriations Act (1871), 160–161
Indian Bureau, 7, 9, 12
indigenous disappearance, 6, 8, 28
Innu people, 36
internationalism, xiv, 23, 34, 36, 154, 186, 199–200, 214n40
Interstate Commerce Act (1887), 164–165
Interstate Commerce Commission, 164, 167
Inter-Tribal Bison Cooperative, 30–31
intersubjectivity, 21
Iraq, 186, 187, 188, 191, 194–196, 198, 200
Iron Shell, 76
Iron Teeth, 129, 133

Johnson v. William M'Intosh, 153–154

Kautsky, Karl, 199
kinship, 23–24, 36
Korea, 186, 188, 194, 200
Kwong Ki-Chaou, 83–84

labor theory of value, xiv
LaDuke, Winona, xiv, 30–36, 200; on collective indigenous mode of relationship, 30–32; on decolonization, 32–33, 36–37; on territorialization, 32
Lakota Nation and people: Blue Water Creek massacre, 66; buffalo economy of,

Lakota Nation and people *(continued)*
21, 60, 61–63, 69, 75, 78, 224n42; creation mythology of, 61–63; Dakota Uprising (1862), 46, 68–69; Fort Laramie Treaty, 47, 64–66, 71, 73–79, 132; and fur trade, 62–63; and gendered violence, 63; historical geography of, 60; and horses, 62; maps, *58–59;* relationship to place, 60–62; "Sioux Treaty Hearing," 64, 79; and Union Pacific Railroad Company, 67–79; Treaty of 1868, 76–79; and war-finance nexus, 63–69, 74–75, 79; winter counts, 62
land grants: to Central Pacific Railroad, 2, 9, 15; and centralization of capital, 157; and corporate debt, 161; and countersovereignty, 2; ecological effects of, 34; and finance capital, 87, 157, 178, 179; Maxwell Land Grant, 46; and Métis rebellion (1885), 49; and mineral rights, 101; and railroad colonialism in India, 43; to Texas and Pacific Railway Company, 46; to Union Pacific Railroad Company, 67, 167
Latin America, 187–188, 193–195
Lean Bear, 134
Lenin, Vladimir, xv, 168, 170, 172–173, 183, 199; on annexation of imperialism, 183; on concentration of railroad ownership, 180; on features of capitalism, 177; on finance capital and financialization, 172, 178–179, 183; on monopoly of production, 175–176; on phases of capitalism's evolution into imperialism, 177; on territorialization, 173, 177; theory of imperialism, 168, 170, 172–173, 175–180, 183, 199
Leon, Sam, 19
limited liability, 157, 165–166
Lincoln, Abraham, 67, 69, 156
Little Thunder, 66
Ludlow massacre, 101
lumber, 14–16, 97, 111
Lushbaugh, Benjamin, 115–117, 119
Luxemburg, Rosa, 200, 222n14, 224n42

Man Afraid of His Horses, 71
Mandan people, 62, 64, 132
Mark, Karl, xii, 20, 62, 150, 153

Marshall, John, 152–156
masculinity, 23–24, 159, 177
mass destruction threat, 188, 194, 196
measles, 117, 122
Métis people, 49, 66
Mexican-American War, 132
militarization, 49, 121, 130, 138
Mizner, Henry, 139–140, 145
modes of relationship, 20; American, 169; and anti-imperialism, 194–200; and capitalism, 64–68, 174–175; Cheyenne, 129, 131, 135, 139–143; and Chinese labor, 82, 100; collective, 22–24, 30; colonial, 26–30, 35; of continental imperialism, 34–36, 168–172, 174–175, 177, 180–184; and countersovereignty, 2, 8, 120–125, 180–182; Dakota, 21–25; and decolonization, 36–37, 64, 184, 185–186, 194–200; definition of, xii–xiii; and exclusion, 100; expropriation of, 10, 65; of imperialism, 34, 177; indigenous non-human, 30–32and infrastructure, 32–33; Lakota, 30–31, 60–61, 64–69, 71, 77, 79, 221n2, 224n42; of migration, 82; Paiute, 10, 13; Pawnee, 105, 107–110, 112, 114, 120–125; and railroad colonialism, 42, 54; and regime replacement, 194; and shareholder whiteness, 151–152, 153–154, 159, 161, 165; and territorialization, 32–33; theory of Deloria, Ella, 21–15; theory of LaDuke, Winona, 30–36; theory of Winnemucca, Sarah, 26–30; war as, 36
monopoly: of agriculture and ranching, 34, 112–117, 124, 188–189; and anti-imperialism, 186, 196; of continental imperialism, 105, 170–173, 175–176, 178–179, 183; and credit, 71; and decolonization on foreign relations, 105–106; destructive effects of, 43; Du Bois on, 170, 171; of indigenous relations, 169; Lenin on, 172, 173, 175–176, 178–179, 183; Lenin on "monopolist giants," 175; Marx on "monopolized earth" and wage labor, 20; monopoly capitalism's effect on Pawnee people, 112–117, 124; and race, 96, 98; and rail networks, 41, 43; resource monopolies, 49, 196; of technology, 196; and territorialization, 32; on trade, 105–106; and

trusts, 162, 167, 177; Union Pacific
Railroad as a, 167; and violence, 32, 96
Moreton-Robinson, Aileen, 57
Mormons and Mormon communities, 66,
97–98, 112, 132
motherhood, 21–24, 26, 28–30
mules, 14, 71, 73–74, 136–138, 141
mutually assured destruction, 200

National Banking Act (1863), 156
nationalism, xiv, 54, 57, 159, 199
Ndebele people, 49–50, 53
neoliberalism, 193, 195, 197
Nitassinan, 36
North, Frank, 110, 114–115, 116, 119–121, 123
North, Luther, 110, 114–115, 119, 121
Not Help Him, Celane, 63
Nyerere, Julius, 195

Office of Indian Affairs, 168
Ogallala Aquifer, 34
One Horn, 76
Oregon Trail, *126*, 131

Pacific Railroad Act (1862), 67–68, 72, 97,
156, 163
Paiute people: and anxiety about whiteness,
4–7, 14, 18, 25; beef distribution, 29, 35;
capitalization of land, 26–29, 96, 173–
174; and Chinese migrants, 1–19; colonial and gendered modes of relationship, 29; vision of Wovoka, 147; and
war, 26–29, 173–174
partition, xiii; and colonial modes of relationship, 25–26; and credit, 115; and
decolonization, 57; and gendered labor,
120; and racial labor, 89; as a key characteristic of imperialism, 177; Lenin on,
177; as ongoing process, 177result of
continental imperialism, 130; and
territorialization, 177; and treaties, 107;
Turner on, 177, 181–182; violence of, 52,
57; and war-finance nexus, 105
Pascal, Loretta, 34
Pawnee Nation and people: agency farmers,
108–109, 114, 117; buffalo economy of,
104, 108, 109, 119–120; annuity goods
distribution system, 112–117, 119, 121;

commercial farming imposed on, 106–
110, 114, 117; and compulsory education,
110–112, 117–118; and continental imperialism, 104–105, 107–110; and countersovereignty, 105–106, 117, 120–125; and
displacement of women's relationships
and work, 120; and finance capital, 123;
and financializing, 114–115; gender
relations and labor, 107–117; and gendered expropriation, 107–110, 123–124;
maps, *102–103;* Mulberry Creek Massacre, 121; Pawnee Manual Labor
School, 115; Pawnee scouts, 104–105,
108, 110, 112, 116–125, 128; property
regime, 119; suspension of self-rule, 113;
treaties, 105–112, 116–117; underground
caches of, 105–106; and war-finance
nexus, 105, 112, 115, 123, 125
Platt, Elvira, 115, 120
Platte River, *58,* 65, 68, 71, 79, *102, 103,* 106,
109, 119, 124–125, 130–132; North Platte
River, 63, 66, 70, 71, 73, 75, 79, *126,* 129;
South Platte River, 73, 119
Platte River Valley, 119–120, 122–124
Plessy v. Ferguson, 165–166
profit, 3, 11, 35, 119, 121, 123; through capitalization of indigenous land, 35, 45;
and Chinese labor, 88–94, 96, 98, 100;
and colonial violence, 141; Du Bois on,
159, 172through expropriating indigenous modes of relationship, 65;
through infrastructure, 65; through
invasion and occupation, 68; Lenin on,
178; and racism, 172; and racial competition, 90–91; and shareholder whiteness,
150, 153, 159; through suffering, 41;
wartime, 45
Promontory Point, xi-xii, xiii, 78, 98;
golden spike ceremony, xi-xiv
proprietary anchor, indigenous land possession as, 43
Pyramid Lake Reservation, 9, 15–16, *18,* 97

quarantine, 21, 51

race: profit and racial competition, 90–91;
racial and class anxieties, 82, 97; racial
labor, 82–83, 86–87, 89–101; racial lines

taxation, 29, 35, 43, 49–50, 54–55, 83, 122, 137, 152, 163–165

terra nullius (empty place), 11, 154, 174–175

territorialization, 77; and corporate charters, 151; and gender, 170; and imperialism, 32; and infrastructure development, 32–33, 65; and Panic of 1873, 47; and partition, 177; and property, 158, 161; and race, 158, 166, 170; and terror or violence, 32

Trade and Intercourse Acts, 156

Trans-Siberian Railway, 52

Treaty of Fort Wise, 133–134

Treaty of Medicine Lodge Creek, 143–144

Treaty of 1868, 76–79

Treaty of Shimonoseki, 50

Truckee River, 15, 91

Truckee River Reserve, 15

Trustees of Dartmouth College v. Woodward, 152

Tubman, Harriet, 149

Turner, Frederick Jackson, xv, 5, 167–182; on frontier as site nationality, 169–174, 180–181; on "Indian question," 180–182; on indigenous peoples, 169–170, 173, 175, 180–181; on linearity of frontier, 180–181; on melancholy, 169; on mercantilistic frontier, 174–180; on nation and frontier, 170–173; on terra nullius of frontier, 174–175; on transcontinental railroad, 179–180

Union Pacific Coal Company, 101

Union Pacific Railroad, Company, xiii, *81, 103;* brochure description of Platte River Valley, 122; and Cheyenne people, 128–147; and Chinese labor, 84, 98; and Dakota Uprising, 68–69; derailing of train by Cheyenne (1867), 128–129, 143; and finance capitalism, 178; land grants to, 67, 167; and Lakota people, 67–79; and Mormon labor, 98; Pacific Railroad Act (1862), 67–68, 72, 97, 156, 163; as means to occupation, 70–79; and Pawnee people, 104, 108, 117–122

unipolarity, 186–187

uranium mining, 33

Utah. *See* Promontory Point

Virginia and Truckee Railroad Company, 16

wage labor, 7, 9–10, 15, 17–18, 20, 29, 116, 122, 124

Waggoner, Josephine, 77

Walker River Reservation, 9, 16

War Department, 168, 173

war-finance nexus: and Cheyenne people, 128, 140–141, 146; and Chinese labor, 82, 90, 93; and continental imperialism, 34–36, 69, 93–95, 105, 131–144, 157, 168, 182–183, 185–187; definition of, 168; and emancipation, 149, 153, 156–165; and Lakota peoples, 63–69, 74–75, 79; and Pawnee people, 105, 112, 115, 123, 125; and railroad colonialism, 45–46, 52–53, 61; and shareholder whiteness, 149–150, 153, 156–157, 165

"War on Terror," 188, 193–194

Waterlily (Deloria), 21–27

Wells, Ida B., 160; *Chesapeake & Ohio & Southwestern Railroad Company v. Ida B. Wells,* 162, 165–166

White Bird, 137, 140

White Crane, 77

white nativism, 14, 18

whiteness: dividends of, 158; as fictitious capital, 149–150; New World Whiteness, 84; and supplanting Chinese workers, 95. *See also* shareholder whiteness

Winnemucca, Sarah, xiv, 200; on decolonization, 29–30; *Life among the Piutes: Their Wrongs and Claims,* 26–30, 34–35, 173–174

Woods, Clyde, 189

Worcester v. State of Georgia, 156

Yates, William Henry, 92–93

Yellow Wolf, 130

Yellowstone National Park, 32

Yick Wo v. Hopkins, 162–163

Young Bear, Severt, 67, 77

Zinoviev, G. Y., 199

AMERICAN CROSSROADS

Edited by Earl Lewis, George Lipsitz, George Sánchez, Dana Takagi, Laura Briggs, and Nikhil Pal Singh